CHIP OFF MY SHOULDER

LONDON: HUMPHREY MILFORD
OXFORD UNIVERSITY PRESS

Chip
off my
Shoulder

THOMAS L. STOKES

PRINCETON · 1940

PRINCETON UNIVERSITY PRESS

SET UP AND PRINTED BY PRINCETON UNIVERSITY PRESS
AT PRINCETON, NEW JERSEY, U.S.A.

4-14-70

Contents

BOOK ONE

FAR TO THE SOUTH

The girls were always beautiful. The men
Wore varnished boots, raced horses and played cards
And drank mint juleps till the time came round
For fighting duels with their second cousins
Or tar-and-feathering some God-damned Yankee. . . .
The South . . . the honeysuckle . . . the hot sun . . .
The taste of ripe persimmons and sugar cane . . .
The cloyed and waxy sweetness of magnolias . . .
White cotton, blowing like a fallen cloud,
And foxhounds belling the Virginia hills. . . .
  (*A Connecticut Yankee's idea of the South*)

This was his Georgia, this his share
Of pine and river and sleepy air,
Of summer thunder and winter rain
That spills bright tears on the windowpane
With the slight, fierce passion of young men's grief,
Of the mockingbird and the mulberry leaf.
For, wherever the winds of Georgia run,
It smells of peaches long in the sun,
And the white wolf-winter, hungry and frore,
Can prowl the North by a frozen door
But here we have fed him on bacon fat
And he sleeps by the stove like a lazy cat.
Here Christmas stops at everyone's house
With a jug of molasses and green, young boughs,
And the little New Year, the weakling one,
Can lie outdoors in the noonday sun,
Blowing the fluff from a turkey wing
At skies already haunted with spring—

Oh, Georgia . . . Georgia . . . the careless yield!
The watermelons ripe in the field!
The mist in the bottoms that tastes of fever
And the yellow river rolling forever . . . !

From *John Brown's Body*, by STEPHEN VINCENT BENÉT, published by Farrar &
Rinehart, Inc. Copyright 1927, 1928, by Stephen Vincent Benét.

1

UNTIL I returned to the South after several years in the North I did not know how much I loved it. I did not know how much a part of me it was. Until I went back home and looked about me and talked to the people and tried to put things together, I did not know how far I had come from the South. Until then I really did not know much about the South, for now I saw it more objectively, saw it with eyes that had seen much of the world elsewhere, saw it with a mind that had grown from contacts with many men and many experiences.

And so, love it as I did, I also hated it.

But I can never pluck it from my soul.

It will not out of me, and I must go back ever so often to warm my heart in its sunshine, for it has healing powers for me. It is blood of my blood and bone of my bone. It is my home, my native land, the land of generations and generations of my family, back beyond the Civil War, back beyond the Revolution.

My wife and I were having breakfast at a long counter, open to the beneficent tropical sunshine of Key West. We had stopped early in the morning before driving to Miami where I was to take a train back to the North and icy, dreary January. The buxom, indolent waitress behind the counter was talking lackadaisically to a man who stood near us.

"You ain't going nowhere, are you?" she asked him.
"I got to write a letter tomorrow," he replied.
There's the casual South.

I have loved it at its deepest reach into the Caribbean, its jewelled toe point at Key West, skipping across the glittering ballroom floor where the Gulf of Mexico joins the Atlantic. The trade winds fondle the palm trees at night gently, and they purr their delight in whispers like the fall of summer rain, bowing their fronds gratefully the while. A white moon rides overhead and lays an inviting, gleaming road to the horizon. The stars let themselves down bright and close like wanton fireflies seeking to bathe themselves in the sea. The days are golden and full of warmth that soothes the blood. You sit on a dock holding a fishing line carelessly, listening with one ear to the chatter of the "conchs," and do not mind whether anything pecks at the bait.

I have found peace at night along the waterfront at Savannah where, as a young reporter, I wandered by day from ship to ship and talked to quiet men who had sailed the seven seas; and at night watched the masts against the sky and heard the slosh of water against the pier and saw, forever stretching away beyond these hardy vessels, the distant waters which they traverse and the distant ports where they drop their anchors.

I have feared the South as I saw its low flat heatlands across middle and southern Georgia and Alabama and Louisiana and Mississippi, land where the blood rises hotly to the call of deep-laid prejudices, the land where white men shoot each other over trifles and lynch Negroes. The sun seems to rot the souls of men here and transform them, every so often, into beasts. The yellow dust swirls across the fields like a plague from some cursed desert of antiquity.

4

tween the States, as it was called at home. Tattered soldiers in gray are slowly giving away before hordes in blue. Their mouths are wide with the shouts of victory, those soldiers in blue. The Confederate flag is there, ripped and torn. Shells are bursting overhead. The blue hordes are rolling over a fence, pouring over a fence. The soldiers in gray are yielding stubbornly.

Above me, in her rocking chair, my grandmother sits and tells me about the war. She told me about my grandfather who fought all through it. She told me how, after the battle of Atlanta, he had been promoted from first lieutenant to command of his regiment because all the other officers above him had been killed. She said he told her how you could walk on nothing but dead bodies for miles about the battlefield. She spoke unkindly of General John B. Hood who had permitted that slaughter of soldiers in gray. "Gallant John Hood"—she bit it out sarcastically. She didn't permit herself to speak of General Sherman. He was the unmentionable. He was a beast.

The gray soldiers retreat in the picture there before me and something bitter is left in my childish soul. It is the bitter blow to pride suffered by the vanquished that must burn through two or three generations before it passes. The victors forget. They can forget. The vanquished cannot. That's something of what still smoulders in the soul of the South. As a youngster I used to find Minié balls in the woods not far from home. They still rankle in the heart of the South.

The South still nurses a beautiful romantic legend of the Old Days on the Plantation. There were some such plantations, but not near so many as we supposed. They represented, however, the ideal of those who did not have plantations and when the South lost them, they lost them.

Deep in its heart the South cannot be proud of a war to preserve human slavery, so it translates it into a war to

9

save its homes and its scattered aristocratic civilization. This gives it an inferiority complex and a thin skin. It rationalizes and, knowing that it rationalizes and that everybody else knows that it rationalizes, it flares up and grows hostile and retreats, sulkily, into its legends. I know because I have felt all those things and done all those things.

There is, too, in the South's resentment, the age-old enmity of the agricultural civilization for the mechanical and commercial civilization. The producer is always at the mercy of the trader by the very nature of things. The South seeks refuge in an assumed superiority of gentility and looks down its nose at those "in trade," that is, the instinctive, inherent South—for the South is now a land of traders and long ago they achieved respectability. But, in the background, there's still something of this hostility. It is a characteristic of the landowner class from time immemorial.

It speaks haughtily of its own "po' white trash," but the "po' white trash" is always somebody else.

The South is a dream lady in crinoline, flirting with her fan.

The South also is a nightmare and a hag.

It is the tenant farmer who toils the year round on his cotton patch which grows increasingly scraggly as the soil wears out, and he gets deeper and deeper into debt. It is his wife who bears children year after year, looks like an old woman at thirty-five and then, ceasing to care because it's no use to care, drags about hopelessly and screeches at her offspring, finding her comfort in her snuff box and the "old man's jug."

It is the tenant farmer and his family who have been driven off the land by the loss of foreign markets for the cotton crop, by the introduction of machinery, and who go into the mills in the towns and cities and work for four, five and six dollars a week and are satisfied because, with the whole family working, that is more cash money than they ever have seen before.

It is children who grow up scrawny and underfed and marry their cousins and go deeper into debt.

It is slavery, white slavery and black slavery.

And often it is cruelty and murder. It is the mob vengeful in its fury. It is the luckless Negro dangling from the limb of a tree. It is the luckless Negro tortured and burned at the stake.

All this is my South. All this I carry in my soul and upon my soul.

I first began to see it consciously from a little cottage on a corner in West End, a neighborhood community of Atlanta, Ga., a typical middle-class residential section with nice houses and trees and a trolley line on the street on which we lived.

2

THE white cups of the Southern magnolia gave forth their sweet incense in the summer, a fragrance forever associated with the South and my childhood. The tree stood in the corner of our small yard, generously sharing itself with the passerby along the street, dropping its petals on the sidewalk. Near the house, along the fence, stood a massive oak—or so it seems as I call it up in memory; a rugged sentinel spreading its brawny arms around and over the house protectively.

I remember this oak tree lovingly as a refuge. The mossy carpet underneath the spreading branches was our house from which we set out on all sorts of adventures, my sister and I and our playmates. The little girls brought their dolls and their tea sets there to play house. For us boys it was now a fort, now an Indian blockhouse, now the quarterdeck of a battleship—for the Spanish-American War was over not so long before and the Russo-Japanese War, in time, echoed its way around the world to little boys playing in the front yards of the South. During a gentle summer rain we would huddle together under the oak tree, feeling cozy, and assure my mother as she came anxiously to the front porch and called us to come in that we were not getting wet.

It gave us a feeling of independence, aroused a latent cockiness that we were out on our own. We didn't need the protection of a house. We had our own house. As the rain became more insistent—on occasion—the front porch began to look far away and individually we would feel a desire to dash for its shelter, but none of us could admit that, of course. So we laughed bravely, if self-consciously, too self-consciously, and boasted about how hard it was raining. It would stop presently, and we smiled inwardly at our fears, or it would come down harder and harder and, when mother called a second time, we would start to argue with her, then someone would weaken, then all would scramble madly to the front porch.

We wanted so much to struggle away from the chrysalis and try our wings. I did on two occasions. I don't remember them. My mother used to tell me about them later. They happened in that period which no man can call up from the dark ages of childhood. Once was when I dashed across the street barely in front of an onrushing streetcar, its momentum picking up second by second as it hurtled down the grade in front of our house. My mother was standing on the porch watching my race with death. She had come out to look for me, just in time to see me make my mad dash. She shivered years later when she talked about it, and would seize me and hold me to her breast. The other time was my first runaway from home, at about the same age. I was found at the home of Joel Chandler Harris, two blocks away. I came to know him later as a rotund little fellow who walked occasionally past the house. In the winter time he was almost concealed in a great coat that fell nearly down to his feet. There was intense excitement in our neighborhood when Teddy Roosevelt came to visit him and sat on the big porch which ran around the house, screened with vines, and talked with our local celebrity. On that porch the author did his writing in good weather. His grandchildren were schoolmates and playmates of mine. When he died, we children stood along the streets as the funeral procession passed in a downpour of rain and tossed drenched flowers into the street in tribute. Afterward there was a Maypole dance and festival every year to raise money to make a shrine of his home—Snap Bean Farm, it was called—and one year my sister was Queen of the May. It was quite a pretty sight as I recall it, the costumes and white dresses standing out stiffly and colored streamers of the Maypole against the fresh green background of the large field which adjoined the writer's spreading house. At gaily decorated booths they sold candy and cakes and everybody in our neighborhood went to the festival.

Within a few hundred square feet was enclosed the first world that I remember.

There was constant activity. The streetcars lumbered down the incline past the house every few minutes and against the Belgian block pavement the horses beat their tattoo, now slow and regular as they pulled a heavy wagon up the incline—like this, p-l-o-p, p-l-o-p; now gay and ecstatic, like this, plop-plop, plop-plop, as blooded steeds proudly drew fine equipages, linked two and two. The coachman sat stiff and erect. The plumes of the women waved a feathery trail behind. It was a splendid sight.

13

I remember the chain gang of convicts which came to work on the street in front of the house. With a continuous clank of the chains they moved about their jobs. I watched them with the wide-eyed curiosity of a child. I knew they were supposed to be bad men. That's what I was told. The guard who stood around with a gun in the crook of his elbow looked ominous. The water bucket was on the sidewalk near our fence and when they came over, sweat running down their faces, dragging their chains, they did not look like bad men. Most of them were Negroes, with a few whites sprinkled in between. One day one of them, a Negro, handed me a grimy letter and asked me to mail it. I was frightened at the task but I took it and slipped out the yard and put it in the box on the corner.

There was always one Negro along who would sing as they worked. That was done purposely to keep them contentedly in motion, I have learned since, a theory that has definite scientific basis. They would raise their picks as he sang and then, altogether, they would strike the ground and grunt "Hump" or what sounded like that. Once, in one of these gangs, I heard a voice that was as magnificent as I have ever heard since in grand opera. He was a huge Negro and when he opened his mouth his voice would ring along the whole street. There, perhaps, was a voice lost to a musical world which would have bowed down before it.

With a whining of wheels farm wagons would crawl along our street, the huckster crying out his wares methodically, with no great show of enthusiasm. He would stop at our gate on the side street. His wagon would be piled high with watermelons and "musk" melons and ro's'in' ears and string beans and gleaming yellow squash and other vegetables. (My father never liked squash. He said it tasted like soap and it was not until years later that I actually knew squash and discovered I liked it. Since he didn't like it we seldom had it, and his dislike was mandate enough for me. My mother

14

was very fond of it and would smile teasingly at him as she ate it, with evidence of relish, and he would make a face and always say he didn't see how anybody could eat that stuff.)

The tired horse moved solemnly, and solemnly he would shake his head. Perched atop it at a rakish angle which no serious farmer could have premeditated was a discarded straw hat to keep off the flies. My mother would go to the wagon with her purse and look carefully over the stock, trading shrewdly, for ours was a cautious budget in those days with three growing children, my sister and little brother and myself.

"Please get us a watermelon," we children would plead.

Life was simple as I look back upon it.

We didn't see a great deal of father. Regularly he took the streetcar at our corner at twenty minutes to eight in the morning. Regularly he stepped from it on the opposite corner at noon, coming home for a nap and our dinner in the middle of the day; then, at 1:30 he caught the car back to town again and at 7 o'clock returned home for supper.

We children used to sit out on the porch steps and watch for him at night. Then, sure it was he, we would dash to get to him first. He wore a derby hat. He would catch up into his arms the first one who got to him. Usually I took the newspapers from him and carried them to the house. He always had a copy of the *New York American* in those days. He admired William Randolph Hearst who was then slugging his way into New York journalism, a brash youngster breaking rules and older heads. There I became acquainted with Bud Fisher's Mutt, the race-track tout he was in those days who always ended in the last picture in a barrel. Jeff had not then been created.

After supper, in the summer time, we children would chase about the lawn after lightning bugs, barefooted. The memory of my childhood that comes back with poignant sweetness is associated with the dusk; the sizzling of the hose playing upon the lawn; the feel of the damp grass upon my feet; the flashing of the lightning bugs, now here, now there; in the background the bed-time song of the July fly, fainter than its day-time noisy whir, rising slowly then dropping away gradually and sounding far away; and, through all, filling the air like a blessing, the sweet perfume of the magnolia.

Gradually my world widened.

It extended its frontiers across the street into a shady grove with big trees where we played by the hour. Through a high hedge, on the opposite corner, we peeked into the spacious grounds where sat, several hundred feet from the street, the big home of Evan P. Howell, once mayor of Atlanta, editor of the *Atlanta Constitution*. Later, when he moved away, it became a public park where was laid a great circular cement sidewalk for roller skating for children of the neighborhood.

Our family moved from house to house, each in turn a little larger, as I grew older, but always during my childhood and boyhood in the same neighborhood. I went to the same grade school for eight years, from first to eighth grade. Life rolled over me in a smooth, accustomed course.

Vividly I recall windy October afternoons, munching sweet red apples and playing tag on our skates and follow-the-leader until we were almost ready to drop and, in front of the fire later, dozing as we tried to study tomorrow's geography and history and spelling and arithmetic lessons.

The world grew still bigger. My legs grew long and lanky and I was a bundle of almost uncontrollable energy.

In time it extended to the woods a mile away. November afternoons there; hickory nuts strewing the ground to be cached in pockets bulging with tops, marbles, cigarette pictures of baseball players which we collected and swapped among ourselves, buckeyes and heavens knows what else; hillsides covered with acorns; the valleys stretching away from them yellow with golden rod; leaves turning into a glory now remembered vaguely; the ruddy feeling on the cheeks; the smarting crack in the lips and the rough feeling of chapped hands.

On the edge of the woods was a spring surrounded by weeping willows and two giant magnolia trees. Hot and thirsty from a summer day in the woods which stretched beyond, where we chased each other tirelessly as Indians and cowboys or in hare and hounds, we gathered about Wilson's Spring and, lying on our bellies, drank deep of the ice-cold water which bubbled up from the sands. Never has water tasted so sweet and clean. There was a hill among the woods which we called Bush Mountain and, in the deep of the woods, a pond—Mac's Pond—where we could go swimming in the raw.

I stood one day, when I was thirteen, in the glow of an autumn sunset on the path down Bush Mountain. Several of us had been wandering through the woods. The others had gone on ahead and were shouting to each other as they bounced down the hill, jumping, throwing rocks. I stopped and looked across the colored landscape, red with autumn, toward the setting sun, and into the aisles of trees about me. Something suddenly tore at me inside. Tears came to my eyes. I wondered. I had a great longing to bow down and worship. A shiver coursed through my body. I clutched my hands and bowed my head.

I had found beauty—and had become a man. I had begun to find myself.

Someone shouted at me from below, asking me what was the matter, calling out that I'd get left behind.

I rushed headlong down the hill. I remember it as if it were yesterday.

Today a chain grocery store stands where our house stood, the first little home that I remember. The spring at the edge of the woods has been filled up and is lost somewhere under some of the houses now built in what was once our wilderness. The trees in the woods long ago have been cut down and now there are rows and rows of houses where once we ran wild and free. It is all unfamiliar. Strange people live there, or they seem strange. I resent them.

When I was growing up we bought our groceries and supplies and medicine at stores in a community center about three blocks down Gordon Street from where we lived. Some families traded with one groceryman, some with another, and some shopped here and there. My mother divided her trade, I remember. The men who ran the stores were personal friends and we knew their families.

I remember when the first chain grocery store, a local chain, opened up. We snubbed our noses at it. We would not buy there. It eked out a bare existence for awhile. Then people discovered that things were cheaper there. Gradually it began to flourish. Thus came the chain store.

The automobile entered our small world. I recall the first one in our neighborhood, a wonder and a marvel and a miracle. On Sunday, after the usual dinner of fried chicken and rice and gravy, a vegetable or two, hot biscuits and ice cream, we children would gather along the sidewalk, enviously, covetously, timidly, and watch the neighbor's car as it stood in front of the house. For he was a hospitable neighbor and every Sunday would invite one of the families to crowd with him and his wife into his car—a high-standing contraption it was, cranked on the side—and go for a ride. A telephone call presently would single out the lucky family. We would wrap up warmly even if it was only a bit chilly. Our neighbor wore a tan linen duster and his goggles gave him a mechanical forbidding appearance like the picture of a man from Mars we had seen in the Sunday newspapers. We would chug-chug six or seven miles out in the country along dirt roads from which the dust whirled giddily and back again and think we had been halfway around the world. The automobile has never been so much fun since.

Soon the horse and buggy era passed.

A strange new age was ushered in of which we were only dimly conscious at the time. Gradually, however, it intruded here and there, over a long period of time and we woke up to what it really meant years later. Then we could try to trace it back and put it together.

But we can only half succeed. Others who come after us must solve the ultimate riddle and reveal the ultimate secrets.

For it all happened so slowly and only slowly could it penetrate the solid wall so long built up about our settled way of life. For life seemed to be fairly simple and settled then. Simple and accepted facts were our religion and our politics and our social ways. Our education only served to imbed them more deeply.

The facts were few. The Southern way of life was the best form of life. All the trouble we had had in the South was due to people who had come from somewhere else to disturb us, strange people we called by the name of Yankees. They had come down first to fight us—and how we had fought them! Then, after they had defeated us, they came down to exploit us—though it was not all clear and definite like that. That was the essential meaning. Those were the essential facts. We wanted to be left alone with our troubles. We wanted to take life simply and not try to change it too much. We liked our groove.

Individual Yankees—and we had families in our neighborhood from time to time, here and there—we learned to like. They were all right when they had become a part of us and we accepted them. They were exceptions. We could not believe, if we learned to like them, that other Yankees were like them at all. We thought their talk was strange and some of their ways, especially the stiff politeness with which they treated Negroes, as if Negroes were set off from the rest of us. The Negroes knew they were different, that Yankees were different, and mimicked them to us.

It seems to me now so utterly impossible that we felt as we did so many, many years after Appomattox, but I am trying to tell the truth as I remember it, for this will explain many things we see in our day and age.

The Civil War was very real to me and to those of my generation. We heard it from our grandmothers and grandfathers mostly. Our mothers and fathers did not talk much about it. I think, trying to analyze our psychology, that it was in fact more real to me, in a way, than to my mother and father. They wanted to forget it and look forward, for they lived closer to it. By the time it got to us through the tales and interpretation of our grandparents, colored with old age and memory, it became a romantic episode tinged with poignancy and sadness like the stories of King Arthur and the Knights of the Round Table which I loved as a child. The American history book I studied in grade school was devoted principally to the Civil War, as I recollect it, and written from a partisan standpoint. After studying its accounts of the battles—and we had to know all about the various campaigns, individual battles and leaders —it was hard for me to understand how the South lost. We learned all the "ifs" which might have given the victory to the South. One thing my grandmother did bequeath me for which I have been thankful. That was respect for Abraham Lincoln. Her view was that had Lincoln lived, the terrible reconstruction era would not have occurred—and the reconstruction era was graphically hideous in her memory.

Our Southern patriotism was constantly rekindled. We observed Robert E. Lee's birthday every January 19. He virtually was a patron saint. On Confederate Memorial Day, which was April 26 in our state, all the schoolboys in the city marched in the parade, swinging along proudly for several miles behind the wagons which bore the aged heroes, too feeble now to walk. We practised marching weeks beforehand so that our lines would be clean and straight and we could swing around a corner in good order. We never observed Lincoln's Birthday or national Memorial Day. It took me years to become accustomed to Memorial Day on May 30, and it never has seemed the hallowed occasion that our Confederate Memorial Day was. I grew up with the ready thrill in my spine at the sound of Dixie. I grew up with an instinctive shout at the point of my tongue when I heard it. That seems strange now. I feel guilty when they play it, for it does not mean anything to me, and immediately all eyes turn upon me, teasing and provocative. I'm expected to do something about it—I don't know just what.

Religion, or the form of it, was an accepted part of our lives. Our family was Baptist. Others were Methodists or Presbyterians or Christians, or occasionally Catholics. From my grandmother's stern lips I learned Baptist dogma, why their form of baptism was the only true form, was the form that Christ had used. (I never knew exactly how she was so sure.) Sprinkling as the Methodists did it—bah! she grimaced and shuddered when she spoke of it.

Sunday was a day for religion and not much else. We children went to Sunday school in the morning and, when we grew old enough, accompanied our parents to church at 11 o'clock. The service usually was long. I can remember the long summer hour of service. The preacher's wife, a big, solid woman, sat right in front of us, and her palm leaf fan moved methodically, as if attached to an electric motor. I squirmed on the hard pew. The air was close though all the windows were open, and the sound of streetcars would come in from outside to drown out the preacher's voice. The preacher, a big, four-square man, would weep unashamed, as he rose to his climax and called upon sinners to repent. We had two aged preachers, retired, who attended our church. They were called upon to pray on alternate Sundays. Both implored the Lord at great length. As one of them would be called upon to pray, the congregation would look around at itself, smile resignedly at one another, and bow collective heads for the ordeal.

There were two bright spots in our Puritan Sundays. One was the big dinner in the middle of the day which was always a special dinner; I used to churn the ice cream and got to lick the dasher. The other was the box of candy that father had brought home Saturday night which was opened, with much ceremony, after our light, pick-up supper on Sunday night. Sundays as I remember them, aside from these pleasant interruptions, were somewhat doleful. We were not allowed to play the regular games which we played on weekdays. The city, itself, observed strict blue laws, and no places of amusement were open. I remember, as a very small child, how the whole family would take a long street-car ride on Sunday afternoon. When the automobile came along, and we acquired one, we would take a long automobile ride. Why that was all right and it was not right to play baseball or football or other games I never could quite understand, though it did not disturb me much. We just accepted that. I recall the first time I went to a theater on Sunday. It was in Washington, after I was grown. I felt guilty and out of place.

For I had been a devout sort of youngster. There was a time when I felt "called" to the ministry, as it was termed. One day a visiting evangelist at our church, who was putting on the annual "protracted meeting," asked who would be willing to go to China as a missionary and I stood up, feeling lonely and uncomfortable, but also proud. No one else got up. I did not go to China as a missionary. Maybe that is why today I feel more antagonistic to missionaries than to perhaps any other class of people. They are always getting involved in China and having to be rescued. And the Chinese people, I think, know what gods they want to worship without any direction from me.

But religion and preachers perhaps did have some influence in rare instances that dug down into me.

Despite all the dogma I did come to see the beauty of soul of Christ the Man who tore away the sham of his day, paid heed to the lowly and distressed who were born to days of hardship and toil, and showed the way to a kingdom on earth within the man, himself; but, at the same time, could give way to a righteous fury as when he drove the money-changers from the temple. I, too, have been swept by frequent, deep-seated angers—and that is part of my story.

There was one preacher who revealed to me the beauty of Sidney Lanier, our own Georgia poet and musician. In a series of half sermons, half lectures one summer he talked of "The Marshes of Glynn" and "The Sun." He was a Congregationalist, Dr. Thornwell Jacobs, later president of Oglethorpe University near Atlanta which he helped to found.

And there was another preacher who gave me a motto.

"Only the best."

New Year's Day, aged thirteen, I was sitting at the bottom of the stairs in our house on a landing printing it out on a piece of cardboard to hang in my room—"Only The Best"—when my father ran down the steps, a wild man, mumbling, terrified, and shouted to me:

"Son, she's gone."

That was the day my mother died. That was one of two days when my world tumbled about my head. It happened so quickly. She had become really ill only that morning. The doctor had gone upstairs an hour or two before. I sat at the bottom of the steps waiting for a report, but not expecting anything serious.

She was such a cheerful soul and so close to me and always such a good sport about everything. I was her first-born. We were each other's best friend. That was our relationship and it was a beautiful one.

Trouble came into my world. It had been peaceful and quiet, like the sweetness of a Southern summer night. Trouble of others came into my world. I began to see the world about me. But yet only vaguely, with no clearness, just here and there something that disturbed me, something I could not understand. The fires that stirred my being later were kindled slowly, a little spark here, a little spark there, that hardly flickered consciously at the time. Looking back I recognize them now.

3

NEARLY every Sunday afternoon, from the time I was about nine until I was thirteen or fourteen, I went with my father to a Sunday school he conducted in a woollen mill district about a mile from home. We left the house soon after dinner and walked there, down along Gordon Street by nice, comfortable homes where, in the summer, people would be sitting on their front porches; past the business center of West End where the grocery stores and drugstore were; under the trestle of the Southern Railroad; then suddenly into squalor and misery where the streets were not paved, a cluster of unkempt, unpainted houses dominated by the mill, a dirty, gaunt, silent monster on Sunday, glaring down through its unwashed, gloomy eyes upon the meager habitations of its weekday victims.

The Sunday school was one of the missionary ventures of our church. There was a sallow, flat-breasted, stern-visaged woman, sharp of features, always dressed in a black dress tarnished with wear, with a missionary's bonnet atop her thin, graying hair, who was employed by the church to work with the mill people. She was pleasant in a strained way, but somehow, haggard and sorrowful. Miss Mamie, we called her. We had her to dinner at our house occasionally. She had, I have thought since, a lovely but tortured soul. She married a drunkard—a widower who worked intermittently at the mill—to take care of his children and, with the earnest belief, I'm sure, that she could reform him and make a man of him. But he was satisfied with the man he was. That marriage came later. She was an energetic, nervous spinster when I first knew her, inclined to be a bit harsh with the mill children at Sunday school if they did not behave. But I never thought she meant anything.

My father's rôle was superintendent of the Sunday school, which meant that he stood on the platform, called upon people to pray at intervals, cheerily gave out the songs and urged people to sing. We would have an opening service of song and prayer and then everybody would divide into classes for Sunday school. My father taught the men and women. Young girls from our Sunday school taught the young people and the boys and girls.

The Sunday school was held in the top of a two-story building reached by a long wooden stairway on the outside. In weekdays the room was used for school and there were a few desks in front with rows of chairs back of them. In the winter the room was heated by a big stove that stood in the center of the room. The air was heavy and fetid in the winter when

25

the stove was going full blast. The Saturday night bath did not seem to be general. I associate that odor of bodies with the Sunday school.

I always had on my Sunday clothes, was brushed and neatly dressed and clean, and somehow I always felt a little uncomfortable, for the other children were necessarily shabbily dressed and I did not want there to be any difference. I felt sorry for them, but I did not want them to know that I felt that way. I wanted them to feel that they were the same as myself. There were two or three boys of my age with whom I always sat at Sunday school and I wanted to be accepted by them. I did not want to feel apart, and yet I felt I was. They would look at me, look at my clothes, timidly. They were setting me off in a class, and I honestly didn't have any class consciousness.

I wanted to help them and I did not know how. I accepted the order of things. I can recall even yet a feeling of heaviness as I set out with my father each Sunday, an antipathy to going to the Sunday school and seeing someone who was poor and didn't have the same sort of home I did, the sort of life I did. I didn't want to think the world was like that. That must have been it. I was always relieved when the praying and the singing and the Sunday school lessons were over and behind me and felt relieved when we came back out from under the trestle again and entered our accustomed world.

There was always a Christmas tree on some night before Christmas and it hurt me to see their eagerness in getting so little—a toy, some fruit and candy in a fancy stocking from the ten-cent store; for I knew I would find many more presents on Christmas morning at home. Pity was born in me from those experiences.

The whole scene comes back to me—the wheezing of the organ on the platform; my father standing there smiling cheerfully and singing lustily; those about me, children, young men and women, middle-aged men and women, old people, all singing hymns about salvation earnestly, and all listening as my father talked, their heads bowed as he led in prayer and as others prayed; and the close odor of unwashed bodies and clothes that had been worn too long.

My father never said anything much about the mill, about conditions there. He undoubtedly had his ideas about what went on in this half world. According to his lights, he was trying to do something. He was trying to save their souls, to teach them patience with their lot. He never quarrelled with the system in my hearing, but I guess I was too young to be told the facts of the uneven economic and social order.

I see him again, standing there, a kindly expression on his face.

He told them about the children of Israel who finally reached a Promised Land.

From knots in their handkerchiefs, from battered and worn pocketbooks, from the bottoms of pockets in stained, unpressed trousers, came presently the coins to drop in the collection box to send missionaries to China and Africa and India to spread the glad tidings of salvation.

4

VAGUE doubts agitated me intermittently. But they were encouraged only rarely in the process of my Southern education in high school and college. Questions were smothered under the comfortable cloak of middle-class conservatism. The occasional itch, like that from the bite of the Georgia "chigger," was rubbed into a temporary and pleasantly inciting glow, only to disappear tomorrow with the application of ointment.

There was one professor in high school who was so bold as to poke around in the social stream of Atlanta. His daily stint was ancient and medieval history which seemed to bore him as it did us. His heart was not much in it. But he had an outside hobby—and his heart was in that. This was the inequitable tax system of the city, inequitable as the politicians administered it. His chief complaint was the favoritism shown our Coca-Cola millionaire, Asa G. Candler, who, he said, paid taxes on a very negligible valuation on the pride and joy of our growing city, the twenty-one-story Candler Building on Peachtree Street, while the average man was taxed closely to the value of his property. Looking back, I don't know how he was permitted such heresy. His study had been thorough and exhaustive. I guess his enthusiasm had to spill over in revelation. I suppose he did not fear that second-grade high school students would be much concerned. He just had to talk to someone. It left an impression on one youthful mind which could have been impressed by more facts about the world in which we live—had someone taken the trouble to explore and tell.

The Candlers, being then our outstanding wealthy family, were treated reverentially by press and pulpit—and by the city government. They had achieved, because the palate of America had taken to a five-cent drink that was stimulating. Asa Candler had risen in the good old American way—as did Henry Ford later—by devising a cheap product for the masses. Until fairly well along in life he had been a small-time druggist, as Henry Ford had been a small-time mechanic with an idea. There was luck in it, of course. We often forget that, as we bow down to the "enterprise and initiative" of our capitalists.

28

Atlanta was the Candlers and Coca-Cola, and the Candlers and Coca-Cola were Atlanta. So the city was known afar. It is of course, toying with the truth to say Atlanta was a city built by a soft drink, but the soft drink contributed much to its fame and fortune, and the Candlers were our royal family and a dominant influence in our city life of that day. Asa Candler was interviewed about civic affairs and business conditions. We elected him mayor once on a "reform" wave, one of those occasions when the populace is convinced that what the city needed was to take it away from the "politicians" and have a "business administration by a businessman." Subsequently, of course, we handed it back to the politicians. The Candlers developed their eccentricities, some of them, and some of them were involved in the usual troubles that come to plague the rich. Even Asa, himself, became involved in a breach-of-promise suit by a New Orleans beauty who supplied his ardent love letters— he was well along in years then—to the court and the public. Vicariously we enjoyed these troubles that only the rich can afford. After all, it was our royal family, and it was nice to have them human and amusing.

The family's prestige was elevated—and somewhat protected—by the presence of a bishop, Bishop Warren A. Candler, a brother of Asa, a powerful man of the cloth in one of the most powerful Protestant flocks of Georgia and the South, the Methodists. His dictum was law ecclesiastically—and in other ways. The bishop pointed the way for the donation of his brother's soft-drink millions to church and education and great was the name of Candler in my time.

It was a potent combination of wealth and religion. Deep into Georgia's economy and politics did its influence spread. As the business grew, as the fountain of never-ceasing nickels leaped higher and higher, it showered riches upon other men and, in time, really big capital bought it out and raised up still other millionaires. (In every family was the knowing one who claimed that he knew he should have bought Coca-Cola stock way back—and look where the family would be now, on Easy Street. He would shake his head sadly. For some had gambled on it, and he could point out their ornate residences and sweeping lawns.) It was only natural that Coca-Cola should enter politics to keep its taxes down and protect its various interests, and this it did.

Cola-Cola speaks effectively in Georgia politics today. It is one of the sacred business institutions, along with the Georgia Power Company, and the textile mills which are sprinkled about the state.

It was something of this which my high school teacher was hinting to us. I have learned all about it since.

Such heresy dared not raise its head at the University of Georgia.

Here, in fact, was a world away from the world—these ancient buildings and old trees at Athens among which I spent some of the happiest days of my life. Those were the careless and carefree years.

There I lived almost entirely in the past, a recluse from the dingy world of dirty factory and run-down farm and problems which we all were dodging. Tradition—and the University of Georgia was steeped in that—conduces to pleasant unawareness. The faded fragrance of the Confederacy still lingered there. The civilization which flowered in the Confederacy still was an ideal, with its proper allotment and distribution of those who were lords and those who served. It tried to impose itself upon the new industrial civilization. So the grandsons of men who had fought for the preservation of that older civilization came to the University to spend impressionable years under a fictitiously benign afterglow and to return home, little the wiser, to assume the rôle of lords and masters in their little principalities, humble though they might be. The existing order was not challenged at the University. It was only perpetuated, father to son, father to son.

None of this I saw at the time, of course. I see it all now as I look back. I did not think it strange then, as I do now, that we were not encouraged to look realistically at the world about us. What I found as I poked about in the past was heart's delight.

College was the Fountain of Beauty for me.

I was content to dream with Athens which sat sleepily upon her hill, patiently tolerating the generations of young men who pattered up and down her streets, gamins for a day and then away to the worries of a hard world. The slow stream of the city's life flowed in and about the college, catching upon its bosom the faded leaves from that ancient tree. For the University was old, as we in America count time. It was founded in 1785.

Ghosts filled the place, ghosts of long dead statesmen who had been young men here and then had gone away to play their parts on the political stage—powerfully in the early days of the country when the Southern influence was predominant at Washington; as rulers in their own right and generals of armies during the brief history of a new nation, the Confederate States of America; less adequately in these latter days when the chains of an ancient tradition, something exemplified in the outworn expression "state rights," employed as an excuse, hobbled their steps and kept them behind the procession toward a new nationalism. They and their Southern colleagues were a constant drag on any progress which recurrent leaders strove to make through the party to which they gave their nominal allegiance, the Democratic Party. They constituted a political chain gang watched and guarded carefully by the overseer of the new industrial oligarchy of the South—always with exceptions, of course.

In the room across the hall from my own room in Old College (a solid, brick dormitory built in 1801) had lived and pondered as a student the diminutive Alexander Hamilton Stephens, Vice-President of the Confederacy, a little man with an enormous head. Bob Toombs, United States Senator and Secretary of State of the Confederacy, was one of our legends. He was expelled from college shortly before graduation but returned on Commencement Day, brilliantly intoxicated, and, taking his stand under a spreading tree before the Chapel—afterwards known as "Bob Toombs' Oak"—he delivered an oration which gradually emptied the Chapel of its Commencement guests and left University officials and graduating students to a cheerless ceremony in a vacuum. Bob Toombs opposed secession in principle, but acquiesced when Georgia left the Union. His conversion was permanent. He remained a rebel to the end of his life. He refused to take the oath of allegiance to the United States when the war was over and died a Confederate. Nor was he content with the controversy of statecraft directing a war. He left the cabinet of Jefferson Davis and took to the field of battle under the Stars and Bars.

These glories of the past were the bread and meat from which we young men drew our sustenance.

It was so easy and so satisfying to look backward.

We young men went to the University, most of us, for no particular purpose, or so it seems now when I look back. Some stayed only a year; some less than a year. Only about half of the freshman class returned next year as sophomores. Graduation in the heat of middle June, swathed in those stifling black robes, saw only a thin remnant of the flock which had bubbled in noisily and joyously four years before. Graduates went back home to business or the law to become, in time, the sober, leading citizens, members and presidents of the Chambers of Commerce, members of the country club "set"; teachers of Sunday school classes. Some entered politics and, in the course of time, sat in the legislature, or in Congress at Washington. A few attained the governor's chair; a few got to the United States Senate. A few took to the arts and sciences seriously and strayed far away. But the bulk remained in the state and trod prosaic paths. There were those who became professional alumni and travelled back to Athens to the football games; got a little drunk; arrogated to themselves the right to denounce the current football coach if he did not turn out a championship team, and ganged up to throw him out and get another. Then there were those who didn't care. I went back for my five-year reunion. Something was gone. I have never been back since—and won't be.

Young men who wanted a University background to help their future careers in the state managed to study enough to pass, to be in a fraternity, to go with the right girls from the right families. They were pleasant and amiable companions in those days. One of my early rebellions was over a lecture an elder brother in the fraternity delivered us freshmen one night about the necessity of going with the proper girls from the proper families. It looked like arrant snobbishness to me, but undoubtedly behind it was the best of Southern college tradition. The Confederacy still lived.

Ours was a small world in the University and the town which stretched away on every side of it.

And our constant monitor was a bell, the Chapel bell, a monster of a bell with a clear and regular and determined clang that penetrated beyond the campus into the farthest recesses of the town and, its metallic tone sweetened by

33

distance, drifted gently into the countryside like an after-thought of prayer. Now its voice was sharp and reprimand-ing as it called you from warm covers of a winter morning, or when it summoned you from idle gossip of a lazy May afternoon into a bare classroom stifling with the smell of chalk and dust. Now its voice was joyful when its call did not mat-ter, for it did not call you; joyful, too, when it began its pæan as some stout freshman pulled the cord up and down lustily to announce an athletic victory. For thus were athletic vic-tories announced and sometimes the bell rang merrily nearly all night long as freshmen relieved each other in regularly prescribed order.

The bell, I know, tolls still. It tolled long before I heard it. It will toll long after I am gone.

It is time and it is timeless.

It rings now in my ears.

To me it rings of permanence in a changing world, of young men who are forever young, for only the young move in that world of the University; of old fables of long ago, for they, too, are permanent.

It rings in my ears and the routine returns—drill an hour every morning three days a week, squads right, squads left, present arms, shoulder arms; sauntering about the campus from class to class; football games on crisp October and November afternoons; the crack of the bat and the plop of the glove on spring afternoons under a blue sky speckled with dainty fluffs of cloud; nights over the books, with frequent wandering of the eyes from my desk in our room atop Old College across the campus toward the city; dances on week-ends—faint perfume and careless laughter under the stars; walks in the moonlight and the smell of flowers; Sunday afternoons and nights trailing around in gangs calling on the right girls, a sport somewhat boring.

34

On Wednesday nights the debating societies had their weekly meetings. The attendance was small but regular. I belonged to Phi Kappa. A very keen rivalry existed with Demosthenian, the other literary and debating society. Each had a hall. The first floor of our building was occupied by the College Co-op; the first floor of Demosthenian by the College Y.M.C.A. The halls were on the second floor. Each society had a long and honored history, perhaps much more honored in the early days when oratory was full of sound, if not meaning. I participated in the annual Freshman Debate, arguing on the affirmative side of government ownership of railroads in which, incidentally, I have believed ever since. Our side lost. I attended regularly in my freshman year, but lost interest thereafter. The societies had their faithful following, mostly young men who had aspirations for the law. Being a lawyer still seemed to be the ambition of so many—then lawyer into politics. Talk is a strong Southern trait, and if you can get paid for doing it before a jury, or in the legislature, or in Congress, why so much the better. But, even if you don't get paid for it, it goes on and on. There's something in the long season of beneficent weather in the South which makes it tempting to stop whatever you are doing and talk awhile, or if you are just strolling down the street, to stop on meeting a friend and talk, and talk. I do it still, when there's work of the world to be done.

Among the solid old piles of brick and stone and the ancient trees I led a sort of hallowed existence and, like an archaeologist, picked and dug among the glory that was Greece and the grandeur that was Rome. Greek and Latin I absorbed in plentiful doses and so with English and all sorts of history. I took only the required mathematics and sciences.

We had a delightful and able professor of Greek whose theory it was that the language taught you to think. I don't know whether it worked out that way in my case, but it did carry me back to sunshine and cloudless skies and white temples and beautiful human bodies and clear minds, to seas which danced with light, into wooded hills where satyrs dwelt and Pan piped, into isolated mountain passes where brave men fought. I travelled with Xenophon and wandered with Odysseus and sat as a witness at the trial of the thirty generals. Greece and all things Grecian fed my spirit to the full.

My Greek professor gave me a satisfying conception of democracy.

"Ninety-nine out of a hundred times," he said, "democracy is inefficient and cumbersome. But then there comes the hundredth time, a crisis, when it is necessary for the people to rise up and assert themselves and protect their liberties. Democracy affords the means for that, and for that it is worth keeping."

That was long before Hitler and Mussolini.

From him I learned to believe passionately in democracy. My faith still is unshaken.

And yet, though I took much American history, I learned precious little about our democracy, that is, as it was working out. My political science course told me how democracy operated, that is, theoretically. I knew all the forms. But I did not learn how those forms were being twisted and used to suppress real democracy. We were not encouraged to be particularly curious. The sweep of great social forces was not brought to our attention. No startling questions were propounded to us to create the inquiring mind. We looked at the world around us passively, without asking too much why it was that way.

We were shaken up a bit by the World War when it swept in upon us and began to break up our peaceful college life. When I came back from a few weeks at Camp Taylor, near Louisville, to resume my college course, there was a restless spirit abroad in the school. The sudden release from war restrictions reacted back into the campus through those who had been under them, even for a brief period. Students began to complain about the food at the Beanery, as we called the dining hall, and to put up broadsides about this and other school institutions on trees about the campus. They were unsigned and were hung out in the dead of night, like the work of mischievous boys. In those days, too, students began to drink more. There was one occasion—and it caused quite a scandal—when several students, dead drunk, were found in the early morning hours stretched out on the campus, near the entrance gate, after a big night. Well also I remember the return of the three soldiers, out of eighteen of us sent to Camp Taylor, who remained behind to get commissions in the reserves. They turned up one day in February in their brilliant new officer's uniforms, and were almost hooted off the campus. To Hell with the war! We had seen the world and we were proud of our disillusionment.

I look back upon those weeks at Camp Taylor on bare plains and little eminences swept by November winds; the chill mornings when we stood about pitching shells to each other and listening to interminable lectures about tactics; raw afternoons spent jumping on and off wooden horses— I never did get on a real horse. And I think of myself as a soldier, a potential officer! I was so immature. I dread to think of what might have happened if I had commanded troops in France.

I recall a drill one day at school during the period of the Students Army Training Camps, the S.A.T.C., when colleges were turned into barracks. This was before I went to

Camp Taylor. I stood holding my gun at "Present Arms." Suddenly I thought to myself, looking down the barrel which ran along my nose: "This is what the world is worshiping today—this is our god." A feeling of disgust and uselessness swept over me. Then there was bayonet practice conducted by a chubby little youngster, about eighteen years old, who had received a commission after a few weeks in Plattsburg, a rosy-cheeked youth. In a high-pitched voice he shouted at us, his soldiers there before him:

"Give 'em the cold steel, boys! Give 'em the cold steel!"

His young guts would have made a pretty mess.

Then there was the day I forgot my own name.

In little batches they were sending the boys from college out of the S.A.T.C. to camp. I received instructions one day to report to the commandant. I knocked on the door properly, stood properly at attention before the six-foot regular army officer who sat straight and erect at a desk, a fine figure of a man, weatherbeaten of face. He asked me my name. For the life of me I couldn't remember it. I stood there staring at him. It wasn't funny to me. I took myself rather seriously. He smiled—a good yarn to tell over evening mess.

"When you can remember your name, maybe I will call you back," he said, not unkindly.

I saluted and departed, feeling like a fool.

I did not get off to the wars with that consignment. But the military machine was gluttonous and later I was called again, and I remembered my name, and eighteen of us set out October 31, 1918, and landed on November 1, my birthday, at Camp Taylor. No band was there to meet us, not even a corporal. (We really expected something.) Carrying our baggage—and my father had presented me with a huge valise which was chockful of unnecessaries—we wandered for two or three hours looking for the 48th Training

38

Battalion. Khaki-clad figures, idling about the endless rows of barracks we passed in our search, hooted at us:

"You'll like it—"

I never did.

We could hear the noisy celebration in Louisville, several miles away, on the night of November 7, the premature Armistice. But they would not let us leave camp. Instead of that they herded us into an assembly hall and told us we were going to be sent to Russia. We gave them what later came to be known as the Bronx cheer. Then the officers, too, relented, and told us how the old army game worked, how a few of us had been picked each day to be criticized publicly for practically everything from morning until night. I had a day of persecution. Though I was a veteran at close-order drill I was called out for not turning a squads right quick enough and publicly reprimanded, and later that day was called from the ranks again and told I had my belt on backwards. For this offense—and that's the way I always wore my belt and continued to wear it—I was made to dog trot half a mile across the parade ground, touch a fence, and return.

College again after my brief military experience in the outer tents of war was a retreat. I was glad to get back to my books and the cheerful companionship of young fellows who had no particular purpose in life, back where the days rolled easily and, as a senior, I could sleep late and have other privileges.

The patriotic spirit, a little tarnished, nevertheless lingered on with us for awhile. I was editor of the college magazine my senior year. One of the younger professors who advised with us on the magazine suggested a War Memorial Issue, with war experiences contributed by alumni who had participated. So I sent out letters and got an amazing number of volunteer contributions.

Our faculty was composed for the most part of gentle men. There was an occasional firebrand who exploded in class with sarcasm. By and large, they were conformists, at least as far as their teaching went. They did not raise any pertinent questions about the existing order, or instil any doubt into future citizens of a state that needed a good dose of doubt. For they knew their trustees who represented the stable economic lords of the state.

Our state university was poor. Professors who had no less a responsibility than moulding the thinking of the future citizens of the state struggled along on meager salaries that the overlords would not have paid some of their clerks, and saw their families grow larger and larger about them. The legislature was niggardly with funds. The state was gerrymandered in favor of the rural districts, which is common in our country, and the farmer representatives could not see why much money should be spent on "higher learning," as it was called. I understand that has changed somewhat in the intervening years, for some of those in college with me and since that time have gone to the legislature and the governor's chair and have paid some heed to the University. During my time one of the professors had to spend a good deal of his time in Atlanta lobbying with the legislature to get appropriations. Matters would have been still worse had it not been for the money we got from the Federal government. That's why we maintained an R.O.T.C. unit and that's why I learned squads right before the war came on.

I did not know then so much about the influence on education of the powers-that-be, the industrial overlords. I did not pay any attention to the solemn, respectable group of men who gathered every June on the eve of Commencement. They were, I was told in a reverent, hushed voice, the "trustees." They were assembling in annual conclave. I could not see that they had anything to do with me, or I with them.

They were for the most part, I know now, good Christian, Confederate gentlemen.

They were interested in seeing that the ideas their fathers had passed down to them should be passed down to their sons—the idea that some men are born to be masters and the others to take orders from them; the idea that the existing social and economic order is right and that those who question it are "agitators" who should be dealt with summarily; the idea that religion is something for Sunday, a necessary nuisance of sitting stiffly in a hard pew, singing praises to God dolefully, listening to some long-winded minister whom they privately regarded as a simple-minded fellow with no "get-up-and-go" as he talks about prophets who lived thousands of years ago, and sometimes of a man called Jesus, but with not too much emphasis on what Jesus thought about the rights of the lowly. The emphasis is on the "meek," which covers those who work in mills and factories and are properly satisfied with their lot, and keep their eyes glued on the world hereafter and not this poor one.

"Praise God from whom all blessings flow—"

It rings out through the still Sunday morning in Georgia city, town and village.

I used to listen to it of a Sunday at the Methodist Church in Athens where freshmen foregathered chiefly because, at the appointed hour of morning service, a whole flock of pretty girls from Lucy Cobb Institute would be herded in to take their seats. A young man was preaching there then. Later he was transferred to another church in a larger city which was the center of a big textile industry. He was so bold one Sunday as to comment on the miserly wages paid in the mills. The paternalistic system ran riot there, with company stores and company houses and a company church. One of the stewards of the church, who was also a trustee of the University, was head of the textile company. So, after the sermon, the stewards gathered in a group about the minister and, gently but firmly, told him he could not talk about one of their number that way. They reminded him that, after all, the mill head was a large contributor to the church—and to his salary. The young man listened gravely. The next Sunday, and the Sunday after, he preached the same gospel again. Then, suddenly, he was transferred to Los Angeles.

"Praise God from whom all blessings flow—"

ך

NEGROES always had been an accepted part of my life. We had Negro cooks who were a part of our household.

There was Ida, a light-skinned cook, a slender, neat efficient woman whom I remember only vaguely. She had been my mother's first servant after her marriage and had taught her how to cook. My mother often used to recall Ida and what a splendid cook she was.

"She taught you—and that's praise enough," my father would say, for my mother was an excellent cook.

Then there was Corinne, a spare, gawky girl, full of laughter, with a spiteful streak that revealed itself occasionally. Her favorite diversion was attending a stock company which played in one of our theaters—Negroes could sit in the second gallery, or "peanut gallery" we called it—and she would mimic the actresses, throwing her body about with an artful and, at the same time, artless gesture.

42

There was old Aunt Lucy, a squat motherly woman who was both cook and nurse for my young brother. She used to roll him in his buggy down Gordon Street every afternoon to the Southern Railroad trestle and there the two would sit and watch the trains go by. She told how he loved to watch the trains. I always suspected the interest was mutual. She was with us for years.

Then there was big-boned, graceless Mary, loud-voiced and raucous, who was adept at picking up neighborhood gossip.

Maud, whose tan face was pock-marked from small pox, remains in memory chiefly for her lemon pies.

Negroes had their place. They had to be respectful, though they weren't always and, when they had been with the family a long time, they virtually entered the councils on domestic matters. Some were temperamental. They might pout when they had, for some reason, to stay on their afternoon off, or when they had to stay later than usual at night. Their big lips then would drop dolefully and they would put on a great show of persecution, mumbling as they went about their chores.

"Lawsy, I can't understand your mother sometimes," one would say in the hearing of one of the children.

We understood all that. If they got sick, we had the family doctor go to see them. We knew they "toted," that is, carried away food at night for their families. That was a privilege which everybody winked at. One of our Yankee neighbors when I was a boy couldn't understand that. She thought it was a frightful practice and she was determined to break it in her household. But she found servants suddenly leaving, and finally she had to fall in with the custom of the country.

There was a Negro boy, son of one of the cooks in our neighborhood, who used to play baseball with us. He was deferential and, when there was a question raised as to whether he had been safe or out, he would always step aside quietly and not enter the quarrel. We recognized a difference between him and us. So did he. He was a good companion. But there was that difference.

Dimly, as in some long forgotten dream, I recall an atmosphere about the neighborhood during the Atlanta race riots, when I was very small. I can remember talk about the home guard, men of the neighborhood who patrolled the streets at night. Nothing ever happened in our neighborhood during that time, but I have a recollection of a tense feeling, something mysterious to me.

There was one amusing and revealing incident.

Oliver, a light-skinned, middle-aged little Negro who came around every morning to take the grocery order, did not turn up one morning. He was so regular and so faithful that curiosity was aroused in the neighborhood when Oliver didn't appear. He was the stable, reliable sort of person who never got into trouble. The family said just that in expressing surprise at his failure to be on hand as usual.

He appeared next morning, a little shamefaced.

He explained he had been arrested for carrying a pistol. Nobody seemed to think that was a crime and did not hold it against Oliver. People felt they could trust him. The incident soon was forgotten, and for years thereafter he appeared regularly every morning at the back door, pencil in hand, hat off. He had the eager look of a fox terrier. I remember that.

One of my earlier recollections is of Judea, the Negro boy who delivered our groceries, shuffling around the corner of the house whistling "It's a Hot Time in the Old Town Tonight." It was a skilful and musical two-tone trill, a tenor and bass combination, each clear and distinct, and I tried in vain for years to learn the trick. As I look back,

I see that picture of Judea. It's a Southern summer morning. The air is fresh before the still heat that comes later. The grass is cool and crisp on my bare feet. Judea grins when he sees me, showing his shining teeth. He wears long pants rolled a time or two at his ankles, hand-me-downs from some white customer. They sag amply at the knees. He wears a fancy vest that hangs loose, an affectation to which he clings despite the heat, and a straw hat that has seen many and better seasons. His shoes are over-size and delicately pointed. There are slits across the toes which he has cut with his knife. Birds chat merrily in the background, somewhere in the big oak tree in the front yard. Gyp, our water spaniel, dashes across the lawn in pursuit of a sparrow which rises giddily a few feet ahead of his nose.

"It's a Hot Time in the Old Town Tonight." Remember it, the Spanish-American War tune back at the turn of the century?

It was just such a morning many years later, as youth counts time, that I bustled cheerily into the newspaper office where I worked in a small Southern town. I was chief reporter, city editor, sports editor, and odd-job leg man. I also took want ads over the front counter and listened to complaints about the paper not being delivered. I was quite a titled and busy fellow.

As I entered, the other and superior half of the staff, whom I shall call Burt, got up from the big roll-top desk he used. There was suppressed excitement bottled up in Burt. It was particularly signified in the light in his bright, eager eyes and the tilt of his slender face, like a dog sniffing something interesting. (Burt enjoyed all the other titles and worked hard at them, managing editor, make-up man, editorial writer, head-line writer, head and sole keeper of the copy desk. In short, he and I got out the paper.)

45

"I've been waiting for you," he said, and he tried to make his voice toneless and matter-of-fact, but he didn't fool me.

There was no reprimand in his voice, though I was a few minutes late.

"There's been a murder," he said, almost apologetically.

"A murder?" I croaked.

He nodded his head and threw his cigarette on the floor, crunching it with his foot.

I was properly impressed. I had never covered a murder. A question ran through my mind: "How do you cover a murder?"

"Yep, out on Hull Mill Road. White woman, farmer's wife, killed. They think a Negro did it. You'd better go out there, I guess. You can go in Joe's car. (He was the business and advertising manager of our small daily.) Get the story and call me from somewhere and tell me what it looks like."

Burt had worked for a time on a big city newspaper. Now he was being the crisp efficient managing editor under whom he had worked. All this passed through my head as I said, equally crisply, "Yep, Burt," and turned about to be the energetic reporter, grabbing up a handful of copy paper from my desk alongside his own.

"You go to the end of Harrison Avenue and turn into Hull Mill Road. You know where that is?"

I wasn't exactly sure, but I nodded. I remembered the Message to Garcia.

"The house is about three miles down that road. The sheriff's already there. You'll know the place. There'll probably be a crowd when you get there."

I started to go.

"I'll get up your sport copy," he said.

"Thanks," I replied, caught up at forgetting a routine duty and not mentioning it myself.

This meant clipping some "canned" sport stories from a mail service, the standings of the Southern and Sally Leagues

46

from a metropolitan daily, writing heads and sending the copy back to the composing room.

A murder! A murder story! I seethed inside, but very nonchalant was my departure, as if I covered murder stories every day.

It was a day for anything but a murder, a picnic among the trees, a lark—but not a murder. The trees were fresh and green. Dewdrops glittered in the grass. I noticed the morning brightness of Nature with only half a mind, however. Dark and ominous were the thoughts that plagued my mind.

I found the place easily enough. Several automobiles were parked along the road. The house was up an embankment in a cluster of trees. I could see several people standing around as I climbed up the rickety steps which led to the yard above. I recognized the sheriff and approached him. I asked him what had happened.

He was a tall casual individual with vague blue eyes. He turned aside to spit tobacco juice as he talked to me. He affected high boots. His air seemed to be one of assumed calm. His manner was blunt.

"This woman was shot early this morning while her husband was away—down at the cord mill. I guess a nigger done it. We've got bloodhounds out now. Hear 'em?"

He stopped talking—and I could hear them, baying across a valley about half a mile away. I listened. They seemed to be running around in a circle.

"You might ask her husband about it. He's that stout fellow standing over there."

I left him and approached the husband, pulling myself together before I spoke to him. He was talking to two women. His face was round and his general demeanor phlegmatic. He seemed to have control of himself. Timidly, I introduced myself, told him I was a reporter. This was an ordeal for me.

47

He talked freely, in a low voice.

"I was down at the cord mill—went down there at 4 o'clock this morning. I heard a shot, but didn't think nothin' of it. Then I heard my dog bark. I came back to the house and when I went in I found her, lying in the front room, with blood all over her breast."

His voice got lower.

"She was dead. I found a gun lyin' aside the house, over there."

He pointed, and I saw the gun.

"One of my neighbors said he saw a nigger a-runnin' across the field there."

I went over to the corner of the house and looked down at the gun. Then I came back to him.

"It was a gun stole from me a few days ago," he said. "I know who stole it—and we're going to get him."

He spit this out, bitterly, vengefully.

I asked a few more questions, trying to remember to get all the essential facts. I did not go into the house to see the dead woman. Dimly I could see women moving about within in their quiet, commanding way. The house was a frame structure with a long porch clear across the front. A dog lay on the porch in the sun, raising his head occasionally as someone approached the porch.

I did not want to see the dead woman. I abhorred death. I had seen my mother dead when I was thirteen years old. Even a painful reminder of my conscience that it was my duty to go inside, to ask more questions there, my duty as a reporter, could not force me into that gloomy shade where she lay. So many things I neglected to learn, as I look back. But I wanted to get away—and I did. I wanted to get away from this peaceful rural scene now clouded with deep tragedy. Down in the valley the bloodhounds still ran around in circles, barking like lost souls.

48

Back again in the office I slipped a sheet of copy paper in my typewriter and wrote the story. Proudly I read it later when the paper was brought into the news room, hot off the press. There it was, the lead story, with my name across the top.

"You'd better make a check at the sheriff's office and police headquarters," Burt instructed.

As I walked into police headquarters, one of the officers I knew was talking over the telephone. I slid into a chair by his desk and waited for him to finish. Presently he put down the receiver with a last word.

"Hold him there," he directed. "We'll be right out."

"They've got a nigger out at a boarding house at Main and Fourth," he said. "Think he may be the one. Come on, we'll go out."

Two other policemen got to their feet casually. I trailed along and, thrilled to the depths of my reporter heart, I rode perilously on the running board of the ramshackle car as it speeded out the avenue to the boarding house. The Negro made no resistance. He was a nondescript, mild-looking black man. I can't remember his face now. The officers handled him roughly. Meekly he got into the back seat of the car. His story was that he had gone there to visit the Negro butler at the boarding house, a friend. He lived in the country near the scene of the crime. He sat quietly as we bumped along back to police headquarters.

I shouted questions at him above the noises of the car. He said he had nothing to do with the crime.

Quietly he sat later at police headquarters until he was transferred to custody of the sheriff. They took him to a cell in the county jail which was on top of the court house, on the fourth floor of the big stone building. He had a previous police record, a charge of attempted rape of a Negro girl which might mean something or nothing. I went back to

49

the office and wrote a new lead for our second and final edition, across which Burt flung a headline: "Negro Held."

Late that afternoon strangers began to appear in town, grim farmers who stood about in clusters on the street corners. Most of them wore overalls. They were neighbors of the dead woman and her husband. They had come for a purpose. They talked that way and they spat their tobacco that way. They swore sullenly that they were "a-goin' to git that God-damned nigger." So I heard from curious friends who had foregathered with them. I did not. I was disturbed and fearful. Disconsolately I ate my dinner and thought of that Negro up there in his cell on top of the court house. Afterward I went to my own white cell in the local Y.M.C.A. where I lived. I sprawled out on my cot. On the plain, white walls I could see the pictures go by—that farmhouse; the people standing about talking in low tones; the husband; the women moving about the house inside; the bloodhounds in the valley. Again I heard their dismal baying, like lost souls looking for a lost soul. Again I saw that Negro, quiet and stolid. What was he doing up in that lonely cell? I saw the cruel eyes of the men in overalls.

A knock on the door jerked me from my nightmare.

It was a friend who lived down the hall.

"There's a mob gathering in front of the court house," he said excitedly. "Looks like there's going to be a lynching."

It was as if someone slapped me in the face.

"Let's go down and see the fun," he said.

Again, the slap.

"I don't think I will," I replied.

"What—and you a newspaper reporter. How're you going to write this up for your paper?"

He called me back to my duty, though I was ready to give up this duty, this so-called profession. I would like to run away from it all.

But I went.

There was a mob. The streets all around the court house were filled with a restless, shuffling throng. I saw there people I knew and saw every day. They talked to one another in low voices. There was an ominous hush and, coming upon this crowd, unknowing, I would immediately have sensed that something evil was afoot somewhere within it. It had a guilty conscience. Occasionally a person would look cautiously about him, as if he realized suddenly that he should not be here and hoped that some people he knew did not see him here.

This was my first impression and my friend and I stood at the edge of the crowd and looked about.

Up front I got the impression of movement, way up front there at the foot of the court house steps. It did look far away. Between me and that spot were hundreds of tops of heads. The street lamps threw a dim light across faces and shoulders.

Suddenly torches flared up in front. They detached themselves from the human base. Flaming and fiery they moved toward the court house door, bobbing weirdly. Then the men who carried them stood out sharp against the building under the flashing, popping balls of fire over their heads. Their faces were streaked with charcoal for disguise. Indistinguishably they cried out and it all sounded far off and inhuman.

Behind the torchbearers came the yeomen of this night's ghastly business, several men bearing a huge piece of timber.

"Now go to it!"

The command came clear.

The yeomen advanced with a rush and there was a dull thud as the timber met the door. Then there was another attack, another thud, and another attack, and another thud. I became conscious of subdued voices around me, against the background of this thud, thud, thud.

"He's on the top floor—the steps are narrow—one man with a gun could hold them back—if he dare—the sheriff's up there with some deputies, they say—he won't dare—he won't dare—but he'll make a stall at it—"

Boom, boom, boom! The stout timber thunders as stout men propel it. The torches jumped about.

"It's down—the door's down."

There was excitement, fear and pity in the exclamations on all sides.

A ghoulish shout of triumph went up from the torch-bearers and their yeomen. The lights disappeared into the building. The crowd sucked in its breath. I prayed for I knew not what. I turned away.

"Look—they're going up—see the lights!"

Higher and higher the torches rose in the building. The shadows danced against the walls within. One man stuck his head out a window and shouted to the crowd below:

"We'll get the bastard!"

"They're on the third floor. See the lights up there."

The crowd became silent. It was as if a clammy hand clutched at its throat. The torches danced about still on the third floor. It seemed a very long time.

"Look, they're coming down—they must have him."

Downward, swiftly downward, the torches moved—to the second floor—to the first—then disappeared.

"They're taking him out the back—let's go!"

I found myself in the moving crowd. Before we got clear around to the back there was the whine of automobile starters, one after another. Then he came, hustled along by several men with charcoal streaked across their faces. Just a frightened shadow—and he was gone, bundled into an automobile. It all happened so quickly.

"Come on—let's get into a car—we can find one."

My friend shouted at me.

"Nope—I'm not going—I'm not going—"

I turned about and began to push through the crowd, now thinning out. Behind me there was the bang of automobile doors closing, of horns honking, of engines racing. The caravan was off to its horrible business.

I returned to my room and sprawled again on my bed.

Did my story have anything to do with bringing this mob here? Over and over again I asked myself the question and over and over again I told myself that the paper did not even get out into the county where the crime occurred. These men had come, I assured myself, of their own volition. Word had spread quickly through that neighborhood. I could not have started them to town. I could not have stopped them.

I dozed off into a light, troubled sleep and saw myself standing before the crowd on the court house steps pleading with them. It wasn't a dream. It was my imagination telling me what I might have done. It was my conscience telling me what I ought to have done. But the realistic side of my mind told me I never would have done it. It was the hero instinct.

I could not abide my own thoughts. I left my room and walked down the hill away from the Y.M.C.A. I wandered this way and that. Finally I turned homeward again and went to my room. I flopped on the bed. Presently someone was calling my name. I stepped to the door, and shouted back.

"Telephone—"

I went down to the lobby. It was Burt.

"We're going to get out an extra. Will you come down?"

When I got to the office I found that Joe, our business and advertising manager, already had written a description of the scene in front of the court house. The extra was his idea and he had sat down and tapped off several hundred words after calling Burt and assembling enough of the composing room staff to get out the paper.

"You'll have to write a lead," Burt told me, "about the lynching itself. Since you didn't go out there you can pick it up from the crowd when they come back. I imagine that'll be pretty soon."

He hadn't gone either.

He was right. Soon after I stepped out of the door and started up the street I saw them. By twos and threes they scurried along the sidewalk toward me, excitedly talking. I stopped a group I knew.

"It was terrible, Tom. They burned him. And the people who were there! Cars were parked along the road for a mile. People who live out Morrison Avenue, in their limousines. Women, too, right up in the front of the crowd. The husband was there. They asked him to identify the nigger. He said it was the right one.

"They tied him to a tree and then built a fire under him. Poured kerosene all over his body. He said ' 'Fore God I didn't do it. 'Fore God, I'm innocent.' He kept shouting that until the flames choked him. God, it was awful."

I wrote the lead for the extra. Soon after it had gone to the composing room I heard the boys begin their screeching.

"Extra! Extra! All about the lynching!"

Their voices died away gradually as they moved away from the building and our part of town, but, now and then, from afar, like a fugitive night bird, would come a faint shout:

"Extra! Extra!"

"Big town stuff," said Joe, rubbing his hands as he stood over me.

I was slumped in my chair before my typewriter.

"We'll sell a thousand of them at least. Pretty good stuff I wrote there, eh, Tom? Like old times when I was a reporter in Memphis."

I slept very little that night.

The morning paper carried a ringing indictment, by a local judge, of the lynching.

Where was he last night?

Where was I last night?

54

Soon thereafter I left the South.

I was headed for New York, the mecca of ambitious newspapermen from the hinterlands. My love for the newspaper had sprung naturally, I always have believed, from my father. At the time I was born he was writing advertising copy for the business in which he later became a partner, and in that capacity he became acquainted with newspapermen of that day in Atlanta. He told me of sitting about the city room chatting with them. Into my very blood must have been infused something of that friendly and exciting atmosphere of the city room, for the first time I ever walked into one, I immediately felt at home.

Among his newspaper friends of that day were Clark Howell, then editor of the *Atlanta Constitution,* and Frank L. Stanton, the poet columnist of the *Constitution,* author of that little lyric "Mighty Lak a Rose." Stanton constantly bubbled rhyme and, in a gesture of warmth toward my father, wrote a poem about me when I was eighteen months old. It was published in the Junior Supplement with a picture of me, laces, curls, angelic expression and all. (This picture my wife cherishes and has framed with one of her own—no laces, no curls, no angelic expression—showing the contrast between little Southern gentlemen and little female damyanks at that period!)

My father got for me letters of introduction to editors in New York. I still have them. I did not reach New York. I stopped for a few days in Washington and got a job there with the United Press. I have been with Scripps-Howard organizations there ever since.

My departure from the South was not altogether a mad, desperate flight from a land over which a dark and evil spirit seemed to brood; a land of injustice and intolerance and poverty of soul; a land flat and hot under the sun, as I had seen it in middle and southern Georgia; a land of bare little towns and cities where so much unhappiness and dirt and inequality existed. There was something of that in the back of my mind, for something of that still rises to haunt me when I think of the South as I saw it as a reporter here and there. But it was nebulous. Outwardly and openly, my flight undoubtedly was provoked by the spirit of adventure found in every young man, the yearning for further fields that look greener than familiar surroundings. I was seeking a career and this always seems easier in strange lands among strange people.

BOOK TWO

THE DELIRIOUS DECADE

PART ONE. THE GRAB BAG

6

WASHINGTON in 1921 was seeking to return to its legendary rôle of the quiet, placid city along the Potomac, seeking to burrow its head in the mud and sleep for a season, to forget. Its body was weary and its nerves frazzled from the night-before of the War.

The thud of the drums was a dull pain in the back of the brain and the wild cry of the brasses like the sounds of a nightmare recalled from childhood. The parade had passed, leaving scraps of bunting and bits of paper that the wind caught up and whirled about the vacant streets.

The soldiers had come home from the wars, exulted through their brief, blaring welcome, all too short and a bit forced they felt. Then those who were whole of body had gone on back to their homes. But the boats coming back brought loads of men who were not whole of body or soul. They were trundled into hospitals to become the pets of indulgent nurses and of too cheerful doctors who told them pleasant lies and, as they lay day after day and saw the sands of life slipping downward before their eyes, they became morose and full of bitterness for a government which had gathered them together, happy-go-lucky young men, hardened their muscles, put guns in their hands and sent them thousands of miles across the ocean to filthy trenches, and

59

nights in the rain, and the eerie hour of dawn before the ceaseless attack.

For what?

And now, the boats were bringing back those they had left over there, quiet now forever, sons missed from some home, now only bodies in wooden boxes, over which a President of the United States, a new President, a kindly sort of man, would pause now and again and try to say something in his confused, stumbling way. Then an eternal sleep under the trees of Arlington, row on row, or in the family plot on a green hillside of the little cemetery back home. Only mothers and fathers knew or cared.

Yes, the parade had passed. The bands had stopped their noise.

Washington wanted to forget. It discovered, in time, that it could not. The country found that it could not forget. It found out ten years later what a heavy price must be paid in trying. For the nation, trying for a time to forget quietly, learned this was useless and tried to forget as the soldier himself in France had tried, in a mad spree of the physical and material senses.

But this spree began some time later.

Now, Washington was tearing down the bunting and trying to live calmly.

I saw only a slow-moving town that showed little trace of the hysteria of a few months before. True, my impression from Union Station was military in effect—the rows and rows of wooden dormitories, like cantonments, which housed the thousands of women and girls who had come to Washington to feed tons of paper into the war machine, to run red tape, instead of soap suds, through their fingers. And, in the Mall back of Pennsylvania Avenue, there were rows and rows more of these same wooden buildings, now housing various agencies, including—as I learned so well later—

60

the one that was trying in vain to force a hardy and stiff-necked race to abhor its accustomed strong drink.

But there was now no war activity and so, when I came upon Washington, the city seemed to be an eddy away from the torrent of national life as it had been in the days before the war, as we had known it back in the provinces, where the President lived and Congress met, from time to time, to quarrel and squabble over matters that did not seem very important to us. It had been just a blur upon the national consciousness.

My first reaction to Washington, as I recall it now, was what I might label provincialism, induced perhaps by the low, squat buildings and the absence of skyscrapers, by the broad streets and sidewalks and a general atmosphere of casualness and unconcern. No one rushed about here, helter-skelter, with a purposeless, a nervous haste, as in other cities I had known. Here there was an orderliness. The stream of life moved at flood tide twice a day, between 8:30 and 9 o'clock in the morning and between 4:30 and 5 o'clock in the afternoon. Then it spilled over the sidewalks and streets. And it had a definite and precise objective. These people knew exactly where they were going. They were going to their cubbyholes in government buildings in the morning and late in the afternoon they were headed to their manifold domestic warrens. The stream subsided soon after 9 and soon after 5 and again the city was at ease.

At times it seemed almost deserted to me. This was true especially at night. I remember the almost appalling life-lessness in the downtown sections when, in those first days, I went out alone to walk about and discover the city. At home we had a white way along Whitehall and Peachtree Streets and at night people went downtown to parade back and forth gregariously. There was life and color and move-ment. Here I would pass an occasional stray soul, and he seemed just as lonely and out of place as I felt. Where was everybody?

Washington, in 1921, was not the white cluster of cold and solemn buildings it has become since under the elaborate building program designed to meet the necessities of depression and provide a stimulant to the building industry and its concomitant trades and furnish work to men. Then it was cluttered up with temporary wooden buildings, thrown up hastily here, there and everywhere without rhyme or reason, to provide shelter for the hordes essential to a government at war. Lower Pennsylvania Avenue about the Capitol was like the side street off the main line of traffic to be found in all large cities—a conglomeration of Chinese gift shops, their windows gay with silk kimonos, cigarette holders, ivory knickknacks, and alive with Chinese children who did not seem to disturb placid fathers and mothers as they slipped about the store and up the stairs to living quarters; small cheap hotels; shops into which tourists were lured to purchase replicas of the Washington monument, photographs of the White House and the cherry trees in bloom along the Tidal Basin, lurid pillows with appropriate designs and "Washington, D.C." in bold letters athwart them; and one cavernous second-hand book store where I used to spend much time wandering among the stacks. There was something informal and very human about this region to me. Nearly all of that has been torn away now.

Washington is cold to the stranger. It is not friendly. I discovered this when I first came upon the scene from among hospitable people in the South. This, I think, derives from the fact that Washington, though a big city by census standards, is essentially the small town. The nucleus consists of the residential group, the "cave dwellers," the shopkeepers and that great mass of civil employes who provide the continuous economic sustenance of the city. This keeps the wolf of depression from the capital's door. These groups are stratified, moving in their own little circles without crossing over the line very often. They, however, recognize themselves as Washington and regard as strangers that portion of the population which, by the very nature of government, is figuratively here today and gone tomorrow.

The top officials, those who press the buzzers and ride in limousines furnished by the taxpayer, who trip through the news columns or stumble through the news columns ineffectually, whose wives' teas and luncheons and dinners and comings and goings are recorded in the society pages— these change from year to year, often, and always from administration to administration. But the underlings, the shock troops, those who perform the simple, fundamental functions, remain from year to year. So though the city is publicly just a stage across which the show moves, it is underneath a changeless order with the basic character of timelessness.

For the first six months I hated the city. Then I became a part of it, began to find out its secrets, to learn its legends. The more I learned the more fascination it held for me. I have loved it more every day since I, in effect, was taken in —not by its people, but by its intriguing personality. It became a study in human beings. It is an excellent laboratory for studying the species of man, and in the raw. For the politician virtually is man in the raw. Politics brings the primeval instincts to the surface. And I did not need any entree, any credentials of passport other than my profession which, because some Englishman a long time ago established that license we call freedom of the press, allowed that nosy creature known as a reporter to walk brashly into the seats of the mighty and take a look and ask embarrassing questions. The task is much the easier because the poor politician lives in a goldfish bowl forever. His every act is a public act. He squirms around there before you in plain gaze, only rarely asking mercy and never expecting any. You see him writhe and wriggle, like a specimen under the microscope. He is capital for our sarcasm and our irony. He is, though, only the human being on parade under difficult circumstances. He is trying to please us, that is, us as the people and the voters; trying to beguile us so that we will retain him as politician and let him go on parading and making his speeches and baring his soul. He is a figure altogether to be pitied. He is not even a hero to himself. He is so human. We see our foibles on display in him. We recognize our blundering, wavering selves. We see how little we are and know, on very rare occasions, how big we can become—for moments.

Democracy, I learned, is a pitiless institution.

But how much fun to watch in operation! Especially when the onlooker has no particular responsibility.

The politician suffers not only from the arrows we hurl into the heart and soul he wears on his sleeve. He suffers from the weather, as do the rest of us who live in this city which the founding fathers laid out in the swamps along the Potomac. It steams in summer and freezes in winter. And always, winter or summer, there is that eternal dampness from the marshes of the Potomac which intensifies both the heat and the cold. The politicians and their camp followers only slightly outnumber—or so it seems—those who look after their bodily ills—the doctors, especially the doctors who look after ailments of the nose and throat and bronchial tubes. Their names are written across hundreds of glazed doors in down-town office buildings and on neat little signs which sit in the lower windows of houses that once were fashionable homes. The doctor is everywhere. And every other person you meet in winter has the sniffles or a cough.

Washington's brief weeks of spring and autumn only are recompense for the chills and the fevers and the heat.

One fine day spring comes up quickly from the South, riding a thin perfumed breeze, and breaks forth in the cherry blossoms along the Tidal Basin, the jonquils in the parks and the dogwood along the bridle paths. Then it is truly heavenly. Thousands of clerks take their lunches into the parks under the trees and a holiday joi-de-vivre permeates the city. The tourists pour into town in restless droves by motor and train and hurry wildly about the city to be sure to see everything there is to see; the hardened citizen (and it takes only a few months' residence to qualify as one) turns up his nose, but only slightly, mutters "Tourists" under his breath in a way that sounds like "Vermin" and then turns away to the beauty about him and forgives, for it is possible to forgive with the pleasing prospect of nature and the spring fever that inspires the laziness from which tolerance is born.

Washington goes down to its winter tribulation through the pleasant portals of winy October, a brief brown interlude when the air becomes fresh again and the haze gathers along the Potomac and about the Virginia and Maryland hills and the burning leaves in the residential sections send up their incense. The trees throw out their flaming signals in warning and then, alas, too soon winter is upon the city. The dampness begins to creep into the bones and the politician is grateful for the warm office and turns, reluctantly, to ponder the troubles of the people. For the people forever have their troubles and the politician is forever troubled about them, professionally speaking.

Endlessly the seasons roll by. Endlessly the elections come and go. Endlessly the fledgling statesmen arrive upon the scene, strut briefly in vain, or strut successfully and stay for years. Forever some are being recalled by the voters. Others remain behind to die in harness and have the flag lowered to half staff while their colleagues adjourn in respect to their servitude. Few quit voluntarily.

But Washington sits placidly forever, like a great white cat with her paws in the mud of the Potomac. She is the sphinx. She is eternal. She is the Republic. Far away men become hungry and desperate. Far away men shout and shake their fists at an economic system which does not give them meat and bread. The angry waves break, in time, upon the capital and the servants of the people rush about madly, doing this and that. They push back the angry waves again. The cat only squirms a little in her sleep.

She is a fat cat, this bureaucratic cat, and she grows fatter and fatter as the country feeds her. The politicians delight to make her purr, and she purrs best when she is being fed and the food she likes best is the dollar that the taxpayer yields up.

When I first came upon Washington, it was confusion personified to me. It was not at all what the history books and the political science books said, I learned in time. It was a monster, this government, and it has grown since. I wandered down miles of corridors in the big white buildings, past hundreds of doors where thousands and thousands of people sat behind desks. What did they all find to do?

Nerves led out from them, I discovered in time, to the giant body which is the United States.

More confusing still was Congress. House and Senate, watched from the galleries, were now babel and bedlam, now quieter than a bank, with a few men reading newspapers, talking among themselves and paying no attention to the speaker of the moment. How did they ever get anything done? I wondered.

In time I learned, of course, that a handful of men really directed each body and I learned that they were not the real rulers, not their own masters. They were merely the puppets dancing to the pull of strings which led back elsewhere, led —for a long period at a time for a great many of them— back to a few men sitting in fine offices far away, America's financial and industrial leaders; led, less often, to what we know as the common people who rise occasionally in their wrath and demand that their interests be considered, and the common people are so many people, divided, of themselves into farmers, laborers, white-collar workers, other groups, and their interests clash. It all cannot be oversimplified. The political leader must oversimplify it for his purposes. He must paint his cause in great black and white strokes; he must divide the populace into sheep and goats.

But I run ahead of myself.

Bit by bit I learned.

To me, when I landed in Washington in 1921 to begin my explorations, there were statesmen. I was timid before them.

One day, very soon after I arrived, I was assigned to make a poll to find out how the Senate stood then on the League of Nations, or on some form of world organization. Republicans, in their campaign, had spoken vaguely of an association of nations. The League of Nations was dead, but the idea still persisted. I had a list of Senators to check. First on the list was Senator Carter Glass of Virginia. I knocked on his door, not knowing that the open-door policy permitted even the mildest constituent to enter boldly and ask.

A tiny little man opened the door. (I don't know how that happened.)

"I would like to see Senator Glass," I said.

"I'm Senator Glass," he snarled out of the corner of his mouth.

"I want to know how you stand on the League of Nations, sir," I began.

"Everybody in the country knows how I stand on the League of Nations," he snarled back, and it was like the crackling of thunder.

He slammed the door in my face.

So I went out and learned how Senator Carter Glass stood on the League of Nations.

Bit by bit I learned.

67

That encounter with Carter Glass was when I first emerged as a reporter after a siege inside the United Press office, and was beginning to rove about the Capitol and find my bearings.

I had been in Washington about three months. Previously I had been sort of an odd-job man about the office, doing a little of this and that, but my major task was to take dictation from the staff men assigned to the various runs about town, the White House, Capitol, Supreme Court, and downtown departments. My job with the United Press had come through the intercession of Lowell Mellett, then head of the Scripps-Howard Newspaper Alliance, who had taken a kindly interest in me when I had called at his office in those first few days of wandering about Washington looking for a place to land. Lowell served for years in the joint rôle of head of the Alliance and editor of the *Washington Daily News,* the local Scripps-Howard newspaper which began publication two months after I arrived in Washington. He started me out in Washington and a few years later in 1933 took me on the Alliance staff, which I joined after a dozen years with the United Press. He has been always a real friend and counsellor. He is now in an important government position.

When I began my work with the United Press I was given command of a small desk, a typewriter, and a midget telephone switchboard. I operated the switchboard, taking the calls on the direct lines which came in from the White House and the Capitol and the Supreme Court, relaying them to the desk, or if the caller had a story, I put on my headphones and took it. From this desk, which was alongside the main news desk, I got my first glimpse into the confusion that is political Washington. I began to learn names and places, the figures and geography of national politics, as I took the

68

stories. It was not long before I grew to love it and know that it was this sort of reporting that I wanted to do.

My boss then was Herbert Walker, now general manager of the Newspaper Enterprise Association. He guided me, tolerantly overlooked my mistakes—and I made two whoppers—and gave me an opportunity to work myself into a regular reporting job. My salary was meager and I was anxious for a raise. (I borrowed from a telegraph operator friend, Gus Tarry, to tide me over week-ends.) Finally I wrote direct to Karl A. Bickel, then president of the United Press. I went all the way to the top. He sent the letter back to Herb with the notation "Who is Stokes?" and Herb in his kind way explained that it was not customary for a reporter to go over the head of the bureau manager. He could have been nasty—but he was the very contrary. That won me to him. He also could have been very nasty, later—and had good grounds for firing me—for a boner I pulled at the White House. Scanning the list of persons who had engagements with President Harding one morning—the list is always posted in the White House Press Room—I noted that some Spanish-American War Veterans were listed to witness the signing of a Spanish-American pension bill by the President. Ah, thought I, I can settle this matter right now. So I dictated a story that President Harding had signed the bill. Later in the day, the ceremony was called off. Secretary of Interior Fall had objected to the bill and dissuaded Harding from signing it. It has not been signed to this good day. We had the bill signed all over the country for hours. I confessed what I'd done to Herb over the telephone and went into the office that night expecting something dire, probably my walking papers. He knew how bad I felt. He did not rub it in. He let it pass with just a word. I've liked him for that ever since, and determined then that if I could possibly avoid it, I'd never make any more mistakes which could come back on him.

My first assignment outside came when Congress convened in December. I was sent to the Capitol as an assistant to the regular staff men there. But, before I really learned my way around, I was switched to the White House. It was to be a temporary assignment, to fill in, but I remained there over a year.

Some of my fondest memories are of that year at the White House. The older newspapermen there gave me a hand and helped me.

We had a small White House Correspondents Association then. We would hold dinners and have a Cabinet officer or two as guests. We never had the President in those days. Later the White House Correspondents Association grew to big proportions and its dinner every spring is one of the occasions of Washington, attended by the President, Cabinet members, and other notables.

My Georgia accent was something I could not conceal. I had not been at the White House long before one of the men who had visited Atlanta suggested that there should be a memorial to General Sherman at Five Points where the statue of Henry W. Grady stands. A collection of pennies was started. I was asked constantly how the memorial was getting along. The project was finally abandoned and the entire fund devoted, according to a letter accompanying the gift, "to a fitting memorial to commemorate the occasion of your marriage."

From the White House I was transferred to the newly organized night service of the United Press for morning papers, then known as the United News, and worked under Raymond Clapper, bureau manager, from whom I acquired a knowledge of politics. He knew the game inside out. My continued association with Ray Clapper has been one of the most pleasant and valuable of my life. In time I covered all sectors of the Washington political front and, later, I was out frequently on trips through the country on general political assignments.

It was with many illusions that I came upon Washington in my early twenties.

My idea of the Washington political scene and the figures who moved about the stage, derived, romantically, from my history of a past era, something associated with the names of Andy Jackson and Clay and Calhoun and Daniel Webster and Abraham Lincoln. My study of American history had been intensified around the prelude to the Civil War, the struggle over the tariff and nullification and the various slave compromises, and about the Civil War itself and Reconstruction. Closer to my time I knew something of Theodore Roosevelt, whom I had seen and heard deliver a speech in Atlanta while I was a high school student, and who appeared to me a man of personality and strong character; William Jennings Bryan, whom I also had heard speak and who was a flaming figure in his early days and a revolutionary in some respects; our own southern Woodrow Wilson who had given us the Federal Reserve Act and other reforms and who bestrode the world like a Colossus in the War days.

Even yet I recall the awe I felt the first time I walked into a White House Press Conference in the presence of Warren G. Harding. The office hallowed the man. He looked like a President. He had a fine commanding bearing. He conducted himself outwardly like a President. He had dignity. To others, veteran newspapermen, who stood about me, Harding was a man who had been an Ohio politician and a genial fellow they had known in the Senate, very human.

71

I learned to look at Harding that way later, as I sat about the White House day after day. I learned to look critically at the other leading figures as I came to know them, to see how they met their problems or were overwhelmed by them.

This all happened gradually.

7

IN September 1921 I came to Washington. This was six months after Harding was inaugurated.

The new administration was settling itself and people had turned back to their own affairs.

It all began auspiciously enough on the surface—the inauguration of Normalcy. The country, tired of the war, rather liked the idea and the word. Harding seemed a well intentioned leader. He was human and friendly. The people saw in him a man much like themselves. There was none of the coldness and austerity of Woodrow Wilson about him, nothing of the superman.

Fine and comely he was, a splendid figure of a man, a modern Saul, as he stood before the great throng in front of the Capitol that March 4 to assume his office. It was a fair day, hallowed by a cordial early spring sun. The thousands who rubbed elbows snugly with one another there were carefree, happy, eagerly watching and hopefully awaiting the dawn of a new era—the Era of Normalcy. They were ready to let go, to relax, to throw off the habiliments of war. Out in the country people looked forward also with hope. Here and there, the bony finger of unemployment began to wag ominously, but not enough yet to disturb. A new administration, it was believed, would make things better. Americans are eternally optimistic.

So he stood there, with a certain air of humility, before the people.

His trip to the Capitol from the White House, one could imagine, was not particularly pleasant. At his side in the open car sat the invalid Woodrow Wilson. Neither man ever could understand the other. They were ages apart. So they sat there with that wall between them as the car hurried down Pennsylvania Avenue, hurried so that the crowds were disappointed with just a glimpse of the two contrasting figures.

It was at 1:18, so the newspaper stop watches recorded, when he took the oath of office. His big, soft hand rested upon a passage from Micah:

"What doth the Lord require of thee but to do justly and to love mercy and to walk humbly with thy God?"

That epitomized the man. But the desire to do justly, to have mercy, to be humble are not armor enough against the trickery of designing friends, of crafty economic interests, and this he discovered. One pities the man; one almost weeps for him.

His inauguration address thrilled no one. It pleased his backers, but they did not make a great deal of noise.

He promised "omission of unnecessary interference of government in business." He was for an end to "government's experiment in business." We must, he said, "adjust our tariffs to the new order." He was doing very nicely. Wealth, he averred "is not inimical to welfare, it ought to be its friendliest agency."

He was in Europe—and out.

The United States would cooperate with other nations but not make commitments. It "will accept no responsibility except as our own conscience and judgment in each instance may determine." The new President declared himself for the United States' participation in a World Court. But a world super-government—and by that he meant the League of Nations—"is contrary to everything we cherish and can have no sanction by our Republic."

There should be no war profits in a future war. (The future war was far enough away not to worry about that now.)

He bubbled with goodwill.

"The earth is thirsting for the cup of goodwill."

He repeated the quotation from Micah, adding solemnly: "This I plight to God and country."

And he ended in the clouds.

"I would rejoice to acclaim the era of the golden rule, and to crown it with the autocracy of service."

During his address he introduced the glucose coating that became such a part of Presidential utterances in the decade which he inaugurated:

"We want an America of homes illumined with hope and happiness, where mothers, freed from the necessity of long hours of toil beyond their own doors may preside as befits the hearthstone of American citizenship. We want the cradle of American childhood rocked under conditions so wholesome and so hopeful that no blight may touch it in its development, and we want to provide that so no selfish interest, no material necessity, no lack of opportunity shall prevent the gaining of that education so essential to best citizenship."

Words, words, words. The typical Harding muddy English.

The new President, friendly to the veterans of the late war as to every other human being, turned to drawn-faced soldiers who sat before him in wheelchairs and said, with feeling, "this Republic will never be ungrateful for the services you have rendered."

May we lift up just a corner of the cover and peep into the future? We see Colonel Charles R. Forbes, director of the Veterans' Bureau, present in the inauguration throng that day, indicted in just exactly one day less than three years for mishandling funds set aside for the benefit of war veterans. (I afterward became familiar with this situation. I covered the Senate investigation of the Veterans' Bureau.) The handsome President who stands there before the people now so trustingly will be in his grave then. May we lift up the cover still a bit further, eleven years ahead, and what do we see? There where those people stood looking upward to the new executive, there, before the Capitol, marched, day and night, around and around in what they called a "death dance," a long line of war veterans, the "Bonus Army," come to demand a cash bonus from Congress. They were driven away, before bayonets, in the administration of another President. I watched the burning of their little shacks in Anacostia Flats and followed them for miles as they fled from the city.

That future President was there, his round face serious, his brow creased by the glare from the sun. He exuded energy, did Herbert Hoover. Also there was Charles Evans Hughes, who almost had won the White House, and who was to project himself and his influence into another era and engage in a mighty duel with another President, from behind the curtain of the Supreme Court.

There, too, was the banker, Andrew W. Mellon, the wisp of a man who dominated the delirious decade, who was, for a time, mightier than Presidents. They were but his mouthpieces. He looked like a dried up dollar bill that any wind might whisk away.

There, too, were Albert B. Fall and Harry M. Daugherty.

They heard him say:

"What doth the Lord require of thee, but to do justly and to love mercy and to walk humbly with thy God."

He had said it twice.

Newspaper accounts of the day told of his departure from his home town and his arrival in Washington.

A goodly throng of neighbors in Marion had gathered in the front yard and in the streets before the green, ten-room frame house on March 2 to say their farewell to the Hardings. Now they stood for the last time on that famous front porch, before their neighbors. The Reverend T. H. McAfee, pastor of Trinity Baptist Church, spoke the words of farewell on behalf of the townspeople and presented the President-elect and his wife with a silver plaque.

On March 3, at one o'clock, the kindly burgher of Marion and his wife arrived at Union Station. (They had arrived here before, as Senator and Mrs. Harding, but not with the fanfare that heralded this approach.) A crowd was at the station to welcome the pair. They were met officially by the Vice-President-elect and the charming Mrs. Coolidge. The two carloads of home-folks from Marion trailed through the station behind them. In the afternoon the Hardings called upon President and Mrs. Wilson at the White House. For twenty minutes the four sat chatting over tea. It was the first time the new President had seen Woodrow Wilson since August 1919. On that other occasion Harding had a rather spirited discussion with the President about obligations imposed upon the United States by the covenant of the League of Nations in event of future war in Europe. He went to the White House with members of the Foreign Relations Committee. After leaving the White House, the Hardings went to call upon Mrs. Champ Clark, widow of the Speaker. He had died the night before.

That night Ohio celebrated its new importance in national affairs with a dinner party given in honor of the Hardings by Carmi Thompson, the perpetual Ohio politician, rolypoly and genial. The elite of what later came to be known as "The Ohio Gang" was present. Harry M. Daugherty was there. So was Jess Smith, the big, bluff, still youthful looking man-at-arms for Daugherty, the department-store owner of

Washington Court House, master of the small-town wise-crack, who moved into a desk in the Attorney General's outer office. The fidgety little physician, Dr. Charles E. Sawyer, who was made a brigadier general and came to look more and more like an antiquated Boy Scout, was there with the plump and motherly Mrs. Sawyer. Dr. Sawyer had come along to be personal physician to the President, with his particular charge the ailing kidneys of Mrs. Harding. Present also were Edward B. McLean, the playboy Washington publisher out of Ohio, and the eccentric owner of the Hope Diamond, his wife, Evelyn Walsh McLean. They all gossiped comfortably. Marion, one small town, had transplanted itself upon another small town, but a small town where the temptations are greater and the fall reverberates across a continent and is not kept a local secret to be whispered about the bridge table, more with kindly curiosity than malice.

Provincial and friendly was the atmosphere as the former small-town editor took up his new chores in the White House.

Ohio's visitors who came to Washington to see their native son inaugurated continued their boisterous merrymaking the following day as their representative in the Cabinet, Harry M. Daugherty, was inducted into office. His régime started with the spirit of a big party. National committeemen paid their allegiance to the new political master. Lillian Russell, now retired from the stage and swishing about royally with her wealthy husband, Alexander P. Moore, the Pittsburgh publisher, stepped up in her best manner and planted a kiss upon Daugherty when he had taken the oath of office. The reception lasted an hour. When it was all over the new Attorney General went over to the White House to see his old crony.

Harry Daugherty had made Warren G. Harding President. He learned the way to the White House that day and it was to become a very well worn path. For Daugherty was to leave his impress on this administration. He was its practical politician. The favors at his disposal were large.

But even larger were those at the disposal of a man of sharply contrasting character, habits and background, the little Pennsylvania banker, who had been cloistered in the countinghouse among his stocks and bonds that represented a financial interest in enterprises all over the United States and in many lands beyond the seas. Few knew Andrew Mellon or suspected the catholicity of his economic interests. Few realized how close he kept his thin fingers upon the pulse of commerce and industry. His conception of politics was spelled out in tariff protection and tax laws and percentages of interest. He saw economics in politics, the economics of his kind, the big bankers, the financiers, the industrialists, those who to him represented the backbone of America. It was only their due to have their interests protected, for had they not made the country what it is? They took their profits as divine right. The people would take what came to them from the brains and industry of the overlords. (And the cupidity, perhaps? But he did not think of it that way.) The richer the upper crust of the economic pie, the better the crumbs that fell to those below. Andrew Mellon's philosophy was deeply instilled. He had no questions in his mind. It was simply his faith.

Considered purely as a human being, he was withal a lonely and tragic figure. So he seemed to me as I watched him and studied him over a period of years as he ruled from Washington. A Midas of modern America, he piled up mountains of gold. That represented achievement among his kind and, yes, to Americans of that day who turned to worship of the Money Masters when the Idealism to which they had aspired during the war, embodied somehow in that

78

phrase about making the world safe for Democracy which the Professor in the White House had coined, became only a bitter and sordid memory. But to him it must have been in reality nothing as he sat among his luxuries, nursing his loneliness, and conversed with his soul. Money, after all, could but buy him a collection of fine art, fine houses and automobiles, well tailored clothes, those specially made little black cigars which he smoked.

I see him as he wandered along F Street, alone, of a night, window-shopping, a lost and hungry soul. I see him, as I saw him so often, behind his big desk at our regular newspaper conferences. There he indulged in that dry wit which often pricked the pretentions of the world, slyly, showing that he knew within him that all was vanity and vexation of the spirit. At first he was a shy and timid and uncertain man before us in his press conferences. He marvelled that his hesitant "Yes" or "No" could become columns on the front page. I remember one day when he held up the front page of a newspaper and pointed to a story about the soldiers' bonus. Almost plaintively he said that he only had said one word "No" when asked whether he would favor passage of the soldiers' bonus, and look!, there was a whole column on the subject. I have often thought that, in time, these front-page stories became like a drug to him, that, figuratively, he hugged the newspaper to his breast and conned it avidly. It made him a master mind, a man of destiny—for a time. Life again was worth living. It had a purpose.

Then, in the early 'thirties when the depression enveloped Washington like a clammy fog that would not lift but only got heavier, he again became the uncertain little man. His economic theories wouldn't fit, his words no longer would act like magic. He propounded into the encircling gloom in vain. Once more he was the lonely and tragic figure wandering down the street at night peering into the windows. In vain he recalled the signs of the past which had lifted

America from its periodic slumps. They appeared on the horizon, those sure signs, and nothing happened. They were mere will-o'-the-wisps dancing ahead in the swamps to drive one mad. I recall one day when crop reports showed favorable signs. He was chatty and optimistic at his press conference. Agricultural recovery had lifted the country from the great and terrible depression that began in 1873 and lasted into 1881. Off he went into the past. He related how, in that time, he had been sent out to Colorado by his father to sell wagons, a young man with a business career. The present vanished for him. He lived in his youth as he talked and talked. America had come from that depression. It must come—and come quickly—from this one. He tried to convince himself as he talked. But the horse and buggy age was over. He could not bring it back.

In those early days of the Harding administration, when he began his reign, he had a philosophy that seemed to fit the occasion, and he proceeded to act upon it guilelessly, as a matter of principle which all should understand.

His own kind, big business, was his particular charge. He would take care of them, and they would take care of America.

Herbert Hoover's was the world of the middle class. The smaller business man was his charge. He was a promoter, and this was a field ripe for promotion. The little fellows liked to look up to a man like Hoover—the little fellows who gathered at Rotary Clubs and sang songs of their own importance, who were not interested in graphs and charts but were glad to know there was a man in Washington who knew all about them.

In typically serious manner did Herbert Hoover go about the business of taking over the office from which he planned to get what he wanted—the Presidency. Briskly he strode into his office in the Commerce Department. Replying to the praise of his predecessor, the new Secretary of Commerce said:

"This department is fundamentally a department of service. It is a department which promises as much or more than any other to aid the government and the people. Its functions are not to control or regulate. They are constructive. If I get the same loyalty of the force that has characterized its work heretofore it will indeed be a great success."

Service; no prying into businessmen's affairs; no regulation; the constructive attitude.

He was given the oath.

"I do," he said in a low voice, and then, looking about impatiently at those gathered for the ceremony, he said, with that timid smile which slipped down into his high collar:

"That ends the ceremony. Now we will have to get to work."

Quickly the fertile mind began to devise big schemes for the enlargement of his department that were well under way when I arrived in Washington. Only five days after he had taken office the Foreign Trade Information Service began to pour out that stream of propaganda that was to make Herbert Hoover a veritable god, an impossible legend, in time. Thus:

"The organization of the Department of Commerce contemplated by Mr. Hoover will make that branch of the government service the most important public body in touch with American business and will give the great Food Administrator a place of dominant leadership in American business."

Nobody paid any particular attention to Albert B. Fall, the western Senator who was named Secretary of Interior. He was to take lightly the Cleveland adage that public office is a public trust, along with the others who created that ugly drama known thereafter as "The Scandals of the Harding Administration." They left their dark blot upon the pages of history. The public mind associates this stigma always with the Harding Administration. It was sensational, stranger than fiction.

Without seeking to minimize its importance, however, particularly as an index as to what men will do in places of trust and as an example of the danger of a weak man in the White House, it was of less consequence in the long run bearing upon the national economy and of the welfare of the masses of people than the policies of Mellon.

These contributed to the philosophy that government is to favor the dominant industrial and financial interests.

Little attention was paid, in the shift of administrations, to the last official pronouncement of Woodrow Wilson, his message vetoing the Fordney Emergency Tariff Act which was read to Congress the night of March 3. It might well have been pondered by those who were now taking over the government. It was uncannily prophetic. Democrats in the House did it the honor of rising and cheering when the reading was concluded. None of them could really understand its future import.

Speaking of the tariff bill, Wilson said:

"I imagine there is little doubt that while this measure is temporary, it is intended as a foundation for action of a similar nature of a very general and permanent character."

In which, of course, he was correct.

After denouncing the policy prescribed in the emergency tariff bill, and forecasting with almost unbelievable accuracy the inevitable result of the course followed later in the delirious decade, he concluded:

"Such a policy is antagonistic to the fundamental principle of equal and exact justice to all, and can only serve to revive the feeling of irritation on the part of the great masses of the people and of lack of confidence in the motives of rulers and the results of government.

"There are only three ways in which Europe can meet her indebtedness, namely, by the establishment of private credits, by the shipment of gold or of commodities. It is difficult for

Europe to discover the requisite securities as a basis for the necessary credits.

"Europe is not in a position at the present time to send us the amount of gold which would be needed, and we could not view further large imports of gold into this country without concern. The result, to say the least, would be a larger disarrangement of internal exchange and disturbance of international exchange.

"If we wish to have Europe settle her debts, governmental or commercial, we must be prepared to buy from her, and if we wish to assist Europe and ourselves by the export of either food, raw materials or finished products, we must be prepared to welcome commodities which we need and which Europe will be prepared, with no little pain, to send us. Clearly, this is no time for the erection of high trade barriers."

And yet—

The same emergency tariff was passed and signed by Harding less than three months after he took office. A month later the administration's permanent tariff bill was introduced and became the Fordney-McCumber Tariff Act of 1922. Our bankers began to make big loans to Europe on what turned out to be insufficient collateral. She bought on our loans and merrily the dance went on as we, in effect, sold to ourselves. Prosperity was maintained as our factories turned out goods to be financed from these elusive credits. In 1930, the United States had nearly half of the gold in the world.

Again, in 1930, we raised our tariffs still higher in the Hawley-Smoot Act. Our vaults were bulging with gold. Europe could not sell to us. Her bonds became worthless. Great Britain went off the gold standard. So did other European countries. They began to withdraw government balances here. Over $700,000,000 went out in a few weeks. Frightened Americans withdrew another billion and a half from our banks and hoarded it. Our gold standard was strained to the breaking point.

America was in panic.

The masses rebelled.

But, in 1921, no one could see that far ahead.

8

PRESIDENT HARDING certainly had no talent as a seer.

He only wanted to be neighborly. So he proclaimed open house. He threw the White House doors wide.

When he stood before his friends and home folks at Marion, he said to them in farewell:

"I have a theory of government that if you do for the nation what you do for the community you do exceeding well, because the nation is only the aggregate of communities. So I am going to play my part in the execution of my duties as Chief Magistrate just as I would play it as neighbor and fellow citizen. But I would like to say to you, neighbors and friends, that I am going to my work with the confidence all will be well.

"I believe in the security of the American Republic. I believe the heart of American citizenship is right. I believe that the hundred millions of America will be back of a rightminded Executive just as cordially as you speak your friendship to me here today. . . . I have made it a practice of my life to speak well of my fellowmen and ever do good. I have neither envy nor jealousy in my heart. I feel that I am like the great citizenship of America.

"There is no hatred there. I could never be prouder in all my experience than to apply this friendly feeling within myself to the inauguration of a period of nation-wide goodwill in this Republic."

Two hours after he and Mrs. Harding had returned from the inauguration ceremonies at the Capitol to take up their abode in the White House on March 4 he issued his first order which was that the White House gates, barred since war was declared April 6, 1917, be thrown wide open to the public. The thousands who were gathered on the streets outside, patiently waiting for a glimpse of the figures of the new administration, swept through the gates, and overflowed the lawn.

As a young reporter stationed at the White House, I watched America stream through the grounds in a long, chattering line, to pass through the lobby of the Executive Offices and into the President's office. Slowly they filed by to receive a handshake from the President. Lynx-eyed secret service men, not too happy over this neighborliness, observed anxiously from every angle, nervous and alert. In the spring, when the graduation classes came to Washington from all over the country, as many as two thousand persons would be in the line which stretched away from the doors of the Executive Office, across the little plaza in front, down the side steps and up the sidewalk of West Executive Avenue to Pennsylvania Avenue.

The President's last official caller of the morning would leave. Pat McKenna, the keeper of the outer door of the President's office, would receive the word. He passed it to the policemen at the door. The crowd would surge forward eagerly.

I remember one wiry little man in the line one day. He had his wife and two boys with him, pushing them ahead of him as he turned aside to me to remark: "I almost saw McKinley once. I just missed Teddy Roosevelt. I didn't get to see Taft or Wilson. But I decided, by cracky, I was going to see a President once. So I put my family in the old bus and drove them down—and here I am."

He grinned, triumphantly.

The two boys, like other boys I had seen in this line, were much more interested in the secret service men.

The White House door was not just cracked a bit—it was thrown all the way open. All sorts of persons capitalized this open-door policy. Anybody could get in and, just as politicians always used a visit to the White House as a springboard for publicity, so smart press agents of visiting theatrical stars and would-be stars exploited it—or tried to exploit it—in those days. During the period of a few months I saw two giants from circuses, one seven feet high, one nine; several musical comedy stars whose press agents always told the story about the performance before the Prince of Wales; kid moving picture actors; and an assorted lot not easily classified, including the Maharajah of Razpiplah from India and three dusky youths from far away Abyssinia—Matthew, Mark and Luke they were named—who had attended Muskingum College at New Concord, Ohio, and thus felt they had a claim upon the new President.

There were those who did have a claim upon the President. Among them were the office seekers. They came, triumphantly, in droves. The Democratic reign was over. Those who had helped to drive the Democrats from power came to claim their rewards, not confessing, of course, how easy it had been, that they had to do but little, had but to stand by and watch the angry reaction from war-time anxieties, war-time restrictions sweep up in a great tide.

Warren G. Harding was a politician. He believed in government by politicians. That was the code he had learned in

Ohio. It was the code by which he had risen to the Presidency. It was instinctive with him to reward his friends and the friends of his friends. Unfortunately, political friends can do more harm in places of power in the national government in Washington than they can in the state house at Columbus, Ohio.

He expressed his philosophy very succinctly a few days before he entered the White House. The occasion was an interview with newspaper correspondents on his train returning to Marion from Florida, where he had been on a vacation. It had been reported that Alvin T. Hert, Republican National Committeeman from Kentucky, might be named Assistant Secretary of War. The rumored appointment was being criticized on the ground that Mr. Hert was a "politician."

"A man who makes a practice of politics performs a patriotic duty and we ought to have more like him in this country," said the President-elect.

There are grades of politicians. Harding was unlucky in so many cases in getting the lower grades.

To the victors belonged the spoils was the watchword of the day.

So, little over two months after he became President, Harding issued an executive order which permitted Postmaster General Will H. Hays to fill every second-, third-, and fourth-class postmastership with Republicans. Civil Service was brusquely discarded.

A year later, under prodding from Attorney General Daugherty so the story went at the time—and for weeks it was a scandal in Washington—the President issued another executive order firing the director of the Bureau of Engraving and Printing and twenty-five division chiefs. Their places were filled with deserving Republicans. Labor organizations protested vehemently. In the following February, the President made partial recompense by an executive order restoring seventeen of the former division chiefs to Civil Service status so they could obtain government employment.

"A man who makes a practice of politics performs a patriotic duty and we ought to have more like him in this country."

The open door let others in who had a claim upon the President.

These were representatives of the big interests of the nation who had contributed to Republican victory and now came to demand their toll. Now was the time to see how "neighborly" the new President intended to be. Not all came directly. They were not so crude. They saw those who had influence with the President. They saw Daugherty and Will Hays and Mellon and Republican Senators and Congressmen.

And lots of other Americans learned about the "grab bag" and organized to get their hands into it. The war had revealed a Treasury that seemed to be ready to supply endless wants. Americans became, to use a common but expressive figure, "Treasury Raiders." They descended upon Washington in droves, big business, little business, the veterans, the farmers —pressure groups. Eagerly they dug their hands into the "grab bag" as at a carnival. It was so easy.

They had learned to look to Washington during the war. Washington became, in truth, the capital of the nation. After the war it became the capital of the world. America had become a creditor nation. Everybody was after credit. Thus began, during those times, what later came to be so deplored as centralization of government. The heart is where the purse strings are and the purse strings were in Washington. The national debt became a thing at which to point with pride.

Smart men began to capitalize the shift to Washington. We call them lobbyists. They were not new—the tribe. But now they broadened their front and came in greater and greater numbers. They filled up down-town buildings. They called themselves "legislative representatives." The lobbyists created new needs. They sold businessmen, economic groups, special interests, even organizations with humanitarian objectives, the idea that they needed someone to "represent" them at Washington. They proceeded to get busy to stir up "needs."

The more I live the more amazed I am at the gullibility of businessmen. Clever lobbyists in Washington soon convince them that there's something very mysterious about the way things are done in Washington. They build up a legend. They convince businessmen that it's impossible to be heard, to state a case for themselves, unless they have someone who knows the ropes, someone who can open the door of someone with "influence." Learning much about businessmen from their naïveté in their Washington approach, one does not wonder at what has happened to the country.

A racket sprang up. Poor old Jess Smith found out about all this and he set out to provide the "influence." It was so easy and profitable while it lasted. Many others found out about it during the Harding administration.

It was after the war that the farmers moved into Washington with their organizations with a will. They, too, would dip their hands into the "grab bag." And why not? Everybody else was doing it. The soft-spoken and skilful Charles S. Barrett of Georgia, representing the National Farmers Union, wrote a book in defense of the farm lobby, in which he said just that. *Uncle Reuben Comes to Washington* was the title. He turned on the other lobbyists for the benefit of the general public in a newspaper interview on what he called "the assistant government."

"The 'assistant government,' " said he, "has one advantage over the constitutional government. It is more effectively trained for its work. It is an association of specialists. Eminent men and women who know all the legislative, administrative and bureaucratic avenues, streets and alleys in Washington belong to this interesting collection of men and women."

The professional farm lobbyists learned quickly. They ate well and called congressmen by their first names.

The farmer really needed a friend in Washington.

He had overexpanded himself and now, with the war demand over, his prices began to suffer from his surpluses. He had gone out and bought himself additional broad acres at highly speculative prices. For Europe needed wheat for the soldiers and the price soared. He dug up the whole western country with his plow—to reap a whirlwind of dust and desolation fifteen years later. During the war he exported wheat to Europe. A decade or so later the winds carried his top soil—free of the Buffalo grass cover which once had pinned it down—toward Europe, dark clouds that rolled away and hid the sun and, in time, settled over Washington to throw a pall over the capital and fear into the hearts of those responsible for the national welfare.

The farmer needed a friend. For wheat had dropped to $1.90 a bushel. It had been over $2.00. And cotton was 11 and 12 cents. It had gone as high as 40 cents a pound to supply the gluttonous artillery.

But Secretary of Agriculture Henry C. Wallace was optimistic—and revealing. Said he:

"We will get through this period. The nation is not going bankrupt. The farmers are not going bankrupt. Neither are they going to lie down on their job. Gradually farm prices will be brought into relation with other prices and we will go ahead hitting on all cylinders."

He urged the necessity of a reduction of prices for the things the farmer must buy, which chiefly would require a lowering of tariffs.

When his son took over the Agriculture Department a dozen years later, a bushel of wheat sold for little more than a loaf of bread and nickel cotton threw gloom over the cotton belt which was not lightened any by the clamor of city brethren for five-cent beer.

Herbert Hoover had his solutions. Insistent among the voices raised for "tariff adjustments" was his. He said they were necessary to check foreign dumping of wool, grain, cotton, dairy products and other commodities. He did not realize then that, once the tariff is opened, the big industries come swarming in for theirs. He found this out, but he did not learn his lesson. For, as President a few years later, he sought in vain to limit tariff revision. The Hawley-Smoot monstrosity was the result.

He also proposed foreign loans, saying a few days after the inauguration:

"Another outstanding economic trouble is that our farmers and our manufacturers are overloaded with food, raw materials and goods that we cannot market abroad, and at the same time great masses of people are cold and hungry. These people can only purchase on credit pending their own economic recuperation, and our own recuperation depends greatly upon theirs. We are thus not facing overproduction but a breakdown of credit links between us and the areas of underconsumption.

"Congress has provided the way for creation of foreign credits by banking cooperation under the Edge Act and the logical and economic thing in the whole national interest is for our bankers to work something out. Foreign credits are better than rotten food."

So the bankers and big financiers were summoned. This was to be their administration.

Headed by J. P. Morgan, they gathered in lordly array about the huge table in the State Dining Room at the White House a few nights later. Secretary Mellon and Secretary Hoover sat with them and the President. The dinner was secret. It was not announced beforehand to the newspapers.

They did not know about it until it was over. Then the reporters scurried about trying to discover what had been discussed. The stories were pieced together, in Washington and from the visiting bankers when they returned to New York. All but one had come from New York.

Benjamin Strong, governor of the New York Federal Reserve Bank, was among the conferees. Others were Charles H. Sabin, president, Guaranty Trust; Paul Warburg; James A. Alexander, National Bank of Commerce; Charles E. Mitchell, president, National City Bank; William Kent, of Bankers Trust Company, and H. C. McEldowney, of Union Trust Company, Pittsburgh, Mellon's bank.

The administration put before them, according to the stories which leaked out, a request that banking interests, in floating loans for foreign nations in the United States, should, as far as practicable, make the condition that the proceeds be devoted to the settlement of outstanding obligations or spent to stimulate this country's industries and exports. This followed Hoover's general theory. There had been a feeling among some officials, it was reported, that wholesale flotations of loans should not be permitted if the result would be to take capital out of the country, it being pointed out that wholesale foreign lending tends to raise the interest rate for home industries. Foreigners, it was said, were willing to pay from 7 to 9 per cent for money. There was a general understanding that banking interests should carefully scrutinize requests for further loans in American money markets, the inference being that they should get busy and get some money to Europe. But the whole matter was put delicately. The administration officials made it plain they were not trying to dictate to the bankers. There was no tendency on the part of the administration, it was emphasized, to insist that all money raised on foreign bond issues should be retained in this country, but simply that a course would be followed which would not injure American industry.

It was all very pleasant and cooperative. The bankers left with the feeling that Harding would do very nicely under the tutelage of Mellon and Hoover. One banker, interviewed by the *New York Times*, returned to New York with the impression that the new President "was a very human sort of citizen, big and broad-minded; that he would take advice, and that he had determined to take men of affairs of all lines into his confidence."

The President revealed a curious, but perhaps somewhat naïve, interest in finance—naïve for a President of the United States. He asked all sorts of questions. He was particularly interested in the stock market and its operations. He wanted to know how much of the funds of the country were taken up by stock-market operations—a very intelligent inquiry if it had been pursued then and there. He was surprised, so the bankers reported, to learn how much of the money that went into the stock market came from the country banks and how comparatively little from New York banks. One banker pulled out a notebook in which were jotted down the loans of prominent banks in the call money market that day to prove his point.

The bankers did "work something out," as Hoover had suggested. The stream of credit started abroad, rising gradually. During the Coolidge era, when the so-called Coolidge Boom was being blown up, between the years 1924 and 1928, foreign investments averaged a billion and a quarter and a billion and a half a year. And, in the end, some of it was no better than rotten food.

Woodrow Wilson had warned in vain.

Harding was ready to deliver. All he needed was to be told how.

There was never any question about tax and tariff revision. That was understood. The only question was which should come first. Only four days after the new administration had settled itself, President Harding called his Congressional leaders to the White House at night for a conference to discuss this problem and the time for an extra session of Congress. The conference lasted four hours. Afterward Harding came out personally to inform the newspapermen who waited in the cold. A "wide difference" of opinion was exhibited, he said.

"This," he said, "is the beginning of the program of cooperation between the Executive and Congress," a slap at the "autocrat" Wilson who had a mind of his own, and also a confession that he was to put himself in the hands of the Republican oligarchy in Congress headed by Boise Penrose of Pennsylvania which had elevated him, formerly one of their own, to the Presidency.

The argument over precedence of tariff and tax legislation went on for several days. Secretary Mellon leaned toward tax revision. Steel and the other big industries and financial interests which he represented wanted to get out from under the burden of the high war taxes. Penrose, true to Pennsylvania, echoed Mellon.

But the tariff won in the end, because of the farmers.

It happened rather suddenly. On March 18 the Cabinet became excited about the plight of the farmer. Facts and figures were marshalled to make a gloomy picture. The next day Harding called for an emergency tariff bill to protect the farmers. Many were unable to understand the sudden decision, and especially this particular solution of the farm distress. They said so, repeating the argument of Wilson against higher tariffs. His arguments were particularly apt, for the same Fordney bill which he had vetoed was reintroduced when Congress assembled in special session April 11. It was passed and signed by the President on May 27.

The farmers got that and later a "dirt farmer" member of the Federal Reserve Board and a system of credit banks, revival of the War Finance Corporation to lend to farmers.

Industry was not long in getting its own tariff bill started. The measure, known later as the Fordney-McCumber bill, was introduced late in June. But, in trying to please everybody, it takes a long time to write a tariff bill. It was not until September of the following year that a satisfactory compromise was reached and the bill passed and signed by the President.

Meanwhile, the big industries got their tax burden eased somewhat in the first Mellon tax bill which became law in November 1921.

Their friend in the Treasury was taking care of them.

9

DURING the steaming, stifling summer of 1922 we sat chafing in our press room and in the lobby of the White House Executive Offices and recounted the successive skirmishes as President Harding sought, with characteristic ineptitude, to bring peace in a far-flung labor war that rumbled along two key industrial fronts —coal mining and railroads. The strife was bitter and blood was shed.

Late one afternoon a group of us sauntered back to the office of George Christian, the President's secretary, looking for some scrap of news for hungry wires and newspapers about the conference Harding was holding at the time with railroad executives and labor leaders in his own office just beyond that of his secretary.

Suddenly, the door which led to the President's office opened. We looked around to see him standing there, his coat off, his big shoulders drooped dejectedly, a tired frown across his worried face. He smiled when he saw us.

"I'm glad to get away from that job in there," he said, pointing back over his shoulder. "It's good to be with you fellows for a few minutes."

Troubles had come rolling down upon him in a veritable avalanche. For weeks that summer he had talked and pleaded, suggested and proposed, dealing now with the railroad shopmen's strike, now with the coal strike. The representatives of each side would come to Washington, talk awhile, go back and try again and then return to talk some more. Meanwhile the country began to be fearful of its winter coal supply and to worry about railroad transportation. The negotiators became familiar figures to us from their frequent visits to the White House. Early we came to get the list of appointments for the day, scan the headlines for late developments elsewhere, and then start the daily watch from chairs tilted back against the walls of the Executive Office lobby. Twice a week, on Tuesdays and Fridays, we gathered about the President's desk for our regular press conferences to see his big frame begin to wilt gradually under the constant strain, to learn, in sometimes blunt answers, that his nerves were wearing raw. It would have been a trying ordeal for any President. It tried this President almost beyond endurance.

Even before Harding entered the White House there were signs of trouble to come. In late 1920 men began to lose their jobs in numbers that could not be ignored and during the spring of 1921 railroads and factories began layoffs and wage cuts and an unemployment problem confronted the new administration and the country. Herbert Hoover took command as the man of the hour, as he alone could take command, and an Unemployment Conference assembled in Washington, canvassed the situation, issued a few suggestions, resoluted, and appointed a permanent committee to make a study which turned up with a voluminous report several years later just in time to catch a new depression for which it did not seem to have the answer, though it contributed some significant information about what was happening to America as its frontiers closed and the labor-saving machine spewed men out on the streets with no new prairies to break with the plow, no new homesteads in the west.

The after-war depression was short-lived, luckily. The wrath was saved for another day.

But labor suffered. For the industrialist, who frightens easily, acted quickly to protect his profits, tightening his lines by discharging men and laying them off, and some saw in this minor disaster the opportunity to beat down an independent spirit among the workers which had come from the dire need for them, at high wages, during the war period. Railroads cut wages. So did United States Steel—the latter making its announcement on the day that Secretary of Labor Davis announced there were 5,735,000 men out of work. Urban Ledoux, the famed "Mr. Zero," set up an auction block in Boston Commons and offered jobless men for work, reminiscent of the old slave markets. There were no takers. As the depression widened he enlarged the scale of his operations and moved upon New York. The police stopped his auction there. Later he moved upon Washington with an army of unemployed.

Railroad labor, thanks to its strategic position during the war, was better organized than any other. Discontent with wage cuts boiled up eventually into strike votes. The Railroad Brotherhoods finally ordered a strike for October 30, 1921, but subsequently this was called off when the Railroad Labor Board, an agency created by the Transportation Act, intervened. But the threatening rail strike was postponed only to yield the front pages to another. King Coal began to mumble angrily in the spring of 1922 and John L. Lewis, then a name

97

which did not mean what it did ten and twelve and fifteen years later, called out his United Mine Workers on strike in April. Guerilla warfare already had broken out along the coal-mine front, in bloody Mingo County, W.Va., where United States troops finally were sent to put down disorders, and in famed Herrin County, Ill., where guns barked and men fell.

Again Herbert Hoover moved into action, and with him Jim Davis whose boast was that he once had puddled iron. (That was before he had risen to the lucrative rôle of organizer of the numerous Order of Moose.) Briskly Hoover pranced in and out of conferences that were held in Washington. Less briskly, Jim Davis sought to play the rôle of conciliator. He was jealous of the Secretary of Commerce. After all, *he* was Secretary of Labor.

President Harding had trouble enough with coal.

Double trouble came when, with lightning rapidity, the Labor Board ordered a series of wage cuts affecting railroad workers during May and June and, on July 1, railroad shopmen walked out on strike all over the country. Harding tried everything. He sought mediation. He pleaded. He threatened. He used every avenue, public statements, proclamations, messages to state governors, messages to Congress. We sat in the lobby of the White House and saw him grow more and more desperate. Disquieting news came in from the widely scattered front. Men were killed. Russian and Italian strikers admitted they had deliberately removed spikes on the Michigan Central tracks which caused a wreck at Gary, Ind. One crew deserted a train in the Arizona desert and the men were driven back to their jobs by orders from union chiefs.

Generally, there was a little hell to pay.

Warren Harding, I am sure, had no antilabor bias. He had fine human instincts. He liked his fellow man. I am certain that he could sit down with the average working man and talk with him and understand his problems. He pardoned Eugene V. Debs on his first Christmas in office, something that the supposedly liberal and humane Woodrow Wilson had refused to do. Harding saw Debs as a human being, misguided perhaps, but a human being who had his convictions about war and the rights of man.

But now he dealt with labor in the organized mass, a big and powerful force not at all like the individual working man that he could talk to and reason with. Here was something vague and inchoate that he could not understand and which, furthermore, threatened the privileges of those to whom he looked as guides and masters. Early in his administration he had called in the bankers and financiers and sat, naïvely, at their feet. Small-town man that he was, he looked up to material success. Railroad magnates and mine owners were in the same class. They were the Big Men of America.

They overawed and dominated him.

He wanted to improve the lot of the working man. But to him the practical method was to induce the Big Men who controlled the lives of the working man to do it. These men had no such instincts. There was a meeting at the White House one night when the President had invited Judge Elbert Gary, of United States Steel, and Charles Schwab, of Bethlehem, and others to dinner to talk over abolition of the twelve-hour day in the steel industry. We waited outside the front portico of the White House for the conference to end. When it was over, Harding sent out word for us to come into the mansion. We were ushered into the little room on the right of the vestibule where Secret Service men kept their watch. The President was there and Judge Gary at his side. Harding asked the steel magnate to dictate a statement to us. Judge Gary obliged. This was entirely fitting and proper to Harding. It lights up the man.

I can see him standing there now, a fine figure of a man in his dinner clothes, towering above Judge Gary.

We thanked the judge when he had finished his statement. Harding nodded his approval. We bade the two good-night.

My eyes were opened. I began to understand lots of things.

But sweet reason would not extricate him from the dilemma in which he found himself as the two strikes wore on and on. These men would not behave like neighbors. Conciliatory words would not break this deadlock. He despaired. The job was even bigger than he had contemplated when he was pushed into acceptance of the nomination for President, for the big, soft-hearted fellow only wanted to be kind and enjoy life like the average person.

I was a participant in another episode that was very revealing.

It was in late August 1922. Almost daily conferences were being held with both coal and railroad groups at the White House. There had been a night conference with Attorney General Daugherty and the chairmen of the Interstate Commerce Committees of House and Senate. There was discussion of legislation to give the President authority to take over mines and railroads as an emergency measure to force a settlement of the strikes. But this idea had not taken so well. It was thought too drastic. A couple of days later, a Saturday it was, the President's conferences started in the morning in a meeting with Senator Watson of Indiana, one of the Republican leaders, and John T. Adams, chairman of the Republican National Committee. We waited and waited in the lobby for them to come out. Finally we went back to George Christian's office and he told us that the two men had left. They had been diverted through the basement and out the side entrance. Any attempt to cover up in this manner always arouses newspapermen and we complained bitterly to Christian.

Meanwhile, reports had come from the Capitol that the President had invited a group of railroad men on a week-end cruise down the Potomac with him on the *Mayflower*. We asked Christian about that. He evaded and was indefinite. Subsequently he sent a formal announcement out to the press room about the week-end cruise, listing as guests Senator Cummins of Iowa, chairman of the Senate Interstate Commerce Committee; Representative Winslow of Massachusetts, chairman of the House Interstate Commerce Committee; Secretary Hoover; Secretary of Interior Fall; Senator Frank Kellogg of Minnesota, a close friend of the President, and Albert D. Lasker, chairman of the United States Shipping Board.

As usual on such week-end excursions it was the duty of press association representatives to follow the Presidential party to the Navy Yard and check them out, to see that nothing happened on the way there. We were required in our jobs to dog the President's footsteps. This was just one of the chores.

Our automobile was stopped at a respectful distance from where the *Mayflower* was tied up, and we got out and watched the party go aboard. I saw George Christian look in our direction and then go over and speak to the President. The President came to the rail and beckoned to us. We went to the end of the dock, the three of us, looked up at the President, and took off our hats. I can see the three of us standing there now. The others were Pete Haupert of the Associated Press, a youngster like myself, and the older Harry Ward, of the International News Service. The President's face was stern.

"Do I ever cheat you boys?" he asked.

"No, sir," we chorused, ignorant of what this was all about.

He then explained that he had given us a list of the guests on the trip. He seemed to have the feeling that we were checking up on him, that we did not accept at face value the official list and had come down to see for ourselves. We took the rebuke, put our hats back on, and went back to the automobile.

Presently, Attorney General Daugherty boarded the vessel. He was not on the list. We noted that, but took it as an oversight and made nothing of it. One of the press association bureau heads wrote a letter to the President protesting against the rebuke to his reporter for merely performing his duty.

At the press conference on the following Tuesday, the President referred to the incident, and again raised the accusation that we were "spying" upon him. This was too much for me. Before I knew it I had spoken up. After I had addressed him—to produce a complete pall of silence among the crowd of newspapermen gathered in his office, I became nervous. My Adam's apple ran up and down my scrawny throat, so I was told later. But, stumbling and breathing hard, I finally said my say. I explained this was a regular part of our duty, that we always were required to accompany him to the Navy Yard on such excursions, adding "to see that there is no accident." That wasn't so good. When I finished, he resumed the subject again, as if I had not spoken, and left the accusation with us. I dared not continue the argument.

The omission of Daugherty's name from the guest list had been noted by Robert Barry, correspondent for the *Philadelphia Public Ledger,* who had discussed the incident at the Navy Yard in his column "The Washington Observer" on Monday morning before the Tuesday press conference. He had gently criticized the President and ended his comment "And it happened the name of Attorney General Daugherty who made the trip, had been omitted from the official White House list." Perhaps Harding had seen that. This was one of the papers read at the White House.

It all seemed much to do about nothing. Nor did I couple the boat-trip conference at that time with what followed.

Only three days later, it was, on Friday morning, that Attorney General Daugherty appeared in Chicago in person before Judge James H. Wilkerson and asked for an injunction, one of the most sweeping in American history, tying the strikers hand and foot, prohibiting them from carrying on or supporting the strike, by collecting dues for strike benefits or in any other way.

The administration had resorted to force. Daugherty had found a way. No wonder then that President Harding was nervous and distraught and inclined to be suspicious. This bold sortie against labor must have rankled in his conscience.

Daugherty's brief was accompanied by a statement of fifty-one typewritten pages. In it he inveighed against any effort of the unions to destroy the open shop principle, saying it would not be done "so long as and to the extent that I can speak for the United States." Despite the outcry and criticism that the injunction threatened freedom of speech, freedom of press and freedom of assemblage guaranteed by the Constitution, the Attorney General stood pat and asked for no modifications in the original injunction when he appeared again ten days later and asked that it be extended for ten days more.

The bold assault came suddenly and without warning. Labor knew nothing about it in advance. Rail executives said it was a surprise to them. Labor protested bitterly. Samuel Gompers, president of the American Federation of Labor, called the injunction a violation of constitutional rights and a reversion to slavery and threatened a general strike. More bitter was David Williams, secretary of the Central Strike Committee, who said in a statement issued in New York:

"It indicates the perfidy of President Harding in offering a so-called settlement to the men and railroad companies, with an apparent understanding it would be turned down by the companies and the present action taken when it became evident the strike could not be broken. It shows why the rail-road executives have refused all reasonable offers of the employes for a settlement of the strike. In fact, it proves they would have been foolish to agree to the strikers' terms, knowing that they controlled the power of government through the Attorney General."

The strike collapsed. As an ironic afterthought, Judge Wilkerson made the injunction nation-wide a few days later, on the day when it was announced that seventy-four railroads had signed the so-called Baltimore agreement which had been ratified by the railway shop crafts in Chicago.

In these days they were sowing the wind that blew up later in the whirlwind. The Supreme Court, now under the guidance of former President William Howard Taft who had been named Chief Justice by Harding, was playing its part.

Three shattering decisions were handed down from on high by that august body.

It declared the child labor law enacted by Congress unconstitutional. Taft delivered the opinion.

One of the severest blows dealt labor came in the famous Coronado coal case decision which held that unions could be sued for damages caused by strikes and that funds collected for strike purposes could be assessed as damages. The Sherman antitrust law, enacted originally to check monopoly by corporations, was used as the authority.

It was after these two decisions that Senator Robert M. LaFollette of Wisconsin cried out in protest at the American Federaton of Labor Convention:

"Even the Constitution of the United States is not what its plain terms declare, but what these nine men construe it to be. In fact five of the nine are actually the Supreme rulers for by a bare majority the court has repeatedly overridden the will of the people as declared by their representatives in Congress and has construed the Constitution to mean whatever suited their peculiar economic and political views."

How familiar that became a few years later!

In the third decision, the Court nullified the District of Columbia minimum wage law for women and children.

That also had its echo in the future.

10

INTO a post-war Washington atmosphere surcharged with bitter disillusion over our adventure in Europe I came, with a tiny flame of Wilsonian internationalism still burning in my soul, a beautiful sentimental little flame that flickered bravely.

Out of the South I came, and the South is international-minded, selfishly, it is true, because the South had looked to Europe, particularly to England, for markets for her cotton. But it goes back beyond that. In the early days the South had looked toward Europe, and again particularly toward England, for the boats which sailed slowly up her rivers laden with silks and satins and brocades and other luxuries which made it possible to enjoy some semblance of civilization in the wilderness. Mere trinkets welded a powerful bond, for such is human nature. For these they swapped their tobacco and later their cotton, to clinch the bond with self-interest. Two wars with England could not destroy a deep-seated kinship.

It was refreshed later during the Civil War when England plainly showed her sympathy for the South and almost joined the Confederacy as an ally at one point, and this sympathy lost none of its potency by the South's realization that England was guided by the desire to see a division within the United States which would weaken a nation that sometime might rise as a rival in the commerce of the world.

Behind me, for generations, was this heritage of kinship, and an unadulterated British lineage.

Woodrow Wilson brought it to life again.

He was virtually a god in our household when he came along to capture the Presidency and move into the White House as the ruler of our nation. My father admired him tremendously. Excitedly he came home one night after hearing Wilson deliver an address in Atlanta before he was elected President. Wilson's book, *The New Freedom,* came into our house and I read it, too. Proudly my father would tell about the Federal Reserve Act of the early Wilson days and explain how the new President had slapped "the money power," as he always called it, by this decentralization of credit control.

Important for us was the fact that Wilson was a Democrat, the first in the White House in my time and only the second in my father's time. But, above all, he was a Southerner. He was one of us. So when Woodrow Wilson eventually led us into a war in Europe, and with that inspiring rhetoric of which he was a master—why that was the only course for our country. Questions were useless. He carried us to still greater heights after the war with his League of Nations proposal, a world organization which would forever after prevent wars, and in which our country would be able to exercise a dominant voice in international affairs.

From these heights we were toppled rudely when the Senate rejected the Versailles Treaty and the League.

So it was in a disturbed mood that I observed the postwar maneuverings of the Republican administration when I came to Washington. Despite my own disillusion over the war I still believed that Wilson was right fundamentally in his ideal. To me he seemed a martyr. Reverence for him translated itself into hostility toward those who had denied him his dream. I could never look from the gallery upon Senator Henry Cabot Lodge of Massachusetts except with aversion. Perhaps this was due, in part, to the supercilious air of rightness with which he directed the Senate as Republican leader, the complete scorn he could exhibit as he turned down the corners of his mouth disdainfully above that short and sharply pointed beard. Perhaps it was because he was a New Englander of the snobbish type. For I came, in time, to like most of the other irreconcilables who banded together to break Woodrow Wilson's heart—Borah, Norris, Johnson, Jim Reed, LaFollette, and, as the years wore on and my viewpoint changed, to admire their courage for standing out against the Versailles Treaty and the League, and to admire the courage of the progressives among them for their battle against the entrenched financial oligarchy which ruled America through the delirious decade.

My viewpoint did switch gradually from Wilson internationalism to virtually complete isolationism as the years passed, for I learned, over the years, how we were drawn into the World War, and saw how the European victors crucified a beaten Germany. I have learned how wars are made, and how, in the end, they settle nothing.

But in those early post-war years, it was with a self-satisfied cynicism, growing from my veneration for Wilson, that I watched the antics of the Harding administration as it backed and hauled, timidly moved in to assist and then quickly withdrew—amusing, almost ludicrous. And, as I saw it then, somewhat tragic.

I recall an incident that illustrates the nervousness of the administration over foreign policy.

One day at a press conference President Harding, beleaguered by persistent newspapermen, let out a hint that the administration still was interested in that vague Association of Nations idea which the Republicans, in the 1920 campaign, had thrown out hesitantly as a sop in substitution for the League of Nations to many outstanding party leaders who were internationally minded.

The State Department always has a representative at White House press conferences who reports back to the Secretary. This word got back promptly. So, only a few minutes later, we saw Secretary Hughes, his lips compressed in a thin line dividing his mustache and his bristling beard, hurry through the executive offices and back to the President's private office. He emerged later with a satisfied look.

As a result of that Presidential slip, which had brought a rebuke to the President from his Secretary of State, the open press conference with oral questions, hitherto the custom at the White House, was stopped. Thereafter written questions were required. They had to be signed by the newspaper correspondents and submitted ahead of time to Pat McKenna, the doorkeeper. Mr. Hughes was taking no more chances. That system prevailed through the Coolidge and Hoover administration until President Roosevelt reestablished the free and open conference with oral questions.

Hughes was one of the internationally minded Republicans who wanted to see our nation play a bold and helpful rôle in world affairs. Harding's neighborliness also extended to Europe. But they were in the straitjacket of what Republicans chose to call "the mandate" of the 1920 election and were under the constant surveillance of a Senate dominated by Republicans who wanted to keep clear of Europe. Senator Lodge had a way of asking embarrassing questions every time Secretary Hughes or any of his satellites abroad seemed to be verging too close upon a cooperative policy. Mr. Lodge was a powerful figure, and a grumpy and sarcastic gentleman.

Like the burned child, we avoided Europe and, also like the burned child, we sneaked up close, every so often, attracted by the magnetism of the forbidden, and then dashed off again to look on safely from a distance.

An outstanding impression of that time is of the "unofficial observers." We always had someone or other sitting about the outer corridors of the League of Nations, someone who sat and listened and sent confidential memoranda to Secretary Hughes. In my mind's eye I envisaged a furtive, bespatted figure who never quite got his hat and gloves off, but slipped timidly here and there, gingerly taking a vacant seat somewhere off there in the back row, then rising, apologetically, bowing and excusing himself profusely, if someone came along who seemed to be looking for a place to sit down. He never gave his right name and he tried so hard to disguise any Americanism he might possess. He was a neutral sort of shadow, afraid to open his mouth, uncomfortable, friendless, but always observing nervously.

Our policy, as I watched it then, was a strange compound. We insisted upon using our "moral influence" as we liked to call it, with a cheerful and superior air, and then, suddenly, as we realized that it carried obligations, that we might become "embroiled in Europe," as the phrase went, we withdrew quickly in horror. Europe, we remembered, must be a complete stranger. It was a typically timid policy that only served to make us unpopular and strictly dishonorable to Europe. No one ever knew exactly where we stood. Nor did we. This has always been one of our chief difficulties in European policy.

Europe could not understand "moral influence." Morals had small, if any, part in European diplomacy. Also we were so brash as to want our money back that helped to finance the war, those huge loans which, when the account was cast and a liberal discount made, totalled up to twelve billions of dollars. Europe could not pay, at least much, so she became uppity herself. She tried to shame us with our own idealism. We were just a nation of Shylocks, she insinuated, because we were so crude as to put the whole crusade to save Democracy on a dollars and cents basis. We were depicted as a materialistic nation, with no instinct for the finer things. That hurt our feelings. We withdrew within ourselves, nursing our wounded pride.

I have generalized about the development of policy as it concerned cooperation with Europe. This I saw over a period of years.

Almost immediately upon beginning my work in Washington I was thrown into the midst of one international gesture by the administration which projected us again into the forefront of world affairs—and seemed, for some time thereafter, to hold high hopes of preserving peace among nations.

This was the Naval Disarmament Conference at which we gathered the leading naval powers about the table. Responsible for this glittering spectacle was none other than Senator Borah of Idaho, that determined isolationist who, while constantly anxious to keep us from becoming involved directly in European politics, raised his voice and projected his influence continually over the years, as now, in the interest of world peace. His voice reached far and in Europe his name was better known to the common people than that of some Presidents under whom he served.

In the Pacific, in our relations with Japan, was a source of friction. England then had an alliance with Japan that would appear to throw them together in the event of trouble between the United States and Japan. Senator Borah took the simple expedient of tacking an amendment to the naval appropriations bill suggesting that President Harding call a naval disarmament conference at Washington, upon which he already had sounded out the President and Secretary

Hughes and found them responsive. So Harding invited the powers.

Accordingly, we witnessed that audacious adventure which began, with pomp and ceremony, in the burial of an unknown soldier in the glistening amphitheater at Arlington National Cemetery. It was truly an august performance. I saw all this from afar, as it were. My post for the first few weeks in Washington was taking dictation of news stories over the telephone. So I was in the middle of it, listening to it, absorbing it, at the small telephone switchboard beside the main news desk, but not of it.

All day I sat, that November 11, 1921, during the Unknown Soldier ceremonies, earphones clamped tight to my head, and took thousands and thousands of words from men along the line—solemn, slow-marching words. Reporters that day were trying to write literature. I could feel them searching for the proper rich and gorgeous adjective, as they paused in their deliberate dictation. Something approaching literature *was* turned out in the fever of that day. Kirke Simpson of the Associated Press won the Pulitzer Prize for his stories that had begun when the body of the unknown hero reached Norfolk on a battleship. George R. Holmes, of the International News Service, now asleep himself near that amphitheatre, won honorable mention.

The opening day of the conference I heard the voice of one of our men, tense with suppressed excitement, ask curtly for the desk, and out over the wires went the flash to announce Secretary Hughes' daring proposal for a ten-year naval building holiday which literally took the breath of a discouraged world—though it shocked some of the international politicians gathered for the conference. The sessions of the conference went into the routine stage and ended, a few weeks later, in a series of treaties designed not only to check the building of battleships and confine and blunt somewhat other instruments of war, but to remove possible causes of danger in the Pacific, by scrapping the Anglo-Japanese alliance and drafting a new treaty defining the interests in the Pacific, in which we were included. Other treaties were formulated and approved to guarantee the "open door" in China—in brief, to guarantee Western nations equal rights in exploiting that country under the protecting guns of warships.

But something had been accomplished. Idealism seemed to have a rebirth—our idealism. We hoped again.

Thus we started that check on armaments which, as the years passed, became more and more difficult to sustain. In time, other conferences were held, but they became clouded with suspicions and jealousies, bogged down in technicalities, and finally, the powers dropped the whole pretense and began a new race of armaments in the next decade.

Leading statesmen who represented our former Allies carried back with them to Europe none of the generosity which had been displayed at Washington—so far as the former foe, Germany, was concerned. They returned home to tie the bonds more tightly about that prostrate nation, to fix impossible reparations, and, when Germany could not pay, they set the troops a-marching again. They descended upon the Ruhr to take over that rich coal province. Germany nursed her hate and bided her time for the hour of eventual vengeance.

The harshness of our former Allies reacted upon Washington. We saw much of Secretary Hughes and his aides as they paraded in and out of the White House. Timidly, now and again, we let Europe know that we disapproved of the blunt tactics of the Allies. The State Department protested the forcible collection of reparations. Roland W. Boyden, our "unofficial" representative on the Reparations Commission, talked very plainly and pointedly once, and publicly denounced the Versailles Treaty. But Senator Lodge let out a squawk and Secretary Hughes politely advised the Senator that Boyden's speech was personal and, again of course, "unofficial."

We would talk and then take it back.

Some of our troops still were stationed along the Rhine, and the Senate became alarmed when the French and Belgians began occupation of the Ruhr. The Senate wanted no more chance of entanglement, so it passed a resolution suggesting to President Harding that he recall the American soldiers. Four days later we were handed the order at the White House. On February 11, the transport *St. Mihiel* arrived in New York and landed the last of our foreign legionnaires on American soil. We had wiped our hands of Europe, in effect.

We still could try to collect our debts, and we did try. The British debt-funding commission came first. It included Sir Montagu Norman, the power of the Bank of England, and Stanley Baldwin, later Prime Minister. The French came later and the Italians and some of the smaller nations. They all called at the White House and then sat down with our debt-funding commission created by Congress. Intermittently, we saw them back at the White House to discuss this or that phase of proposed settlements. England, having negotiated first, got the settlement nearest her real obligation. The others were treated more liberally. Simultaneously with the initial payments campaigns for cancellation began.

We discovered that we had a domestic debt of our own. The newly organized American Legion decided that the soldiers ought to have a cash bonus. They had fought to save Democracy. It once had seemed a glorious adventure. Now they thought a little cash would be appropriate. The American Legion set up its lobby in Washington, in time to be joined by other similar organizations—the Veterans of Foreign Wars, the Disabled American Veterans. They began to dig their hands into the "grab bag." American Legion commanders became familiar figures about the White House. They were cocky with their demands. For the soldiers' bonus became a gaudy and alluring political issue. Congress passed a soldiers' bonus bill. Harding vetoed it. But the campaign went ahead. It popped up again and again. An insurance bonus was passed later as a compromise, but it never satisfied. The former soldiers wanted cash. Finally they got it in the Roosevelt administration.

The League of Nations was effectively shelved. A few prominent Woodrow Wilson Democrats raised the ghost from time to time in the early years after the war. The ghost finally was laid by the Democratic Party at the 1924 Madison Square Garden Convention after a dramatic fight one night led by Newton D. Baker, Wilson's Secretary of War.

I was sitting in the front row of the press section as Baker delivered his oration, only a few feet from that small figure who thrilled the convention—but did not win it. I can recall it vividly, for it moved me deeply. Chills ran up and down my spine as the former Secretary of War, in his climax, knelt down on the platform and raised his hands to heaven. I slowly raised myself to my feet behind my typewriter as he lowered his voice almost to a whisper. The great throng in the convention hall sat silent, transfixed.

The words he uttered look cold now and do not stir me.

"I have one other debt," he concluded. "I beg your patience while I pay it. I served Woodrow Wilson for five years. He is standing at the throne of God whose approval he won and has received."

He raised both his arms outstretched and the thousands shook the hall with their applause.

Then he knelt—and the crowd froze into absolute silence. He raised his hands upward.

"As he looks down from there I say to him: 'I did my best. I am doing it now. You are still the captain of my soul.' I feel his spirit here palpably about us. He is standing here, speaking through my weak voice, his presence—not that crippled, shrunken, broken figure that I last saw, but the great, majestic leader is standing here, using me to say to you: 'Save Mankind! Do America's Duty.' "

As he rose to his feet the convention was swept with hysteria. Delegates shouted, whistled, stamped their feet. The band struck up "The Battle Hymn of the Republic" and followed that with "Onward Christian Soldiers." Delegates sang the chorus.

But when they voted a few minutes later, they overwhelmingly defeated Baker's plank favoring the League of Nations.

However, both Republican and Democratic Party leaders supported United States entry into the World Court of the League of Nations, the arbitral body. Both President Harding and Secretary Hughes appealed, but in vain. We still are out, despite successive pleas by every administration since. The Senate adopted a protocol of entry in the Coolidge administration but with reservations which proved unacceptable.

Out of the desolation which war left in its wake in Europe came the Phoenix of Revolution, a bold, perky bird which smirked at old rulers, pecked out their eyes, a bird which strutted and preened its feathers as the masses first exulted with praise and thanksgiving, then began to doubt, then found themselves under the heels of Frankenstein's monsters.

From Washington we watched.

Across the eastern horizon there appeared a cloud that spread terror into the capitalistic heart. A new nation was rising from the wreck left by ruthless Czars. There was a song on its broken lips. The Bear that walked like a man began to dance to the tune of the brotherhood of man. It was such a brave and noble experiment in government. The newspapers pictured a gruesome figure with long black whiskers, a cruel leer on a tyrannical face, a bomb clutched in long bony fingers, and labelled it "Bolshevism." We were admonished to quake in our boots.

This was Communism running riot across half a continent and hadn't Attorney General A. Mitchell Palmer, with his frequent Red raids, laid bare the terrors of Communism? The Baptist soul of Secretary Hughes was well-nigh petrified. No, said he, we could never recognize the monster in the East. Absolutely not. So hopeful souls like myself, idealistic persons like myself, gobbled up all the books we could find on Soviet Russia and spoofed the spooky Mr. Hughes and American capitalists. Proudly we proclaimed our faith in Russia. We were justified for a long time. It was the "liberal" thing to do, to glorify Russia and to plague our "conservative" friends. We took a sadistic delight in it. We loved to frighten them with our defense of her experiment and to cry aloud our "radicalism." It was easy across thousands of miles. We could not foresee the Mongolian Stalin and his mock trials, his blood purges.

Nearer this way a one-time Socialist editor began to cast his shadow across southern Europe and the world. Benito Mussolini led his black-shirted legions downward across Italy and into Rome and the word Fascist entered our political lexicon.

Only those who read their newspapers very carefully remembered afterward the name Adolf Hitler among those involved with General Eric von Ludendorff in the abortive beer hall revolution—and it meant nothing even to them. Napoleon wrote a history of the world in a Parisian garret, and an Austrian painter wrote *Mein Kampf*.

But the average American paid little attention to these foreign events. Americans wanted to forget Europe. The Harding administration, I am convinced, accurately gauged the American people when it kept gingerly aloof from Europe. Harding was from Main Street, and I think he interpreted Main Street aright in this. We look back now and speculate whether history might have taken a different turn had we cooperated in Europe, sat in with the League of Nations as a partner. But we only speculate. We can never know. We do know, those of us who watched the events of that day, that the people of the United States wanted to withdraw from Europe. Our grand and noble gesture had failed.

Deluded, we turned to new games at home, games played around the fleshpots.

The sordidness of war, casualty lists day by day, the cheapening of life, the actual vision of cold-blooded death by so many of our young men who had gone to France—all these hardened and toughened us. We sought release—and what a low, physical release it was. We wallowed. We proudly broke laws of man and God.

"What the hell!" we shouted.

While the soldiers were in France a moralist minority had tortured national prohibition out of a self-righteous Congress and self-righteous state legislatures. Such students of national behavior as Woodrow Wilson and William Howard Taft, to mention but two, realized the futility of legally imposed morality. But we never do anything by halves. Hadn't we emoted ourselves into a war three thousand miles across the ocean, like modern knights errant saving the Lady Fair from the Dragon?

In my early days in Washington the archangel of national prohibition was a fat little fellow by the name of Roy A. Haynes, a nondescript, second-rate Ohio politician, a bubbling, somewhat shy spirit. It was one of my duties during part of that period to cover prohibition enforcement head-quarters, then housed in one of the temporary war buildings along the Mall. There, on a big table outside his office, were piles of mimeographed statements every day telling about how many stills had been captured in this town and that by prohibition agents, how effectively prohibition was being enforced. Haynes exuded optimism. It was, after all, his job. We laughed at him. His name became a national byword. Vaudeville actors could always get a laugh with it, so sure-fire it was. In time he became indrawn and knew the cynicism that lay behind our questions at press conferences. He knew we were kidding him secretly. He was succeeded by another, and that one by another, and so on, through those years, each in time becoming discouraged, and getting weary of seeing himself lampooned. Poorly paid prohibition agents took bribes and created scandal after scandal. Simple fellows in the prohibition army who should have remained on the farm shot people down in cold blood.

Yet the nation drank more and more, risking the dangers. For some were blinded and some were poisoned and died. A few went to jail or paid fines. Big syndicates were formed to bootleg liquor. A national industry was created. Gangs machine-gunned each other in the large cities as they fought for the right to exclusive territory. We looked on in bewilderment.

The nation revelled in its lawlessness. In most homes—or so it seemed, though it could not have been—was the fruit jar of raw alcohol, quickly transformed into gin by the simple expedient, that we all learned, of adding water and juniper drops. We had cocktail parties that began at 5 o'clock in the afternoon and still were going strong at 3 and 4 the next morning. Men and women, ginned up, sneaked off with each other's wives and husbands, for that was also the period when we crowned sex with a dark halo and tried to free ourselves from inhibitions and pampered ourselves with the doctrine of promiscuity.

Luxurious speakeasies sprung up like mushrooms in our cities and now this dimly lit dive was the fad, now that. For the thirsty male there was the gloomy little room with a bar up some alley where we climbed the rickety stairs and were stared at by Bill or Joe or Frank, recognized, and admitted. The atmosphere was dank and foul. Now, looking backward, it all seems so impossible.

We were on the loose. What an age!

Greenwich Village in New York set the style for freedom in living, art and literature. We examined sex and the family relationship and found it passé, old-fashioned. We read magazine articles about companionate marriage. We read magazine articles about no marriage at all. Men and women proudly "lived together" in those days without the bond of holy wedlock. (Many of them sneaked off after a time and got married.) The new poetry appeared that only the author could understand. Novels blossomed in which the characters skipped from one bedroom scene to another. That was called "realism in literature." Four-letter words were sprinkled through the dialogue. Nymphomaniacs became the heroines of literature.

Symbolism in art appeared, borrowed from the French. We "ohed" and "ahed" over crazy shapes and lines, over purple trees.

This freedom luckily did not burrow down to the roots of our civilization, which remained about the same. It was the froth which boiled to the top and remains as the sign of an era when we look back upon it. Generally it was an age of cynicism. The small towns aped the cities in drinking bouts at the country club and petting parties among the night shadows on the golf course. The flapper, that saucy young thing with bobbed hair and with dresses up to her knees, who drank from hip flasks and was ready to offer her kisses to him who asked and enwrap herself in any strong pair of arms, was the presiding genius of the younger generation. F. Scott Fitzgerald limned her as he had seen her at Princeton and she popped up throughout the land to disturb orthodox parents who became unorthodox later when she had settled down to have babies.

Unobtrusive and simple-minded men who never had cut a dashing figure found their release in the hooded order called the Ku Klux Klan which started in my home town of Atlanta, Ga., and eventually spread far and wide under the skilful management of men who knew human psychology and made a fortune out of it. It was based on the primal desire of man to be, in some respect, better than or different from his fellow man. It capitalized the morally and intellectually weak who have a hard time finding an inferior. The necessary inferior was created by pointing to minorities of race, color and creed. They were portrayed as different because they were in a minority. The prospective Ku Kluxer was told that they were not like him, a white Protestant. He, the white Protestant, was better than the Jew, the Catholic, or the Negro. This difference was emphasized and then traits were discovered which could be deplored and looked down upon. This created the relish for persecution. The persecution of another gives the bully, the weak-minded, a feeling of strength.

To all this were added mysteries and secret rites. Like ghouls they gathered about the flaming cross at night. They had passwords and special passports. Their identity was cloaked behind the flowing sheet. There were titles to tempt ambitious gullibility. The member felt himself a personage because he was part of a movement that was feared. He was somebody. He justified himself in a religious fanaticism that harked back to the Druids and the blood sacrifice. His primeval instincts were released.

Like wildfire the Klan spread among the mediocre, and in our world there are so many. Then the wily politician seized upon it, for the politician always is on the lookout for votes in big blocks. In time the Klan became too powerful for him and he cringed and fawned before it. The hooded order captured whole states—Texas, Oklahoma, Indiana.

I can remember the very beginning of the Ku Klux Klan. I recall signs about Atlanta "1,001 eyes are watching you." We wondered what they meant. For a long time, under the early leadership of William J. Simmons, an old man with a mystic cast, the Klan did not grow rapidly. But smart men saw the possibilities and took it over. Old Man Simmons became merely the patriarch, the symbol. In its heyday I have ridden past the "nightshirt factory" at Buckhead, in the outskirts of Atlanta, and seen the plant blazing with its lights. Twenty-four hours a day they were turning out the sheets and the hoods.

The *Atlanta Journal* became interested in the signs, discovered they signalized some new secret order, and the city editor decreed a story. He sent out his feature writer, Ward Greene, with the staff photographer, Matt Winn. They learned that they could not be admitted to a meeting for a picture. So they devised a scheme of their own. They hired a group of Negroes at 25 cents a head, covered them with sheets, and took the first picture of a Klan meeting! Ward Greene, novelist and executive of King Features now in New York, told the story many years afterwards.

The *New York World* exposed the Klan to the nation and, like most such exposures, this only whetted the appetite for the order. It grew and grew. It was forced to the attention of President Harding. He asked Attorney General Daugherty to investigate. Subsequently, in the usual gesture, Simmons himself, the Imperial Wizard, asked the President to investigate. The Senate looked into it. And still it grew. Now it had fastened itself upon politicians. It marched triumphantly into national politics in 1924, after Harding's time, as a factor against the nomination of Alfred E. Smith as Democratic candidate for the Presidency.

In their retreat from the grim after-war realities, other simple and humble Americans sought an avenue of escape through Fundamentalism in religion. Perhaps it was a violent reaction against the freedom and excesses of their less moral neighbors, disappointment also perchance at the dimming of the light of idealism to which they had been led to look with hope now blasted. Now, again, with the war excitement over, they encountered the same troubles they had known before Woodrow Wilson had raised his banner aloft —factories closing, jobs going, strikes breaking out here and there. They began to occupy themselves with a movement against the theory of evolution. Here was a devil to whip. Here they could wreak their vengeance on the intellectual elite, against the thinkers, against the aristocracy of brains which seemed to them to wear its haloes with a snobbish air.

The new crusade against the "free thinkers" was whipped up by William Jennings Bryan, the tired warrior who had streaked across the political firmament at too early an age and now had worn out his welcome in this field where, for so long, he had been a superior being. With his political bob curling about a pate now growing bald, with an evangelical and fervent glint in his eye, he appeared altogether a modern Savonarola as he thundered against the heretics who held that man came from a monkey. His voice still rang clear and silvery. His august presence still magnetized an audience.

How effectively was disclosed when he almost won from the Kentucky legislature a condemnation of the theory of evolution. A resolution was defeated by only one vote after he had harangued the legislators. So potent was the Bryan crusade that the Council of the American Association for the Advancement of Science, meeting at Harvard in December 1922, felt it necessary to reassert the validity of the evolution theory. The seeds that Bryan was planting sprouted later in Tennessee when a young schoolteacher who taught the evolutionary theory became a cause célèbre as the center of a trial in which Bryan was pitted against the agnostic Clarence Darrow. From that ordeal Bryan slipped quietly off the earth and was laid to rest on a hill in Arlington in a drenching rain.

In time from France came another apostle to give us faith in ourselves, the famed Dr. Emile Coué. All America repeated:

"Every day, in every way, I am getting better and better."

But our saving sense of humor translated this into a joke, too, in time.

We were not getting better and better.

We were becoming more befuddled, and so was the man at the head of our state.

11

WARREN G. HARDING did not have much longer to worry, though he did not know it. He did not suspect, when he stepped aboard a special train at Washington in mid-June 1923 for a transcontinental journey that was to take him to Alaska, that he was headed down the last trail, that he would return to the nation's capital again in a box about which flags would be draped, to lie for a few hours in the East Room of the White House, to lie for a few hours in the rotunda of the Capitol, to lie for a few hours on a train that took him back to Marion whence he had started with such high hopes.

There is evidence that it would not have mattered much if he *had* known. Undoubtedly he had begun to suspect the treachery among his friends, the bosom friends he had trusted. He must have heard what was going on. It is known that he had called Charlie Forbes to account one day in his office, told him, in righteous fury and in strong words, to get out of his sight. I remember the day that Forbes, usually the urbane and cheerful, came out of the President's private office a confused and bewildered man. That, I learned later, was the day the President had denounced him as a faithless steward. Rumors were about of his possible resignation. We asked him about those reports that day and he denied them.

Yes, Harding knew this piece of perfidy and he must have suspected more. He must have been sorely troubled as he left on his tour. As he crossed the country he stopped here and there for speeches. He seesawed across his record as he seesawed across the country. He must have been trying to justify himself. The whole performance revealed the crazy-quilt pattern of his record and his thinking. He tossed the little baubles into the air to catch a glint of sunlight. They did not shine very brightly. He must have recognized that he was a failure, that doom was crashing down upon him. He discovered how lonely a friendly man can be—when trusted friends take advantage and leave their benefactor desolately holding the bag.

At St. Louis he pleaded again for a Permanent Court of International Justice entirely separate from the League of Nations. (The League still was untouchable.) The Senate had denied him that. He was straightening out his record for people who really didn't care. At Kansas City he proposed a merger of railroads into regional groups. (He must have thought again of the trainmen's strike.) He urged prohibition enforcement at Denver. It may not have seemed ironical to him, but how ironical to talk of prohibition in a city where full-blooded men—men even like himself—were wont to gather for a spree in the old days, where real silver dollars embedded in the floor winked up at the customer in the Silver Dollar Saloon of Silver Dollar Tabor! According to the story at the time, Harding had given up drinking. The President, he had decided, must abide by the laws that he asks other people to obey.

He advocated nationalization of the coal mines at Cheyenne. (Those months trying to settle the coal strike must have tormented him still.) At Idaho Falls he talked of co-operation with consumers to end the high cost of living. Here he was treading gingerly on issues that mattered. At Helena he suggested that capital as well as men be conscripted for the next war. He promised an extension of irrigation and reclamation at Spokane in the midst of that land where water is uppermost in the minds of men who are trying to get a living out of the volcanic ash which needs only water to make it blossom like the rose. In Portland, where the I.W.W., the Wobblies, had tasted power, he came out for deportation of agitators who menace the country, and thus he stepped back into the shell which his big-business backers had built about him to keep out the facts of life. Still he trusted the Powers that Be, the Big Men of America, for at Tacoma, before embarking for Alaska, he told how steel magnates had pledged him they would abolish the twelve-hour day in their mills as soon as possible. They did establish the eight-hour day. United States Steel made its announcement a few days later.

He boarded the boat, a pathetic creature. He wanted to be kindly, to help his fellow men. And see how shabbily they had treated him! Nowhere had he left anything that contributed to his ambitions for himself, only dark secrets of the misdeeds of his friends that were to be shouted from the housetops after he was gone. He had been so futile and ineffectual.

He had no understanding of the fundamental problems of the nation. Glibly—and sincerely, no doubt—he talked of lightening the burden of toil at his inauguration. Yet he had consented when Harry Daugherty had bound labor in the chains of injunction before Judge Wilkerson at Chicago. He had said that "we want the cradle of American childhood rocked under conditions so wholesome and hopeful that no blight may touch it in its development." Yet he had not said a word when the Supreme Court held the act prohibiting child labor unconstitutional. He did not dare. The Court was sacred. He had expressed, in his inauguration message, a hope for "an America of homes illumined with hope and happiness, where mothers, freed from the necessity of long hours of toil beyond their own doors, may preside as befits the hearthstone of American citizenship." But the mills and mines and factories owned by his big-business friends did not always pay wages enough for a man to keep a wife and family in food, clothes and shelter, and consequently some women must leave the home and toil long hours. But had he spoken out when the Supreme Court held that it was contrary to the Constitution for the District of Columbia— and by that token any state—to have a law fixing minimum wages for women workers? He had not. Reform went to sleep on this particular front for fifteen years.

He had given the farmers more opportunity to borrow themselves more deeply into debt. At the same time he sat by, acquiescent, while Congress levied tariff taxes that made them pay more for what they had to buy in town. He had been faithful to his masters. Not only had he given them tariff protection but he had begun to lift taxes from shoulders well able to bear them.

A popular song typified his era:

"The rich get richer and the poor get children."

Two stars glittered in his crown of thorns. One was the institution of a sound budget system, with a Comptroller dependent solely on Congress—with no allegiance to the Executive—to check on how the money Congress appropriated was spent. The other was in the field of foreign affairs—his disarmament conference. He could not take overmuch credit for either. But there they were, on the record.

On the way to Alaska, so the story ran, he was told by Herbert Hoover about the treachery of men he had trusted. Small wonder that death took him so easily once illness had laid him low in a San Francisco Hotel.

I remember the screaming of extras in Washington the night he died in San Francisco. I went out and bought one and then fled, posthaste, to the office. He had been pronounced better that day and then, suddenly, death had come to release a tortured soul from its misery. But he died a President in full honors. For days, it seemed, the funeral train advanced slowly across the country. Hushed and muffled rhetoric filled the newspapers.

I was at the White House the night his body was brought to the austere mansion that is never quite a home. The caisson wheeled up the gravel drive, slowly crunching its way, stopped under the porte cochère, and the casket was carried up the steps by marines as the horses nervously shuffled their feet. Just as they lifted the dead President across the threshold a shooting star pirouetted down the heavens, a flash of fire that disappeared behind the State Department. I noted that to the rewrite man on the desk in our office when I went to our telephone in the press room in the executive offices to dictate the running story.

Harding's body lay that night in the East Room among the ghosts of the past. In the center of the huge room sat the simple coffin with its four wreaths of flowers. A marine stood at each corner of the casket. A faint light at one end of the room was reflected in the polished floors and in the tall mirrors above the mantel. It sparkled in the three ornate chandeliers overhead, and, like the wan sliver of the new moon, dimly outlined the banks of flowers which stretched away on every side, a vague and lush garden of night. The perfume permeated the gloom.

Other Presidents had slept thus in this historic room—William Henry Harrison, Taylor, Lincoln, Garfield and McKinley. Normally the East Room is a joyous and gay corner of the American empire, light and airy with its big windows and French doors leading out to the terrace. Children have frolicked blithely over its waxed floors in the squares and oblongs of sunlight which danced through the windows. Here it was that the Theodore Roosevelt children played. Here, too, in the dimmer days the babies of Emily Donelson, niece of Andrew Jackson, took their first faltering steps. Here Dolly Madison had been the vivacious belle of many parties while her quiet husband looked on and smiled gravely at her. Here, too, on a rainy day she had hung out the Monday wash to dry. Not many months before President Harding had been the host of a happy gathering here. Sedately he stepped out to waltz with a young girl while Mrs. Harding danced with Secretary George Christian. It was a pretty scene.

Mobs stormed hilariously into this room with the dust of unpaved Pennsylvania Avenue on their feet at President Jackson's farewell reception. They laughed and shouted, shoved and slapped backs, the while tramping into the floor bits of the big yellow cheese which the house had provided for its guests.

Harding would have enjoyed that, relished the easy comradery of those earlier times. But Jackson fought for these common people. He was their idol. Harding had earned no such admiration. He was from them, but never of them.

Thus death came to the White House.

I had seen its approach once before. It had come near, hovered for a few days, then passed.

This was when Mrs. Harding was seriously ill. For three nights we sat about the lobby of the executive offices or sprawled in the press room to one side on a "death watch." Three times I saw the pale light of dawn come creeping across the White House lawn and through the trees and walked outside the executive office to taste its freshness, to hear the birds chatter as they stirred into a new day, to get the muggy feeling out of my bones and my spirit. Through the night we sat about the dimly lit lobby and talked, or got up and paced nervously up and down the marble floor, or tried to read. At such times the body is restless, for the mind must be constantly on the alert for the word that may come from the sick room. One night I heard from Cole Morgan of Universal Service the story of how the *Atlanta Georgian,* on which he had worked at the time, had scored a beat of several hours on the lynching of Leo Frank because O. B. Keeler, then a cub reporter who lived at Marietta near the scene of the lynching, had found out about the horrible affair and had called up to catch Cole at the office. Cole and "Fuzzy" Woodruff, that legendary Southern newspaperman, had pulled printers and enough staff together to get out an extra. I recounted my one terrible ordeal with a lynching. The dark and disturbing South from which I had fled rose up again before me.

We reminisced about the dramatic moments of our lives, the stories we had covered, while a President's wife fought for her life in a sickroom not far away.

As I look back, there is an amusing commentary. We smoked, those nights, cigarette after cigarette. We put the burned matches back into the boxes and took our stubs over and threw them carefully into the fireplace. Such caution—

as if we had been at home under the eyes of neat and watchful wives! Mrs. Harding was responsible for what would have seemed an affectation, or a fixation. One day she had come into the executive office, scanned with some show of distaste the cigarette stubs and matches littered about the chairs where we sat, and then and there delivered us a lecture. This must stop. She was positive about that. Thereafter we got into the habit of putting our burned matches back into the boxes. The habit persisted with me for years. One day absent-mindedly I replaced a lighted match and the whole box went off in my hand!

After she got well and was convalescing she invited us over to the White House to see her. She sat in a wheelchair. On her head was a boudoir cap and about her neck the perpetual black ribbon which it was said she wore to conceal wrinkles. We chatted a few minutes, and then she had a Secret Service man show us through the upper floor where the President and his family live. From that visit dates my memory of the huge bed in which the giant Lincoln slept while a Civil War raged.

She it was, this iron woman, so ambitious for the younger man she had married, who was the heroine of the long day of pomp and ceremony when Democracy paid its honors to her late husband.

"Here she comes!"

The crowd gathered about the White House portico whispered to itself, then lapsed into silence as she walked slowly toward the steps. The caisson bearing the President's body had rumbled away after the clattering cavalry. Thousands of smartly dressed troops were tramping the heated pavement of Pennsylvania Avenue on their way to the Capitol under a merciless sun of late August. The crowd watched the widow intently as she proceeded across the porch on the arm of the faithful George Christian. She wore deep mourning and a heavy black veil. Slowly and firmly she descended the steps and entered the waiting automobile. Her face was pale. Her lips were tightly set.

Down Pennsylvania Avenue to the Capitol I followed the procession. Every sixty seconds the guns of Fort Myer boomed over the city—minute guns. Church bells clanged their death notes. The band bewailed, in the measured sobbing tones of Chopin, man's brief and sorry tenure on earth.

A far greater multitude than had gathered two and a half years ago to witness his one triumphant day, his inauguration, now flooded the plaza before the Capitol and overflowed into the surrounding streets to watch the final official rites for Warren G. Harding. In front of the Congressional Library little boys were filling pop bottles from the stream of water pouring from the fountain and selling them for a nickel apiece to cool parched throats. They dashed about eagerly and merrily at their business enterprise, unaffected by the death of a President of the United States.

In the throng here today were many who had heard him say, as he closed his inaugural address:

"What doth the Lord require of thee but to do justly, and to love mercy, and to walk humbly with thy God?"

Mrs. Harding was my story that day. I followed behind as she entered the rotunda where the service was to be held. Her entrance was from the passage leading to the Senate. Already the vaulted room was filling with the nation's leaders and foreign diplomats and the tiny noises, whispering, rustling of clothes, grew into big noises as they echoed and re-echoed from the dome. Mrs. Harding came in with George Christian. She gripped his arm tightly. They had to wait for a moment at the door. There was a movement at the center of the rotunda. The casket was being placed on the catafalque and the tired and worn young guard of honor was having trouble getting it set just right. Mrs. Harding observed this, but as from miles away.

"Ready?" she asked the policeman who stood at the entrance as the marines finished their task and withdrew.

He nodded respectfully.

She and Christian then walked to their places. She did not falter, but quietly took her seat near the casket.

In the midst of the service, from high above, came a loud report, as if a door had slammed shut. Eyes strayed upward, but nothing amiss was observed. Later, at the office, I learned that William Slavens McNutt, the short-story writer, who was doing a special story for us, was responsible. He had sought the balcony up toward the dome as a vantage point to witness the ceremony below. In order to see over the high stone railing he had turned a bucket upside down to stand upon. It had slipped from under him.

After the service Mrs. Harding returned to the White House and the public was admitted to file by the coffin and look upon a President in death. Between 12:30 and 4:30, when the doors were closed, it was estimated that 35,000 persons had passed by. Still waiting outside in two long lines which wound away for blocks were between 15,000 and 20,000 others who had stood in vain. A few hundred at the front of the line tried to force their way into the rotunda, but were held at bay by policemen. They were piqued that they had missed so narrowly a chance to see a President lying in state, annoyed that they could not exchange comments with their more lucky neighbors across the banisters after supper. But they had put up a fight over it. That, at least, was something.

At 5 o'clock President Coolidge, the members of his Cabinet and the civil and military guards of honor arrived and were escorted into the rotunda. Previously the military escorts had been drawn up in formation on the esplanade before the

Capitol and the caisson had been backed into position at the bottom of the steps. The new President and his Cabinet walked slowly past the casket, all keeping their eyes straight ahead. Postmaster General New, who had been a Senate colleague of the dead President, and Attorney General Daugherty were visibly moved.

Presently they emerged and started down the long, broad steps. Vividly I recall it, as if it were only yesterday. With silk hats in hand they descended in a crude sort of echelon. The sun was dropping behind the dome and the steps and the plaza were in shade. Its rays still lighted the Congressional Library a block away. On the coping far above sparrows jabbered. Time seemed to stand still for a moment and implant the picture upon the memory, as when a faded moving picture film of long ago flickers to a stop and everyone is suddenly frozen into the pose of the moment.

Then the film starts again. The marines appear at the top of the steps bearing the casket. Slowly they descend and lift it upon the caisson. The command is given, and the slow procession to Union Station a few blocks away begins. The August afternoon is redolent with "Nearer My God to Thee," the holy perfume of sound.

In the station we seemed to return, suddenly, to life again. There people went about their eternal little ways. They were buying tickets, buying newspapers, sending telegrams, scanning in that last-minute hurry the racks of magazines. They paused only a moment for death, made conscious of it through the strains of "Lead, Kindly Light," which the band played softly against the background of noises that the living always link with a railway station—the coughing of engines, the occasional shriek of a whistle down the corridor of tracks which lead away to the world, the whirr and buzz of electric baggage trucks which dash in their zigzag courses.

Those who had business to do, who had trains to catch, pushed and threaded their way through the silent crowd which stood in the vaulted concourse in final tribute to a President of the United States who was leaving Washington forever.

Mrs. Harding did not arrive until just before time for departure. Already the flag-shrouded casket had been placed aboard the train, the same special train which had borne him across the country from the coast. She walked slowly down the length of the train. George Christian still was at her side. General Sawyer also accompanied her, stepping along in his nervous, staccato fashion. Just as she prepared to board the train she turned about and spoke to Mrs. Edward B. McLean, her close friend and confidante.

"I'll meet you when you return," Mrs. McLean was heard to answer.

The President's widow was assisted up the steps by George Christian and went into her compartment. A moment later Christian returned to the platform.

"Is everything ready?" he asked.

The conductor nodded.

"All aboard!"

The cry rang through the station and was echoed down the line.

Slowly the train moved away.

That night Mrs. McLean entertained the new President and Mrs. Coolidge at dinner.

The King is dead!

Long live the King!

12

C ALVIN COOLIDGE—President! My God!"
That, and many other unholy outbursts to the
same effect, echoed at intervals from the group
which sat about the office as the story of President
Harding's death came pouring in over our wires from Larry
Martin, our staff man with the President's party at San
Francisco.

We would saunter over and take another look at the wire,
by twos and threes, over the operator's shoulder, as if to make
sure it really was the truth, then we'd sit down or wander
about and break out again, unbelievably:

"Imagine—Calvin Coolidge, President!"

But it really was true, for soon another story began to come
in from Plymouth, Vt., from Paul Mallon, who had been
assigned to stay with the Vice President when Harding had
fallen ill. It told of the news coming to the farm of John
Coolidge, the new President's father. Early in the morning
Paul's story came through about the oath being administered
to the new President of the United States by his father, by the
light of a kerosene lamp. The kerosene lamp was strangely
symbolic. That's about how far Calvin Coolidge had come in
his social and economic philosophy.

History has proved our reaction on the night of Harding's
death to have been accurate. But it took some time.

It was not his social or economic philosophy about which
we were concerned. We didn't speak much those days in
such terms, at least the practical, day-by-day newspapermen
with whom I moved. It was just Coolidge, himself. He didn't
seem to us to measure up to what a President should be, in
any particular.

To me he was a timid person with a perpetual brief case
who sidled in and out of the White House for the semiweekly

Cabinet meetings. He walked in rapidly, his head cocked to one side, looking neither to right nor left, and hurried out first when the meeting was over. Never was he without that brief case. (I still wonder what he carried in it.) Yes, there was one exception. That was the day he came in with Mrs. Coolidge's knitting bag instead of the brief case. That made a little feature story. He grinned, sheepishly, when one of the newspapermen called it to his attention.

The impression I had of Coolidge the person, and still have, is of a country fellow who had just come to town, a shrewd fellow, with a crude kind of rural humor that smacked of casual, cryptic barnyard chatter. This impression, as far as physical appearance contributed, was heightened by the fact that he always wore his hat gingerly on his head, not comfortably. It always seemed just a shade too small. It sat too far up on his head. He looked as I've seen the farmer look on Sunday. He was overly neat, stiff of manner, as if not quite accustomed to his position. His nature was sharpened by occasional meanness and he had a sadistic streak that expressed itself in practical jokes which often plagued the Secret Service men who were the victims of his pranks.

He was a political accident, as, so far as the Presidency was concerned, was Warren Harding. He came up the political ladder because he would go along with the organization and keep his mouth shut. He did his job and got into no unnecessary controversies. He was projected into the national limelight for a time as Governor of Massachusetts by the Boston police strike, and largely through a one-sentence telegram he sent to Samuel Gompers, president of the American Federation of Labor: "There is no right to strike against the public safety by anybody, anywhere, any time." Republican leaders at the 1920 convention had selected Senator Irvine Lenroot of Wisconsin as the Vice Presidential nominee, in a hurried session after the wearing struggle over the Presidential nomination, but a delegate from Oregon, Wallace McCamant, jumped up on a chair, nominated Coolidge, and swept the convention along with him. Nobody knew anything much about him except that he was supposed to be safe and sane and in favor of law and order. The sudden and unexpected death of a President elevated him to the White House.

The elevation stunned him, phlegmatic as he was.

Being President was something quite different from presiding over the United States Senate, attending dinners, and making an occasional, dry prosaic speech. He was a copybook maxim personified, shoved into a post which, properly occupied, requires imagination, feeling, large knowledge, and ability to grow with the office. He lacked these qualifications, though he might have made some effort to enlarge his knowledge, which he did not. He just sat, mostly.

His philosophy was primitively laissez-faire. He believed in letting things run themselves. He thought the existing order was all right. (It had been kind to him without much effort on his part.) Not knowing how it might be changed for the better, nor apparently caring very much, he had no field of positive action. He was a negativist. When anything disturbed the existing order—why, just stop it. His only achievements were negative in character. He is remembered chiefly for vetoing the soldiers' bonus and McNary-Haugen farm bill and the Norris bill for government power development at Muscle Shoals. They interfered with the system he found, the system which the well-to-do, the elect, had created. He approved of the system.

One other thing stands out in his administration, the successive tax reductions for the wealthy which Secretary of Treasury Mellon decreed. Democrats in Congress succeeded in forcing some of the reductions into the lower brackets, but generally the effect was to take the load off the back of the wealthy. That excess was diverted into overexpansion and stock market speculation. Presto—the Coolidge Boom!

Presto—Coolidge the god!

137

He was one of the millions of poor who idolize the rich. Where so many are envious, he was only worshipful. He looked up to men who made money. That, to him, repre-sented achievement. He believed in thrift and economy for the average man, for that was the way, according to the American legend, that the fortunate millionaires had made their start. He subscribed 100 per cent to the Horatio Alger theory.

He preached economy in government. He did not cut very deeply, for the four and five billion dollar budgets which the country regarded as natural after the war continued; but tax returns were lucrative and the budget was kept balanced. He dramatized economy in the White House executive office staff by giving a prize of ten dollars—which he paid out of his own pocket!—to the employee who could suggest the best way to economize. A formula which included substitution of the old-fashioned drinking glass for paper cups and using notepaper on both sides and using pencils down to the bitter end won the award. Public health organizations screamed about the drinking glass. He decreed the economies none-theless.

He admired men who had piled up money and, therefore, he took the country along the path prescribed by one of their shining lights in his Cabinet, Andrew Mellon. He liked Mellon who, in some ways, was much like him, a quiet fellow who went about his business without much noise. He didn't like bustling, energetic, active fellows who had big ideas about the world and were ready, at the drop of a hat, to assume command and issue orders. Therefore he did not like Herbert Hoover. He called him "The Wonder Boy."

The sudden thrust of the Presidential mantle about his thin shoulders staggered him for a time. He really was a timid person those first few days. He promised to carry on the Harding policies—whatever that might mean—and then lapsed into silence for a month.

During that month he was built into a myth. It was one of the greatest feats of newspaper propaganda that the modern world has seen. It really was a miracle. He said nothing. Newspapers must have copy. So we grasped at little incidents to build up human interest stories and we created a character. He kept his counsel. Therefore he was a strong and silent man. The editorial writers on newspapers which were satisfied with the status quo, the big Eastern journals, created the strong, silent man. Then, in time, as the country found out he was not a superman, neither strong nor silent, they emphasized his little witticisms, his dry wit, and we had a national character—Cal. Everybody spoke of him fondly as "Cal." He was one of us. He was the ordinary man incarnate.

"Did you hear what Cal said?"

He wouldn't rock the boat. He wouldn't interfere with business. He would live and let live.

Hurray for Cal!

We stood, twice a week at press conferences, and saw the man, not the myth. He was the same man who had sidled in and out of Cabinet meetings, but with more confidence. He talked, in his nasal twang, out of the corner of his mouth. Often he passed up important questions of national policy and expatiated at length about some trifle. I remember him talking on and on one day, when there were important matters we wanted him to discuss, about whether boys should be allowed to fish in the Tidal Basin. It was a purely local issue. The little sermon was good of its kind, whimsical and small-townish.

There was the day, too, when someone asked him about a life of George Washington which Rupert Hughes had written and which the Daughters of the American Revolution, currently in annual session in Washington, were deploring. He turned about and looked out the window behind him.

"I see the monument is still standing," he said.

There were those moments.

139

They made the homely philosopher, but not the statesman.

It was impossible to destroy the legend of "Silent Cal" in the country, but he was, on occasion, garrulous as the old man who sits in front of the country store. He showed this occasionally at press conferences. He showed it to visitors who would find him interested in some particular subject, when they came to call about some government problem, and who would have to sit while he talked and talked.

He was lazy physically. Often of an afternoon when there were no engagements and no pressing business—and during the days of prosperity no one was concerned much about Washington or national affairs—he would rear his chair back, throw his spare legs on a corner of his desk, and take a nap. One Memorial Day I recall the grumbling among attachés who had to stay around merely because the President had come over to his office and spent the afternoon napping there. He kept Senator Smoot of Utah and the French debt-funding commission waiting for a long time one afternoon because he was taking a snooze after lunch. No one dared to disturb him. He had a nasty temper on occasion.

Figuratively, he slept through two administrations while the wrath to come was boiling underneath, a simple fellow asleep on a volcano. But he had waked up and slipped off down the hill and was not there when the lava started to boil forth. The "Wonder Boy" was full in its path.

The timidity and conservatism of his character is no better revealed than in his trips on the *Mayflower*. He rarely took a long cruise. He seldom ventured down into Chesapeake Bay. The yacht was usually taken a few miles down the Potomac near Mount Vernon and there anchored. Often he just sat on the deck and stared at the water. His guests were left to Mrs. Coolidge—and themselves.

Warren Harding was the big, blundering human fellow who got mixed up in events and was pushed about by his friends.

Calvin Coolidge sat by and did not worry and said "No" when he didn't like what was going on.

During his occupancy, the White House might have been just any house along the highway of the world. To Calvin Coolidge it was just another home to live in, a bigger house, where you could give orders and somebody would run and fetch.

I recall a story one of the Secret Service men who is no longer at the White House told. It was in the first few days of the Coolidge régime. He was shocked one afternoon to find the President sitting in a rocker on the front porch which faces on Pennsylvania Avenue.

"Mr. President," he said, "the other Presidents always use the back portico."

"I want to be out here where I can see the streetcars go by," came the reply.

13

IN a few months Calvin Coolidge must have been glad to be off the front porch, and inside the White House. He could see the streetcars from the front porch, but he could also hear the screaming of the newsboys and what they were screaming was not pleasant to him. Even inside the White House it was almost necessary to stuff ears with cotton to keep out the noisy din which went on, day after day, in the United States Senate—about Albert B. Fall and Harry M. Daugherty and Charlie Forbes and a host of bizarre minor characters smelling, some of them, of the bar and the poolroom, who moved in and out of that melodrama "The Scandals of the Harding Administration."

Harding was dead. Coolidge had to weather the storm that the late President had left behind him. He did not have long to wait. Hardly had he sat himself down at that big desk in the private office of the President of the United States than the long-gathering thunder clouds broke with a crackling vengeance that terrified many politicians, not least of them the spare, red-headed man in the White House.

Beginning in late 1923 and running, at white heat, in the early months of 1924, was that series of investigations which told the sorry story of corruption and treachery—of Forbes' administration of the Veterans Bureau, of Secretary of Interior Albert B. Fall's leases of naval oil reserves, of Harry M. Daugherty's régime at the Justice Department. I had a front row seat at all of them.

They cracked their sensations suddenly, and without much warning.

Vague rumors had floated about and been discussed by us in the press room at the White House. A Minnesota Republican Congressman, Oscar E. Keller, tried to impeach Daugherty, largely on the ground of alleged failure to prosecute big corporations, including some controlled by J. P. Morgan, under antitrust statutes, but the House had thrown his case out overwhelmingly. Other rumors were about. But they had led to nothing. No one seemed greatly concerned, at least publicly.

We knew of course, that Senator LaFollette of Wisconsin had introduced a resolution authorizing an investigation by the Senate Public Lands Committee of Secretary Fall's leases of the Teapot Dome, Wyo., and Elk Hills, Calif., Naval Reserves to Harry F. Sinclair and Edward L. Doheny, respectively, and that Senator Walsh had spent several months in preliminary inquiry before public hearings were opened. It all started when some constituents of Senator Kendrick of Wyoming, a Democrat, wrote him in the spring of 1922 that an oil man named Sinclair was beginning to drill for oil in the Teapot Dome Naval Reserve, and from this it developed that the two leases in Wyoming and California actually had been granted in secret without competitive bidding. Fall explained the secrecy on the ground that it was a national defense matter.

The irony of it all to me—the amazing disclosures that came later—was that we newspapermen at the White House sat, all the time, at the outer gate, so to speak, and had known nothing. That, I know, was not the spot where anything would leak out. That is the last place. But the utter calm in which we lived there from day to day seems very strange when I look back upon it. There were clues, but they were isolated.

There was, for example, the day that Forbes came from the President's office, ruffled. Afterward he went to Paris and cabled his resignation from there. Soon after he left, it was announced that President Harding had ordered an investigation of his administration of the Veterans Bureau. Charles F. Cramer, chief counsel of the Veterans Bureau, had resigned a few weeks earlier and later committed suicide. Jess Smith had killed himself in the apartment which he shared with Daugherty on the night of May 30, 1923, while the Attorney General was at the White House. Fall had resigned his Cabinet post earlier that year and had gone back to his ranch in New Mexico.

Yes, there were clues.

But, even had we suspected, we could not have imagined the scope of the real story which I watched unfold later before Senate committees, in lurid and unbelievable chapters. My assignment was shifted from the White House in late 1923 to a roving one at the Capitol writing special stories for the United Press night service for morning papers. For weeks I followed the investigations.

Looking back upon it now, it seems that those investigations ran on for years. Sensation was crammed so upon sensation.

Literally hordes of curious and queer characters were dug up, sat down before Senators, and required to spread their private lives, their little secrets, their innermost thoughts, upon a record that rolled through the Government Printing Office eventually to make several volumes. Wit and humor enlivened the proceedings. Tragedy, too, is written in the record.

It is all a blurred nightmare to me now. Even at the time it was confusing. There were missing links. The testimony led occasionally down interesting alleys, but the trail was not pursued to the end in numerous instances. Some mysteries never were entirely cleared up. They never will be—which is just as well.

But the Senators got enough. They got enough to reveal one of the darkest eras of the nation's history.

Little vignettes, etched in dramatic strokes, stand out now, clear and concise, against the shadowy background that is the fog of memory. They were engraved upon the mind of an impressionable young reporter with the bitter-edged knife of disillusion.

Vividly I recall a day before the Special Senate Committee which was investigating Forbes' administration in the United States Veterans Bureau. The reasons, I suppose, are two. One is because of the central figure that day, a peculiar and eccentric army sergeant, the fussy, conscientious type you find handling supplies, who somehow attracts about himself an aura of self-sufficient efficiency, as if he were in personal charge of all the wealth of the Indies. The other was his amazing story. He was stationed at the Veterans Hospital at Perryville, Md. He told his story with relish, intermingled with an element of surprise, self-surprise, that seemed to overwhelm him ever so often. Here am I, he seemed to say to himself, before United States Senators. This is my hour.

The story itself had to do with the sale of supplies from the Perryville hospital to a private contracting firm on orders from Forbes. They were supposed to be "surplus" supplies, but they weren't. The little discrepancy in the transaction was that supplies—sheets and pajamas, particularly—were being sold at a big discount to the private contractor while the government was purchasing new supplies of the same sort at a higher price. The sergeant, who was in charge of the loading, reeled off the figures—29,700 new unbleached sheets which had cost $1.27 each were being sold for 25 cents apiece; 43,000 new, unbleached sheets which had been purchased from the navy for 84 cents apiece were being sold for 16 cents, and so on. The incident that stands out was his description of how, on one occasion, brand new sheets which were carted in one door of the hospital were carried through the other and loaded into the private contractor's lot and never even stopped in transit.

The sergeant told his story wide-eyed, as if it had just dawned on him what had happened. It was hard for him to believe it now. This was extravagance. This was waste. This was graft! And he had seen it with his own eyes.

Dr. Sawyer disclosed to the committee that it was this sale of supplies at Perryville which had aroused President Harding. He had learned about it and informed the President. The latter called in Forbes and ordered him to stop it. When it continued for two or three days longer, the President called the Veterans Bureau director before him, reprimanded him severely, and asked for his resignation.

But that was only a minor part of the story. I don't know why it stands out so, unless it is the absurdity of the whole business and the eccentricity of the sergeant. The flavor returns today, the ceaseless carting in and out of supplies at government expense—a ghastly joke perpetrated by an official who held one of the most important posts in the government, a post which had been awarded him because he was a pleasant sort of fellow who talked well and had a fund of good stories and an adventurous background that seemed to appeal particularly to Mrs. Harding. On a junket to Hawaii, Harding had met Colonel Forbes, who had ingratiated himself with the then Senator.

The real damaging phase of the testimony came from the lips of Elias H. Mortimer, a contracting agent who turned state's evidence. Casually he told of gay parties here and there as Forbes and his lieutenants made "inspection trips" about the country. Mortimer seemed to have a shell of hard reserve. A slender fellow he was, thin of face, speaking from behind a mask. He told about alleged bribes to Forbes from those he represented—the contracting firm of John W. Thompson and James W. Black of Chicago and St. Louis. They received choice contracts for veterans' hospitals. Black had died. Forbes and Thompson were indicted by a Chicago grand jury while the Senate investigation was in progress. There were two counts—conspiracy to commit bribery and offenses against the government and conspiracy to defraud the government. Both men were tried later, convicted, and went to jail.

Charlie Cramer, general counsel of the Veterans Bureau, had done away with himself, so he did not face the music. He was charged in the indictment with having accepted a promise from Thompson and others of $100,000 in return for approval of contracts.

Several months later I witnessed an episode in the aftermath of the Cramers and the Hardings. I was sent out to write a story of the sale of the furnishings in the Cramer home because it had been, before that, the home of the Hardings when the late President was in the Senate.

The professional auctioneer made the most of the Harding association with the household goods as he tried to dispose of them. Mrs. Cramer, the widow, of the tall, striking type of beauty, hovered about as the auctioneer went about his business. She wore the big willowy hat fashionable then.

In vain the auctioneer appealed to sentiment.

"Why, the stuff is being given away," Mrs. Cramer said in a testy aside. "It ought to have some value for the sentiment attached to it. It is exactly as the President left it."

The auctioneer tried banter with the small group looking for bargains.

"You people are the worst I've ever appeared before," he complained. "You've got padlocks on your pocketbooks."

He smiled wanly at his attempted wit.

A small Wilton rug was offered. The bidding went to three dollars.

"Three-fifty," a woman said meekly. "I hate to see our President's things go for nothing."

But others had no such concern.

There was a January afternoon when a handful of us sat at the press table in the Senate Public Lands Committee room, half-dozing, idly drawing designs on the copy paper in front of us, occasionally mumbling to one another under our breaths. Some geologist was giving what is known as "expert testimony" about drainage of oil lands, with reference to the Teapot Dome Naval Reserve in Wyoming. Senator Walsh of Montana kept prodding him with questions, his keen blue eyes constantly watchful, his nose poked up inquiringly like a fox terrier's. As he glanced down occasionally at notes before him, the Senator would stroke his mustache with his first two fingers, an unconscious sort of gesture. (This mustache now was a neat, civilized affair, closely cropped, but once we had known it as a sweeping set of handle bars that curved down entrancingly athwart each cheek to recall the picture of Uncle Will or Uncle John that used to hang on nearly every parlor wall.) The Senator was patiently laying the foundation for the exposé that was to shake the nation. He was exasperatingly painstaking. All this testimony, we knew, must be important, must have its significance, but it was not going to make any screaming headlines for our newspapers. The Senator was not looking for headlines, at least just yet. He was a craftsman doing a job. So we let the enervating warmth of the steam heat creep seductively through our bones, with only half an ear to the geologist and the Senator. Outside the bare arms of the trees shook and shivered under the whipping of January blasts. Once more I tried to catch, in a crude sort of sketch, the stern face of Walsh, that visage that reminded me of a Hebrew prophet of old.

Then, suddenly, everything changed with the mere cracking and slow opening of the big double doors. For these were interesting personages who now entered, one by one, quietly.

The first was diminutive Theodore Roosevelt, Jr., Assistant Secretary of Navy. He slipped in almost as an intruder. But proud and self-possessed, as always, was his sister, Alice Roosevelt Longworth, who followed him. Her eyes swept quickly over the room, an actress sizing up an audience which she is sure she can capture. Her bearing was confident and supercilious. Then came Congressman Nick Longworth of Ohio, her husband, suave Nick with his gleaming bald head, dignified by his sober tailoring, his face impassive.

Last came a tall, pale young man with a sensitive face. Shyly, he lowered his head as he stepped before the small audience gathered here for what the newspapers had promised for days was to become significant and interesting, and which thus far had proved unutterably dreary.

The realization that this might be the moment for which they had waited swept, like an electric current, through the audience. We at the press table became alert. Alice Roosevelt did not lend her presence to just the ordinary committee hearing. Something of import must attach to an occasion which attracted her. The audience glanced again and again toward the representatives of the Roosevelt family, hopefully. The wait was not long. The expert witness finished, was thanked by Senator Walsh, and dismissed. The Senator directed his eyes toward the Roosevelt clan and, as if by previous arrangement, young Teddy arose and asked to be permitted to speak to the committee. He left the others and advanced to the committee table and addressed Senator Walsh and his colleagues. His brother, he said, had some information he wanted to give the committee. Expectantly, all eyes centered now on the thin young man who got up from beside his sister, walked to the committee table, and took the witness chair. In confused and halting words he told his story. He was Archie Roosevelt. He had been, until the day before, a vice-president of Union Petroleum Company, a Sinclair export corporation. He had resigned because of the information he was now about to give the committee. This related to a conversation he had with G. D. Wahlberg, personal secretary of Harry F. Sinclair, who had told him, so he testified, that Sinclair had sent $68,000 to Albert B. Fall's ranch in New Mexico. Sinclair had left for Europe a few days before. Archie had bought the tickets. Sinclair's name was not to go on the passenger list. Archie said that Wahlberg had confirmed the story the night before in a telephone conversation in which his brother "Ted" had listened in.

Wahlberg, it turned out, was in the committee room now. So this had all been prearranged by Senator Walsh. Wahlberg was called to the witness chair when Archie had finished his story and gone back to his seat.

The Sinclair secretary was a trying and tortured, and amusing, witness. He denied Archie's story. Then the Senator pinned him down. He squirmed about in his chair, nervous and uncomfortable. What he had talked about to Archie, he insisted, was "six or eight cows," which the young Roosevelt seemed to have heard as "sixty-eight thous." It was "six or eight cows" that his employer, Sinclair, had sent to the Fall ranch. Even the Senator, usually most serious, joined in the merriment which rippled through the committee room at this explanation, though only to the extent of a reserved grin loaded with doubt. But his blue eyes began to flash, as he hunched himself forward in his chair, as if about to spring upon the witness, an effective gesture he employed, and started to work with that accusing finger of his and those penetrating eyes. He could not break Wahlberg, however. The Sinclair secretary persisted in his story until Walsh, like the cat who has grown weary with the mouse, let the matter drop, looking around grimly as if to say: "Everybody knows you lie."

We had our story!

And, not least of it to me, was a family coming to court, so to speak, voluntarily, to preserve its honor. I could imagine a family council over this affair, and the discussion, and the pacing up and down, and, in the background, a President of the United States who once had spoken roughly about "malefactors of great wealth," and about graft and corruption in high places.

The Montana Senator always resented the assumption that this was the incident which opened up the Teapot Dome scandal. For already he had pieced his story together from a clue here and a clue there but, methodical prosecutor that he was, he was building up his case carefully, step by step, from the bottom. This incident, however, did "break" the story as far as the newspapers and public were concerned. For the Roosevelt name had tremendous news value. The drama now moved from geology to persons. Every day the headlines got bigger.

There was the rainy night that Albert B. Fall came back to Washington from New Mexico to take the witness stand. Reporters were scattered all over the station. The train arrived on the lower level. The former Secretary was spirited away in an automobile and we never got to see him. Madly we jumped into taxicabs and chased the party to the house of a friend with whom he was to stay. The butler advised us that Mr. Fall would see no one. He had nothing to say.

He told little when he went on the stand the next day before the committee on the ground he might incriminate himself. But Senator Walsh extracted the story, bit by bit, over the days and weeks, from a host of witnesses.

Boiled down, the volume of testimony showed how Edward L. Doheny, the oil magnate, to whom the Interior Department had leased the valuable Elk Hills Naval Oil Reserve in California, had "loaned" Secretary Fall $100,000— delivered in currency by Doheny's son in the famous "little black bag"; how Harry Sinclair, to whom Fall had leased the Teapot Dome Naval Oil Reserve in Wyoming, had turned over $260,000 in Liberty Bonds to the Secretary, which Sinclair said was for purchase of a third interest in Fall's ranch at Three Rivers, N.M. Both of the leases had been made secretly, without competitive bidding. Fall got control of the leasing when Harding, early in his administration, issued an executive order transferring jurisdiction over the naval oil reserves to the Interior Department from the Navy Department. Senator Robert M. LaFollette of Wisconsin had initiated the investigation by a Senate resolution—but little credit did he ever get for his public service.

The cases dragged through the courts for years.

They became hopelessly confused in appeals and counterappeals and side issues. Sinclair, for example, was tried for contempt of the Senate because he refused to answer questions propounded by Senator Walsh and was sentenced to serve six months. He was convicted also on a charge of jury tampering in the major conspiracy trial of himself and Albert B. Fall and sent to the District of Columbia jail for ninety days. When a millionaire went to jail it was news, especially in those days, so we covered his daily routine when he first entered the District jail. He was put to mixing pills in the pharmacy. He once had plied that trade. Sinclair, the happy-go-lucky, was a model prisoner.

President Coolidge promised immediate, adequate and un-shrinking prosecution of all those found guilty of fraud in the oil cases in a Lincoln Day address before the National Republican Club in New York while the investigation still was in progress, and he appointed Owen J. Roberts, a corporation lawyer of Philadelphia, a Republican, and former Senator Atlee Pomerene of Ohio, a Democrat, as special counsel.

They had their troubles getting the involved story before juries in the District of Columbia. Looking back upon it, it seems that through the years we always were covering some phase or other of these trials.

Only Fall went to jail on a basic charge.

That was seven years after the investigation—in 1931. He was convicted for taking a bribe from Doheny. The latter, who admitted the "loan" of $100,000 was acquitted on the bribery charge. He and Fall were both found not guilty on conspiracy charges growing from the lease of the Elk Hills Reserve. Likewise Fall and Sinclair were acquitted on the Teapot Dome lease charge.

The nation finally got its verdict from the Supreme Court, its highest tribunal. It expressed its opinion plainly on the whole mess. The Court upheld cancellation of both the Doheny and Sinclair leases, passing on the civil suits, on the ground they were surrounded by fraud and corruption.

Owen J. Roberts emerged from the trials with a reputation that served him well later.

When the Senate refused to confirm the nomination of Judge John J. Parker of North Carolina to the Supreme Court, President Hoover named Roberts who, because of his conduct of the oil cases, was quickly confirmed, without much inquiry into his views on economic and social problems.

And thereby he became involved in one of those quirks of fate—or history.

For subsequently, Justice Roberts became a thorn in the flesh of the Roosevelt New Deal. He frequently supplied the necessary vote to nullify important New Deal acts and thus was a factor in that great battle over the Supreme Court precipitated by Franklin D. Roosevelt in his second term, a battle which divided the nation for a time in one of the greatest debates of its history.

Justice Roberts also was the key to the tempering of the Court's course finally, when, under the influence of Chief Justice Charles Evans Hughes, he swung over to provide support for later New Deal reforms and thus checked the war on the Court which, it seemed for a time, would result in a victory for the President and a loss of prestige for the Court.

But the really interesting speculation revolves around the possibilities had Parker been confirmed. On the federal circuit bench, Judge Parker followed the New Deal very closely in his decisions. Had he been on the Court during the Roosevelt era, he undoubtedly would have stood with the President on most of the controversial issues. Acts nullified by 5 to 4 decisions would have been sanctioned, instead of being nullified. The whole course of the New Deal might have changed.

One of those intriguing "ifs" of history.

There was another afternoon. We waited, pencils and copy paper ready, for the opening of the so-called Brookhart investigation into the Department of Justice and the régime of Harry M. Daugherty. Senator Smith Wildman Brookhart of Iowa was chairman of the committee. Senator Burton K. Wheeler of Montana was its prosecuting arm. The session was scheduled to start at 2 o'clock. It was already beyond that time. The crowd gathered for this spectacle was growing restless.

Again a door opened, the big doors into the corridor. Again they released their quarry—and a story.

Senator Wheeler, who had been missing for two days to pique our curiosity, stepped briskly into the room. Accompanying him was a slender, fragile woman. She must have been beautiful at one time. The Montana Senator lost no time in getting the committee down to business. It was called to order by Senator Brookhart and then the mysterious woman was brought to the witness chair. Her name, she told the official reporter, was Roxie Stinson, of Washington Court House, Ohio.

The room was alive with little noises. The spectators, as one, leaned closer to hear. She had a soft voice. The eternal "How does she spell it?" rattled along the press table from one man to another, to be satisfied, as is usual, by the reporter closest to the official stenographer who inquired and then relayed the word back down the line.

Wheeler began to question her.

She was the former wife of Jess Smith, now in his grave. They were divorced. But they had been friends until his death. Jess Smith contributed to her support and when he returned to Washington Court House, as he did frequently, he always saw her and told her what was going on down in Washington.

Just before he had killed himself, he had been a worried, harassed man. He was frightened. He was, she said, "in constant fear of being closed down upon." He had told her, so she testified: "I am not made for this; this intrigue is driving me crazy. If I could just come home, but I am in now and I have to stick by Harry."

Harry, she explained, was Harry Daugherty.

She told of "deals" in which he said they were involved, deals about oil, liquor, stock market deals. Carefully each time, as she proceeded with her story, Wheeler asked her if by "they" she included Daugherty, and each time she said she did. She told of Jess coming home from Washington once wearing a belt with $75,000 in it.

Bulletins were scratched feverishly as we strained our ears to her modulated voice, translated her testimony to paper. Messengers flew back and forth with the copy. The room became alive and vibrant. She was talking in a low voice, but she might as well have been shouting. For she was shouting. Newsboys soon were shouting. On and on the quiet voice flowed. Names were mentioned. The committee was getting tips for days to come.

Burt Wheeler, who had won local fame in Montana as a prosecuting attorney, was delivering. It was, we learned later, by the barest of chances. Only a few days before he had heard about Roxie Stinson. He had gone personally to Ohio to see her and had brought her back on the train. This witness must not escape.

A parade of other witnesses popped from the Pandora's box that she had opened with her soft voice.

Daugherty fought back, viciously. He struck directly at the Montana Senator. Wheeler was indicted on a charge of using his influence to prosecute a private claim before the Land Office, a charge of which he later was acquitted. Nervous Republicans sought to persuade Daugherty to resign. He refused to budge. He told President Coolidge that he could not retire before he was given a hearing. Wheeler had held up opening of the inquiry on the understanding that Daugherty would quit. Senator Borah of Idaho went to the White House one night and, in the presence of Daugherty, insisted that the Attorney General should prove to the President why he should not resign. Still Daugherty hung on and Wheeler began his investigation.

Sensations continued to pour from the committee, with some fiction undoubtedly mingled with fact. The suspicion cast at its Attorney General was reacting against the administration and the party—and another Presidential election was coming in November. The fire got too hot for Coolidge. Finally, after much dilly-dallying, he euchered Daugherty out of office, but not until he had dissipated forever—at least for all of us who knew what was happening—any idea that he was a strong man. He cringed figuratively before the bluff, hard-boiled practical politician that was Harry Daugherty. The Attorney General protested bitterly to the end and left office shouting his defiance to high heaven—not sparing the President in his public abuse.

Daugherty was twice tried and twice the jury failed to agree. The indictment finally was dropped.

He refused to go before the grand jury. In a written statement to the judge he explained how he had been personal attorney for both the President and Mrs. Harding and that his relations "were of the most confidential character as well as professional." Later he refused to testify at the trials. His lawyer, the famous Max Steuer, issued a statement explaining that his client might be cross-examined "about matters political that would not involve Mr. Daugherty concerning which he knew and as to which he would never make disclosure."

One of the most damaging incidents in the case was the burning of ledger sheets in the bank of his brother, Mal Daugherty, at Washington Court House. Those destroyed covered his own personal account and those of his brother and another labelled "Jess Smith extra." As to this, Steuer said "if the jury knew the real reason for destroying the ledger sheets they would commend rather than condemn Daugherty, but he insisted on silence."

Involved in the Daugherty trial was the so-called American Metals Company case which had to do with moneys allegedly paid to Daugherty, his brother Mal, John T. King, Republican National Committeeman from Connecticut, and Thomas W. Miller, Alien Property Custodian, for settlement of a war seizure claim.

Tom Miller was tried on the American Metals Company case charges, was convicted, and sent to jail for eighteen months.

The others got off.

Daugherty retired to Florida to live under the sun.

The steam which blew the lid off Teapot Dome scalded others.

The Senate, riding high under the lash of Democrats, passed a resolution demanding the resignation of the portly Edwin S. Denby, Secretary of Navy, from whom control over naval oil reserves was transferred to Fall. The charge against Denby was negligence. They said he should have known what was going on as Secretary of Navy responsible for protection of the Navy's interests. He resigned and quietly left Washington.

Senator Pat Harrison of Mississippi demanded that young Teddy Roosevelt should get out, too, because he was Assistant Secretary of Navy and shared responsibility in the Navy Department with Denby.

"If TR had been there—he would have spoken out and raised hell." That's what some people were saying.

Young Teddy heard a good deal about this later from the lips of Al Smith in the campaign for governor of New York which resulted in his defeat by Smith. The son of the Rough Rider President spent a season or two as Governor of Porto Rico, a season or two as Governor General of the Philippines, both of which places he was said to have filled creditably. He disappeared from politics and returned to public notice only for his hunting expeditions into Asia and an occasional speech. A nice young man, with the too obvious mannerisms of his father. (He perhaps could not avoid that —but they somehow didn't seem to suit him.)

The steam from Teapot Dome wafted far.

14

I HAD come to Washington, as I have said earlier, with many illusions. In my childhood and youth, my life had been calm and ordered and somewhat idyllic, only rarely troubled by doubts and misgivings. College had been a refuge from the harder facts of life. I lived like a monk in a monastery, behind a wall which kept out the noise and tumult of a changing world and gave me opportunity to tend the garden of the past and walk among its blossoms and inhale its fragrance.

Slowly, the contact with the reality of the political process had broken down walls and shattered illusions.

Gradually, during my early years in Washington my eyes had been opened to certain rude and somewhat surprising actualities; among them, the influence exerted by powerful outside forces upon the political figures who conducted government there. This I had seen, though only vaguely then, in the ease with which government had acquiesced in tariff and tax favors for the dominant units in American industry, business and finance; in the way in which Harry M. Daugherty had moved ruthlessly against labor to protect the interests of the railroads. Anyone who raised his voice against this invasion was classed as a radical.

So I was no longer naïve.

But the revelations of the Senate Committees which had looked behind and beneath the surface of "Normalcy" were almost too raw meat for a still youthful stomach, bringing to light, as they did, the direct approach to figures in high places. These were cash transactions. It was low-down, blatant thievery of the strictly American variety, not heretofore in my time associated with the national government—by blunt straightforward crooks who figuratively were ready to deliver the Goddess of Liberty off the Capitol Dome for a price.

The dark stream of scandal which oozed from the crannies and crevasses of the Harding administration stained indelibly the politicians caught in its path. It drowned others who, unable to stand the sting of their own consciences and the sure retribution they foresaw, lay down quietly and let the mud smother them off the earth.

It washed away, too, my idealism about the national government, coming as a climactic chapter in the process of education which had included courses in the gentler and less discernible purchase of favors.

It overshadowed the latter for the time being, though in time I came to see that the continued influence, during the delirious decade, of the dominant economic overlords in legislation that affected their interests did more permanent damage. The cash corruption, once disclosed, could be punished or at least dramatized so that it would be stopped. The other was accomplished within the law, or within the law as it was interpreted in those days, and was harder to make plain to the rank and file of voters.

The chip on my shoulder began to shake uncomfortably. This was the Southern chip which represents a belief in things as they are, a challenge to prove things otherwise.

There is nothing in any way literal about this chip. I am not a combative type of person in the usually accepted sense.

"You—with a chip on your shoulder—rot—," says my wife.

I try to explain to her, as I am trying to explain now.

I am only combative over what appears to be injustice. That will arouse me. This applies personally as well as in the broader sense.

In the end it was injustice, the discovery of it in so many directions from watching the process of government in Washington and seeing it, at first hand, in trips over the country, that slowly enraged me and shook the chip off my shoulder, the chip of acceptance of things as they are, the chip of acquiescence. My eyes were opened. I was no longer a Southerner, using that term to describe an attitude, for Southerners are not the only ones guilty of it. But, politically, that attitude is most notably represented at Washington by Southerners in Congress which is extremely important because they are the backbone, year in and year out, of one of the nation's two great parties and it is that party through which reform and change have been brought about in recent years.

But I get ahead of myself.

There will be more of that later.

I must be frank.

I have written of the Washington of fifteen and twenty years ago, in my early years as a newspaper reporter. It is impossible, at this distance, to recall states of mind as I went about my daily work, to put the finger upon a change of view here or there, to say that this event affected me in such and such way, impossible, except for those events which shake a man to the roots. The process of education is slow, at least it has been so for me. I have drawn the picture of

Washington of that day, partly as particular events impressed themselves upon me, partly as I look back upon it and reconstruct it in the light of my development since. Everything I saw in those days made its imprint upon me, but just exactly how, I naturally cannot say now. There is a sum total today, of which the parts were pieced together over the years. That sum total represents those forgotten incidents which went into my mental and spiritual outlook. Therefore, the picture of that Washington of the early 'twenties represents a composite attitude, of which events then and events since, all reacting upon each other, have produced a viewpoint.

I look back, for instance, upon those weeks and months of the two great industrial conflicts of Harding's administration, during which I sat daily in the White House at the outer door of the President's office. They taught me much about the fundamental struggle between capital and labor, but how much that contributed to my attitude today I cannot tell. They did educate me to certain facts and reveal more clearly the system under which we live and its inevitable recurring conflicts. During that time I learned how the law may be used for other ends, presumably, than those originally intended. This was a lesson from the Daugherty railroad labor injunction. The issues were confused in my mind then. They have become clearer with further knowledge since.

My suspicions were aroused over big-business influence upon government in the tariff and tax bills of the early 'twenties, though I cannot say that, at the time, I saw it all as clearly as I do now. But the seeds of doubt were planted.

Warren G. Harding, I first saw as a big and fine man. Cabinet officers held my respect. I assumed they were men of character chosen to fill important office.

Then I saw Warren Harding in the wrack of tormenting problems, twisted and tortured. I came to see him as merely the agent for the forces which had made him President, and the dupe of faithless friends who were ready to use and betray him.

The revelations of the Senate committees shattered my faith in government, for a time.

Out of this episode I learned what a danger to our Democracy is a President who is not qualified. Harding had chosen some of his assistants, Cabinet officers and other administrative officers, just as if he were picking a group of friends for an outing or a poker party instead of selecting men who were to administer the affairs of a great nation. Harry Daugherty, whose chief occupation had been as lobbyist about the Ohio state legislature, certainly was not fitted by training or experience to be the chief law officer of a country with the conflicting problems of the United States. Albert B. Fall happened to be one of Harding's Senate friends. The fact that Charles R. Forbes was a gay, dashing fellow who attracted the Hardings hardly was reason enough to give him one of the most important posts in the administration. Naïve indeed and inexcusable was the appointment of his home-town friend Daniel R. Crissinger, lawyer and head of a small bank, as Comptroller of the Currency, but even worse was the elevation of the small-town banker later to be head of the Federal Reserve Board. Coolidge retained Crissinger in this capacity and he was directing head of the board during the speculative boom—ending finally in the crash—which financial authorities since had claimed could have been checked by the board. Other appointments of Harding were subject to criticism but they happened not to have come into the line of fire.

Harding, of course, had his "Best Minds," as the newspapers termed Hughes, Hoover and Mellon and was praised for choosing these men who, in the early days of the administration, usually were thought of by the public as "the Cabinet." Their prestige, however, hardly was sufficient to offset the weaker brothers when the latter's doings were exposed to the light of day.

The Harding administration scandals opened my eyes when they shattered my illusions.

So low, then, could government sink!

They provoked a scepticism with which thereafter I began to look at men and events. Harding, the first President I had seen at close hand, had awed me at the outset with the aura of the office he held. I was prepared to look henceforth at Presidents, beginning with Coolidge, and at other figures, more objectively and analytically.

Naturally my attention shifted to those who were criticizing and attacking the administration, not only for graft and corruption, but also on its basic philosophy—a group which included, among others, Walsh and Wheeler of Montana, Borah of Idaho, Norris of Nebraska, LaFollette of Wisconsin, and a group in the House which embraced the so-called "Wisconsin Insurgents" headed by the aging Henry Allen Cooper and John M. Nelson—LaFollette's little yeast in the other body—and La Guardia of New York.

Walsh and Wheeler were being abused and traduced.

The others were dubbed "Radicals" by both Republicans and conservative Democrats.

But they had energy and courage and ideas.

They were voices in the wilderness.

PART TWO. VOICES IN THE WILDERNESS

15

REVOLUTIONS begin in a small way. They start with a cloud about the size of a man's hand. Sometimes they take years to pile up into the ominous dark bank which covers the heavens and sweeps all before it with a burst of thunder and lightning. Often they dissolve into thin air, as far as the eye can see, under the glaring light of some sun or other, such as, for example, a great period of apparent prosperity. But they reappear in time.

I saw one rise from the West back in the Harding administration. I did not realize its future implications. In 1923 I could not see 1933. None of us could. But I think, looking back now, that there was some connection.

Unruly and streaked with rebellion was the Congress which assembled a little riotously in December 1923.

Thirteen months before, in November 1922, it had been elected on a wave of discontent in the Western farm region and sullen discouragement in the cities. Prosperity was on the way back, but when the elections were held many men were out of jobs. The cities were beginning to look up again as Congress gathered. But gloom still prevailed on the farm. Prices had slumped when the war demand for wheat had ceased. Farmers had bought more land at inflated prices to feed the war boom. Now they had bigger mortgages and heavier taxes.

Particularly unruly and rebellious was the little band of "Wisconsin Insurgents," Republicans in name only. They found new allies in Congress from the neighboring "radical frontier" in Minnesota and North Dakota and Montana and Iowa. These recruits had been catapulted into office on a wave that was swelled by independent political movements in that section, the Non-Partisan League and the Farmer-Labor Party.

This nucleus of rebellion looked to Senator Robert M. LaFollette of Wisconsin for leadership. The veteran Senator discovered that his little band of insurgents in House and Senate held the balance of power between Republicans and Democrats. For the Republican majority of the previous Congress had dwindled to a thin margin. Democrats had made considerable gains in the election.

The LaFollette forces prepared to press their advantage. Their revolt broke simultaneously on both sides of the Capitol.

In the House they forced a liberalization of rules, in coalition with Democrats, designed to break the stranglehold on legislation by Republican leaders. They accomplished their coup by holding out their votes, necessary for the Republicans to elect a Speaker, until their demands for rules changes were met.

For several days they held up organization of the House, with the usually arrogant Republican leaders at their mercy. During these days the little group plotted their strategy in numerous conferences and, during this time, I came to know these rebels who were to give the appointed leaders occasional sleepless nights. The acknowledged leader of the insurgent bloc was the dogged and determined John M. Nelson of Wisconsin. An able lieutenant was Fiorello H. LaGuardia of New York, a veritable dynamo of energy, courageous, and full of fight. I watched the little Italian develop into one of the ablest members of the House in my time. To the venerable dean of the Wisconsin delegation in these days, the amiable Henry Allen Cooper, the insurgents looked for sage counsel in plotting the rules revolt.

LaGuardia attracted me particularly. He was in the thick of every legislative battle during this period. In the halcyon days of Coolidge prosperity it was his bouncing spirit which so often jerked the House from the doldrums, which enlivened it, which tweaked the noses of the political and economic powers of those days puckishly, and often with effect. No game was too big for him, no task too hopeless. He occasionally started fights that looked futile. Then suddenly the leaders, whether they were Republican, as then, or Democratic, as a few years later, realized they would have to treat with the rebellious New Yorker.

He was a lively little monkey who, by turns, amused and alarmed party leaders. To make the monkey simile really perfect, I might say that he munched peanuts from a bag often as he sat, his plump little body alert on the edge of his seat, his watchful eyes trained on the battle which went on before him. Up he would pop, shouting, to intervene, to denounce, to cry down with scorn or irony.

No party could claim him. No leader could hold him down. He was always an independent and an excellent captain of guerillas. At one time or another he was elected on three different party tickets. But no label could describe him, or bind him.

Vividly I recall the day that he upset the best laid plans of the then Secretary of Commerce Herbert Hoover. In the face of the British rubber monopoly, which threatened American rubber goods manufacturers with high prices, including of course the automobile tire makers, Hoover sponsored a bill which would permit the American manufacturers to

166

combine in buying pools, thus exempting them from the anti-trust statutes. LaGuardia didn't like the bill. He saw potential danger in thus letting down the antitrust bars. Many Democrats saw eye to eye with him. He fought the bill in committee, but the regular Republicans overrode him and the Democrats. The measure went to the floor. During the lunch hour the day it was before the House, LaGuardia saw his chance. Republican whips were not on the job. The Republican side of the House was only sparsely populated. He moved quickly to strike out the enacting clause and, before the careless whips could get into action, the vote was over and the Hoover bill was dumped, head first, right out of Congress. Republican leaders seemingly were not too enthusiastic about it anyhow and it never saw the light again.

Nor was this the only time that LaGuardia tripped the leaders.

But I have talked along too much about him. He happens to be one of my favorites. He was one of the men of that day who helped to open my eyes to economic and social evils and he became one of my personal friends.

In the Senate in those days were others who contributed to my education. My attention was directed toward them by the beginnings of revolution in that body, its rebellious core now refreshed and revivified by fresh blood from the West.

It was a newcomer, and a Democrat, Senator Burton K. Wheeler of Montana, who precipitated the opening skirmish there which gave the LaFollette forces and the progressive Democrats a running start in a session that was to see a series of battles directed at the economic rulers of America—and their agents in the administration.

Wheeler and the insurgent Republicans tied up the Senate for days, prevented the regular Republicans from organizing, just as the little band of insurgents had done in the House when they forced rules changes from the party in power there.

An angry and sudden "I object! I object!" from Wheeler opened the fight in the Senate. He interrupted the routine ratification of committee slates when it came to the Interstate Commerce Committee which handled railroad legislation. He made it plain that he did not want Senator Albert B. Cummins of Iowa as chairman of that committee. Others came quickly to his aid, and a deadlock ensued.

The plot was to elevate Senator LaFollette, who was ranking member of the committee, to its chairmanship, and thus provide an opportunity for him to dramatize the transportation problem in which the Western farmer was keenly concerned as a shipper who wanted lower freight rates for his products. LaFollette was for government ownership of railroads, a fearsome doctrine to the administration and its friends.

Once Wheeler had cleared the way, the lines quickly formed. The Senate insurgents rallied about LaFollette. Democrats nominated Senator Ellison D. Smith of South Carolina, their ranking member, popularly known in the years of his service as "Cotton Ed" because of his interest in the welfare of that Southern staple.

This combination prevented the necessary Republican majority for Senator Cummins. The basis of the fight against Cummins was that he was president pro tem of the Senate and should not occupy two important posts. This was a flimsy barrage for a fight that reached much deeper. Cummins had come to the Senate many years before as a progressive, nay, almost a radical, but in the years since he had become tame and harmless and highly acceptable to the regulars. (This happens so often.) They wanted to keep him at the head of the important committee.

The Senate balloted for several days. It was like a miniature national political convention. Finally the LaFollette forces effected a compromise in which they threw their votes to Senator Smith in exchange for pledges of assistance to get consideration by the committee of measures in which they were interested. Accordingly, the Senate witnessed the spectacle of a Democratic committee chairman in a Senate nominally controlled by Republicans.

These two battles at the opening of the first Congress with which Calvin Coolidge had to deal interested and enlightened me. I learned something about the mechanics of government and legislation. From the rules fight in the House I learned how difficult it is for a minority ever to get even a hearing for its bills. I learned how powerful in legislative matters is the handful of party leaders. Parliamentary rules and procedure are too tedious matters for general public interest, and I won't go into them here, but I found out what effective weapons they are. They are necessary, of course, in party government; but they can be used by a reactionary administration to suppress all progressivism.

Powerful economic and social forces, which finally had broken through the dikes in the 1922 congressional elections at numerous points—chiefly in the West—now hurled themselves against the established régime at Washington; and their agents, in the House rules fight, sought to pry open the bottlenecks there so they could get a hearing for relief measures on the floor, and, in the Senate, to seize a forum in a committee chairmanship to agitate for lower freight rates as another avenue of help.

This was the background of the battle I saw break at the opening of that Congress. It led far back to humble folks on the farms and in the cities who had complained of their troubles at the ballot box.

I became conscious of the waves which washed upon Washington from the hinterland as I watched from the gallery and in committee room the movements of the representatives who had come from the areas of discontent. The performance was fascinating then; it has been so ever since.

Likewise I saw the resistance of the established order in those who spoke for them.

The tide ebbs and flows.

In that 68th Congress, which sat from December 1923 to March 3, 1925, it beat angrily against the cliffs of Republicanism.

It rolled up angrily, and then subsided.

I watched the seas of discontent break at several points, and I watched the figures, new and old, who stirred the waters up.

Many new figures took their seats in Congress to become disturbers of Republican peace.

The warning of heavy winds—but not of hurricane force —came in the primaries in 1922 in the defeat of the elder statesman, Senator Porter J. McCumber of North Dakota, chairman of the Finance Committee, co-author of the Fordney-McCumber Tariff Act which, though it had raised rates on agricultural imports, did not seem an adequate solution to the farmers in his state. Governor Lynn J. Frazier, supported by the Non-Partisan League, beat the tariff bill sponsor for the Republican nomination and was elected.

From Minnesota the Farmer-Labor Party, then seeking to make itself a factor in the northwest, sent Henrik Shipstead to the Senate in 1922 and the lusty-voiced Magnus Johnson a year later. Burt Wheeler had come to the Senate from Montana in 1922 and he did not turn out to be good news for the Republicans when he began to dig into their Justice Department presided over by Harry M. Daugherty.

Smith Wildman Brookhart, who promised to eschew the tuxedo and full dress of Washington society and to wear overalls in the Senate (but never did), succeeded to the Iowa seat left vacant by the resignation of Senator William S.

Kenyon—and neither was he good news to orthodox Republicanism. (Kenyon had been neatly elevated to the federal bench by President Harding to fill a fortuitous vacancy. He had proved troublesome as head of the newly organized farm bloc and was too curious about the steel trust in which Harding's friend, Judge Elbert H. Gary, was such a power, as well as about other sacred cows of Republicanism. Progressives saw Kenyon leave the Senate with keen disappointment. There was a sort of poetic justice, however, a few years later when Judge Kenyon, from the eighth circuit court of appeals, spoke out very bluntly in condemnation of the Teapot Dome scandal when it came before his court.)

These men were typical of the election wave.

It broke most noisily in the campaign for farm relief, for this was the biggest single area of distress. Also it was the most vocal, deriving from its size. Already I have described how the farm lobbyists had descended upon Washington. That, of itself, was a sign that there was business in that sector, that there was a definite economic ill which could be capitalized. Republicans never did appreciate its real meaning until several years later when the rebellion then seething became a real revolution and wrenched the farm states away from them and threw them into the laps of the Democrats.

The attitude of Republicans was, as I sensed it from contacts with them during that era, that the farm problem was a political problem, something that had to be tolerated, a source of disturbance that could be soothed from time to time, with soft words and a little pap of some sort. They did not take it too seriously. They yielded slowly, compromising as they could. Few seemed to see it as a fundamental economic problem which, if not coped with, would infect the whole structure of the nation.

The problem then occurred, so far as the politicians were affected, in wheat and in the surpluses which were piling up with the expanded acreage and the gradual loss of foreign markets. To meet the surplus problem, the farm representatives in Congress began to rally about a palliative known as the McNary-Haugen bill, a clumsy piece of machinery. It set up a revolving fund appropriated by Congress to assist in marketing the surplus and provided that, if the surplus were dumped abroad, any losses in this direction and in other marketing arrangements would be met out of an "equalization fee" assessed back upon the producers.

Coolidge, in twice vetoing this measure, included in his denunciation the complaint that it was a "price-fixing" bill, to which the farm representatives retorted that high tariffs on industrial products to protect manufacturers also were price-fixing devices and that farmers paid for this out of their pockets.

While the controversy raged between the White House and Congress over a period of three or four years over the surplus problem in wheat, other things were happening in farming, some incidental to this, to which little attention was paid; but they became glaringly apparent a few years later when the whole economic structure gaped open and revealed what was going on inside.

The machine was making its inroads on the farm, not only in the West but in the South. The tenant farmer, who eked out a bare existence, particularly in the South, was being driven from his home and job. He was no longer needed. This of course was a slow process.

"Coolidge Prosperity" blinded all but a few to this human erosion underneath. Few and rare are the political leaders and ordinary politicians who go out and take a look at what is happening. They are affected only by what the voters throw up in their faces. The tenant farmer was not vocal. The farm organizations paid little heed to him. He had no money for dues. In the South his kind did not vote very often because they could not afford the poll tax, little as it was. Nor did the economic masters want this "poor white trash" to vote.

was nothing wild, however, in his general attitude toward big corporations. He was conservatively genteel in that respect.

Senator Walsh, who had interested himself in the Trade Commission report, reentered the plot.

He got a resolution through the Judiciary Committee, with the help of Senators Norris and Borah, for a Senate investigation of the peculiar circumstances surrounding the Aluminum Company case. But, after a hard fight, he was defeated on the Senate floor. The resolution was voted down, 36 to 33. Senator David A. Reed of Pennsylvania, who was always alert in protecting the interests of the Mellon economic and political dynasty in their home state, successfully led the fight against the Walsh resolution.

Walsh had tackled Mellon and been rebuffed.

Another Senator tried.

This was the multimillionaire James Couzens of Michigan. Couzens had come up with Henry Ford, made a fortune, quarrelled with the automobile magnate, sold out his interest and entered politics. He was independent, able and courageous, one of the most attractive figures about the Senate in recent years. His label was Republican, but party did not mean much to Jim Couzens.

He became curious about the Internal Revenue Bureau, which is an adjunct of the Treasury Department. He got through a resolution to investigate certain matters which had interested him, among them, huge refunds to big corporations, including some Mellon concerns. He found that his inquiry would require expert counsel, so he hired Francis J. Heney of San Francisco who had made a reputation as an investigator and prosecutor on the Pacific Coast. He was paying Heney out of his own pocket until the Senate could formally authorize employment of counsel. Heney's appointment to investigate Mellon's bureau raised a storm. Coolidge sent a message to the Senate. It bristled with fury. He denounced Couzens for hiring counsel out of his own pocket. He denounced the Senate for singling out Mellon companies for investigation, for calling for documents from executive departments. He lectured the Senate on its place in the government. The rôle of Congress was to make laws, not to administer them. That was the function of the Executive. He saw the government breaking down if this sort of procedure kept up.

Couzens' investigation was delayed by the Senator's illness for some time, but finally got under way. But the Michigan Senator felt the lash, too. The Internal Revenue Bureau called on him for payment of nearly $11,000,000 which it claimed was due from him on his sale of Ford stock. The claim was presented only a few days before the statute of limitations expired. Couzens said the memorandum on which the claim was based had been in the Internal Revenue Bureau for three years. Its original purpose, he contended, was for political use against Henry Ford, his one-time business partner, when the automobile manufacturer ran against Truman Newberry for the Senate in 1922. The case subsequently was dismissed by the Board of Tax Appeals.

An interesting series of events:

Coolidge springs to the defense of Mellon when the Aluminum Company is attacked despite the findings of a government agency and the opinion of the Attorney General, well versed in law, that the complaint is valid.

That Attorney General, Harlan Fiske Stone, removed from a spot where he might prove dangerous to Mellon. (Elevated to a position, it is granted, which he deserved and where he proved himself worthy.)

Couzens' investigation of the Mellon régime denounced by Coolidge.

Couzens attacked with a huge tax claim that later proved without merit.

It was heresy to criticize Andrew W. Mellon. He was the untouchable, though ostensibly a public servant.

This certainly looked to me like government for the privileged.

Working about Washington in those days you got the feeling that the people were a long way off.

Rugged George W. Norris of Nebraska was the revolutionary spirit of that day who bridged the gap to our own.

I came to admire him greatly as I watched him plod ahead patiently with his dreams.

I came to admire him as I watched him stick pins, in his ironical way, into the pretensions of the elect and the mighty.

Norris had a vision of public power widely utilized and widely distributed to the common masses of whom he has been the faithful and loyal champion through all the years of his public career. He began, in those Coolidge days, with the material at hand, the Muscle Shoals property of the government in Alabama. His idea was for the government itself to develop electricity at the plants so strategically located there to transmit its blessings through the whole southeast.

In time George Norris began to open the eyes of the country, too, to the unnecessarily high rates that private power companies were charging for this resource which, he argued, belonged to the whole people. He showed how a monopoly was being built by a few giant corporations that were piling holding company upon holding company, an evil illuminated subsequently by the Federal Trade Commission's very thorough investigation and by the collapse of the pyramided Insull power empire. Norris graphically illustrated the devious holding company network by a chart which he called "The Spider Web." It did look like a giant spider web. The octopus spread its tentacles into politics and even into the schoolroom to protect itself and retain its hold. Here again I saw the creation of a super-government outside of government.

To those few who directed this network George Norris became an ogre. They fought him bitterly. Not all saw the full consequences of the program he envisaged in the Alabama project, the dream he dreamed of an expansion of this idea. Nor did Congress of that day. With the help of progressive Democrats and his own Republican insurgents he won enactment of his bill for government operation. He won it by ceaseless and tireless work, by constant vigilance, by a knowledge of parliamentary and legislative tactics equalled by few. I remember sitting in the gallery one day when he held at bay the opponents of government operation and the sponsors of bills for private operation. (Several private companies were trying to get their hands on this project and Republicans generally favored this disposition. Henry Ford was one of the bidders. A bill to accept his bid did pass the House, but later he withdrew his offer.) Norris chased the Senate around in a circle for hours by a series of clever parliamentary maneuvers which divided his foes who favored one or another of the measures for private lease. At the end of the day, grimly triumphant, he saw his foes routed. His bill still was not enacted, but neither were any of the others. Eventually he won his fight.

But Coolidge would not tolerate government operation. He vetoed the Norris bill. The Senator had to wait for his dream.

George Norris had another dream of reform. This was his proposed constitutional amendment to abolish the "lame duck" sessions of Congress, with which was coupled provision for inauguration of the President and the opening of Congress in January. Under the system then operative, a Congress elected in November did not take its seat until thirteen months later, in December of the following year, unless a special session were called after the subsequent March 4, when theoretically the new Congress came into being. Con-

178

gressmen repudiated by their constituents came back to serve in the second or short session, running from December until March 4, when Congress must expire automatically. Through the offer of jobs an administration could, and often did, use these defeated Congressmen, these "lame ducks," to block measures to which it was opposed, but for which the voters may have indicated a preference in the mandate of the election in the previous November. Furthermore, the automatic expiration of Congress opened the way for filibuster in the closing days and here, too, the "lame ducks" could be useful.

Norris won the Senate to his proposed amendment by an overwhelming vote early in 1924. But the reform was postponed into the 'thirties. The House continually blocked the proposed amendment.

Norris in the Senate and LaGuardia in the House cooperated in another reform in the field of labor law. This was a bill to prohibit the use of injunctions in labor disputes such as the sweeping one by which Harry Daugherty had throttled striking railway workers in the Harding administration. Some years later this reform became a reality.

From the sporadic skirmishes in Congress in the early Coolidge years, growing from the minor revolution at the polls in 1922—almost destitute, it is true of any final accomplishment—there emerged the vague outlines of the two philosophies of government which clashed in that period and which have continued to clash since.

On the one hand was the Coolidge-Mellon philosophy that government should intrude as little as possible into the lives of the people, should give business a free hand, encourage and nourish those with large resources so they might expand and in their expansion bring prosperity to those below. The practical results of such a philosophy I saw in the gradually enlarging influence of the big interests upon government, their acceptance of this as almost divine right, and a tendency in the administration of government to defend this right and label as "radicals" those who would question or interfere. I do not think Coolidge had any realization of the ultimate end of such a philosophy. He merely accepted and looked on and interceded where he saw it challenged.

On the other hand was the philosophy of the progressive group, embracing the insurgent Republicans from the West and some Democrats largely from the West, that government should actively enlist itself in the protection of the people wherever their interests were endangered. They saw and warned of the probable results of a government in which the big and powerful exerted the dominant influence.

Their philosopher was Robert M. LaFollette.

His was the most effective critique of the Coolidge-Mellon philosophy and he was the clearest exponent of the counter philosophy which he and the insurgents and progressive Democrats championed. He had formulated a program upon which he was to stand in his independent race for President in 1924. This is a good point to summarize that philosophy as it was summarized in the preamble to the platform upon which he stood in 1924:

"Under our representative democracy the people protect their liberties through their public agents. The test of public officials and public policies alike must be: Will they preserve, or will they exploit, the common need?

"The reactionary continues to put his faith in mastery for the solution of all problems. He seeks to have what he calls 'the strong men and best minds rule' and impose their decision upon the masses of their weaker brethren.

"The progressive, on the contrary, contends for less autocracy and more democracy in government, and for less power of privilege and greater obligation of service.

"Under the principles of ruthless individualism and competition, that government is deemed best which offers to the few the greatest chance of individual gain.

"Under the progressive principle of cooperation that government is deemed best which offers to the many the highest level of average happiness and well-being.

"It is our faith that we all go up or down together—that class gains are temporary delusions and that eternal laws of compensation make every man his brother's keeper."

With eyes alight, and with hope, the progressive forces looked forward to the 1924 battle at the polls.

16

FROM towns and cities and villages on plain and prairie, in mountains and river bottoms and coastal lowlands, from Minnesota and Georgia, from Maine and Nevada, from Ohio and California and all the other states and the possessions beyond the seas—from all that is the United States of America—there converged upon New York City in the heat of late June 1924, when it was muggy in the canyons among the tall buildings, some 3,000 American citizens. There were men and women. There were young, middle-aged and old.

There were big men among them, men who had risen above their fellows, and there were ordinary folks. They came with their ideals and their bitter little prejudices. They were human beings. Some were Methodists and some were Baptists and some were Presbyterians and some were Catholics and some did not worry about religion. Some of these last were Christians and some of the others were not. Some belonged to a hooded order known as the Ku Klux Klan, or were beholden to it as politicians, big and little, and some were Knights of Columbus. Some were Rotarians and some were sceptical of all such organizations. Some were sociable and jovial, free-living, and liked to drink whisky and enjoy life and thought the Eighteenth Amendment and the Volstead Act were the blight of the age. Some were hard-faced and strait-laced and Puritanical and thought of liquor only as the Demon Rum, and the prohibition laws as the salvation of the age.

They were the duly elected delegates and alternates to the Democratic National Convention. Some were whole votes and some were half votes and some were quarter votes and some were eighth votes.

They were less than a ripple among the billowing millions in that human sea which is New York City. As individuals they were lost among the millions. But, in their organized capacity, when they gathered in old Madison Square Garden, when they were all together under that vaulted roof with the flags and the bunting, they were the Democratic Party in action. They were somebody. They were columns on the front page—"the convention," solemnly. They were the potential medium of great economic and social forces. They were the guardians of a share of political liberty. They were democracy.

They had come to nominate candidates for President and Vice-President of the United States and to adopt a platform of party principles. They had come to organize their lines to try to root from the White House that slender, red-headed New England adage with his wry face and his tenacious hold on the voters which was hard to explain. They had come with hope born of scandalous Republican doings down there in Washington, too confusing for them to understand, but which they counted upon, when the stump speakers began to howl, to help their party. They had come to listen to speeches about the perfidy of Republicans and to shout their approbation and their defiance.

Some had come, too, partly as a lark. They thought they could get this business done quickly and then cavort about the big city.

How little did they know when they streamed into the convention hall for preliminary ceremonies and the rousing keynote speech by the usually jovial Pat Harrison, the Senator from Mississippi who rolled his words about in his mouth like a tasty cud of tobacco, and then spat them out, moist with a soft Southern coating. You could almost hear the plup in the white road and see the little cloud of dust curl upward and drift away. Pat was indignant. Republicans now were the enemy, not the genial friends with whom he sham-battled in the Senate back in Washington.

The delegates settled back comfortably—for a time.

I went to New York, too, by way of Georgia and the South and experiences in Washington that had turned me slightly cynical.

This was my first political convention.

From the press gallery I looked out upon it. Like sunflowers the cardboard placards neatly bearing the names of each state perched on the ends of their long standards above the heads of the delegates. They designated the state delegations, but they did not differentiate or distinguish them, for this was impossible. The delegates sat, row on row, beside one another, one state merging into another, and they were as diverse and as alike as any crowd of Americans who got together. They were friendly enough now. I did not realize, when I first looked upon them, how agitated they would become later when primitive emotions swept over them, and how these standards, caught up in the melee of passion, would pitch and toss like sunflowers caught in a hurricane.

Back and behind them now on every side, in the galleries which rose toward the roof, sat thousands of spectators, come to see something new upon the face of New York, in their time—a national political convention. This arena was more accustomed to other entertainment—the pounding of gloves upon bodies, spotlighted in the center there, with the mob screaming from seats in the shadows; circuses with their torpid elephants swinging from side to side as they walked; dog shows with the "ohs" and "ahs" and "isn't-he-sweet" comments of society women, as they looked upon bewildered animals; horse shows where sleek and shiny steeds pranced gracefully; six-day races, where lithe young men, pedalling bicycles, whirled about a giant saucer, like balls on a roulette wheel.

My first view of the convention was brief.

My job was elsewhere. I was assigned to cover the Resolutions Committee at the outset. There I saw the vials of prejudice begin to simmer and spit—to boil over afterward on the convention floor. The Resolutions Committee, or Platform Committee as we chose to call it, held its sessions in the old Madison Square Garden Hotel nearby in a spacious room in the rear of the main lobby. As usual, the doors were barred tight against reporters. We gathered in a large room adjoining, picking up what scraps we could from members who emerged from time to time, and by holding our ears close to the flimsy partition between the rooms.

From there, during the day and night vigil, we heard the noise of the preliminary engagements in the convention hall, the rise and fall of jubilation as the delegates warmed themselves up for the grand battle to come, like the rush of wind through a forest far away. Supporters of the various candidates shouted for their champions as they were nominated, and punctuated the seconding speeches, some of them gaudy and long-winded, with more applause and cheers. A mighty roar permeated our refuge when Governor Al Smith, the idol of New York, was hailed before the convention. The galleries were packed for the home-town boy from the East Side. Another tornado of sound was stirred up, to drift to us, when his rival was nominated—William Gibbs McAdoo, who had come out of Georgia, to burst upon the citadels of finance in New York as a promoter, who had become Secretary of the Treasury in the Wilson administration and then director of the railroads in that war-time experiment of government operation, and was known for a time as "The Crown Prince," when he married a daughter of the President. These were the two leaders over whom the convention was to tug and scrap like cats and dogs.

All that went on, as it were, far away.

Here, in our cauldron, they were preparing the brew which was to poison this rivalry, and, years later, stir men to wonder at the nightmare through which they sat for nearly three weeks. We, in our hide-out, became acutely aware of this when the politicians inside the room we watched quarrelled bitterly all night over the Klan. The question was whether it should be denounced by name in the plank on freedom of religion, freedom of speech, and freedom of press. Senator David I. Walsh of Massachusetts, a supporter of Al Smith, led the fight for denunciation by name. Opposing that was William Jennings Bryan, who was a McAdoo supporter. The angry murmur, rising now and again to bitter, tempestuous tirade, filtered through the thin partition as we strained our ears. Early in the morning Bryan sought to calm the storm with prayer. At his suggestion he led in the Lord's prayer. These men wrestled with their souls, but could find no balm. A majority plank was adopted omitting reference to the Klan. Walsh and his allies brought in a minority plank pledging the party "to oppose any effort on the part of the Ku Klux Klan, or any organization, to interfere with the religious liberty or political freedom of any citizen, or to limit the civic rights of any citizen or body of citizens because of religion, birthplace or racial origin." (Incidentally, I missed that praying incident, this being my first experience in a national convention. John D. Erwin, now Minister to

185

Honduras, then working for the *New York Evening World,* scooped all of us.)

The bone then was pitched on to the convention floor to be gnawed over by the delegates like a ravenous pack of wolves. The session seethed with hate, such as is possible only over a religious issue.

Klan elements in the convention were backing McAdoo. Al Smith was a Catholic. But the line was not as sharply drawn as might appear. Senator Walsh of Montana, for instance, who was a Catholic, was a warm supporter of the McAdoo candidacy. McAdoo had other Catholic support. Smith had many Protestant supporters.

But there were many bitter-end partisans on the religious issue and their feelings saturated the convention.

Rising above the tumult, like a lighthouse to which all could look with absolute faith, was Montana's Senator Walsh as presiding officer over this holocaust. He was calm, fair and judicious throughout, one of the outstanding parliamentarians in the country. No one could find any fault with him. His was a difficult and delicate task. (He was one of my few heroes—George Norris is another.)

For the convention was a veritable madhouse during the debate and balloting which followed. Scenes come back upon me, as if they happened only yesterday. Amazed at his skill, I watched the wizardry of William Jennings Bryan, now an old man. He rose to face a torrent of boos. In a few moments, as his melodious voice carried to the farthest corner and into the galleries where the partisans of Al Smith were gathered, he had the multitude silent and hanging upon his words, and, presently, he pulled applause from the audience, as the magician jerks a rabbit from the hat. It was a masterful performance. Angrily and sullenly, however, some glared up at him all through his speech, muttering under their breaths.

There was the uproar when Mayor Andrew Ervin of Athens, Ga., whom I had known about town as a pleasant young man when I was in college, delivered his stinging speech against the Klan. When he finished, he was carried about the hall on the shoulders of excited sympathizers. A parade was started. State banners were pushed into line. Men and women fought over other banners, some trying to get them into the parade, others resisting. The New York band, trying to do something appropriate for the young Southerner, played "Marching Through Georgia" and you could feel Georgia gorges rise over that!

Hanging upon the outer side of the press gallery rail, I watched this wild night, darting off, every so often, to get the facts about a fist fight, to find out the name of some delegate who did something that should go into the story. I was one of those assigned to do the leg work for the men who were dictating the running stories over the wire.

The balloting took hours. Votes were changed from time to time. Delegations were polled. Our roll-call keepers were nearly frantic as they tried to keep tally. So were the official roll-call keepers. At 2 o'clock the counting was done, and one vote was announced as the margin by which the majority plank was carried, though a subsequent official check the next day put the total at 546.15 to 541.85. (What fractions of votes we had to worry over!)

What followed in the days afterward is now a dizzy blur. I look back upon hundreds and hundreds of haggard faces. I saw them, eventually, as in a haze. The dust from the tan-bark sifted through the hall. Women swung their souvenir fans back and forth, back and forth. Harried men mopped their foreheads, yanked their necks about nervously in their collars, squirmed in their seats.

But nothing, the heat, the weariness, the humid nights in cheap hotel rooms, could shake them. Nothing could break the deadlock between McAdoo and Smith. The former got almost a majority of the convention on one ballot—the 69th, but two-thirds was necessary. Smith reached his peak ten ballots later, 368, which compared with McAdoo's top of 530. Negotiations were tried. They were futile. All sorts of proposals were offered. They were rejected.

"Call the roll!"

I heard it for days. The clerk would begin:

"Alabama."

Back would come the ceaseless refrain: "Alabama casts twenty-four votes for Oscar W. Underwood," in the booming voice of Governor W. W. Brandon.

It always seemed to get a response, a laugh at first, toward the end, a wan smile. It was the symbol of that convention for thousands who heard the proceedings over the radio, and yet it meant nothing at all except that Alabama was faithful to her Senator.

Days and nights merged together. Never did I work so hard, chasing through the hall to find out about this and that, when the convention was in session, writing a story myself for the night service late in the afternoon, then scurrying about hotels covering meetings of delegations, of leaders. One night I saw McAdoo, by no means a young man, but spry as a college boy, jumping up and down on a table as he made a pep talk, swinging his arms like a cheerleader. I dropped wearily on my bed in early morning, to be called only a few hours later to get out again; and once I rebelled when the phone jangled at 6 o'clock and shouted resentfully to one of the top bosses: "Go to hell." But I got up and dragged to the United Press workroom in the Waldorf-Astoria to receive my assignment for the day.

Lunch usually meant a quick hot dog from the stands scattered along the areaway which ran around the outside of the convention hall proper, munched among tired delegates who strolled up, disconsolately, to refresh themselves from the ordeal, chatted awhile, and then strolled wearily on back to their seats. I wouldn't eat hot dogs for years after.

The dreary show finally ended, after months it seemed to me then, though I checked some time later to find it was only sixteen days—and in an anticlimax.

The deadlock between two men who then posed, at least, as champions of the people broke in a compromise nomination of a Wall Street lawyer, John W. Davis, once of West Virginia, counsel for J. P. Morgan, to lead the Democratic Party against an opposition well entrenched with Mellon and big business and finance. What irony!

But nobody cared then.

"The nomination isn't worth a nickel," was the common expression.

The party was hopelessly split.

To give the ticket a smack of flavor for the masses, to conciliate the still powerful Bryan, the leaders nominated for Vice-President his brother, Charles W. Bryan, Governor of Nebraska. We used to watch this placid gentleman curiously. He sat every day in a chair close to the platform near the press section. He wore a black skull cap. He was never without it.

After the nomination of Davis on the 103rd ballot, a movement was started on the floor to nominate Senator Walsh of Montana as Vice-President. He checked it quickly by adjourning the convention. I went up to the platform later to ask him a question about procedure. Two Catholic priests were talking to him, earnestly.

"Remember, Mr. Senator, every seventh Vice-President becomes President," I heard one of them say.

He smiled courteously, and shook his head slowly.

The leaders gathered to pick a Vice-Presidential candidate in a room under the platform before the night session.

I approached Senator Harrison when the meeting broke up.

"It's Bryan," he said, "Governor Bryan."

"Naw, Senator, you're kidding."

"No, I'm not," he insisted. "You'll find out in a little while."

I did.

But there was some trouble convincing the delegates. The plan was to have one roll call, in which complimentary ballots would be given to favorite sons, and then for the switches to be made later to Bryan before the roll call was closed officially.

It all happened early Sunday morning and the real story of that muddled, closing session never has been written. Senator Walsh had left the hall and turned over the gavel to a substitute. The crowd was unruly and virtually unmanageable—and above all, it didn't care.

I remember members of the Wisconsin delegation, jumping to their feet in twos and threes, and shouting:

"We want Berry! We want Berry!"

They referred to George L. Berry of Tennessee, head of the typographical union, later United States Senator, who was then, and in 1928 and 1932, a candidate for the Vice-Presidential nomination.

"Why not nominate Coolidge," shouted wags from the gallery where Smith had been the favorite.

"We want Coolidge!"

The sorry business finally was ended and enough changes were wormed out of worn-out delegates to name Bryan.

Some of the delegates already had gone home in the few days before. Their money had run out. So had their interest and enthusiasm. The convention hall was only partly filled for this farewell performance, and many had straggled out before the ballot was finished. Now the rest of them, as the gavel rapped adjournment, wandered to the doors and out into the night.

Again, something of my South, the South I had loved but was beginning to see more realistically now from a distance, that evil spirit of the South which breeds on intolerance and injustice, asserted itself. It infused its poison into a great political party.

Mayor Ervin had stood out boldly, only to light up the dark background of religious prejudice in his country and mine.

He flamed for a moment and then the flood caught him back into its bosom, and the light was extinguished.

Delegates from Southern states voted overwhelmingly against the minority plank denouncing the Ku Klux Klan. Of the 266 convention votes of the 10 Southern states, in which I include Oklahoma and Texas, 231 were cast against the Klan plank, only 35 for it. Of the latter, 24 were from Alabama, its entire representation. The Alabama delegation at the 1924 convention was under the thumb of Senator Oscar Underwood. He had fought the Klan publicly, exhibiting rare courage for a Southern Senator in those days. The other votes cast for the plank denouncing the Klan by name were scattered among the eleven other Southern states.

The Southern vote for the majority plank, which omitted direct reference to the Klan, was not half of that cast for it, however. The Middle Western votes for the plank which evaded the issue reflected the infiltration of the hooded order into the politics of the states there—in Indiana, Illinois, Michigan, Iowa and Kansas; and this was likewise true of the border states of Kentucky and Missouri and the Pacific Coast states of Washington, Oregon and California.

But in the attitude of the Southern delegations at that convention, with exceptions, I noted the resurgence of religious prejudice. I could feel its influence instinctively, knowing the Southerners and the South.

John W. Davis, the suave, the cultured, the gentleman, would suit them. He was a fine-looking, handsome candidate, and he spoke eloquently and well. That he was a Wall Street lawyer, closely identified with the big interests whose influence over the Republican Party their platform had deplored, would not matter. He was just the right type for the good, respectable folks in the South who did most of the voting. They would rather lose with him, gallantly, of course, than to see their ticket headed by that man Smith.

As I recall my feelings at that convention they were confused. (Toward the end, through sheer physical exhaustion, they were numb.) Neither of the leading rivals who fought each other to a standstill stirred my enthusiasm. I was still too close to the South to be attracted to Smith, the East Side product who retained the stamp. His kind was alien to me. I came to admire him later, to enjoy him when, as a reporter, I saw much of him in another campaign. There came a day, too, when I was sorely disappointed in him—but that was a long time afterward. As for McAdoo the revelation during the Teapot Dome investigation that he had been counsel for Doheny threw a shadow of doubt across my mind. Perhaps it was because it came, suddenly, when the mud was being splattered on every side and everyone who was touched —even if only barely—became questionable in my mind. He gave up his connections promptly with Doheny when they were revealed, when it was said this might affect his candidacy for the nomination, and that did not sit too well, either. I came to feel very strongly about that whole Teapot Dome episode and to suspect anyone drawn into it. (That was probably my youth.) McAdoo of course, had nothing to do with the oil lease. He was handling other business. Doheny had, from time to time, employed three other ex-Cabinet officers of the Wilson administration.

"How about oil?" the McAdoo foes had shouted up at Bryan when he spoke to the convention.

It popped up, intermittently, during the long battle at Madison Square Garden.

I abhorred the Ku Klux Klan, but I had never come into contact with it before, as in this crowd of ordinary American citizens suddenly gone berserk, and now I saw its deep-seated and underlying dangers. I realized what capital might be made of such a racial and religious issue by insincere politicians who would seize whatever side would profit them most, and there seemed to be evidence that this was a mixed affair. I cannot challenge the motives of those who pushed the Klan issue to the fore, for we do not know what is in the hearts and minds of men, but I suspected at the time that sincere convictions did not motivate everybody concerned. I had never been part of a minority group. I had no experience of persecution. The sudden reality of everything involved in this bitter struggle stunned me. Once the issue was raised, it seemed to me that the proper thing for the convention was to take it, deal with it and put the party unflinchingly on record against it, however it might have been injected into the convention.

In his speech advocating the majority plank which omitted reference to the Klan, Bryan had called the convention's attention to issues which to me had become important as I had watched the Harding and Coolidge administrations—the farm distress, the growth of monopoly and concentration of economic power.

"They say," he had declared, "that we are cowards. My friends it requires more courage to fight the Republican Party than it does to fight the Ku Klux Klan. Here we have farmers driven into bankruptcy, a million driven from the farms in a single year. We find monopoly spreading. We find nearly every great line of industry in the control of gigantic combinations of capital. And while we have distress in the country that cries aloud for relief, and while we have a war-torn world across the Atlantic that needs our help and our guidance, these minority men say that we lack courage if we do a big work instead of starting out on a little hunt for something that is nearly dead and which will soon pass away."

Bryan, of course, was begging the question. The natural answer was that it did not take more courage for the party to fight the Republican Party than to fight the Klan; that it could do both—denounce the Klan and then turn its attention to the other—and as Bryan regarded them—bigger and more fundamental problems. But Bryan subsequently rendered his own arguments invalid—or so it seemed to me— in accepting the J. P. Morgan lawyer as the candidate of his party. This seemed contrary to the long crusade he had made, beginning in his own campaign for the Presidency in 1896 against McKinley, his crusade to make the Democratic Party the vehicle and representative of the masses. John W. Davis seemed to be aligned with those against whom Bryan had raised the sword so often in the past.

Bryan was a faded and futile hero.

My first convention turned out to be a delusion.

The torch that had been raised by Senator Walsh and Senator Wheeler and the insurgent Republicans who had fought along with them, Norris and LaFollette and LaGuardia and the others, suddenly had been doused in a bucket of prejudice and passion and hate—as far as the Democratic Party was concerned.

But there was a torch raised out at Cleveland, Ohio, in a dark and dingy hall.

17

THE challenge of "Fighting Bob" LaFollette was flung to the Republican Party of Coolidge and Mellon, to the Democratic Party and its Wall Street lawyer candidate, and to the world at large in a convention at Cleveland, which knew what it wanted, took only two days to do it, and required only a nomination by acclamation without any monkey business about balloting.

By a happy chance I saw the fledgling third party born in the gloomy auditorium of the Brotherhood of Locomotive Engineers. The variously assorted groups which sponsored this Conference for Progressive Political Action, as it was called, had set the date for July 4, judging this would give the Democrats, who assembled June 24, sufficient time to get their job done. The Railroad Labor organizations which were the backbone of this venture looked with favor upon McAdoo who had been friendly to them during war days, and it was reported that if he were nominated this convention might endorse him and thus conduct a unified crusade against the might and power of Republicanism.

But the deadlock at New York persisted. There seemed no chance of McAdoo's nomination by that time. So the conference got down to business on July 4. I was dispatched from the New York convention—the top flight talent being required to stay there—to help cover the Cleveland meeting.

One of my memories is of walking down Euclid Avenue and observing a straggly group gathered about the monument in Cleveland's public square. Someone was making a speech. Moving closer I recognized Representative Theodore Burton who had been keynoter of the Republican Convention here a few weeks earlier. For some reason the scene struck me as ludicrous. He was delivering a Fourth of July address. The group was not particularly attentive. People would stop for a moment, as I did, and listen, then stroll on. The Congressman had the look of an owl. He was a big, ungainly gentleman. He had a large head which sat forward of his stooped shoulders and he peered down along his nose as he talked. He was earnest and sincere. His manner was placid, as usual, and it did not seem to concern him that the crowd was little interested in what he was saying.

This simple ceremony impressed me, I suppose, because it was such a contrast to the uproarious scenes I had left behind in New York. Republicans did have a quiet, unworried way of doing things. It stood out, too, because of a reference to Burton later by Mayor Peter Witt of Cleveland, a salty-tongued gentleman, in his welcoming speech to the Conference for Progressive Political Action. He spoke of Burton and his keynote address to the Republicans. He referred whimsically to the fact that Burton was a bachelor and had not tasted all the experiences of the world, despite his long political career and his study of affairs, and closed with that couplet from Tennyson's "Sir Galahad"—"ne'er felt the touch of woman's lips, ne'er held woman's hand in mine."

But this crowd here was serious.

Labor was here with its grievances. A solemn fellow with little humor was Bill Johnston of the International Machinists, whom I had seen about Washington. He was chairman of this conference. Here also was Representative John M. Nelson, my friend of the rules fight days, a weathered and diminutive veteran, rugged and devoted, who later became chairman of the executive committee which directed the LaFollette campaign.

This conference attracted some of the determined and fervent type of "liberals" who associate themselves with such political movements and furnish fire if not a great deal of practical assistance. They revel in splitting hairs and quibbling over details. (While I sympathize with the aims

196

of many liberal groups, I am occasionally rebuffed by their intensity, which occasionally becomes arrogant, and by their assumption frequently of self-righteousness. If they would smile occasionally and not take themselves too seriously I would feel more comfortable with them.) But there was no disturbance of any consequence here. Labor, in political action, is hard-boiled and practical. The conference did repudiate as communistic the program adopted by the Farmer-Labor Progressive Convention at St. Paul, held several days before and barred its representative, and, for its pains, was branded as "the most reactionary political convention held this year," by William Z. Foster and C. E. Ruthenberg of the Workers Party of America.

The big moment of the July 4 session was when Bob La-Follette, Jr., his father's secretary, then a comparative youngster of twenty-nine, appeared on the platform and read a statement from the Senator announcing that he would submit his name for filing as candidate for President in every state in the union. The Senator, himself, was not present.

It was late in the afternoon when the young man was called to the platform. He appeared then, as he does now, much younger than his years. His round, boyish face seemed to glow against the forbidding dull atmosphere of the hall. In a loud and ringing voice—in which was the pride of a son—he read the statement to the conference. It was a blistering condemnation of both the Republican Party—which the Senator was now leaving by this defiance—and the Democratic Party. They had betrayed the trust of the people, the statement declared. He expressed his hope that the November election would bring an uprising of the people that would insure a new progressive party.

The conference wasted no time, now that it had its champion. The next day it adopted the LaFollette platform and endorsed the Senator for President in exuberant acclamation.

Then it let itself go in an hilarious demonstration that was genuine and needed none of the artificial stimulation which I had seen pumped into demonstrations in New York when the various and sundry candidates were placed in nomination. Only in its demonstration for the Senator did it imitate the customary mechanics of the usual national political convention.

There was no mock nomination of "favorite sons" put forward to be traded off later in negotiations between leaders. There was only one "favorite" son here. There were no state lines drawn, no state banners. This was a national movement for the people as a whole with no glorification of individual states to emphasize local prejudices. There was no quibbling over whether the Ku Klux Klan should be denounced by name. Everyone knew what Bob LaFollette thought about organizations which thrived on prejudice and operated under cover of secrecy and in the darkness of night. They did not have to write it down in a platform, spelling it out. They adopted a simple plank pledging enforcement of the constitutional guarantees of freedom of speech, press and assemblage.

The conference did not pick a Vice-Presidential candidate. That was left to the National Committee of the Conference in cooperation with the LaFollette-for-President Committee. Two weeks later, Senator Wheeler of Montana, a Democrat, who had helped to show up the rottenness of the Harding régime by his investigation into the Justice Department, was delegated as the Wisconsin Senator's running-mate.

"Fighting Bob" LaFollette now was ready at last to strike out on his own at the age of sixty-nine.

For over a quarter of a century he had been picking energetically at the bulwarks of reactionary Republicanism. In the 'nineties he had cut loose from the Republican doctrines of those times, and, formulating a progressive program, had won the governorship of Wisconsin. There he had originated reforms which, carried on since by his sons, have made that state a laboratory of social and economic experiment. In 1906 when he was sent to the United States Senate he got his opportunity to fight for the "Wisconsin idea," as it was characterized, on a national scale. Often he fought alone. From time to time allies gathered about him, as in the revolt in the session of Congress preceding the 1924 election.

Until now he had worked within the Republican Party. The birth of the Republican Party was associated with Wisconsin. Its cradle was at Ripon, Wis., where in 1854, the year before Bob LaFollette was born on a Wisconsin farm, earnest men concerned about slavery in the South had gathered to organize a new political movement. In his youth, the young LaFollette had cherished the Republican Party as the party of Abraham Lincoln, the party of economic and social justice. In his maturity he saw how far it had drifted from its moorings.

But still he worked from within.

For years he had offered a Wisconsin platform to the Republican National conventions. Each time it was rejected. That had happened again in 1924, only a few weeks before, at the Republican Convention here in this city which had renominated Calvin Coolidge. Gradually, however, his reforms were written into the law of the land, always some years after he had enunciated them.

He still was in the vanguard ahead of his times.

Now he was cutting himself adrift at last.

The terse, pungent platform upon which he based his crusade in 1924 was a contrast, in plain-speaking and brevity, to the evasive, turgid, long-winded documents composed by Republicans and Democrats which hid from the realities and left the reader (and few there are of such documents) in a bewildering fog of words.

Bob LaFollette could not live long enough to see the country catch up with this platform. He died less than a year later, victim of the hard campaign which carried him over the country in a vain effort to dispel the clouds which confounded the electorate.

He would have had to live a long time.

Eight and ten years later some of his objectives would become those of the New Deal of Franklin D. Roosevelt, and some would be still the subject of dispute and still potential issues in the shadowy campaigns yet ahead.

Later the Franklin Roosevelt régime enacted laws to protect labor's right to bargain collectively which LaFollette had advocated in 1924. Later the New Deal put through Congress a tax on undistributed profits, which the LaFollette 1924 platform had proposed—only to lose this reform as the conservative wing of the Democratic Party began to regain its ascendency toward the end of Franklin Roosevelt's second administration.

For years before 1924, Bob LaFollette had proclaimed his distrust of the courts. His 1924 platform appealed for "abolition of the tyranny and usurpation of the courts, including the practice of nullifying legislation in conflict with the political, social or economic theories of the judges." Franklin Roosevelt, eleven years later, took this same attitude in charging the courts with holding back the tide of progress. His particular target was the Supreme Court which he accused of arrogating to itself legislative authority to override the will of the people as expressed through Congress. LaFollette's platform urged election of federal judges without party designation to limited terms and, as for the Supreme Court, he advocated during his campaign that Congress be empowered to overrule its decisions by a two-thirds majority. Franklin Roosevelt's remedy, proposed a decade later, would have forced judges over seventy to retire or face the prospect of having a new member appointed for each one over seventy who remained, or, as his enemies charged, to "pack" the Court.

The LaFollette 1924 platform urged direct public control of money and credit by reconstruction of the Federal Reserve System and the farm loan system. Several years later the Roosevelt New Deal centralized monetary control more strongly in the Federal Reserve system, but stopped short of the 1924 LaFollette objective.

In 1924 Senator LaFollette wanted public ownership of the nation's waterpower and creation of a superpower system. The Roosevelt administration, several years later, moved in this direction through creation of the Tennessee Valley, Grand Coulee (Washington) and Bonneville (Oregon) projects.

Looking to the future, if we accept LaFollette of 1924 as a prophet, public ownership of railroads would seem to lie ahead.

The LaFollette convention was like a breath of fresh air after the contamination of strife and hatred in that dreary treadmill in New York. When I left New York for Cleveland I had supposed that the Democratic convention would have worked itself out of its dilemma, ready for a conclusion, by the time my task was done in Cleveland, and that I could return to Washington. But I discovered I was sadly mistaken. Back to New York I was called to plunge again into that maelstrom, to consume more hot dogs, to be dragged from my bed at ungodly hours, to follow and record the disgusting antics of my former friends, the Democrats.

The progressive forces in the Democratic Party and the Republican insurgents, who had started so bravely in that minor revolution in Congress in the 1923-1924 session, lost their golden opportunity in the turn of events. Republicans could not have ordered it better themselves—a Democratic

Party torn asunder as the outgrowth of the bitter convention fight and led by the Wall Street lawyer; a third party which would tend to split the progressive voters within the country.

Still Republicans were worried. That is the natural instinct of the politician, even when it seems certain that everything is in his favor. There were three parties in the field. This presented the possibility of a stalemate that would throw the election into the House of Representatives, an eventuality for which LaFollette supporters hoped. The Republicans emphasized this possibility. Look, they exclaimed in horror, the election may be thrown into the House and there the Democrats might join with the LaFollette insurgents, still the balance of power there, as they had in the rules fight several months before, and that "radical LaFollette" might be elected! It was enough to terrify conservatives.

In their platform Democrats had a very neat line which they undoubtedly regretted often:

"A vote for Coolidge is a vote for chaos."

Republicans twisted this very nicely around the possible danger that a three-way race might result in LaFollette's eventual election and coined a slogan:

"Coolidge or Chaos."

It has often been assumed, and I think with some justification, that many conservative Democrats were influenced to vote for Coolidge on account of the fear that such an impasse as Republicans were stressing might develop. Some mildly liberal Democrats could not swallow LaFollette and, as far as fundamental political and economic philosophy went, there was little choice for them between Coolidge and Davis. The South, of course, would vote Democratic in the normal way—now that "that man Smith" was not the candidate.

At Clarksburg, W. Va., I saw John W. Davis open his campaign. If the weather is any augury, he was singing his swan-song then and there. A thundercloud out of the West Virginia hills broke that night upon the throng gathered for the notification ceremonies just as the Democratic candidate began his acceptance address. The rain splattered in upon him as he stood at the front of the pavilion thrown up for this occasion. There was no shelter for the rest of us. Fraser Edwards, who was covering the story for our day service, obligingly—like the good fellow he is—held a piece of beaverboard over my head and over the head of our telegraph operator as I tried to write a running "picture" story of the damp occasion for our night wire. It was impossible, even with that protection, to keep the copy paper dry. Fraser sat up on the press table and from above, full in the fury of the storm, he shouted down bits of "color" which included, I remember, an old mountaineer—mythical I have always believed—who was singing: "It Ain't Gonna Rain No Mo'." Nobody could sing in that flood from on high.

The subsequent Davis speechmaking campaign, which Fraser followed, was described by him, very aptly I thought, as "a kid-glove campaign." The Democratic nominee, he said, "just won't take off his gloves and take down his back hair and go after 'em." Davis's speeches were fine examples of rhetoric, but they did not seem to stir up the voters. He exhorted about the Harding administration scandals—which anyone would have thought, a few months previously, would have tossed any administration mercilessly out of office—but the story was too confusing for the average person to understand and many voters, undoubtedly, were willing to accept the Republican explanation that it was just "a political fishing expedition" and their added reminder that, anyhow, that was under Harding. Coolidge was running now, and he was honest, and the country could depend on him to see that anyone who was guilty of fraud or corruption was prosecuted.

Another Coolidge campaign slogan was:
"Keep Cool with Coolidge."

The President kept outwardly as cool as ice and as calm as a Buddha. His notification ceremonies were in old Constitution Hall in Washington, the headquarters of the Daughters of the American Revolution, before a select audience of officials. The austere hall held only a few hundred. During the campaign he remained for the most part quietly at his desk in Washington, as if there were no question at all that he would continue there, and disregarded the shouting and the tumult of the Democrats and Progressives. He just stayed on the job. He received delegations from time to time who came to pledge their support.

It seems almost a miracle now, looking back upon it, that LaFollette rolled up nearly 5,000,000 votes, when the handicaps and obstacles are considered. He had to throw up an organization quickly. The two major parties had both organization and money. He had to combat the fear mania dramatized by Republicans. The country was fairly prosperous, so far as surface indications revealed.

But, when the returns of that election are analyzed, a very interesting and significant story emerges. It was not a Coolidge landslide, nor the smashing victory that might be deduced from a mere recital of the electoral vote, which was: Coolidge, 382; Davis, 136; La Follette, 13.

Coolidge was, in reality, closely pressed. The same groundswell of dissatisfaction with the Republican régime that had been exhibited in the 1922 congressional election, particularly in the West, still existed. Coolidge was lucky that there were two parties in the field against him.

For, in addition to the twelve Southern states carried by Davis and the one, Wisconsin, which LaFollette carried, Coolidge's vote was less than a majority of all votes cast in fourteen other states. The combined vote for Davis and LaFollette in those fourteen states was greater than his vote. He received a plurality in those fourteen states and thus they were added to his list and he received their electoral votes.

The electoral vote of the twenty-seven states in which Coolidge did not get a majority of votes cast was 248; leaving 283 electoral votes in the states in which he did get a majority of all votes cast. This would have represented a close election.

Of these twenty-seven states, a dozen were in the South (including Texas and Oklahoma in that geographical category); four were border states, Maryland, Kentucky, West Virginia and Missouri; and the rest were in the West, Arizona, Idaho, Iowa, Montana, Nebraska, Nevada, New Mexico, North and South Dakota, Utah and Wisconsin.

This reveals Coolidge's strength largely concentrated in the East, the industrial Middle West, and the Pacific Coast. He was weak in the farm states, both West and South—the latter, of course, normally Democratic.

Dissatisfaction with both old parties in a large section of the West, including the Pacific Coast, would seem to have existed in 1924 among many voters. LaFollette ran ahead of Davis in ten states, all in that region—California, Idaho, Iowa, Minnesota, Montana, North and South Dakota, Oregon, Washington and Wyoming—in addition to his own state of Wisconsin.

I have tallied these votes up because I think they help to an understanding of the true situation in the country at that time. Something was going on underneath, especially in the farm states. The revolution that turned the country upside down eight years later was in the making. Just speculating idly, one might draw the conclusion that had the Democrats nominated a progressive candidate—but not Al Smith—and had LaFollette withheld his independent movement, Coolidge might have had a very narrow escape in 1924. Again, speculating idly and looking forward a bit, the result might not have been so one-sided in 1928 had the Democrats nominated a candidate other than Smith. For, from my experience in that campaign, I am convinced that the combination of religious prejudice and his wet stand and an antipathy to his type of New Yorker, weighed heavily against Smith in the Midwest, just as it did in the South where Hoover captured four states and broke the solid Democratic phalanx in that section.

But that is mere idle speculation.

The fact was that the back of the little revolution was broken for the time being. Republicans regained their ascendency in Congress. They proceeded immediately to discipline those who had left the party and followed LaFollette for President, depriving them of their priority on committees.

LaFollette was shoved into the background by his Republican colleagues. He took it philosophically. For he was accustomed to persecution. He had been virtually outlawed because of his opposition to United States participation in the World War. His Senator son, Bob, Jr., recalled to me recently, with a smile, those days during the war when, as he explained, his father was relegated to a dank office in the basement of the Capitol and was "Chairman of the Committee on the Potomac Mud Flats."

Yes, the revolution had to wait for another day.

The insurgents, and those among the Democrats who were of like mind, were wilted and shrunken under the burning sun of "Coolidge Prosperity" in the next few years and cried aloud in vain.

Again they were voices in the wilderness.

18

I SIT on the front porch of a cottage at the beach in middle June, thinking back to Coolidge's second administration. I am stripped to the waist. It is hot and close. The tide is beginning to come in. The waves wash regularly up the sand about two hundred feet away, edging closer. The sound of them rises and falls. Now there is a slushing roar, now a growling echo as they subside; then, there is silence for a moment, and I look up. The sea is still there, and again there is a big wave, and a resounding roar, to prove it. A few clouds are beginning to pile up in the east. It looks as if we'll have a little rain later.

A shout comes up from the beach. Several little boys jump about in a circle and their dog barks, excitedly. Probably a crab washed ashore. An airplane zooms overhead—and everybody along the beach looks up at it, shading his eyes and watch it sail away into the distance, just as if he had never seen an airplane before. A man is casting his line from a jetty not far away. Suddenly he begins to reel in energetically. There he has it. A small fish wriggles on his hook. He is chagrined. The little boys race over and stand about, hands on hips, looking down at the fish. The man looks the other way, annoyed, as he rebaits his hook and casts again.

Still I am thinking back to the second Coolidge administration. Then the light dawns on me. Here it is before me. A hot lazy afternoon. Clouds in the offing, but not disturbing. People excited about little, everyday affairs. Nothing serious is on their minds.

I've been pondering, trying to remember what happened in that second Coolidge administration. It's a blur. It's like this afternoon which is like so many afternoons here in June, so that when I go away and look back, I'll just remember the ocean rolling in, and people on the beach, and little boys dashing about madly and shrieking and the little dog that trots along with them and the occasional airplane that flies overhead.

This is something aside and apart from my regular life and the sameness of it leaves just a single impression of a scene, like a photograph of long ago. That was Washington in the second Coolidge administration, a vacation for awhile from the realities that had gone before and the realities that were to follow. The things I remember most of that day are things that happened outside Washington. America was living away and apart from Washington then. Washington was a forgotten city almost.

From my notes I observe that the day after Coolidge and Dawes were elected the stock market began to boom. It kept on booming for nearly four years, nearly, not quite. That dizzy gambling game set the tone for the whole era.

America was off down Prosperity Road, a road filled with shiny new automobiles and new little houses on each side with their radios and their gadgets—a gay road paved with good intentions to pay the next instalment.

It was several years later when Huey Long conceived his slogan about "Every Man a King." In those days, the ambition was more modest. It was "Every Man a Capitalist." There was a very simple way to become a capitalist. That was to buy a few shares of stock. Big corporations encouraged this. They saw that if an employee owned a few shares of stock, he would get the capitalistic viewpoint and he wouldn't go running off after every politician and agitator who wanted to regulate business. He would feel he was a capitalist, that he had a share in the business. Of course he didn't. That was nicely arranged. The real capitalists would manage his affairs for him—without his help. They had no fear of widely diffused stock that couldn't be voted. Later it all came out what had been done with some of this stock managed by a few men.

It was only a step from owning a little stock in the big corporation you worked for to buying a little stock in other corporations, and buying and selling this, in time, became a game. The big fellows found out about this and operated the market so the little fellows could come in and play. This all went along very merrily for the little fellow without any trouble while Coolidge was President. He didn't do anything to stop it, in fact he rather encouraged it; but it just happened that a spree of this sort is good for a certain length of time, and Coolidge happened to be out of office when it came time to pick up the pieces and go home and see if you could scrape up a little something to eat. Then some people discovered that there were things they enjoyed about the home, the automobile, the radio, the new sofa, the new suits and dresses that hadn't been paid for yet. Some people had to let the instalment man take them away and when he took them away he couldn't do anything with them, not even sell them again. For nobody wanted to buy.

It seemed so easy to go in and put a few dollars down. That stock was going up again. Instalment buying became a national habit and then, suddenly, it all backed up, and there was no use of making more things, and so they shut the factories down, and men were out of work and there was hell to pay.

It was not all as simple as that—but that was a part of all of it—when the reckoning day came.

In the giddy days there was no thought of the wrath to come, in the giddy days of Coolidge.

People thought of Washington only in terms of Coolidge and Mellon. They wanted Washington just to sit still. All they wanted out of Washington was a nice, rosy statement at intervals from Coolidge, or Mellon or Hoover that business was fine, so the stock market could jump up another peg or two, and for Congress to take Mellon's advice and cut taxes some more. Congress did take Mellon's advice periodically until finally he had shaved down the taxes on the big fellows to a maximum surtax of 20 per cent on incomes of $100,000 and above. They didn't want those radicals and insurgents fighting with Coolidge and taking the bit in their teeth to regulate business or inquire into businessmen's affairs.

This is my impression of the psychology of the times as it beat back upon Washington. Calvin Coolidge was a symbol to the people in that day, a symbol of the golden age, a sour little man sitting there presiding over "Prosperity." He was not a national leader. But nobody wanted him to be a leader. He was absolutely uninspiring. His speeches were dull and colorless, with no lift in them. In his messages to Congress he followed a neat pattern, with his topics properly divided and labelled, written as we were taught to write "themes" in school. His other speeches were dry, dealing mostly with truisms, such as the necessity of the people exercising their franchise (to keep government out of the hands of politicians!); the meaning of the flag (living under the American flag, he said, gave assurance of the best occupation, or job, to be had anywhere in the world); prosperity (the country was entering a new era of prosperity—this two years before the crash); and always, constantly, law enforcement, the necessity of obedience to law—by which, largely, he was talking about the prohibition law.

People listened to those law-enforcement speeches, and then ordered another case "just off the boat" from the bootlegger.

We had a little flurry during 1926 when the "wets" in the Senate forced public hearings by the Judiciary Committee on the Eighteenth Amendment and the Volstead Act. That was quite an achievement in those days, even to bring the subject before a congressional committee for talk and controversy. I remember the excitement it created and how the newspapers covered it with meticulous detail. We sat about the press tables and wrote thousands of words for days. Prohibitionists defended the law, with the arguments we knew now by heart. Wets attacked the law, with the arguments we also had learned by heart. Officials in charge of enforcement defended themselves. It all came to nothing. The special subcommittee which had conducted the hearing recommended to the full committee that consideration of numerous bills to change the laws be postponed indefinitely and concluded that there was no legal authority to hold a national referendum on prohibition, which had been proposed. A wet committee minority squawked, and wets generally squawked, but that was all there was to it.

A few days later we found out something about the operations of wiry and able Wayne B. Wheeler, legislative representative of the Anti-Saloon League, who had put the Eighteenth Amendment and the Volstead Act over and who now was holding the lines successfully against a slowly rising tide. He told the Senate Campaign Fund Investigating Committee that the League, in the period between January 1, 1920, when prohibition became effective, and December 1, 1925, had collected $3,444,623 and spent $3,430,285. He also revealed that the League had paid fees to members of Congress to deliver speeches for prohibition, and had collected money to help elect and reelect members who supported the prohibition law.

Wayne Wheeler was always an intriguing figure to me. I saw and talked with him many times in his dusty little office on the second floor of the Bliss Building, a remodelled residence, a few hundred yards away from the Capitol on Capitol Hill. There in a drawer at hand he had the record of every member of Congress on every bill affecting the question of prohibition. He kept close tab, and kept his files up to date. He was a fanatic, but one of the ablest and most practical I ever encountered. His only measuring stick of a member of Congress was whether he was for or against prohibition. If he was against, he did everything in his power to defeat him, and this meant going right into the district to spend money and propagandize. If a member was for prohibition, no questions were asked. It did not matter to Wheeler if that member personally was against prohibition, whether he was insincere, whether he drank liquor, himself. All he cared about was how he voted. Slowly, he fixed Congress so that he had his majority. But he did not relax then, as the collections and expenditures of the League showed. If anything, he worked harder. He was a quiet gentleman, mild mannered, but oh, how persistent! His voice was soft and his general demeanor was soft. He slipped about the Capitol, in and out, in and out, through the years, like a Cheshire cat, always with that professional smile on his thin face. You almost felt that his feet were padded. I recall him stepping into an elevator one day at the Waldorf during the 1924 Democratic Convention. Timidly, he stepped back into a corner. Among the few people in the elevator was a wet leader from Ohio who was outspoken and rabid about the prohibition laws, a stocky, husky gentleman. He made a sarcastic remark to Wheeler, in a loud voice. The diminutive little dry general just smiled in his wan way, but I thought I detected about the eyes and the lips, just a shade of triumph. The wets could shout all they pleased. They could be sarcastic and mean. That did not matter to him. He had them where he wanted them.

He died in 1927, at the age of fifty-seven. Anyone who knew him could have forecast then that prohibition could not do so well thereafter, what with the nation's sentiment slowly shifting. He left no one who could fill those small shoes.

What a help he would have been to some progressive cause, with his quiet determination!

I have digressed. But Wayne Wheeler was a very important influence in that era, one of its guides.

I was speaking of Coolidge and his dry, uninspiring speeches. Once he strayed into a slightly unorthodox path when he urged higher wages for the unskilled worker. (The skilled worker was getting good wages in those days.) But he didn't do anything else about it. His saying so—effective enough when it had to do with favors for the well fixed— was not enough for the under crust. Even in those days, the textile mills were moving South, to take advantage of surplus, unskilled labor from the farm, something which I learned about much later. Labor organizers, too, were moving into that field. Disorders occurred in North and South Carolina and the name Gastonia, the mill-town which was to figure a good deal in future strikes and disturbances, came into the news. Blood was shed in conflicts in that locality.

That was in the next year. The speech about unskilled workers he delivered in Indiana in 1927 on his way to his summer vacation in South Dakota. He was more in his accustomed rôle when at Pittsburgh a few months later, at a celebration at Carnegie Institute, he said that America's wealthy men were using their riches to spread democracy and for developing the liberal arts. (Some of them we learned later, were doing other things, too, especially in the handsome offices of big banks in New York City.)

Coolidge was no hero.

My quarrel with him constantly—stemming from my growing interest in what some of the progressives were trying to do—was that he seemed to lack those qualities of leadership that I expected of a President. From those progressives I did get some sustenance for idealism. They were trying to look beneath the surface to the common man to find out what was going on among the plain people who were not swept up into the vortex of specious prosperity.

Herbert Hoover phrased it well shortly afterward in a telegram on the occasion of his nomination when he said: "The Presidency is more than executive responsibility. It is the inspiring symbol of all that is highest in America's purpose and ideals."

Coolidge was nothing of that sort. He was as bare and bleak as a New England rock farm.

The public found its heroes elsewhere in those days.

One was that determined young man, Charles A. Lindbergh, who streaked out of the West, calmly let it be known in New York that he was going to fly to Paris in a little ship called "The Spirit of St. Louis," was laughed at as "The Flying Fool," until he actually did what he said he was going to do and then became "The Lone Eagle" and a hero to a whole nation.

I was assigned to the Navy Department during the spring and early summer of 1927, for the naval communications service was proving to be very efficient in bringing information covering stories which ran along during that period, the numerous trans-oceanic flights which began with the futile attempt of the two Frenchmen, Nungesser and Coli, to fly from Paris to New York, and the Nanking incident.

On the morning of Lindbergh's second day out, when the whole of America was tense over this daring youngster, I was talking to a naval aviation expert. He said with a doleful smile:

"He's crazy. The flying fool is right. He's probably in the 'drink' by now. We'll never hear from him again."

The Navy's interest was in its own Commander Richard E. Byrd, who had taken weeks to prepare for a flight, and was still sitting about New York waiting for all auguries to be exactly right for his big plane to take off for Paris with its crew of four. Byrd had flown over the North Pole the year before. His subsequent flight to Europe, which ended up on the edge of the ocean, was an anticlimax. The kid who dashed off by himself was the nation's darling.

I stood at the Navy Yard and watched the cruiser *Memphis* move slowly up the Potomac River. Lindbergh stood there on deck. In his face at the time I found all sorts of expressions which I duly recorded for the United Press. All day we reporters chased him about, chronicling his every act.

He was the hero, and President Coolidge and everybody else made their obeisances to him. His exploit started numerous others and people were trying to fly all the oceans that summer. Some succeeded and some disappeared never to be heard from again.

From the Navy Department, too, we covered the capture of Nanking by the Chinese nationalists headed by Chiang Kai-Shek, and the shelling of the hill where sat the Standard Oil compound, to which many Americans had fled. I remember this particularly, because of one amusing situation. We were getting more about what was going on in China from the Naval Communications than the news cables were bringing. It was a gold mine for news. Ray Tucker, then working for the *New York Evening Post,* turned up at the Navy Department press room and sensed the story we were getting there. He scanned the bulletins we already had received, jumped to a telephone, and calling the telegraph office, said: "Start some messenger boys down here. Keep them coming in a string. I'll have lots of copy." In his eager, enthusiastic way, he began to pound the typewriter in a running story that took the play away from the cabled stories from China that day in his paper. I can see him now, rubbing his hands exultantly. But, for the amusing situation. The young lieutenant commander in charge of the press room, who was excited over the story himself, was handing us bulletins, it turned out later, before sending them to the State Department where they should have been sent in the usual course. It was the function of the State Department to give out such information. We were getting it hot off the wireless, uncensored. We got lots of stuff that the State Department would have withheld. Secretary of State Kellogg discovered what was happening and called up Secretary of Navy Wilbur, who, in turn, called the young officer before him and reprimanded him. We heard about it and went to the Secretary on behalf of our friend and Wilbur let him off with a lecture.

The young officer had his chance to be amused at me.

There was an admiral named Hough in charge of American naval forces in the Far East. In time, our warships did their share of shelling. It was quite a dramatic affair—perhaps more so as we took it from thousands of miles away, and gave it our imaginative touch. I went about the Department talking to men who had known Hough. Then I composed myself a story in which I called him "Give 'em Hell Hough."

When the officer saw my story he smiled and began to kid me.

"A nice story," he said, "but 'Give 'em Hell, Hough!'"

He laughed.

"He's a very quiet, mild-mannered man."

Those were pleasant days.

Steve Early, then with the Associated Press, and Marvin McIntyre, then with Pathé News Service, who later became secretaries to President Roosevelt, were among the group which sat about the press room then. There I learned that both were much better bridge players than I.

Congress was only a sideshow in those second Coolidge administration days. It had its exciting moments, but the rebellious element, the progressive Democrats and the insurgents, seldom came from their skirmishes with anything substantial gained. The regular Democrats and their leaders were content to stage mock battles about issues that didn't matter a great deal. They made their share of noise and enjoyed the little irritation they occasionally caused at the White House.

President Coolidge, from the White House, mostly said "No," at least to anything new or novel. He vetoed the McNary-Haugen bill twice; he said "No" to Norris' bill for government operation of Muscle Shoals; he said "No" to pension bills and bills to increase the pay of postal employees. He had nothing new to offer himself. He let his leaders in Congress initiate the routine measures thought necessary for the time, and his leaders showed no disposition to disturb the placid status quo. Their idea was to let well enough alone, and things in the country seemed well enough to them.

Congress got through its sessions early. There were no special sessions then. Coolidge spent the whole of every summer away from Washington. Cabinet officers sought cooler retreats. Congress was away. Washington was left, a hot and deserted village. We had difficulty ever getting it in the front page. For myself, I was set to dabbling in amateur science in those eventless days, interviewing scientists at the Bureau of Standards, the National Museum, the Department of Agriculture, about work in which they were engaged. (I am thankful for that experience, for I did get an insight into the value of research and did learn to appreciate the "pure scientist," usually an absent-minded fellow with a faraway look in his eyes who was poring into mysteries far beyond me, alone with his dream and content with it, searching out things that might, in time, change our lives in many ways—and for the better; and he worked away without thought of his material rewards. Some of these men, I discovered had meager salaries; and yet they stuck to their research, year after year, big names in their fields, yet not capitalizing upon it as they might.)

One controversy I recall which excited us for awhile was caused when President Coolidge dispatched marines to Nicaragua to help the existing government, which was properly protecting the interests of American financiers, from a revolution led by a gentleman named Sacasa. Some of the Democrats and Republican insurgents in the Senate raised the cry of "dollar diplomacy," and thought this interference in a Latin American nation's internal affairs was none of our business. Secretary Kellogg threw a lot of documents at the Senate Foreign Relations Committee to try to prove that Soviet Russia was mixed up in all this, that a Bolshevik "hegemony," as the State Department called it, was being created in Central America. Coolidge said it had been proved that Mexico was sending arms to the revolutionaries. We were having our troubles with Mexico about that time, too. She was confiscating lands of American oil companies in the first harbinger of a new policy of "Mexico for Mexicans" which has extended down to our day.

President Coolidge had a way of picking men to take such problems over for him, and settle them. He sent Henry L. Stimson, former Secretary of War, subsequently Secretary of State in the Hoover administration, to Nicaragua, and Stimson straightened that matter out, supervising an election which upheld the existing order, quietly disarming the revolutionists, without any retaliations permitted. To Mexico he sent Dwight W. Morrow, partner in J. P. Morgan and Company, who proved to be an able and realistic diplomat. Morrow amicably adjusted the oil controversy for the time being.

In the one really disturbing domestic dilemma, an anthracite strike in Pennsylvania, President Coolidge also delegated powers very shrewdly and satisfactorily. He called Governor Pinchot to Washington and talked to him at the

White House. He turned the job over to Pinchot, told him to settle the dispute. One of our reporters who knew Pinchot described a scene in the library of Pinchot's Washington home on "N" street after the governor had come back from the White House. Pinchot was delighted that Coolidge had turned the problem completely over to him. Excitedly he walked up and down his library, rubbing his hands.

"I didn't think he'd do it—I didn't think he'd do it," he kept repeating.

He could not have known the President very well.

The really sensational event of the Coolidge administration was the simple act that presaged its end.

"I do not choose to run for President in 1928," broke upon Washington like a thunderclap.

I have heard Paul Mallon, who was covering Coolidge's vacation in South Dakota that summer, describe how the President, at one of the press conferences which were held in a little schoolhouse, handed out typewritten slips of paper with those ten words upon it. What a mad scramble for the wires! We searched out the few politicians who still were about Washington in the summer recess to get their reaction. Senator Smoot of Utah looked at the bulletin, read it over and over, scratched his head.

"I don't know what it means—I don't believe he means it," he finally said.

This cryptic statement of the President, so typical, provoked a great national debate. He must have enjoyed that privately, in his way. He couldn't mean it, said some. He was just bluffing, was the reaction among many. Editors went to their thesaurus of idioms and discovered, and so pointed out, that "I do not choose" is a strong phrase in Vermont, that it means, plainly and simply "I won't." Whatever he might have meant—and you can get up an argument today in Washington—there was one man who took the idiomatic Vermont meaning that the editors had discovered very literally. That was Herbert Hoover. He immediately started his campaign for the office for which he had itched for eight years, and toward which he had directed every step that he took. The Mississippi River had broken from its bounds that spring to give Herbert Hoover another opportunity to show himself as the great organizer and humanitarian that he is. For weeks he had directed gigantic relief operations from a river boat. Even Nature helped him toward the pinnacle.

President Coolidge sat on the mountain top and watched the sun of Prosperity sink slowly toward its setting and came down in the afterglow, gathered his belongings from the White House, and he and Mrs. Coolidge moved out one rainy day.

He retired, still a god.

"It always rains on moving day," he is credited with saying to Mrs. Coolidge as he arose and looked out the White House window that March 4.

But the real downpour began later.

The clouds have rolled clear across the heavens, as I write. The lightning streaks across the sky and the thunder rumbles grimly. Now the rain begins to fall, in big drops. The people along the beach hurriedly pick up their belongings, clutching umbrellas, beach chairs, robes and books, and dash hurriedly for shelter.

Then the heavens open. The water comes down in sheets.

BOOK THREE

THE MAN WHO

19

A CHUNKY, broad-shouldered Negro, his face a glistening coal black, stood up in the Georgia delegation at the back of the convention hall and shouted for recognition:

"Mr. Che-e-e-rman!"

Senator George Moses of New Hampshire, permanent chairman of the 1928 Republican Convention at Kansas City, shouted back:

"For what purpose does the gentleman arise?"

The Negro threw back his head, opened his mouth wide and bellowed:

"Hoov-ah!"

Delegates howled in glee. Their Georgia colleague knew what he was here for. He had succinctly stated the purpose of this national convention, the nomination for President, at last, of the man who had looked forward since 1920 to this day.

Herbert Hoover was nominated. California was ready for this hour. She had provided noise-makers of all sorts which she distributed lavishly. California delegates started a mad parade around the hall, following behind their own band which blared "California, Here I Come." Delegates from other states swarmed into line. Again, from the press box, I watched one of those scenes that still give me a thrill— pumped up, arranged, and artificial though I knew it was. For over an hour the jubilation filled the great hall.

This was the climax. But it had not been quite so easy as that.

For Andrew W. Mellon's permission was necessary first. The little man still was a power. The motions of getting Mellon's approval were preliminary to this ecstatic scene here at night on the convention floor—and they were comic. They struck me so then, comic and somehow a bit tragic—for representative democracy.

Herbert Hoover came to this convention with nearly a majority of the delegates already in his pocket. He was supposed to be the choice of the rank and file, the popular choice, not the choice of the politicians, the bosses. That was the way in which his candidacy had been built up.

But there was one boss who must be appeased and convinced. That was Mellon.

The little banker arrived in Kansas City with such welcomes as are accorded conquering heroes back from the wars. For days the newspapers had prepared the way; had emphasized that the final word on the Hoover candidacy was his. For the man who had sat behind Coolidge for five years, who had been the symbol of Coolidge Prosperity, was thought not to look so kindly upon Herbert Hoover. There still was talk of a "draft Coolidge" movement which kept the Hoover forces on edge and it was suspected that perhaps Mellon was a party to this. "When Mellon Arrives" —ran the newspaper headlines.

And now he was here, timid and blinking in the aura provided by Kansas City at the railroad station. There was a band to meet him and a large crowd of people to see the god who ran the prosperity machine and reduced taxes and was so encouraging always about how good business was. The god drew within himself at this welcome. He had not expected it. He was not one for public display, nor one to be displayed publicly. He fingered his little black cigar

224

nervously and his mouth opened and closed, in that way he had, with soft sounds emerging, difficult to distinguish, hardly complete words.

His entourage let it be known that he would have a press conference at eight o'clock that evening in his hotel suite.

Then the great man would speak and the world would know.

But there was another man there from Pennsylvania with some pretensions as a boss in his own right, the dumpy William S. Vare, the Republican boss of Philadelphia. He sent word around to the newspaper offices that he would have a press conference at 7:30. This was getting to be fun.

In a drove we descended upon his hotel suite at the appointed hour. He came into the sitting room, his pudgy hands clutching some typewritten sheets. He said that he had a statement. In a moment he was in the midst of a surging mob of newspaper reporters who reached for the papers in his hand. He was bewildered. I can see him now trying to protect himself as we grabbed at the typewritten pages. The mob had seen there were not enough copies and everyone was trying to get his now. I got one—that was what I was there for; and, as those of us who were lucky left, I looked back to see the politician still standing there, looking about as if dazed.

But he, it turned out, had done a very nice night's job for himself. He said in his statement that he thought Pennsylvania should be for Herbert Hoover. He controlled a block of delegates. He had beat the great Mellon to the draw. He was trying, single-handed, to force Mellon's hands and swing the state in line behind Hoover. Vare had a selfish motive. His election to the Senate in 1926, in which, incidentally, he had defeated the Mellon candidate, Senator George Wharton Pepper, had been challenged on account of the huge sum spent in the campaign—nearly $2,000,000—and he still was waiting for a decision as to his right to occupy the seat. He wanted Hoover's support in this personal emergency. (Eventually he was refused his seat, but he saw an opportunity at this time to curry favor with Herbert Hoover.) I wrote a story that night about how the Philadelphia boss had stolen a march on the great Mellon and, when I returned to Washington later, I was told by our man at the Treasury that it aroused resentment among the Mellon lieutenants there. It was lèse majesté of the rankest sort, unmitigated heresy, to the Mellon sycophants.

But this night's business had just begun.

The Mellon press conference was postponed. There were to be conferences of leaders. I had learned about conferences of leaders at New York four years before, and I prepared myself for a long evening of gumshoeing.

Paul Mallon and I were assigned to the conferences which were being held on various floors of the Muhlbach Hotel. Paul followed Vare from his hotel to the Muhlbach, took the same elevator, and got off when Vare did at the sixth floor. The Philadelphia boss ambled hesitantly down the corridor, looking anxiously to either side, finally spied a stairway and then walked down to the third floor! In the numerous conferences that night were representatives of Calvin Coolidge, including his secretary, Everett Saunders, former Congressman from Indiana. The political leaders were sneaking up and down the stairways, like house detectives. Every now and then one would pop through a stairway door and slip down the hall to another room. I ran into Mellon once, a furtive little figure, as he made his way from one room to another.

So this was the way Presidents were selected!

I was assigned the next morning to cover the meeting of the Pennsylvania delegation when the Mellon word was expected. After the meeting had been formally opened, the Pittsburgh banker-boss got to his feet and in his shy, stuttering manner said that he thought Pennsylvania should give its votes to Herbert Hoover. That's all I needed to know. That's all the world needed to know. That's all Herbert Hoover needed to know. I dashed away with the news.

But Herbert Hoover did not escape without a foretaste of trouble to come. The farmer, who rose up to plague him and to smite him four years later, was present at Kansas City—both in the body and in the spirit. Delegations of farmers were on hand. They held meetings and paraded and even tried to get into the convention hall. They were checked, however, at the door. A Republican convention was not yet, after all, a public forum for disgruntled groups. Everything must be done in order.

The farmers had their champion, their candidate, in a personage of rather contradictory lineage, when you considered that Former Governor Frank O. Lowden of Illinois was a man of some means and had married into the plutocratic Pullman family. He was a farmer in his own right, yes, a gentleman farmer who sat placidly among his plentiful acres at Oregon, Ill., with his blooded cattle and his agricultural experiments, and cared not for the cost. The phlegmatic calm of the squarish gentleman farmer was not disturbed by surpluses, by low prices, but he had a political interest in all these matters. He had seized upon the McNary-Haugen bill formula and this was his platform before the farmers to challenge Herbert Hoover.

Calvin Coolidge had raised up trouble for the man he called "The Wonder Boy" by vetoing the McNary-Haugen bill virtually on the eve of the convention. This had aroused the farmers and had given them—and Lowden—a cause.

The gentleman farmer entered the convention with a nice chunk of votes and a then friend of the farmer as his political general—the silver-haired Lester J. Dickinson of Iowa, who had achieved some recognition among the farmers as head of the farm bloc in the House.

Herbert Hoover had on his side an even more formidable figure. Senator William E. Borah of Idaho delivered himself up, influence, statesmanlike presence, magnetic voice and all, to the nomination of the Great Engineer—much to the annoyance of some of his progressive friends. Again he was the unpredictable Borah. He fought off in his magnificent manner the threat of McNary-Haugenism. It was defeated in the Resolutions Committee and, laid before the convention in a minority report, was gracefully embalmed in the sweet and suffocating tones of the Idaho Senator's condemnation.

This offered Gentleman Farmer Lowden an opportunity for the grand gesture. He took it. He wired the convention that he was no longer interested since his cherished "equalization fee" solution of the farm problem had been discarded. He asked that his name be withdrawn. (He saw the Hoover juggernaut steaming up for his destruction.) His telegram was read to the convention by Dickinson, and we wrote finis in the press section upon that little bit of excitement—and wondered how long Bill Borah would stick by Herbert Hoover.

Borah's hand had been in the making of the farm plank which, among other things, called for creation of a Federal Farm Board to supervise the marketing of surpluses. The Idaho Senator served Herbert Hoover nobly, too, in smothering another element of discontent, and this task was much to his liking. He relished the skirmish with the wets—it was hardly more than that—who wanted the Republicans to declare for repeal of the Eighteenth Amendment and the Volstead Act. Borah was a sincere prohibitionist. He bowled over the wet opposition in the Resolutions Committee which then adopted the plank he had drafted pledging vigorous enforcement of the Eighteenth Amendment and the Volstead Act. Dr. Nicholas Murray Butler offered from the floor a plank urging repeal of the amendment and the act. He was hooted down without the further embarrassment of a roll-call.

The mildly revolutionary spirit which I had seen astir in one quarter of the Republican Party in 1924, which had broken loose and spread itself through the land under the direction of Senator Robert M. LaFollette and attracted the support of nearly 5,000,000 voters, now was only an inert bird with broken wings. Liberalism of the militant and aggressive sort had been supplanted by a middle-class fervor which was concerned with material blessings for itself. Its god was Herbert Hoover. Many who had followed Bob LaFollette professed to see some symptoms of liberalism in Hoover, resorting to that species of wishful thinking with which so-called "liberals" deceive themselves. They were amazed later at their own self-hypnosis.

There was an echo of "Fighting Bob" in his son, Robert M. LaFollette, Jr., who had succeeded to the family seat in the Senate. "Young Bob," as he then popularly was called, was awarded the privilege of presenting the minority farm plank advocating the "equalization fee" principle of the McNary-Haugen bill. He was a zealous and eager young man preaching to hard-hearted but friendly elders. The latter took it all in good spirit—just a young fellow feeling his wings—and the hall thundered with the most sincere personal ovation of the entire convention. The young man's face glowed and his voice rang with earnest fervor as he evangelized from the pulpit that his father had deserted. He performed rousingly. Perhaps, in the hearty welcome of the convention there was, beyond a spontaneous tribute to a young man beginning his political career, a feeling among some of the older heads who had smarted under his father's thrusts that they might win the son over with kindliness. They did not know their young man.

He was a true-blue chip off the old block.

He was to me, also a young man looking for some faith to which to cling, a momentary flash of inspiration in a grey wilderness of conformity and orthodoxy which that 1928 convention represented to me. The Great God Borah had failed me, as he had done before, and was to do again, and yet I knew then, as I knew so often later when he disappointed me, that my personal admiration for the man would burn anew from time to time. I gave Young Bob a hand in a story I wrote, thus letting off a youthful enthusiasm which had no other outlet in this dull political event.

The perfect touch of irony, such as to satisfy the most cynical and furnish the satisfying jest, was the nomination of the solemn Senator Charles Curtis of Kansas as Vice Presidential candidate. Curtis, like Lowden and Senator Jim Watson of Indiana and a few others, had come to this convention as a candidate for President. He had for Herbert Hoover the distaste of the old-line politician. During the preliminary maneuvering the Kansas Senator had issued a biting blast at Hoover in which, among other castigations, he had challenged Hoover's Americanism. He referred to Hoover's long residence abroad. Curtis spoke as an aboriginal American. Indian blood flowed in his veins. When time came for the leaders to fit the picture puzzle together, the piece which they found best suited for the Vice Presidential space was none other than Curtis. He accepted.

I can see him yet as he stood before the convention gulping at his pride under the Klieg lights. He had eaten his bitter words, but he was suffering from indigestion, you could see. His bald head gleamed, as if still feverish with the indignity of second place on the ticket. His mustache twitched, in pain, as he tried to smile. It was only a contorted grin that creased his swarthy face.

In the press section we nudged each other and chuckled cruelly.

Politics begins to affect you that way in time.

A railroad journey and I was among the Democrats at Houston, Tex.

What I recall most vividly about this convention—and I assume that's true of everyone who was there—was the constant line of people waiting for the elevators in the Rice Hotel, and the terrific heat. If you were patient enough, you could get up to your room eventually. The United Press workroom was on the seventh floor and that was high up. We commandeered a freight elevator by slipping fifty cents to the Negro boy at frequent intervals.

There was not much doubt about the outcome there. The Democrats had decided to make good for Al Smith, who had run well in the primaries that year. His 1924 rival, William G. McAdoo, had cleared the way by announcing several months ahead of time that he would not be a candidate.

But the Southerners still resisted. They rallied about "favorite sons," Senator George of Georgia and Representative Cordell Hull of Tennessee, in an effort to seal an alliance that would check Smith from the necessary two-thirds. The other substantial candidate was the bitter-tongued Senator Jim Reed of Missouri. Reed had been a violent anti-prohibitionist. In a move to realize his ambition, and to curry favor with hostile Southern drys, he had issued a statement backtracking on his strong "wet" stand through the years. Ambition will do strange things to a man. But the "allies" that we have at so many conventions—and the newspapers always can find them—could not rally sufficient strength. Al Smith won on the first ballot and Senator Joseph T. Robinson of

Arkansas, Senate minority leader, and permanent chairman of this convention, was nominated as Vice Presidential candidate.

Little incidents color my memory of that Houston convention.

One day early in the convention workmen came into the hall with huge bags which they attached to ropes and drew up to the roof of the convention hall. I inquired what they were—but the workmen maintained a mystifying silence. During the session that day one of the bags began to let go its cargo. Slowly balloons began to drift down upon the heads of the delegates. Printed in gold letters across the red surface was "Jesse H. Jones for President." Houston had its own candidate, its banker, real estate owner and liege lord. Too bad that the show was spoiled. For the balloon shower was scheduled for two days later when the banker's name was to be put in nomination for President. When it came it was an anticlimax.

I was assigned to cover the prayer meetings which a group of Southern women held at noon every day to implore the Lord against the nomination of "that man Smith." Every day they gathered and angrily and resentfully complained to the Lord like clucking hens. It was a sorry assignment in my eyes. But, for that convention, I was, among other things, "woman's editor." After a few of these prayer meetings I went in one day to the room of the late Robert J. Bender, then general news manager of the United Press, and bewailed my assignment bitterly. I was tired, I told him frankly, of being "woman's editor." He was lying on his bed resting. He almost went into hysterics. My serious manner, my description of my troubles, somehow struck his sense of humor—and he had a good one. He rolled and howled. I saw the joke myself.

"You've done a good job," he said. "I'll try to get someone else to take it over—but it's all so funny."

I retained the title—for a long time, at least in Bob's eyes. He was such a grand fellow.

I guess it must have been in this capacity that I was assigned, the night that Smith was to be nominated, to write about his wife who was in Houston for the convention and occupied a box along the side of the arena. I clung to the side of the box and watched her face and her actions as her husband was declared the nominee and the usual demonstration started. She wept a little and waved her hand at the tumultuous delegates as they paraded about the hall.

For the second time I heard Franklin D. Roosevelt of New York nominate Al Smith. In New York I had seen him pull himself to the microphone on his crutches and praise his friend and term him "the happy warrior." Before that, in 1920, he had nominated Smith at the San Francisco Democratic Convention. Now he was standing behind Smith again. I was much impressed by Franklin Roosevelt on those two occasions. His face fascinated me and his delivery was pleasing and effective.

Al Smith was not at this convention. But he gave it a very proper jolt by telegraph. Despite the fact that the convention had adopted a plank pledging enforcement of the prohibition laws and making no mention or suggestion of a change, Smith boldly told the delegates, in effect, that he would not be bound by this section of the platform and felt it his duty as party nominee to point the way to a change.

"It is well known," he declared, "that I believe there should be fundamental changes in the present provisions for national prohibition, based, as I stated in my Jackson Day letter, on the fearless application to the problem of the principles of Jeffersonian Democracy. While I fully appreciate that these changes can only be made by the people themselves through their elected legislative representatives, I feel it to be the duty of the chosen leader of the people to point the way, which in his opinion leads to a sane, sensible solution of a condition which I am convinced is entirely unsatisfactory to the great mass of the people."

Some of the Southerners were wrathy.

"We told you so," they said.

Some of them accused him of accepting the nomination on false pretenses. They said he should have sent his message before the balloting.

They had done their duty. They had nominated him.

Let him try to go out and get himself elected.

That was the attitude in many parts of the South.

It was whisky, yes—partly. It was religious prejudice, mostly. And it was also a man from the East Side, from alien New York, who talked out of the corner of his mouth and said "foist" instead of "first"—not a great deal different from the pronunciation one hears in the South.

Hoover and Smith.

The great battle of 1928 was on.

20

THIS was the battle of the high stiff collar and the brown derby.

The high collar was the sort that Herbert Hoover wore when I first knew him as Secretary of Commerce. It pushed up under his round, chubby chin. It stood for the sound respectable citizen, the solid businessman, the man who busied himself about community affairs, the orthodox, the conservative. It stood for his wife who was interested in her clubs and her movements. It stood also for the man and woman who had not quite reached the solid businessman circles and the women's club circles—for they had not yet acquired the necessary income—but they were looking hopefully toward it in these days when the country seemed on the verge of what the popular economists called "The New Era."

Al Smith was the man of the brown derby. To the solid citizen and his wife and those who were aspiring to that class, the brown derby was the symbol of the class below, the class represented in New York's East Side and in the East Sides of their own towns and cities, what they would call, raising their noses slightly, "riffraff." The brown derby and Smith, to them, represented the "mob." (It recalled too well what some of them had come from.) It also represented the barroom and the pool parlor and the flashy sport. To the rebels in American society—and they reached up and down through all strata; to those who loved life and a drink of whisky and a glass of beer—to these Al Smith and the brown derby represented freedom and gaiety and the full, rounded existence. He represented a revolt against stuffiness—and America was very stuffy in those days, in some respects.

This also was the campaign of "Onward Christian Soldiers" (standing somehow for an aroused and militant Protestantism) against that lively air "The Sidewalks of New York." How weary I grew that year of both!

Al Smith's campaign was a circus with bands and clowns— of which he was the chief; with animals and sideshows and a cold bottle of beer as you left the tent.

Herbert Hoover's was a somber crusade of uplift to a high plateau where every man would be a capitalist and could belong to a country club.

I saw much, as a reporter, of both the high stiff collar and the brown derby.

But before I began to follow Al Smith in that cavalcade through the West, I was assigned for a few weeks to cover Democratic and Republican campaign headquarters in New York City. There I came to know the stolid, serious little multimillionaire, John J. Raskob, chairman of the Democratic National Committee and manager of Smith's campaign. We saw him, day after day, in those elaborate and munificent political headquarters which he had provided in the General Motors Building. It was a paradox that Raskob was managing Smith's campaign. His kind fitted much better with the Hoover crowd—big business and all that. But Smith's campaign, directed as one would suppose to the common people, had this same paradox running all through it. Big Money had its hands about Smith, too. He was not the defiant rebel. He catered as well to the man who had it and expected to get more of it. He was not out to do any uprooting—except of prohibition. He discussed fundamental issues, but he never went too far.

Raskob was a devoted and hopeful campaign director. He saw rainbows easily—as might be expected of a man who had no previous political experience, who did not know that all the money you passed out to party hacks did not necessarily go into rounding up votes, who did not know that the promises of party hacks, their optimistic reports, had to be discounted; that you can trust few people in politics, and you want to be careful even of those. One day he came into the regular press conference at noon with reports from Pennsylvania. Then and there he predicted that Smith would carry Pennsylvania. We gave him a respectful hearing and reserved our smiles until later. He was such a nice, pleasant fellow. I liked him.

236

There too, at Democratic national headquarters, I met Mrs. Eleanor Roosevelt for the first time. (In my capacity, of course, still as "woman's editor." I was supposed to get a story on the woman's angle from time to time.) She was directing the campaign among women. I interviewed her about her activities. She was helpful and pleasant.

At Republican headquarters one day in New York (I shuttled between the two sets of offices all day long), I witnessed an enlightening episode. We had been tipped that something important might be expected. We waited in the reception room. The door opened and Senator George Moses, Eastern campaign director, entered with an elderly figure on his arm. Then I recognized him. It was the Democratic Senator Robert L. Owen of Oklahoma. The Senator had a statement to make, Senator Moses advised us, with an air of "Boys, listen to this!" Owen announced he was for Herbert Hoover. He was bolting the party—not the first nor the last in that campaign. Owen had some standing as a Democratic leader. The quarrel still goes on today as to whether he, who was Chairman of the Senate Banking Committee in the Wilson Administration, or Carter Glass, who was Chairman of the House Banking Committee, was the real author of the Federal Reserve Act.

Owen was bolting. Senators Furnifold Simmons of North Carolina and Tom Heflin of Alabama, also refused to support Smith. This was an inkling of what was going on in my South.

Later, at Albany, I climbed Capitol Hill every day for Smith's regular press conferences. They alternated between his offices there and the governor's mansion. The conferences were at noon. Smith was a late riser. We liked that. We also liked the frankness with which he answered questions in his husky voice and his salty expressions and his very human touch.

Then came the great adventure in the West with the man from the East Side to whom that country and its people were alien, and to whose people and viewpoints he was an alien. He came buoyantly down to the luxurious special train at Albany that night of departure—and he had on a brown derby. So he was going to wear it after all. We discovered that this had been the subject of much controversy in the family. But Smith, like Abraham Lincoln with his Cabinet, voted his lone "Aye" and the "Ayes" had it. That was settled. The home-town folks of Albany gave him a hearty send-off; I dispatched a lead about the brown derby going into the West—and we were off.

Of that campaign trip there is one outstanding impression —the train rolling slowly to a stop; fields of eager faces going by the windows, eyes virtually boring into the train looking for "Al," and then always and forever, the notes of "The Sidewalks of New York," expertly and in rhythm by uniformed bands in the big cities, less expertly in the medium towns and, in small towns, a raucous blast that swept in upon the train from the amateurs gathered together, sour notes, raw notes, but still recognizable:

"The Sidewalks of New York."

In the big cities, and occasionally in some of the smaller ones, we paraded. The multitudes had gathered, as for a circus, to see this strange fellow from New York. And he never disappointed. He was ever the consummate actor— brown derby cocked jauntily, then off and up in his hand in friendly welcome, cigar in the corner of his mouth. Through long lanes of Midwestern and Western folks we drove. In Denver they gave the procession a baptism of ticker tape, reminiscent of Al's own New York and in that parade he sat back on the folded-up top of the car, waving his derby up at the windows of the buildings, grinning at the people along the sidewalk. We got off at Butte, Mont., for a parade through that drab little mining town, with its scores of saloons in that dry era. Tiny little tots were lined up in front of a Catholic school that we passed, the sisters standing there with them, and, as we went by, they said in unison:

"One-two-three-four, who are we for—Al Smith."

Everywhere they turned out to see him—curious crowds, but cheerful and cheering, for the most part. The impression was of the West up in arms for this fellow, that is, the impression to one who did not go below the surface, who wanted to see it that way as did Al and his political associates, who wanted to accept the inquisitive throngs as an outpouring of loyal support, which, of course, it was not. Mostly it was curiosity. These folks went back home, at least a majority of them, thought it all over, and then voted in November for Herbert Hoover.

One night at dinner, after we had come all day through eager and excited crowds gathered in Kansas towns, a New York reporter who had stuck rather closely heretofore to the metropolis, wanted to bet me that Smith would carry Kansas. I told him it was impossible. I would not take his money.

Gradually I had been storing up impressions of these Midwestern and Western people. I had talked with local newspapermen. I heard the stories of the "whispering campaign" going on against the man from New York. Midwestern people, I decided, were a good deal like Southerners in some respects. I saw how the religious issue would react here against him; also, his anti-prohibition views and his general type—the "city feller"—who was regarded suspiciously by the simpler folks on the western plains and in the small, homey Midwestern towns.

This is not second-guessing after the fact. On the train returning from that Western trip, upon request from my New York office for a memorandum as to Smith's prospects in the states we had visited, I wrote a report in which I analyzed my impressions about as I've set them down here and concluded that there were only two states in which Smith had a chance, Wisconsin and Nebraska, with his chances better in the former than the latter.

Incidents here and there, small things it is true, seemed to me significant.

As we were pulling out of a small town in Nebraska little boys ran along by the train shouting: "Alcohol Al! Alcohol Al!"

We stopped one night for a few moments in a small Indiana town. I walked along the track outside to get some fresh air. People had gathered to see the train and to get a glimpse of the Democratic Presidential candidate. Many were clustered about the private car "St. Nicholas" furnished by Smith's wealthy friend, William F. Kenny, who was along on this trip. It was used by Smith and his immediate party. They craned their necks to see inside. I could see Smith there, leaning over. I judged he was patting a dog that was along on the trip.

"I bet he's shooting craps," someone in the crowd said, with a sneaky chuckle.

In Oklahoma City there was resentment in the air.

We rode through thousands and thousands of people who lined the streets, several deep, but they were not enthusiastic. There was hardly any cheering. For the most part they looked on silently. The Ku Klux Klan had befouled the atmosphere here. It was that night that Al struck out bluntly against religious intolerance and bigotry and the "whispering campaign." He paid his respects to Senator Robert L. Owen, curling his lips sarcastically as he spit forth his scorn.

240

More lightly he dealt with Mabel Walker Willebrandt, the woman assistant attorney general in charge of prohibition enforcement who had gone out to Ohio to address Methodist Church groups and had aroused criticism of her speeches as designed to stir up religious prejudice. Humorously he referred to "up in Mabel's room." It was one of his best efforts. His mimicry was delightful.

As we left Oklahoma City and rolled along through the countryside, a report passed along the train that a cross was seen burning far away on a hillside. I did not see it. But the report was symptomatic of the sensitivity to the Klan issue among those on the train.

Al Smith had to make his own speeches in his own way. When he was to speak we would get during the afternoon, and sometimes not so early in the afternoon, the prepared text of the speech he was to deliver that night so that we could write our leads and get off an advance story. But, in the hall, before the crowd, he would discard his text and talk as the occasion inspired. He followed the general theme of the prepared text. But he made it fresh and alive when he spoke. That always meant a new lead at night to catch up in print some of the clever phrases that he would blurt out on the spur of the moment. His speeches were a constant joy. He was more than a speaker. He was an actor. (He used to tell us proudly about his amateur acting at the parish hall when he was a young man.) On that trip every speech was just as much fun to me—and I think to the other newspapermen—as to the fresh audience he faced. That is not usually true of the speaker you must follow, day in and day out, in political campaigns.

But there was one subject on which he did not trust himself to ad lib—and this discloses a bit of political trickery. This was farm relief. He opened his campaign at Omaha, Neb., with a farm speech. On farm relief he had sought the advice of George N. Peek, who was then campaigning for the McNary-Haugen bill with an organization called The Committee of Forty-eight. Peek was active all during that period in behalf of farm legislation and was, for a time, associated with the Roosevelt New Deal later as AAA Administrator. Peek had worked out a formula for Smith on farm relief for that opening address which was his major appeal for the farm vote. They had spent a long time at it. We were late getting that first speech. The formula mentioned the McNary-Haugen bill, but it did not specifically endorse it. But, when Smith shouted the magic name to the audience that night and into the radio the impression was that he had come out for it. The audience burst its buttons. Always after that, when he mentioned farm relief, he would pause, pull out his paper, and say:

"I gave a prescription for farm relief in my speech at Omaha. And here is that prescription."

He always read it. He did not trust himself to speak extemporaneously about this delicate subject. He stuck to his prescription.

Al Smith was a godsend to the newspaperman—for comfort, convenience, and necessity.

Never was there a campaign train set-up such as was provided for newspapermen on that 1928 Smith train. On such trains the newspaper reporter usually works in his compartment. In addition, on this train, there also was provided a special Pullman car with a score of typewriters, useful for the visiting correspondents who would get on for a day or so crossing their own state, and also useful when it was necessary to write late at night, as I did, because you would not disturb those who wanted to sleep. The train was equipped with a complete mimeographing office set up in a baggage car, so that, only a few minutes after a press conference on the train, there would be delivered at our compartments a complete question and answer on the Smith press conference.

We had daily conferences with Smith in the club car at noon. These were especially valuable on long hops where there would be few stops and no major set speech, therefore no outstanding spot-news development, for the cross-fire at the press conference, with his keen wit and his perpetually amusing wisecracks, would always furnish us a good, live column of stuff.

There was such a conference one day in North Dakota. For hours we had been riding across that bare country. Someone asked Smith how he liked it.

"You just sit by the window all day and see nothing," he commented.

He was a born New Yorker.

In time we got back. Covering Al Smith was one of the most enjoyable experiences of my life.

It was with keen disappointment then that I was waked one morning, soon after we returned to Albany from that Western trip, by a telegram from the office instructing me to report to Washington to cover Herbert Hoover. Paul Mallon, who had been with Hoover, was to take over Smith. The office wanted to have two men on the staff who would be familiar with the next President. The switch now would assure that. So I reported back to Washington.

The contrast was marked, to say the least.

I was aware of this soon after I walked into the big stone residence on Massachusetts Avenue, just off Sheridan Circle, now an embassy, which was Hoover's political headquarters. There he kept office hours during the day. His home was just around the corner on S Street. There was much formality here. Reporters seldom saw Hoover, himself. The whole prospect was gloomy and forbidding. Nor did I get a very good introduction in my transfer to Hoover. I walked through the big glass doors that first day and was greeted by a newspaper friend with a shout:

"Well—a spy from Al Smith, huh?"

One of the Hoover attachés who sat at a desk, a very proper young man, looked up, startled. He always seemed to regard me suspiciously thereafter.

Hoover's office was on the second floor and we picked up our news from a steady stream of visitors and occasional official announcements. From those days in the big house I got the impression, which was enhanced as the campaign progressed, of a man who was withdrawing himself, who was becoming very cautious, who was uncertain and indecisive. There was a transformation from the bold public figure who had been presented to the country in the days before his nomination. He seemed to want to hide away. He hesitated to speak plainly and in a forthright manner. Perhaps it was due to the pressures coming in upon him from conflicting groups—on one hand, the push of those "liberals" who had promoted his nomination and were sure he was one of them, and the pull back, on the other hand, of the interests who were represented in Andrew Mellon's support.

This was illuminated vividly one day.

After his opening speech at Elizabethton, Tenn., he was quoted in an interview in the *Knoxville News-Sentinel,* the Scripps-Howard newspaper there, as being in favor of government development at Muscle Shoals. Subsequently, it was indicated that this was not exactly his view, and the question was raised as to his exact stand.

We were promised a statement. All day there was much activity about the headquarters. The late James Francis Burke, counsel of the Republican National Committee, was in consultation with the nominee. Finally, about six o'clock, we were handed a statement. The other two press association men and I rushed down to our telephone booths and stepped inside. I read the statement hastily, before picking up the telephone to dictate to the office, then I read it again slowly and carefully. I could not understand it. I could not say in a one paragraph lead what it meant. Confused, I stepped out of my booth. Simultaneously, the other two men stepped from theirs. Almost in one breath, we all asked:

"What does it mean?"

We tried to figure it out again.

I finally solved my problem by dictating that "Herbert Hoover tonight issued the following statement" and then gave the office the text. The editorial writers could bother their heads over what it meant. I heard later there was plenty of bother.

A few days before election we started a swift transcontinental train journey to the Pacific Coast so that Hoover could vote at home in Palo Alto. We stopped briefly at Louisville, St. Louis, and Pueblo, Colo., for speeches.

On this trip I began to observe the almost physical horror, the evident recoil, when Herbert Hoover made a public speech. He was a timid person before a crowd. He would hide his face in his manuscript and go to the task as if it were something that must be borne. He would plod through it without relish or enthusiasm. This surprised me for I had sat before him many times at press conferences when he was Secretary of Commerce. He was easy, fluent, expressive, and in those days was a source of much information. But how he hated to face a crowd, even a small one, in a political rôle!

We stopped at a tank town in Nevada for water. Stretching away on every side was that bleak, raw country with the stern, bare mountains in the distance. It was just at dusk. Hoover went out on the back platform for a breath of air. A few persons gathered about the rear end of the train. A weathered little old man spoke up and addressed the Presidential candidate and Hoover chatted with him. Hoover told how he had worked in a mine in this country when he was a young man. Then the little old man said:

"What are you going to do about lead, Mr. Hoover?"

A political inquiry. Hoover was abashed. He awkwardly turned the question aside. He had no political small talk.

Election night is, usually, a gala night—at least before the counting gets well under way. It was a gala night at the Hoover home which sits atop the hill on the campus of Stanford University, that is, so far as the college friends who had gathered in the big drawing room were concerned. But not for Herbert Hoover. He went about it all in a businesslike, statistical manner. In the room was a big blackboard which he had prepared, neat and authoritative, with the names of the states and the electoral votes of each. He moved about quietly before the board, a stubby pipe in his mouth. Press association wires set up in the basement were bringing in the returns. Methodically, while the numerous friends in for the occasion chatted with Mrs. Hoover, the man most concerned would quietly post the figures. Later moving pictures of the campaign trips were shown and Mrs. Hoover's voice rose out of the dark in explanation. Hoover moved about now here, now there.

Early in the evening the landslide became apparent. Our United Press wire was the first to bring in Smith's message congratulating Hoover on his election. I rushed this bulletin upstairs from below and it was read to the party. There was a ripple of reserved hand-clapping, no hilarity. These people seemed to be infected with the reserve of their host. His personality permeated the room. He showed no outward excitement.

Immediately I sought out George Akerson, Hoover's secretary and our press contact, to inquire about an answer. I supposed it would not be long delayed. But we didn't get the reply that night. It was not until two o'clock the next afternoon that it was handed to us. Shortly after the Smith message was read Hoover retired to his den with Akerson. (I have always imagined that this composition of a reply to Smith became a major task. I can imagine him bending to it with all his energy. He wanted to say just the proper thing. It was easier for Smith to congratulate the victor than for Hoover to write a message back to the vanquished. Hoover had his difficulties with composition, anyhow, and, despite that, he insisted on writing his own pronouncements. That was true later of his speeches and state papers when he was President.)

Up the hill, later in the evening, came the Stanford students. They stood outside in the night and serenaded the new President with college songs. It was a touching scene. He must have recalled his own college days here so long ago now. He and Mrs. Hoover stood on the balcony above the entrance. George Akerson objected the next day to my story in which I said that tears came into the eyes of the newly elected President, but I told him that my wife had been standing close by, that she was a good reporter, and I would have to stand by her report. They didn't seem to want him to appear human, even when he was.

Two weeks later we sailed away from San Pedro on a good-will mission to Central and South America on a battle-ship. Hoover's avowed purpose was to promote friendly relations, which meant to smooth out some ill feeling caused by what was popularly called "Yankee Imperialism" as practised under the Coolidge régime, and to safeguard our trade with our neighbors to the South from encroachments from abroad. This trip also offered a very convenient escape from the politicians who now were beginning to plague the new Chief Executive.

247

Just as we were leaving Palo Alto late in the afternoon for Los Angeles and San Pedro, a disturbance was created by the appearance of a group about the train waving banners denouncing "Latin American Imperialism" and carrying other slogans about American policy in Nicaragua where Calvin Coolidge had dispatched the marines. The President-elect already was safely in his private car, but the Secret Service men were worried. I was worried, too—but about the story—and my spirits were low at leaving and running off to South America. There was little time for farewells. As the train started off I shouted down to my wife to be sure to get the story and call the San Francisco United Press office and give it to them. She got it.

For the next six weeks we lived on a battleship, with forays ashore into quaint and dirty little Central American towns, into South America's big and handsome cities, always with a fanfare of parades and processions, smart and gaily capar-isoned cavalry escort, and among people who, for the most part, were hospitable. Our journey was broken in a trip across the Andes and the Argentine pampas in a special train from Santiago, Chile, to Buenos Aires. We had left the battleship *Maryland,* then flagship of the Pacific Fleet, which had brought us down the west coast and, at Monte-video, we went aboard the old *Utah* for our trip back up the east coast and home.

Soon after we were aboard, Hoover gathered us together and explained in a general way the purposes of the trip. He suggested that our ship should be called "Friendship Mary-land" instead of "Battleship Maryland" which we did not take seriously. (That was a smile—we didn't have so many on this adventure.) It was also suggested, since this was a deli-cate mission and South American governments and people were very sensitive, that we should be very careful of our stories off the battleship, for the inference would be that they represented an official viewpoint since the President-elect was aboard. Because there were eighteen newspaper correspondents on the trip who had to file dispatches, we had to work out some sort of a schedule. We held a meeting for this purpose. George Barr Baker, one of Hoover's assistants, suggested that the copy be turned over to him for filing. Subsequently we found out that he also had taken over the duties of an editor. The copy must have his approval before the naval communications operator would send it. Baker would read the copy and, on occasion, suggest to the correspondent that this or that be deleted. The explanation was that most of us were domestic correspondents unfamiliar with the South American field and its problems and, on account of our unfamiliarity, might say something that would offend and that this would react upon Hoover as coming from him. As soon as we reached the first stop for a visit, stories went out from the land cable offices about this arrangement, and we had a mild censorship scandal.

I repeat this story only because it gives a clue to the Hoover approach. The "censorship" was not terribly confining, because we could file what we pleased at our frequent visits ashore; but it was the principle of the thing that aroused resentments aboard ship.

I had an associate aboard who was thoroughly familiar with Latin America and its problems. That was Harry W. Frantz, cable editor of the United Press in Washington, who had come out to the coast to join the party for the journey. He wrote the major stories on the Latin American problem for the United Press on the trip while I devoted myself to the human interest angles. Harry had covered numerous South American missions in years past, and he was something of a father confessor for the correspondents aboard who had dealt largely with domestic affairs previously.

There was another incident that left a sour taste with reporters on that trip.

We anchored off Antofagasta, Chile, that little town which bakes in the sun on the edge of those drear nitrate plains. Hoover received the American Minister to Bolivia, Jay Kaufman, and a party of Bolivian officials for a conference. (War had just broken out between Bolivia and Paraguay over possession of the Gran Chaco which later caused so much pain in our State Department.) The newspaper correspondents were told that transportation would be provided ashore for them to visit Antofagasta during the luncheon and conference of President-elect Hoover and the officials, but that we must be back within an hour. It came time to sail and when noses were counted among the correspondents, it was discovered that three were missing. They had not yet returned to the battleship. They were William Philip Simms, foreign editor of the Scripps-Howard newspapers, the late Rodney Dutcher, Washington correspondent of the Newspaper Enterprise Association, and Edward Price Bell, chief of the *Chicago Daily News* foreign service. We waited for a few minutes. Hoover became impatient and ordered the battleship to sail. It was a harrowing experience for the three men, we learned later when they finally caught up with us at Santiago. They had met an Englishman who lived in Antofagasta and he invited them to his club. He promised them that he would see that they got back to the ship, as he had boats himself available for that purpose. After a friendly visit they emerged from the club to find that the battleship was no longer on the horizon. Then they were confronted with the problem of rejoining the party, somehow. Luckily they got hold of Minister Kaufman and he arranged transportation for them on a hand-car, one hundred miles to a military aviation field. This ride was not particularly pleasant. The army planes available would hold only two passengers. Simms and Bell got off first on that long flight across the Chilean nitrate wilderness and mountains and were landed at Santiago. Dutcher was taken up in another plane. I have heard him describe the incident. They got up about a mile, he said, and one of the wings began to shake loose, so the plane had to return and land. He had to wait for the other plane to come back from Santiago. He got into that city just about half an hour before the party was to leave for Buenos Aires.

At Buenos Aires and Montevideo we witnessed an out-cropping of anti-American feeling. A demonstration was staged about the American Embassy where President-elect Hoover was quartered, by a boisterous crowd who were chased away by the Argentine cavalry. As we approached the dock at Montevideo, across the River Plata from Buenos Aires, an angry cry "Viva Sandino!" burst from longshore-men gathered there. Sandino, the Nicaraguan rebel, was a symbol of anti-imperialism all through South America. We were not on the battleship, having come across from Buenos Aires on a river steamer.

We had what we called a "White Christmas" on the battleship, that is, we were all garbed in our white summer clothes. It was spent in tropical waters on the way home from Rio de Janeiro. We arrived at Norfolk early in January in a cold rainstorm. Hoover retired to his S Street home in Washington to receive visitors and plan his administration. We reporters had to stand outside on the sidewalk and catch visitors as they came and went. Washington had one of her occasional heavy snows and news photographers took pictures of us standing in two feet of snow "covering Hoover." After one of these appeared in a local paper, headquarters were moved to a hotel and there we had a press room where we could be out of the weather.

In late January the incoming administration moved its headquarters to Miami. There the Belle Isle estate of J. C. Penney, chain store magnate, was turned over to the President-elect. A temporary office was set up in a little building near the entrance to the grounds for the Hoover staff, but he remained at the house. There he received his visitors. We camped all day long in a summer house also near the entrance and convenient to the temporary offices.

President-elect Hoover we saw only at a distance all during that month we spent in Florida. We caught a glimpse of him occasionally as he rode by in his car. He did not hold a single newspaper conference. We were never inside the house.

On Thomas Edison's eighty-second birthday, President-elect and Mrs. Hoover went to Fort Myers to celebrate the occasion with him and Harvey L. Firestone and Henry Ford. These three took a vacation together every winter. The trip to Fort Myers was made with a party of friends on the yacht of Jeremiah Milbank, sailing around the Keys and back up the west coast. We went across state by automobile to cover the President-elect while there and also, incidentally, the annual "interview" which Edison delivered himself of each year. There was a question as to whether the official party would return to Miami Beach on the yacht or overland by car. If he returned across country it was our job to follow him. I stayed up until two o'clock trying to get the decision before writing my story for the next day and was finally advised that the President-elect would return on the yacht. The next morning when the two other press association men and I were at breakfast we heard a rumor that he had already left by automobile. We were finally able to get hold of a telegraph operator at a point near where the yacht was anchored, who verified the fact that he had left two hours before. We started a wild dash across the state, two hours behind the next President of the United States whose every movement we were supposed to follow like hawks. In the case of the President or the President-elect it is customary to keep reporters correctly advised on such a trip.

During those days, because of the lack of contact with Hoover, we did much of what we call "thumbsucking" for inspiration for "dope" stories. Some noble forecasts and dreams were imposed upon the American newspaper reading public in those days. We discovered later that every member of the future Hoover Cabinet had been to Belle Isle to see him. But they came to the house at night when we were not around. A sports reporter for a Boston newspaper who was in Miami printed the story that Charles Francis Adams was expected to be Secretary of the Navy. He recognized him in a restaurant one night.

We did get a break when Al Smith visited Hoover one day.

We were allowed to select one of our number to go to the house, watch proceedings, and come back and tell us about it.

We learned something about Herbert Hoover in those days.

21

HOUR after hour at the Kansas City Republican Convention we had heard orator after orator talk about Herbert Hoover as "The man who did this" and "The man who did that." It happens at every convention. But never had a human being been so lauded, not only there but in the campaign which followed, as had Herbert Hoover.

He was the nation's "The Man Who."

Speakers who proclaimed his virtues, qualifications and experiences at the convention had a wealth of actual material at their command, which did not require the exaggeration to which the political speaker is addicted. Immediately they had his administration for eight years as Secretary of Commerce, which had endeared him to the middle-class businessman (Some of the big ones did not care so much for him.) He had made the Commerce Department one of the major departments of government as had been predicted when he took it over. Back beyond that was his relief work in Belgium, his reign as Food Administrator which made his name known to every housewife. And, back beyond that, was that vague, shadowy, glamorous Hoover, a man who had wandered into the far places of the earth as a promoter and a mining engineer, a figure of romance to the ordinary man. A man of India and Australia and Cathay and all the storied lands of the East.

Yes, Herbert Hoover had many attractions. He made a fascinating person to read about.

One of his chief attractions as a Presidential candidate, as the people looked upon him in those days, was that he was not a politician. The politician was in rather bad odor. The smell still hung over from those rapacious gentlemen who had made merry in the Harding administration. Calvin Coolidge even had talked once of the necessity of people using their franchise and voting—to keep the government from being taken over by "politicians." (And he was an astute politician, himself—which is not said in disparagement.)

The businessman had come to be glorified. He glorified himself, and his country glorified him. Why then, let's have a businessman as President! That's it! That's what we need in Washington, a businessman who'll keep these politicians in their places. We need a good sound business administration.

Hoover's qualifications for the high office, as they were assessed by the nation, seemed to be plentiful. He had proved himself an organizer and an administrator. Looked at coldly and realistically, with all the glamour cast aside and the fine phrases swept away, he did stand in many ways high above Harding and Coolidge. He seemed to have a breadth of understanding. He seemed to think in big, broad terms. He had seen much of the world. His intelligence was of a high order and he appeared to be motivated by generous impulses.

Why, then, did he fall so far? Why did his name become a slur on men's lips and a cruel joke?

He could not possibly have lived up, of course, to the man-god created in the minds of the people. He was too much "The Man Who." No one could have lived up to that legend, and it was bad for him that he started out that way. It would have been bad had times been good and his task not almost a superhuman one. It was tragic in view of the times in which he stepped into the Presidency.

An orphan boy, living with relatives, growing up in a still pioneer West, Herbert Hoover had few natural advantages when he started out. He had to fight for what he got, and he did fight his way up to the very top. He got little help and sympathy and he asked none. He dealt always with cold realities. He was a businessman, a promoter, and this, of itself, required a certain hard surface, a certain cold calculation.

How Herbert Hoover saw himself and his career and his country is indicated in his last speech to the Gridiron Club in Washington, December 10, 1932, just before he left office. The election was over. The Presidency was behind him.

"I notice in the press generous suggestions that my countrymen owe to me some debts," he had said on that occasion. "I have said in part elsewhere that on the contrary the debt is mine. My country gave me, as it gives every boy and every

255

girl, a chance. It gave me a schooling, the precious freedom of equal opportunity for advancement in life, for service and honor. In no other land could a boy from a country village without inheritance or influential friends look forward with unbounded hope. It gave to me a certain measure of success in my profession. It conferred upon me the honor of administering the world's response to the appeal of hundreds of millions of afflicted people during and after the war. It gave me high place in the war councils of the nation. My country called upon me to represent it in the reconstruction of human and economic relations between former enemies on the Continent of Europe after the Armistice. It gave me an opportunity for service in the Cabinets of two Presidents. It gave me the highest honor that comes to man—the Presidency of the United States. For this fullness of life—for the chance to serve in many emergencies, I am indebted to my country beyond any human power to say."

A poor orphan boy who became President.

What he did, others could do. He spoke the philosophy of the self-made man of his era. Despite the turmoil and trouble in the country, despite the paralysis in the economic system, he still saw America as the America in which he had grown up. This explains the stubborn fight he made throughout his administration to keep what he considered the democratic ideal—local responsibility, with the federal government keeping as far as possible from direct responsibility in the lives of its citizens.

He saw the rôle of the federal government as that of guide and coordinator.

He had never asked its help.

In the orphan boy who fought his way upward we can detect something of the reason why he could not understand the cry from the public for the federal government to intervene and why the people in need, who saw this in him, came in the end to abhor and hate him, to make a mockery of his name, and to say, ironically "The Great Engineer."

In his recital of the high services he had performed for his country there is, between the lines, the cry of a defeated and lonely man into the void, a question:

"Why could I not have succeeded as President?"

He had been a success in his own eyes and in the eyes of the world up to the Presidency.

In his 1932 campaign, he had gone back again and again over his record, telling what he had done.

Why had it all come to this?

Herbert Hoover still is asking the question. Today he is burning once again for an opportunity to sit in the White House and to show that he can master the only job at which he did not attain the success he had elsewhere; either that, or to see the man who succeeded him swept from office and another man, if not Hoover himself, with Hoover's ideas about government installed there to change the process and prove that his philosophy was the proper one. He wants vindication.

One of the supposed qualifications stressed in his campaign was that he was not a politician.

To this may be traced some of his undoing.

The experience of the man who gave him the oath of office, Chief Justice William Howard Taft, like himself the only other man in recent years who had come to the Presidency without a previous ordeal in elected public office, might have been a warning to Herbert Hoover.

Travelling with him and living close to him in the 1928 campaign, I had come to know his uncertainty in a political rôle. I had the added advantage of the contrast with a man who had spent most of his life in politics. Al Smith loved the crowd. He loved to talk to it. He had lived with it all his life.

Hoover was uncomfortable in the presence of mobs of his fellow citizens. He did not understand them. He shrank within himself.

Never before had he dealt with them as voters. He never had been a candidate for public office. He had never had to treat with man as a political animal, which is different from dealing with him as a businessman across the conference table; or dealing with him in great unidentified masses, such as was the case in his relief ventures; or dealing with him and his family as mere units in the economic system, which is part of the duty of a Secretary of Commerce.

Hoover basically had little patience with the political process as he found it operating practically in Congress—though he continued to fight for his theoretical ideal of democratic government. He had little instinct for dealing with politicians. They found that out and made life miserable for him.

He had been accustomed to handle large affairs. He made the decisions. He pressed the buttons. He gave the orders. They were carried out. That had been his way as a businessman and as Secretary of Commerce. He could do that still in administrative matters as President. But that is not possible in dealing with the men of Congress. They are not beholden to him. They owe their allegiance to the voters back home.

Herbert Hoover had none of the little political tricks that help a man in public office. He did not have the beguiling ways, the little meaningless niceties. He seemed to have little concept of human psychology. He lacked the sense of humor necessary to the politician. He was always deadly serious in the political rôle, though, in small groups, I discovered that he did have a rather good sense of humor. He never let it escape to the public where it would have done so much good. He lacked resiliency. In the prize-fighter's jargon, he did not know how to rock with the punch. (And how many he got!) He had a glass nose and a glass jaw. It was not until after the

258

Presidency that he acquired the humorous phrase in his speeches. (The times of his Presidency, it is true, did not offer much opportunity for humor. But a touch now and then might have helped. People could laugh, they proved.)

He spoke loftily of "the imponderables," of "the ebb and flow of economic life," when people were thinking of their bellies and of bread and meat. They weren't in a mood for lectures or high thinking or fine phrases. He could have used a ghost writer with a flair for the common phrase, the lowly human impulse, but he insisted on toiling through his speeches laboriously himself.

From the Hoover experience, I am convinced that the politician makes the best President. There are weak politicians, of course, like Harding, and politicians who just sit on the lid, like Coolidge. Of that type I am not speaking. But, given a man with broad understanding, knowledge and capabilities, I think he is only made ripe for the Presidency by experience which has taken him before the voters and made him responsible to the voters. That, I know, narrows our choice, because of the mediocrity of the run of American politicians.

Often I speculate upon the possibility if Hoover had been elected President in 1920, when he was a potential candidate. He was shunted aside, first by his indecision as to whether he was a Democrat or Republican, and, then, when he decided that he was a Republican, by the bosses of the Republican Party who did not want him. They were afraid of him in those days.

If elected then, he would have come to the office when he could have enjoyed the full reach of his powers without interference by the crushing, confusing forces of depression. It is impossible to imagine that his Cabinet would have included any Falls, Daughertys or Forbeses. In those flush times, he

259

might have gone down as one of our great Presidents. He had an understanding of the danger of the inflation and stock market speculation into which the country ran head-on under the Coolidge-Mellon direction. He had something to say of that at the time as a member of the Cabinet. He might, as President, have so managed affairs that the depression which hit him full blast in 1929 might have been minimized.

But this was not 1921.

This was 1929.

"The Man Who" came too late.

In a political trip through the country in early 1936 I talked with Hoover at his home in Palo Alto. I got the impression then that he approved of a good many of the Roosevelt objectives—but not of the methods—and that he had planned numerous reforms himself for his administration. But he was overwhelmed by the depression. There's no doubt about that.

22

IT was raining the day Herbert Hoover was inaugurated. But no one considered that an ill omen.

The new President was my assignment. For that day of his assumption I wrote a story decorated with homely, human details, how he had arisen, as usual, at seven o'clock and, as usual, had his breakfast alone at eight. I spoke of him as another farm boy who had become President, but I pointed out that he had wandered far from the farm over the highways of the world and entered the White House an international figure, a cosmopolite, with a rich background of experience in big affairs.

He held the promise of energy and action and he overshadowed, with his powerful physique and his air of nervous alertness, the smaller man with the long nose and glum expression who sat beside him in the automobile which took the outgoing Calvin Coolidge and the incoming Chief Executive down Pennsylvania Avenue to the Capitol.

Herbert Hoover came to the Presidency under most favorable auspices, it seemed that day. He came with high hopes and big plans, we who had travelled with him for weeks had been led to believe. We were not sure just what they were, but, in those days in Florida when we reporters cast back over the man's career, we forecast vast enterprises on many fronts.

The people looked to him to perpetuate the Coolidge Prosperity. That's about all they asked.

The rain of inauguration day passed and the spring sun cast a warm and pleasant glow over Washington and the White House—for a few glorious days. The anticipation of a new era of constructive activity, of large projects of some sort, served to conceal the anxiety and concern which, we learned later, disturbed Herbert Hoover even in those outwardly halcyon days.

For he was not wholly unaware of trouble to come when he took the oath of office on March 4, 1929, though he could not divine its extent—and luckily for him. He knew that corrosive influences were at work. He knew that stock-market speculation was far beyond bounds. He could sense the danger. He was informed sufficiently to know what this might mean, in time, when it hit the rebound and reacted upon business and industry and banking. Undoubtedly he felt that he would be able to check the spree and taper it off without too much damage.

We who patrolled the White House in those first weeks saw the signs. Secretary of Treasury Mellon and Federal Reserve officials were in and out of the White House, mysteriously. Their worry became public when Secretary Mellon passed out the advice at a press conference, offhand and casually, and as if he were just passing a friendly warning to us who sat before him, newspapermen who usually had our week's pay spent before we got it, that the market offered an opportunity for the prudent investor to buy bonds. Bonds, he said, were low in price compared to stocks. Thus, in a roundabout and devious way, he cautioned against the continued speculation in stocks. This was quite a delicate operation. Hoover and Mellon talked softly in parables. They did not want to scare the country and business.

They needed to have no worry on this score. The speculation went on right merrily. Big banks and corporations paid no heed. They kept on pouring their funds into the market, fuel for the raging fire, at almost unheard of rates of interest. The roulette whirled only the faster. Charles E. Mitchell, chairman of National City Bank, thumbed his nose at Washington—and again we saw that even the new President could not command Wall Street. Mitchell scornfully offered more money for stock-market speculation. The government could not stop him. In the high days of Coolidge prosperity bankers and financiers were not used to anybody in Washington butting in and telling them what to do. They had come to think of themselves as a law unto themselves. They were not yet ready to turn in their chips and go home. Senator Carter Glass of Virginia shrieked at Mitchell from the Senate for ignoring the Federal Reserve Board and warned of the wrath to come if the dizzy speculation were not halted. (A few years later the Virginia Senator had his hour of vindication when Mitchell sat before the Senate Banking Committee and admitted some errors in that reckless era.)

Once before Hoover had watched from the inside, as a Cabinet member, an inflationary, speculative cycle which, when Calvin Coolidge first had entered the White House, seemed about to throw the country into a depression. Privately he had been a sharp critic of the Federal Reserve Board's easy-money policy upon which the board had embarked in conjunction with the Bank of England as a means of relieving conditions abroad. He protested to Daniel R. Crissinger, the small town banker whom Harding had left as a legacy to Coolidge in the important place at the head of the Federal Reserve System. He wrote to Crissinger in November 1925: "As to the effects of these Reserve policies upon the United States, it means inflation with inevitable collapse which will bring the greatest calamities upon our farmers, our workers and legitimate business."

Ironical it was that Hoover should be so prophetic, for he caught the blow that he had forecast full on the chin. Prophets usually are on the side lines and are not standing on the spot when the earthquake tears the ground apart beneath them. It struck with that series of shocks on the stock market in October. Thereafter, for nearly four years, Herbert Hoover was a harassed and tormented man. The fissures opened by the stock-market collapse revealed underneath a disturbing weakness in the whole economic system. The stock-market crash was but a surface indicator. It was the seismograph. Hoover became more and more morose at his press conferences, despite the statements he issued in tireless succession about recurring happy signs on the horizon.

But trouble began for Herbert Hoover even before the stock-market crash.

It started only a few weeks after he took office. It came from the usual source of trouble for Presidents—Congress;

and over a subject that always is troublous to both Presidents and Congress—the tariff.

We had wondered at Kansas City how long Bill Borah would stick with Herbert Hoover.

Not long, we had figured. We were right.

Over the tariff they split. The Idaho Senator exerted an influence upon regular Republican Party policy during the campaign and shortly thereafter such as he had not done before nor has he done since. This was because Hoover relied much upon his counsel as a link between the regular organization and its less regular Western wing. It was an alliance of convenience for the Republican candidate, but it led him into trouble.

Borah was very effective in the campaign. He was a tower of strength for Hoover in the West with the farmers. From the stump he ridiculed Al Smith's knowledge of the farm problem. In the South he crusaded for prohibition. He was again the persuasive political siren, America's Number One Orator in action. Large crowds gathered to hear him as he wrapped a glittering mantle of liberalism about the Republican Party and its candidate. Many who were not sure about Hoover of themselves were willing to accept Bill Borah's judgment—and did. Hoover owed much to the Idaho Senator. He undoubtedly was a factor in the South where four states broke loose from their traditional Democratic base to give their electoral vote to the Republican candidate.

Borah still was afraid of Al Smith's flirtation with McNary-Haugenism in the West as the campaign neared its end and he came ambling into Hoover headquarters a few days before we left for California. He convinced the candidate that, to insure the West, he should pledge himself to call a special session of Congress, if elected, to consider farm relief legislation. Borah proposed a double program—the federal farm board for handling surpluses which he had argued for in the campaign, and readjustment of tariffs on agricultural products to protect the farmer still further from foreign competition. Hoover issued a public statement promising such a special session just before we headed west for California.

The President and his progressive mentor clashed when it came time to outline the administration's program. Borah insisted that the President confine tariff adjustments to agriculture and was under the impression that Hoover agreed with him. So the Idaho Senator was very much surprised when, in his message to Congress, Hoover recommended "limited revision" of industrial rates to take care of economic changes since the 1922 act, in addition to increases for agriculture.

That was the cue for the special interests. They came bolting through the door which the President had opened and encamped about Washington and the Capitol. Again it was the old familiar story. Hoover should have known what would happen. He had watched the scramble over the 1922 act from inside the administration as Secretary of Commerce. In the House, Congressmen hurried forward joyfully to get their share and satisfy the local interests within their districts —and the bigger interests which were so powerful politically. Before the House members had finished they had jacked up rates all along the line.

Borah now had a real fighting issue and he seized it boldly. When the House bill reached the Senate Finance Committee he proposed a resolution in the Senate to limit revision to agricultural schedules and those related to agriculture. He lost by a single vote, 38 to 39. Then he joined forces with the Democrats in a coalition when the bill came into the Senate. He and Senator Joseph T. Robinson of Arkansas, Democratic leader, directed the strategy. Once again the Idaho Senator was the vibrant, brilliant, clever guerrilla chieftain of the League of Nations battle—though the cause did not, of course, lend itself to popular dramatization as did the League of Nations fight. It was difficult to make tariff rates a subject of conversation among the plain people, even though their interests were affected.

Borah went through this fight to the end, belying the frequent charge that he starts fights but does not go through with them. Nor was he here the lone battler. Throughout he worked with others. He lost because the Democratic ranks finally were broken by pressure from constituents back home who wanted special favors. He became a victim of the familiar log-rolling process—"You vote for my tariff and I'll vote for yours."

The tariff started a cleavage in the Republican Party between the Eastern and Western wings, the latter the progressive element, which grew wider and wider as the depression struck and the two factions constantly divided on issues arising from the economic collapse. Borah openly deserted the man he had helped to make President and liberals and progressives in and out of Congress began to regard Hoover with suspicion. They lost confidence in him. Their earlier disappointment turned to bitterness in time, the more intense because they had thought him one of their own. The antagonism was intensified by the realization that they had misjudged him, that they had deceived themselves.

Hoover's dilemma was the same as I had observed during the campaign, only more acute now because there was a specific, concrete issue involved. He was caught again in a tug of war between the conservative and progressive forces of his party. He did not satisfy either. Now one side, now the other, would dispatch emissaries to the White House. The regulars, speaking for the big interests which had supported his election, sought to swing him behind rate increases. The progressives, with Borah as their agent, courted his aid in withholding these favors from the entrenched economic interests.

We would talk to them at the Capitol when they returned from their sessions at the White House. Each side claimed his support. The President was peculiarly unfortunate in his Republican leader in the Senate. James E. Watson of Indiana had fought Hoover's nomination at the Kansas City Convention. He had been a candidate himself. Now, in a position of power at the Capitol, he did not exert himself on Hoover's behalf, but rather the contrary. He made no secret of his antipathy to the President. He expressed his delight over the President's discomfiture. His broad humor fattened on Hoover's misfortune and bubbled with Indiana vulgarisms.

"You can't follow a man who has St. Vitus dance," he would chortle to a group of us in the Senate lobby.

He would wink and grin and his big belly would heave up and down as he chuckled.

Watson was the typical, old-line politician who always had taken his orders from the dominant economic interests. He had been particularly active for them in writing tariff rates. He was G.O.P. personified, frankly and openly. He represented all that was reactionary in the Republican Party. His political philosophy was concentrated still in what we think of as the "full dinner pail" days of McKinley. His distrust and dislike of Herbert Hoover symbolized that of the cynical regular Republican politician and the interests he served. They looked upon the man who now was President as "unstable." It was this attitude toward Hoover among Old Guard Republicans which had attracted "liberals" to him. Now they, too, were disappointed and began to talk of him as a "reactionary."

He seemed to satisfy nobody.

The tariff bill satisfied Watson's friends.

I sat in the gallery the day it was passed when Jim Watson rose in his place and chirruped cheerfully:

"Happy days are here again!"

He licked his lips and slapped his big hands against his bountiful flanks. Optimism exuded from his big frame. He predicted cheerfully that prosperity would return in sixty days. If the tariff is high, then America is all right. That was Jim Watson's gospel, the essence of his political faith. He could not understand why all would not now be well, why the unemployed would not disappear as do the morning mists under the heat of the sun. And he was high placed in the nation's councils and management! The sad thing is that there were so many others like him. Fix up the big fellows and they will fix up the country. That was his motto.

For all practical purposes Hoover might as well have been one of them—as his one-time progressive friends now said—though he knew so much better. If you are with us, they now said to him in effect, there is still time to redeem yourself. Stand up courageously and veto this bill. They begged him. They petitioned him. But he signed it with a statement full of excuses. Tariff revision, he said, was a pledge of the Republican platform and "platform promises must not be empty gestures." He submitted estimates of comparative rates under this and previous acts in an effort to show that the Hawley-Smoot tariff was not excessively high.

I learned something of tariff-making in those days, thanks to the investigation conducted by Senator Thaddeus Caraway, the sharp-tongued gentleman from Arkansas who hauled the lobbying interests before him and pinned them down mercilessly. Especially revealing was pudgy little Joseph R. Grundy, tariff lobbyist de luxe, president of the Pennsylvania Manufacturers Association. He told unabashed how he had raised money among the protected industries of Pennsylvania to pour into campaign funds to keep Republicans in office. He had helped to raise $800,000 in Pennsylvania in 1924, he testified, and in 1928 he had raised $700,000 alone in the eastern part of the state. He had lobbied for higher rates in every tariff measure since the Dingley bill of 1897, he said. He was now spending $2,000 a month out of his own pocket to maintain an office in Washington to influence increased rates in the Hawley-Smoot bill.

It was also during consideration of the Hawley-Smoot tariff bill by the Senate Finance Committee that it was disclosed that a high official and tariff expert of the Connecticut Manufacturers Association, Charles L. Eyanson, was sitting in executive sessions of the Committee on invitation of Senator Hiram Bingham, Connecticut Republican. Eyanson had been "loaned" to the Connecticut Senator as an expert by the Association. Bingham, the tall, handsome former professor, was tortured on the Senate floor for this indiscretion during debate on a resolution of censure which was passed. The Caraway Committee branded the Senator's action as "beneath the dignity of the Senate and tending to shake the confidence of the American people in the integrity of legislation" in a report to the Senate on the incident.

The loose strands come together to weave the rotten pattern of the delirious decade.

It was on October 29, 1929, the day of the major earthquake in Wall Street, that Joe Grundy appeared before the Caraway Committee to propound the doctrine of government by the few and the big and the powerful. He was a mild-mannered little man, with the look of Santa Claus about him. He had bushy white eyebrows, rosy cheeks and a cherubic face. He had that well-kept look. But he was very sure and positive, a bit supercilious and somewhat arrogant, as he told the Senators his conception of government, and the conception of his kind. Big business had an inalienable and vested right to write tariff bills. Big business had the right to line the party purses with gold to get what it wanted. The states of small population, "the backward states" he called them, should "talk darn small" in government. Pennsylvania was one of the few which could talk loud to Congress.

To complete the picture of the whole, sordid era he related how Harding, with whom it began, had been chosen by the bosses in the "smoke-filled room" in the Blackstone Hotel at Chicago in 1920. He was there. So were other representatives of the Pennsylvania industrial barony. So was Daugherty. He did not answer directly when asked whether Sinclair, Fall and Jake Hamon, the Oklahoma oil king, were present, but he was sure Doheny was not there.

Only a few days before Grundy told the Senate Committee how government should be conducted—and how it had been conducted—Albert B. Fall had been convicted and finally sentenced to serve a year in jail—the first Cabinet officer in American history to go behind the bars.

And now the tinselled towers of Prosperity were toppling.

I can remember still the grim forebodings of those days. The stock market plunged, then wavered, then plunged again. We in Washington were very conscious of it, because the country seemed to believe that somebody, or something, in Washington was responsible for the golden days, and now surely somebody or something in Washington could perform the magic act that would halt the downward plunge.

People were losing their shirts. Couldn't Mellon or Hoover or somebody do something? But the machine that men created, the stock-market machine which turned out Prosperity—or so America thought then—turned out to be like any other machine, an inert, uncomprehending thing that could not hear or see. Mere men talked softly to it. They whispered sweet words. They caressed; they cajoled.

Secretary Mellon felt called upon to do something. He was the god. Now he had an opportunity to show what a god he was. He met in all-day sessions with the Federal Reserve Board. They were advised of pools being formed by bankers, the mighty men of America, in Wall Street, to steady the tumbling price structure. But big men in Washington and big men in Wall Street ran around in circles. They were helpless.

Our economic prophets were crying down the wolf. Professor Irving Fisher took umbrage at Roger Babson who had issued a pessimistic survey. Professor Fisher said on October 15 that stock prices had reached "a permanent high plateau."

"While I will not attempt to make any exact forecast," he said pontifically," I do not feel that there will soon, if ever, be a 50- or 60-point break below present levels such as Mr. Babson has predicted."

The next day was October 16, and there are men in Wall Street today who shudder when they think of October 16, 1929. More vividly still they can recall the master crash thirteen days later, on October 29, when smart men became hysterical and it looked to some who thought they knew the stock market as if the world was coming to an end.

President Hoover, in the White House, coined the phrase that was to hound him—about business being "fundamentally sound." The reserves were called out by the administration the night of October 29 in the soothing person of Dr. Julius Klein, the affable and confident gentleman whose well cut double-breasted suits seemed to inspire confidence. The Assistant Secretary of Commerce was altogether a well disposed gentleman. His genial smile paraded so comfortably about his cheerful face. He threw his whole personality into a radio address that disturbing night of October 29. All was

well he assured the dazed investor and the half-crazy specu-
lator. The stock market, the doctor said, was not a barometer.

Anybody who perused the financial pages closely would
have learned the bitter truth—though perhaps unwilling to
believe it—in excerpts from a survey by the Guaranty Trust
Company published two days ahead of the deafening crash
on October 29.

The small investor was "a sap," though the Guaranty Trust
said so more politely. What it did say was: "Although there
has always been an element of mob psychology in the actions
of the investing public, this elements has been increasing
many-fold by the changes in recent years. The small investor
is, then, to a large extent the victim of his own imagination.
His attitude toward the market seems to have been based on
the view that there was no limit to increasing earnings, re-
investing funds, and thus, still further increasing earnings.
But the country's business concerns can not go on indefinitely
fulfilling the demands of the public imagination."

Obviously.

But the Big Men of America had led the little fellow to believe that. Nor had he heard anything to the contrary from
the protectors of the public interest down there in Washington—from Coolidge or Mellon or Hoover.

23

AMERICA'S little man was confused, bewildered and frightened. Only a few months and he would be frantic and panicky. Factories would shut their doors behind him. He who hung on to his job, perilously, would wonder when he might join the doleful procession.

Confused, too, were the leaders, the political guides and the economic monitors.

The Delirious Decade had come to its ghastly finale.

It had started with a kindly man who talked about "Normalcy." It had seen, at the outset, a minor depression. It had been splashed with the worst political corruption the nation ever had witnessed. This was forgotten as the country went spinning dizzily into the greatest period of prosperity it ever had known, a veritable golden age. Now it all had ended with this, the greatest depression of history.

Except for the corruption, which was not typical on quite this scale, it was the usual American cycle—from depression to depression in eight or nine or ten years. But was this just the typical American cycle, or was it the cycle to end such cycles? Had vague forces which seethed underneath for years, vocal on occasion, suppressed for years at a time, finally come to the top to presage a change in what we had known as the American system of government?

Was this, in brief, a Second American Revolution?

We now know enough to recognize that we are in the midst of something cataclysmic. We are too close to know just what it is or how it will turn out. We can not see objectively from the middle of the hurricane. All we can do is to shout questions into the whirling confusion. What can we save of the world as we once knew it? Twenty or thirty years from now, perhaps sooner, perhaps later, it may be possible to look back and see what really happened in 1929 and how it linked up with what had gone before.

We do know, as we look back now, that a great wave swept in upon Herbert Hoover when the economic machine cracked under him and proved unable to provide work, and to clothe and feed America's millions. We know that this wave seeped right into Washington and compelled the federal government eventually to take over responsibility for the welfare of its people.

Did this wave represent the final surging over of that mass which had foamed up behind William Jennings Bryan in the 'nineties; which had cheered Teddy Roosevelt on for his mild crusade against trusts and courts; which had made a champion of Woodrow Wilson when he called for the "new freedom" for the common man and tried to regulate industry and business?

Was this the revolution which had broken in vain against the Harding-Coolidge bulwarks in the early 'twenties under the leadership of LaFollette and Norris and Walsh and Wheeler and John Nelson and LaGuardia?

Did it break through with such a thunderous roar because it had been bottled up so tightly in the Harding-Coolidge era by the unknowing and arrogant economic lords of America and their political representatives who would not read the signs or could not read the signs? For years they had been forging their instruments of control through legal devices and dodges which had kept them beyond the pale of the law. They had erected giant economic structures with power over the many, exercised by the few, which had brought blessings in the way of mass distribution of necessities, but which were allowed to go their own way without social control. They had protected their power by buying their way into government. They had become stronger than government. Many had not used their power wisely.

The people, who are the government when they want to be, began moving into battle formation, but blindly, not knowing to whom to look for leadership, not knowing exactly what they were fighting for, but ready at last to be led.

This is where the danger arises, but they can hardly be blamed for their revolt.

Herbert Hoover met this force head on.

Like King Canute, he tried to sweep it back.

He made what was probably the last stand for a type of society and government that is gone, the sort I had known as a child, the sort, as he had pointed out, that had given him the opportunity to battle his way to the top.

Again and again—in his messages to Congress and in public speeches as President, later in his campaign speeches—he set forth his ideal of American democracy as he saw it. He stood for local responsibility as far as possible, and against centralization of government in Washington. But he conceded the need of protecting the rights of citizens where the states did not properly safeguard them and for this he would extend the regulatory powers of the central government. Such extension, however, would require a real showing of failure of local governmental agencies and would not be applied willy-nilly. The boundaries as he tried to outline them were hazy and indefinite. He discovered this when he faced the practical problem in a great national emergency.

The government, he held, should not de dominated by selfish business interests on the one hand, or, on the other, by a bureaucratic oligarchy which would seek to operate business and everything else from Washington. When he moved into the White House, he took over a government in which selfish interests had exerted large influence for the previous eight years. When he moved out, he left behind him machinery to combat the depression that was susceptible to enlargement and extension of bureaucracy. This embraced the Reconstruction Finance Corporation with its wide lending authority, including relief loans to states and self-liquidating public works loans; the Federal Home Loan Banks, the relief organization he set up to coordinate local relief activities but without any power to distribute money.

Over and over he restated his philosophy of the separation of federal and local functions, but gradually he was driven back, step by step, into compromises.

The issue was crystallized most sharply in his administration by his resistance to direct federal appropriations for relief for the unemployed. This was the cross upon which the American people crucified him.

Reviled and cursed by the mass of the American people, he clung to this cross to the end.

It took a raw kind of courage.

My reactions are those of the average American citizen. To me his attitude, in those days, seemed to have in it nothing of courage but to be blind, unfeeling and unreasonable. Personally I felt angry and resentful toward him and I could guess how the people who were suffering must feel toward him. Politically, of course, his attitude was stupid and suicidal which, in the backward glance, casts it in a more favorable light than was possible at the time.

Herbert Hoover, in his turgid, confusing and colorless English, tried to explain his philosophy numerous times. I think it is best and most succinctly outlined in a speech he delivered before the American Bar Association in Washington in October 1932, during his campaign against Franklin D. Roosevelt. I have been better able to understand his position in dispassionate retrospect, more aloof now from the heat and fevers of those troubled months, and I think it is worth while for the reader of today to go along with me in a few excerpts from that address. He referred to "one of the most delicate relations of our republic."

"We must," he said, "maintain on the one hand a sense of responsibility in the states. It is the local communities that can best safeguard our liberties. We must, therefore, impose upon the state the maximum responsibility in those regulatory powers over economic functions.

"It may even be necessary in the long view of the Republic that the people of some states, whose governments are negligent of the interests of their own people, should be inadequately protected rather than destroy the initiative and responsibility of local communities and of all states and undermine the very foundations of local government. On the other hand, we must be courageous in providing for extension of these regulatory powers when they run beyond the capacity of the states to protect their citizens.

"In the ebb and flow of economic life our people in times of prosperity and ease naturally tend to neglect the vigilance over their rights. Moreover, wrongdoing is obscured by apparent success in enterprise. Then insidious diseases and wrongdoings grow apace. But we have in the past seen that in times of distress and difficulty wrongdoing and weakness come to the surface and our people, in their endeavors to correct these wrongs, are tempted to extremes which may destroy rather than build.

"In the separation of responsibilities between the federal and state governments on matters outside of the economic field, we have constantly to resist the well meaning reformer who, witnessing the failure of local communities to discharge responsibilities of government, to extinguish crime, and to set up agencies of government free of corruption, to move apace with the thousand social and other advances which the

277

country sorely needs, constantly advocates and agitates that the powers of the federal government be applied, that we may have a rigid uniformity of reform throughout the nation. Yet even here it is better that we should witness some instances of failure of municipal and state governments to discharge responsibilities in protection and government of the people, rather than that we should drive this republic to a centralization which will mean the deadening of its great mainspring of progress, which is the discovery and experimentation of advancement by the local community."

Hoover called this the real liberalism. He clung to this philosophy even when the storms beat about his head. He clings to it still.

"Men who are going about this country announcing that they are liberals, because of their promises to extend the government in business, are not liberals, they are reactionaries of the United States," he said in his final speech at New York City in the 1932 campaign.

The controversy over labels, which still rages, thus began.

While Herbert Hoover stoutly resisted direct federal relief appropriations to the end, he utilized the influence and offices of the national government on a wide front, and also such resources as comported with his philosophy, in an organized effort to turn back the tide of depression and readjust the nation's economy to the shocks of this catastrophe. Midway in his term he assured Congress that he would ask every resource of the country to prevent starvation if voluntary help was insufficient, thus tacitly intimating direct relief appropriations, but he never conceded that this final step was necessary.

On a minor scale, President Harding had recognized national government responsibility in a time of depression— and this for the first time in the nation's history—when he had called a conference to consider the unemployment emergency and had delegated Hoover to direct its activities. That depression had passed without disturbing developments.

But it was Herbert Hoover, as President, who really recognized federal responsibility in an economic emergency in a major way and who thus, in effect, established a new concept of government, even though he sought to restrict it and to deny its ultimate implications. That is often overlooked, both by Hoover, himself, and by his critics, friendly and hostile. He was caught in a rising tide of nationalism and swept along with it, though struggling desperately against it.

He did not hesitate nor equivocate when the stock-market crash reverberated through the country to sound the alarm, but acted quickly. On November 19 he summoned railroad presidents and asked them to help by maintaining their normal construction work. Two days later he assembled the captains of industry, a blue-ribbon list, in a morning conference and that afternoon he talked to leaders of organized labor. He announced a pledge by the industrialists not to cut wages.

Eventually the industrialists forgot their pledge. The administration could do nothing about that. In fact the futility of this wage-pledge gesture became evident in a letter some months later in which Secretary of Commerce Robert P. Lamont virtually condoned wage-cutting in the face of continued depression. It was a reply to one from an industrialist who claimed he could no longer operate on his existing wage scale and must cut it. Mike Flynn of the *Wall Street Journal,* a colleague with whom I worked at that time covering the Treasury, Commerce, and Justice Departments, heard about the letter and we got hold of it and printed it, much to the discomfiture of the White House. It became apparent generally that wages were being cut, pledge or no pledge, as the depression deepened. Men were being laid off, too, in wholesale batches.

The people expressed their grievances in the 1930 congressional elections. Democrats came within a hairline of capturing the House on election day. By the time Congress assembled in December 1931, thirteen months later, they had a slim majority due to the death of Republicans meanwhile and election to their places of Democrats. Triumphantly they took command and elected Representative John Nance Garner of Texas, Speaker. He had been Democratic leader for two years prior to his elevation to the Speakership.

I sat in the gallery at the beginning of that session and heard an Alabama Congressman, George Huddleston, then regarded as a "left-winger," get up and demand loudly and bluntly in one of those dramatic forensic displays of which he was capable, that the government appropriate $50,000,000 from the federal treasury for relief of the unemployed. Republicans, aghast, deplored loudly. This, then, was what was coming under Democratic leadership of the House when the country required statesmanship! Democrats likewise were dismayed and they rushed one of their most effective spokesmen, Representative William Bankhead, also of Alabama, now Speaker, into the breach. Bankhead assured the House—and the country—that the Democratic Party was conscious of its responsibility and would act constructively. The rebel was hushed up and explained away satisfactorily.

House Democrats proceeded warily in the early days of their rule.

But Democrats in the Senate were not so soft-spoken and timid. They had become active in behalf of direct relief in the previous short session ending March 4, 1931. Though Republicans still were nominally in control there the whip was really in the hands of a coalition of Democrats and

Progressive and Insurgent Republicans. The latter threw the direct federal relief issue smack into the Senate early in the session. The issue was raised over a bill appropriating $45,000,000 for loans to drought sufferers for purchase of seed and feed for their cattle. Distress was particularly acute in Arkansas and reports portrayed an emergency there. Democratic Senate Leader Joe Robinson, who was from that state, proposed an additional $25,000,000 appropriation to feed human beings—"human relief" as it was called—to be distributed by the Red Cross which then was dispensing drought relief. Borah and others joined with the Democratic leader. The Senate voted $20,000,000.

Hoover chose to make his stand here at the outset against direct federal appropriations for relief. He insisted that relief should be financed by voluntary public contributions to the Red Cross which was then planning a campaign for further public support. Chairman John Barton Payne sided with the President, insisting that the Red Cross could meet human relief needs for drought sufferers if Congress would provide loans for seed and cattle feed.

Republicans rallied behind Hoover when the bill went back to the House. I covered a hearing by the Appropriations Committee on the $20,000,000 for human relief added by the Senate. The hearing was public, which was unusual procedure, but the Committee thought the occasion justified it. Payne appeared and informed them that the Red Cross would not assume the task of dispensing relief money voted out of the federal treasury. I dashed away to the telephone with this piece of news.

It created quite a sensation. Hoover and Payne both were severely criticized in angry debate on both sides of the Capitol. Was Congress going to vote money to feed cattle and not to feed human beings? This question was asked bitterly. Hadn't Congress in the past voted money for

Hoover to feed foreigners in distress? The President's stock took a quick plunge downward during this row. Democrats capitalized his attitude. But the House backed him up and the Robinson appropriation was defeated.

Condemnation was heaped upon him in the Senate. A number of Senators threatened to force an extra session to vote direct relief. Hoover issued a public statement defending himself and explaining his position. He pointed out what he had done to provide relief, including loans for drought areas, increased appropriations for public works, the organization of business and labor to assist in holding the lines, mobilization of the Red Cross and local agencies. He reiterated his position that "our American system requires that municipal, county, and state governments shall use their own resources and credit before seeking such assistance from the federal treasury."

"I have indeed spent much of my life in fighting hardship and starvation both abroad and in the Southern states," he declared. "I do not feel that I should be charged with lack of human sympathy for those who suffer, but I recall that in all the organizations with which I have been connected over these many years, the foundation has been to summon the maximum of self-help.

"I am proud to have sought the help of Congress in the past for nations who were so disorganized by war and anarchy that self-help was impossible. But even these appropriations were but a tithe of that which was coincidently mobilized from the public charity of the United States and foreign countries. There is no such paralysis in the United States and I am confident that our people have the resources, the initiative, the courage, the stamina and the kindliness of spirit to meet this situation in the way they have met their problems over generations."

He added that he was willing to pledge himself "that if the time should ever come that the voluntary agencies of the country together with the local and state governments are unable to find resources with which to prevent hunger and suffering in my country, I will ask the aid of every resource of the federal government because I would no more see starvation amongst our countrymen than would any senator or congressman. I have faith in the American people that such a day will not come."

Unemployment continued. The financial structure got shaky.

He was gradually forced back.

A few months later, in October 1931, he turned again to the financial leaders in an emergency that held dangerous potentialities.

He tried to throw the cloak of secrecy about this meeting. It was held at the apartment of Secretary of Treasury Mellon on Massachusetts Avenue one night. Thirty of the nation's big bankers and financiers were gathered in the luxurious Mellon domicile where hung some of the art treasures the little man had culled from the world's finest galleries. The President left the White House and went to the Mellon apartment for the secret session.

Futile were the attempts to keep the meeting secret. We learned about it, but we did not learn, until some time later, of the dire story of threatening disaster that President Hoover laid that night before the assembled captains of American finance. He had written it out carefully in a memorandum which told of the imminent danger to the whole American banking system due to the panicky withdrawal of gold by frightened foreigners, the feverish hoarding by people in the United States, the calling of loans to smaller banks by big city banks which had to protect themselves from the foreign drain—a vicious circle that dragged into the danger zone not only the banking system, particularly in the agricultural South and Midwest, but farmers and home-owners who could not meet their mortgages. Out of this came the National Credit Association, a pool formed by the bankers with a capital of $500,000,000 to rediscount assets that were not eligible for discount by Federal Reserve Banks and to make loans to closed banks so they could make early partial payments to depositors.

From this in time came the Reconstruction Finance Corporation, modelled on the old War Finance Corporation created in 1918 to give financial support to industries essential in prosecuting the war and to banking institutions that helped finance the war. President Hoover recommended creation of the Reconstruction Finance Corporation and thus moved the federal government into the emergency on the financial front. It still exists.

A giant venture, the world's biggest bank, it carried out his theory of salvage which was to bolster up the banks and business institutions of the country, to pour money from the top. In essence, it was state capitalism. If I read Herbert Hoover's fundamental philosophy right, this represented a departure. This certainly put the government directly into banking and business. It created a framework from which almost anything—and many things abhorrent to Herbert Hoover—might grow. But it was a necessary retreat. The nation was tottering on the edge.

Hoover, himself, admitted what a Frankenstein's monster the R.F.C. might become. He excoriated proposed extension of its authority by Democrats to lend broadside—to individuals, trusts, estates, partnerships, corporations, associations, joint-stock companies, states, political subdivisions of states, municipalities and subdivisions of them.

"This expansion of authority," he said, "would mean loans against security for any conceivable purpose on any conceivable security for anybody who wants money. It would place the government in private business in such a fashion as to violate the very principle of public relations upon which we have builded our nation, and render insecure its very foundations. Such action would make the Reconstruction Finance Corporation the greatest banking and money-lending institution of all history. It would constitute a gigantic centralization of banking and finance to which the American people have been properly opposed for the past one hundred years."

It was capable, then, of transformation into something that violated every tenet of the Hoover philosophy.

Democrats in the House, under the leadership of Speaker Jack Garner, had helped to load the relief bill with provisions to which Hoover objected. "Cactus Jack" was riding high. He sponsored a measure for $1,200,000,000 for public works, including post offices, which was inserted in the omnibus relief bill. After the President had vetoed the original relief measure, Congress modified it to meet some of his objections. The $1,200,000,000 item was cut to $322,000,000, and the broadside loan authority eliminated. Hoover then signed the bill.

Some of its provisions showed how he was being beaten back slowly.

It provided $300,000,000 for loans to states for direct relief, which, at the time, nobody ever expected to be paid back. It wasn't. Subsequently these loans were cancelled by Congress—wiped from the books. Hoover compromised here, but his face was saved. He still preserved the principle for which he had fought. The bill also authorized loans of $1,500,000-000 for productive public works, self-liquidating loans.

The President was criticized by Democrats for the pour-it-in-from-the-top theory of the R.F.C., the salvaging of what they called "the big fellows," while on the other hand, he was stoutly resisting direct appropriations for the "little fellows" at the bottom of the economic heap.

In his 1932 campaign, at Detroit, he answered this attack as voiced by his opponent, Franklin D. Roosevelt.

"Practically the only evidence of the attitude of the Democratic candidate upon this program [the R.F.C.] is the sneer that it has been designed to help banks and corporations, that it had not helped the common man," the President said.

"He knows full well that the only purpose of helping an insurance company is to protect the policyholder. He knows full well that the only purpose in helping a bank is to protect the depositor and the borrower. He knows full well that the only purpose of helping a farm-mortgage company is to enable the farmer to hold his farm. He knows that the only purpose of helping the building and loan associations is to protect savings and homes. He knows full well that in sustaining the businessman it maintains the worker in his job. He knows full well that in loans to states it protects the family in distress."

A partial answer perhaps. Herbert Hoover could have had a better one later. Roosevelt kept the R.F.C.

Hoover had to yield here and there, but when he left office his record was clear on one issue. Congress had not voted any money for direct relief, other than the state loans and appropriations for public works. The latter, he had conceded early in his administration, was one of the proper ways to provide relief. He had abhorred creation of a federal relief agency for distribution of money. This he had averted. How long he would have been able to stand up against the tide had he been reelected, no one knows. He made no promises of direct federal relief in the 1932 campaign. He stuck stoutly by his principles. He had to pay for it in the abuse which was poured upon him.

A dejected, lonely, and pathetic figure he was as he went about that 1932 campaign defending himself. Once or twice he spoke out against the torrent of criticism that rolled in from every side.

"I shall say now the only harsh word that I have uttered in public office," he said at Fort Wayne on October 5, 1932.

"I hope it will be the last I shall have to say. When you are told that the President of the United States, who by the most sacred trust of our nation is the President of all the people, a man of your own blood and upbringing, has sat in the White House for the last three years of your misfortune without troubling to know your burdens, without heartaches over your miseries and casualties, without summoning every avenue of skilful assistance irrespective of party or view, without using every ounce of his strength and straining his every nerve to protect and help, without putting aside personal ambition and humbling his pride of opinion, if that would serve—then I say to you that such statements are deliberate, intolerable falsehoods."

Bitterness spoke feelingly there.

The day before, at Des Moines, in the state of his birth, he had touched upon his personal tribulations in speaking of the efforts he had made to check the tide of depression and bring economic recovery.

"In all these great efforts there has been," he said, "the constant difficulty of translating the daily action into terms of public understanding. The forces in motion have been so gigantic, so complex in their character, the instrumentalities and actions we must undertake to deal with them are so involved, the figures we must use are so astronomical as to seem to have but little relation to the family in the apartment, the cottage, or on the farm.

"Many of these battles have had to be fought in silence, without the cheers of the limelight or encouragement of public support, because the very disclosure of the forces opposed to us would have undermined the courage of the weak and induced panic in the timid, which would have destroyed the very basis of success.

"Hideous misrepresentation and unjustified complaint had to be accepted in silence. It was as if a great battle in war should be fought without public knowledge of any incident, except the stream of dead and wounded from the front. There has been much of tragedy, but there has been but little public evidence of the dangers and enormous risks from which a great national victory has been achieved.

"I have every confidence that the whole American people know in their hearts that there has been but one test in my mind, one supreme object in the measures and policies we have forged to win in this war against depression: That test was the interest of the people in the homes and at the firesides of our country. I have had before me but one vision: That is, the vision of the millions of homes of that sort which I knew as a boy in this state."

Herbert Hoover wrote these words himself. They bear unmistakable evidence of his tortured struggle with the English language. They are stumbling and clumsy. A literary adviser could have turned a phrase and polished a sentence to stir an audience with the trickery of words. But something from the heart cries out still from the printed page.

As in his battles with Congress, Hoover saw again in his campaign fight with Franklin D. Roosevelt a conflict between two philosophies of government.

"This campaign," he said in his closing speech at Madison Square Garden, October 31, "is more than a contest between two men. It is a contest between two philosophies of government."

The Garden was packed that night to the outermost corner by a howling crowd of earnest Republicans. They gave the candidate a great ovation. We newspapermen who had accompanied him from Washington almost missed this fare-well speech. New York's "finest" mounted on extraordinarily big horses, barred our way at every entrance. The President was being very closely guarded now because of the ill feeling manifest particularly in the large cities. Credentials, badges, White House press cards, cards signed by Hoover's secre-taries, meant nothing to these stalwart Irishmen. But, finally, somehow, we got through at the last minute.

In this speech, Hoover revealed, as he had previously, a foresight of what would come after him in Washington if Democrats should carry out the general aims which Roose-velt and others were proclaiming in the campaign, though he cloaked his predictions with the usual political exaggera-tions about altering "the whole foundation of our national life" and "dictator" and the like. He forecast "the enormous expansions of the federal government"; "the growth of bureaucracy such as we have never seen in our history"; "the most gigantic expenditures ever known in history."

Republicans caught up quickly the reference Roosevelt made to the Supreme Court in his Baltimore speech. The Democratic candidate added it, extemporaneously. I was following the text as he spoke. Roosevelt had said: "After March 4, 1929, the Republican Party was in complete control of all branches of the government—the legislature, with the Senate and Congress, and the executive departments, *and I may add for full measure to make it complete, the United States Supreme Court as well.*"

President Hoover avidly picked up this tempting morsel in his speech at Indianapolis on October 28.

"Aside from the fact that the charge that the Supreme Court has been controlled by any political party is an atrocious one, there is a deeper implication in that statement. Does it disclose the Democratic candidate's conception of the functions of the Supreme Court? Does he expect the Supreme Court to be subservient to him and his party? Does that statement express his intention by his appointment or otherwise to attempt to reduce that tribunal to an instrument of party policy and political action for sustaining such doctrines as he may bring with him?"

It was over four years to February 5, 1937, when Roosevelt sent his Supreme Court reform bill to Congress.

The fight that Herbert Hoover conducted during his administration and carried right through his campaign in the face of virtually certain defeat, his fight for a theory of democratic government that he cherished and held dear, was not so clear in those disturbing times as it becomes in retrospect. It takes on a more vivid outline now, because of what followed. The federal government subsequently did move in on all fronts. A bureaucracy was necessary for this, as he predicted, and likewise his forecast of huge expenditures was borne out.

These developments, coupled with the greatly increased powers lodged in Washington, have created new problems that cry for solution today, among them, how far can centralization and nationalization go before they take away something from democratic forms and privileges as we have known them?

This is a vital issue in our times.

Herbert Hoover had a clearer vision than I, at least, gave him credit for when he was in office.

During those days in Washington we were overwhelmed with the rapid headlong charge of depression and swiftly moving events as President and Congress tried to meet it and fought stubbornly inch by inch over means of meeting it. We had no time nor opportunity to get off at a distance, figuratively, and take a look and try to determine what might be the eventual result of this or that policy.

Personally, I was in entire sympathy with the effort to vote direct appropriations from the common treasury for relief. Hoover seemed to me at that time to be quibbling over something that was vague and illusory and had no substance whatever. He seemed to be an inhuman figure sitting there in the White House fighting over definitions that were not important. To me the government is the people, not something high and mighty set off on a pedestal, veiled in mysteries. It must act for the people. I still think that it is the government's function to provide food and clothing when the economic machinery breaks down and can't provide them. It is acting merely as the common treasury to which "the haves" contribute to help "the have-nots."

But we know now that the federal government's problem, once it spreads itself out in many directions, becomes an increasingly complicated and confused one. In moving into new fields it creates new needs, new demands and new pressures. It also is infused constantly with new strength and acquires new powers. There is always danger that such power may be misused.

Hoover saw this.

He may loom a bigger figure in history than he appeared when he was a tried and sore President during the dark days of depression. He proved himself no politician. He swept, vainly, against the tide. The smart politician rides with it.

His reward was curses and sneers and defeat.

24

SENTENCES, phrases, popular tunes, little scenes drift back across memory to light up again those troubled years.

"Business is fundamentally sound."

"Prosperity is just around the corner."

Unemployed men selling apples on street corners.

"Brother, can you spare a dime?"

And, cynically, as the depression's grip tightened:

"Do you remember how he was going to abolish poverty?"

"A chicken in every pot and two cars in every garage— what a laugh!" (Hoover never said that. It was a slogan in Republican campaign literature.)

Hoover the butt of cruel jokes.

Men in breadlines. Men and women in lines in front of banks trying to get their money.

Newspapers striving for sweetness and light, printing little boxes of "business cheer," fugitive and slight items, about ten men going to work here, twelve more there, a small new plant being built here, one there—all adding up to nothing much. Business leaders interviewed and found spouting some new theory that should soon bring "a turn of the tide." Professional financial and business writers inventing formulae, new ways to say the bottom has been reached.

During one Congressional recess in those years I covered what we knew then as "the downtown run," including the Commerce, Treasury and Justice Departments, among others. From time to time I interviewed Dr. Julius Klein, Assistant Secretary of Commerce, and I learned the jargon of those days, the jargon of hope, how this or that sign might bring "the upturn" for which we looked so vainly. I learned how inventories were very low and that this should mean shelves soon must be replenished and how this would react, in turn, upon the manufacturer. But it didn't work out that way. Businessmen were buying only from hand to mouth. I learned new things about the business "curve," how it might act, but it acted the way it had been acting, that is, sliding gradually downward. Finally we grew hopeless about signs. Nothing seemed to work as the orthodox economists thought it should.

Often in those years I was about the White House. It was a gloomy place. We got few smiles from Herbert Hoover. His face was somber and serious even when he thought he saw a ray of light here or there. We knew it wouldn't mean anything. We thought he was stubborn the way he fought back at Congress and that life would have been so much easier for him if he would stop fighting and let Congress have its way. And, always, it seemed, he decided to fight Congress at the time when he had no chance to win. His Congressional leaders would canvass a particular situation, find he was sure to be defeated, advise him to lay low. He would pick just that time to step out and swing lustily and Congress would swing back, making his set-back all the more pointed to the public.

I spent much of those years at the Capitol and there heard little complimentary about Herbert Hoover. Even his own party leaders defended him dispiritedly. Privately some of them criticized him. He was almost entirely friendless among the politicians at the Capitol. His leaders thought he pushed them too often into unnecessary battles.

After the depression spread broadly in the land, Hoover had an increasingly hostile Congress. He never did have a Congress upon which he could depend during his whole four years. In the Senate there was always the effective coalition of Democrats and Insurgent and Progressive Republicans. He had a paper majority there in his first two

293

years in office, which meant nothing. The 1930 elections all but wiped this out, leaving the standing 48 Republicans, 47 Democrats, and 1 Farmer-Labor. This permitted the Republicans to organize the Senate and retain its posts of nominal control, its committee chairmanships; but the coalition was in the saddle and it rode higher as Hoover's prestige fell in the country. He had a majority in the House his first two years and the House was an effective backstop for him, as when it turned back the first Senate assault, in the drought relief appropriation, against his principle that the federal government should not provide funds for direct relief of the unemployed. Democrats took over after the 1930 Congressional elections and their paper majority of two did not indicate their real strength. For there, too, the Republican Insurgents joined with Jack Garner in his sorties against Hoover.

In the Senate, which was rampant and on the loose in those years, Hoover could not rely on Jim Watson, the designated Republican leader. He began more and more to consult with Senator Charles L. McNary of Oregon, present Republican leader, at that time assistant leader. The two had known each other as boys and young men. A loyal Hoover Republican band was organized known facetiously as "The Young Turks," under the leadership of Senators Fess of Ohio, Vandenberg of Michigan, then a somewhat brash and nervy newcomer, and Allen of Kansas. But their efforts were futile. McNary disdained them as impractical and amateurish.

The rift between regular and insurgent Republicans was widened beyond repair by an incident that provoked angry and lengthy debate in the Senate. I was on the United Press desk at the time. One of our staff men, Joseph H. Baird, heard about a dinner of New England businessmen which was to be addressed by Senator George H. Moses of New Hampshire, Senate wag and wit. It was at that dinner that

Moses flippantly referred to the Western insurgents as "sons of the wild jackass." He did not know any reporters were present. There happened to be only two, Baird and the representative of a Boston newspaper. Joe wrote a box about Moses' phrase "sons of the wild jackass." It appeared the following morning on the first page of the *Washington Post.* Senator Norris took one look at it, and, as soon as the Senate convened, was on his feet and for hours he threw vitriol into the face of Moses and the regulars he represented. Vandenberg started a movement to discipline Moses by removing him as head of the Senatorial Campaign Committee, which was charged with assisting in the reelection of Republican Senators. A meeting of the campaign committee was called one night at the Capitol. We waited outside the room where the committee had gathered in executive session. Finally it broke up. Vandenberg emerged, derby cocked down over his eyes, appearing a bit shamefaced. He declined to talk and referred us to Moses, the chairman. Moses was smiling and triumphant. The coup of the "Young Turks" had fallen flat against his hard-boiled, practical political cynicism. He still was chairman. Subsequently certain Western officials of the regular Republican organization were found to be behind an attempt to defeat Senator Norris in the 1930 primary by running a grocer from Broken Bow, Neb., of the same name, George W. Norris, against him. The revelation that the G.O.P. organization was involved in this plot created a sensation and intensified the bitter resentment of the Western insurgents against the regular Republicans. Moses was suspected but he could not be tied up with it. Norris was reelected. Two years later Moses was swept out of office and sent back to Concord to exercise his wit upon the home-folks. It was always a good wit, acid and tart. But it had overreached itself. His "sons of the wild jackass" symbolized the feeling of many Eastern Republicans toward their Western insurgent brethren and reacted disastrously for the party. It foreshadowed the subsequent bolt of Norris and young Bob LaFollette and Bronson Cutting of New Mexico and Hiram Johnson of California to the Democratic standard of Franklin D. Roosevelt. The Westerners came more nearly to expressing the feeling of the country in that day.

They were dissatisfied with Hoover's farm relief program embodied in the Federal Farm Board and its $500,000,000 revolving fund to help dispose of surplus crops. They were successful with Democratic support in adding the export debenture plan, a panacea of those days, to the Hoover bill in the Senate, but after the measure had been thrown in and out of conference committee and back and forth from Senate to House, President Hoover finally got the debenture plan eliminated. The House consistently backed him up. The Farm Board, in time, acquired great stocks of wheat and cotton and the basic problem still was unsolved. Prices continued to tumble.

Midway in the Hoover régime came the one-year moratorium of World War debts owed us. This was part of a moratorium on all intergovernmental debts which Hoover negotiated to relieve Germany, temporarily, of burdensome reparations payments. Germany faced a severe financial crisis which threatened her complete collapse. The moratorium was approved by Congress which, however, refused Hoover's appeal for a readjustment of war debts. He proposed re-creation of the World War Debt Funding Commission for this purpose. All the debtor nations, with the exception of Finland, subsequently defaulted and have paid nothing since. Finland always paid on the dot. So war debts went out the window.

We had our jokes in those days, sources of irony and sarcasm among ourselves. One was the Wickersham Commission on Law Observance and Enforcement which was created by Hoover to investigate enforcement of law, including the prohibition laws. The body, which was headed by George W. Wickersham, Attorney General under Taft, and included many notable figures in the legal world, surrounded its deliberations with great secrecy. It was one of my charges during part of its life—and a burden it proved to be.

Its final report to the President was a strange and mystifying document, with general conclusions and minority reports that conflicted. Almost any deduction could be drawn from it, depending upon how you read it. As a group, the commission voted against outright repeal of the Eighteenth Amendment, but two favored repeal and six were for modification of the Volstead Act, so that, as a whole, a majority in their individual capacities were for a change. The other four members were for a further trial of enforcement. The commission, which covered other phases of law enforcement than prohibition, was engaged on its task a year and a half. Its report was used by both sides.

During its deliberations and in the period immediately before a number of things happened to intensify feeling over the prohibition laws. Dry agents used their firearms loosely and shot innocent persons. The public outcry provoked a statement from President Hoover deploring such incidents and giving assurance that the Treasury Department "is making every effort to prevent the misuse of arms." An official report released sometime previously disclosed that 190 persons had been killed since the Eighteenth Amendment had become effective, 135 citizens by prohibition agents, and 55 prohibition agents who met death in line of duty. Congress passed the "five and ten law," as it was called, sponsored by Senator Wesley L. Jones of Washington, a Republican, which provided a five-year jail sentence or a $10,000 fine, or both if the court so decreed, for first offenders under the Volstead Act. A woman in Michigan who had been arrested four times for violating the prohibition law was given a life sentence under Michigan's "habitual criminal" law which was repealed a few months later when public sentiment revolted. International complications, eventually amicably settled, arose when the Coast Guard sank the British ship *I'm Alone* which was suspected of rum-running. A Coast Guard cutter hailed it within the twelve-mile limit and chased it one hundred miles into the Gulf of Mexico and sank it. One sailor lost his life. Senator Howell of Nebraska, a Democrat and a dry, got excited about prohibition enforcement in Washington, which he claimed was lax, and said President Hoover could make Washington dry if he insisted on it. The President called on the Senator for definite facts to support his charges and proclaimed his determination to make Washington dry as a model for the rest of the nation. Senator Brookhart of Iowa, a Republican prohibitionist, "told all" in the Senate one day about an affair he went to in a Washington hotel with other Senators some years before where, of all things, liquor was being served. That was a three days' joke.

All the fire and fuss over prohibition enforcement seemed a little silly when lots of people were more concerned with getting something to eat.

Into our financial vocabulary in those Hoover days, too, came the phrase "balance the budget." That was something we did not have to worry about before. The late Ogden Mills, Under Secretary of Treasury, introduced it. Tax receipts were running behind as business profits dropped. We no longer had the Coolidge surpluses. Mills, many times a millionaire, waxed hot and eloquent about the necessity of balancing the budget. I remember how one day during Senate consideration of the tax bill it was suddenly discovered that the measure would be short of balancing the budget, and Senators dashed about and gathered up all sorts of odds and ends upon which to levy taxes. They were dumped into the bill. Some of the "nuisance taxes"—sales taxes they were—were repealed later; but some of them we still have with us. "Balancing the budget" became a game that was played furiously but never successfully. Deficits began to pile up in the latter part of the Hoover administration. But a "balance the budget" fetish was created. It was hailed as the cure for all our economic ills, then, and down to our own day. Men still use the incantation "Balance the Budget." It is the mumbo jumbo of the conservative economist, the businessman, the banker. It is a magic wand. It is also a refuge from serious and constructive thinking about what is wrong with America. It has its importance, but it is far from being all-important.

Ogden Mills, "Little Augie," as his close friend, Jack Garner, was wont to call him, became the presiding genius at the Treasury when the depression struck. Mellon, disconsolately, took a back seat. Mills began to assume command at press conferences. He would sit at Mellon's side and when the Secretary would mumble an answer to a question, the Under Secretary would speak up and say: "The Secretary means thus and so." Mellon's rôle was Secretary of Prosperity—and there was no more of that. The halo which had hovered over his grey head for so long disintegrated in these days. The god disappeared and a hopeless old man was discovered in his place.

Mellon's right to continue as Secretary was challenged in the Senate at the outset of Hoover's administration, because of his corporate interests. The argument was that he had not really divested himself of his great industrial and financial connections as required by law of the Secretary of Treasury. Senator McKellar of Tennessee had raised this question several years earlier, but to attack Mellon then was like preaching evolution to a group of religious fundamentalists. The Senate, after an inquiry, decided not to disturb his reign. But, in the House, a pert young Texas Congressman, Wright Patman, who had made himself a nuisance for a long time to the powers that be as champion of the soldier bonus, took up the cause many months later against Mellon and made it very embarrassing for the elder statesman.

Hoover long had wanted to drop the discredited pilot of finance. This gave him his opportunity. Mellon was sent away to London as Ambassador.

The gods were becoming tarnished.

Hoover looked no more like "The Man Who" of brighter days, either.

Then, toward the end, came the "Bonus Army." By the tens and scores and hundreds, war veterans out of jobs descended upon Washington from all parts of the country and camped in old buildings on lower Pennsylvania Avenue near the Capitol, and in hastily constructed shacks in the mud flats along the Anacostia River. Finally some 10,000 had assembled. They demanded cash payment of the bonus. They walked round and round the Capitol in a "death march," night and day, relieving each other, picketing Congress.

Hoover asked Congress for an appropriation for their transportation home. Congress voted the money. About half of them took their fare and left. But the others stayed. Congress adjourned without passing the bonus. Still the remnants of the army stayed.

I did not cover the "Bonus Army." We had a man stationed with it constantly. He got to be friendly with the leaders and men through his day-by-day association. He took no stock in the claim later by Hoover that there was a large Communistic element among those who refused transportation and remained.

I know nothing of that. But unforgettable and still vivid is my experience on that last day and night when they were driven from the city. I had been at the Capitol and was on my way to the office on a streetcar in the middle of the afternoon. From the window I saw a crowd gathered on Pennsylvania Avenue not far from the Capitol, about the old houses and shacks in which a number of the men were squatting. This property belonged to the government and orders had been given for the men to move out so that the houses could be torn down to make way for the new building program. That day the police had been ordered to clear the land.

I got off the car.

I learned that the men had resisted and a war veteran had been shot and killed by a policeman just ten minutes before I got there.

There was an ominous hush about the crowd. People were talking in low voices. We had a man there and I talked to him. He had just learned from the office that the President had ordered out the troops from Fort Myer to clean this place out and that they would arrive soon. I checked with the office and found out that the troops already were lined up back of the War Department and White House. I hastened there and arrived in time to get in one of the press cars which followed the troops slowly down the Avenue. Major General Douglas McArthur was in command.

I stood in the street and watched the soldiers move into action with their bayonets drawn. No resistance was offered. They routed the men from the houses and then set fire to the shacks that had been thrown up on the property. I can see the soldiers now, rushing here and there with torches. The fire crackled and the flames rose and the smoke billowed upward.

General McArthur, his chest glittering with medals, strode up and down the middle of Pennsylvania Avenue, flipping a riding crop against his neatly pressed breeches. The thought crossed my mind—isn't this a travesty—the Chief of Staff directing this expedition here? Yet there he was, pacing up and down, as the handful of soldiers went about their task. It seems strange to me still.

There was a simulation of real warfare a few moments later when the troops began to toss tear bombs around. People who had gathered to watch this sortie by the United States Army began to fly in all directions. My eyes filled up and I raced madly to get out of range. We finally got out of the war zone and could wipe our eyes and breathe freely. But, when I started back up Pennsylvania Avenue toward the office, walking in the street, a trooper came along on his horse and told me to move on, which I was doing. He had his saber ready in his hand and nudged his horse's nose into my back to hurry me along. Aroused, I was talking back to him, but he was winning his point. Slowly his horse was nudging me forward. I finally jumped free and proceeded on my way, considerably miffed.

But this was just the first engagement of this war. The second was that night.

During the late afternoon the big question was whether the troops would be sent to clean out the camp along the Anacostia River. We saw McArthur in his office late in the afternoon. He was a handsome man, a fine figure, the consummate soldier in his bearing. He was friendly and easy in that conference with us, not the same stiff, serious general of armies I had watched earlier pacing up and down while his troops burned out the Bonus Army's camp.

We got no definite word on the further stages of the campaign but gathered that the army might move on the Anacostia Camp, so I was assigned to go there and await developments. A number of us gathered about the bridge from which a path led down to the flat river bottom and the shack community there. All sorts of rumors were about of possible trouble if the troops tried to clear out this camp. There were reports that some of the men had firearms. Rumors fly thick and fast in such a situation, particularly when it is as tense as that. From a nearby telephone through which we kept in touch with the office, we learned that Hoover had ordered the troops to proceed to Anacostia. He finally had decided and had given the orders to General McArthur.

I don't remember the exact time, but it was around ten o'clock as I recall that we heard the troops were on their way.

Quietly we waited on the bridge.

"Here they come!"

The word passed around. Down the hill they marched. The only sound was the shuffle of feet as they approached. The shack community now was pitch dark. All lights had been put out. The troops marched on to the other end of the bridge. Now they were here. At an order they turned on to the road and disappeared into the blackness.

The lost feeling comes back to me now as I recapture the picture. I watched those soldiers step off, two by two into the dark.

Every nerve alert, I waited for a shot.

This, I said to myself, may be the end of this country as we know it. The United States Army turned on to American citizens—just fellows like myself, down on their luck, dispirited, hopeless. My mood was one of despair. It was an experience that stands apart from all others in my life. So all the misery and suffering had come finally to this—soldiers marching with their guns against American citizens. I had nothing but bitter feelings toward Herbert Hoover that night.

I didn't try to put myself in his position and ponder what I would have done. I couldn't. But this—

No shot was fired. In a very few seconds, I suppose it was—though it seemed much longer to me waiting there—torches began to flare in the flats, and in their sputtering light, I could see shadows scurrying about. The soldiers were setting fire to the shacks. Soon the conflagration was general. We ventured into the war zone. Here and there we walked among the fires. Some of the occupants watched their shacks burn quietly, standing beside piles of their few belongings. Then, one after another, they gathered up their possessions and wandered away. The dome of the Capitol was outlined against the flames. It was only a few blocks away. Soon the community was vacant and deserted.

Later I followed the vanishing army up Good Hope Hill (which still seems ironical) and out the Marlboro Road they went. Some of them were camping for the night along the road. I stopped and talked with them. They accepted their lot. They were going somewhere else—just where they did not know.

I wonder what's ever become of them.

I saw Herbert Hoover led up to his Calvary.

It was at Detroit.

When we newspapermen, the advance guard, stepped outside the station, we found a howling mob there. They were shouting imprecations at the President. Hoover remained inside the station, with Governor Wilbur Brucker, who had come to meet him. The Secret Service men were alarmed. But, presently, the mounted police rode down the mob, scattered them, and Hoover came out and got into his car. We travelled in a fleet of limousines provided by Henry Ford.

Never can I forget that experience. We drove to the hall where he was to make his speech through miles and miles of silent men and women gathered along the streets. They looked on, glumly. Occasionally there would be a hoot and a jeer.

"There they go—riding in Henry Ford's limousines."

I heard that cry at one point in our progress.

But for the most part they just stood and looked on sullenly.

At the hall where Hoover was to make his speech, we found the usual stalwart crowd of regular Republicans. They put on a good show. They waved American flags and shouted for several minutes when the President was introduced.

When he got up to speak, his face was an ashen grey. His hands, hanging limply at his side, were shaking.

He defended his program, telling how it had "saved" America.

He said it was "creating new jobs and giving to the whole system a new breath of life."

"Nothing," he said, "has ever been devised in our history which has done more for those whom Mr. Coolidge has aptly called the common run of men and women."

He had fallen back upon Coolidge, now in his grave, but Coolidge was no longer the saint he had been.

An orphan boy—he had fought his way to the top.

America of his youth, the land of opportunity, had opened her doors for him. He had opened many doors for himself.

Finally he opened the door to the Presidency.

But America did not seem any more the land of opportunity.

America closed her heart to him.

Now he was the orphan boy of his country—friendless and alone.

BOOK FOUR

THE CRUCIBLE

25

I CAN never forget the man who stood, high above, on the platform at the East Front of the Capitol on March 4, 1933.

The day was dark and drear. Clouds hung heavily as if ready at any moment to open their funnels and pour a torrent upon the huge crowd below.

He stood, bareheaded, as the raw wind pecked at his hair.

He spoke and his voice had an electric, vibrant quality that magnetized the multitudes before him.

"This nation asks for action and action now," he cried.

The crowd thundered back its acclaim. Little boys, hanging from trees and lamp posts, unknowing, clapped their hands and whistled shrilly.

His face was stern. Tightly he gripped the sides of the reading stand. He knew—as those before him could not know—the gigantic task which had been imposed upon him a few minutes before as he took the oath of office.

To millions of Americans in despair his voice was the symbol of hope. As we listened, it seemed that the pall of gloom was lifting a bit. It was an overwhelming gloom. The newspapers brought word of banks closing all over the country. The structure seemed to be giving away at every point. Desolate men, even now as he spoke, trailed in gaunt lines about windy corners to get a bowl of soup and a piece of bread. Farmers looked out across their acres and wondered how they would meet the mortgage. Families in financial straits watched neighbors evicted and wondered how long before they would be on the streets. Businessmen scanned their balance sheets and knew not how they would survive. America was in panic.

This *must* be the Deliverer from the troubles which encompassed us on every side.

Certainly it was a complete change of management. The old order had been swept out in the election the previous November.

Standing behind the new President, when he took the oath of office, pulling their cloaks tightly about them against the wind, looking drearily into the future, were the apostles of the old order, the key men of the delirious decade which began with Harding and wound so merrily for a time through that wild dance that had ended so disastrously.

Back whence they came to power now went Senator Reed Smoot of Utah, the high priest of tariff protection; Senator George H. Moses of New Hampshire who had given the revolution now manifest a push with his quip about "the sons of the wild jackass"; Representative Willis C. Hawley of Oregon, the school teacher become statesman for a time, who as chairman of the House Ways and Means Committee was co-author of the Smoot-Hawley Tariff Act; Senator Jim Watson of Indiana who had flapped his long arms so cheerily in his fashion and proclaimed that passage of the Smoot-Hawley Tariff meant "happy days are here again."

Ironically, the bands played "Happy Days Are Here Again" on this occasion—but not for Jim Watson, or for any of his like.

Herbert Hoover's round face was like the mound of dough before it goes into the oven, drab and puffy and expressionless. I watched him as he sat on the front row of the Senate during the ceremonies of swearing in Vice President Garner. He looked as if only vaguely conscious of what went on here and not the least bit interested. I wondered what he was thinking as I wrote a running descriptive story of the scene. He vouchsafed no smile. Mrs. Hoover, on the front row of the gallery to my left, likewise was grim and glum. This, perhaps, was one of the most trying ordeals in the lives of this couple who had dined with kings and potentates and realized now that so many millions of their own countrymen only prayed for this hour when they would be shuffled out of the White House.

They wanted to forget the name Hoover and everything it connoted.

There was no mention of him, except derisively, that night in the buzz of conversation about Washington. Franklin D. Roosevelt was the man of the hour, his name the charmed sesame to open the door of hope and new life. Washington trembled with excitement. It still vibrated to the voice from the front of the Capitol. People read his speech again and recited sentences and phrases and speculated avidly what he would do. There was general agreement that he would begin to act. Washington is cynical and blasé; it had been unusually so in the closing months of the Hoover administration. But little doubt crept into the conversation that night. Washington was ready to believe, to have faith. It looked forward, too, to a great adventure. That was in the air. And the adventure would occur right here, in its sight and hearing. If Washington reacted thus to a man and a voice, what must be happening out in the country where people were crushed and desperate? Washington still was above the storm by its very nature. Depression touches but lightly the capital, a city with no industry except the industry of government and its only business that of the entrepreneur who sells food and clothing and the necessities to a stable population with a steady income supplied by the taxpayer. Washington was ready for the drama. Eagerly it waited for the play to begin.

It did not have long to wait.
Action began dizzily on every front.

The hope of a nation was crystallized in this man.
But no one knew yet exactly what to expect of him.

His triumph had been easy. The nation had revolted—the biggest electoral revolt thus far in its history—against a system under which it had suffered. The election sweep was negative in character. People were voting more "agin" than for. Anything, they felt, would be better than Hoover.

Roosevelt had been expediently vague in his campaign speeches, that is, for the comprehension of the voters at that time. Read now, in the light of developments, with the backward glance, they are clear. He suggested the general outlines of a program, but at that time we could not visualize its ultimate shape in any detail; for we had not been accustomed to thinking in terms of the national government moving in on many fronts. He was vague, too, because he was not, at that time, sure of his own future movements. He only knew that he faced an enemy known as Depression, that he was ready to enlist whatever weapons and recruits were necessary, and that he was prepared to throw the full force of the national government into the battle. On some few points he was sure. He had fairly definite ideas about reforms in the existing economic and social order which he long had envisioned, more to do with long-range national policy than immediate recovery, on some of which he had made a beginning so far as is possible within the structure of an individual state while governor of New York. These included a new approach to the electrical power problem through government intervention; elimination of abuses in the financial structure, including banking and the stock market; conservation of national resources; social security.

He had promised a "new deal"—and that was a term every-body could understand. It was about time for that.

Hoover had accused him of seeking to change the basic form of government. This was generally accepted as an exaggerated political bogey-man. Some hoped there would be basic changes, but they had little hope that the man Roosevelt they had come to know through his campaign speeches would go very far.

Still, he was an unknown factor in many respects when he stood before the people that March 4, 1933.

So he had been, as far as the general public was concerned, before his nomination at Chicago.

The name "Roosevelt" had supplied most of the glamour for the public at large, and many thought that the venerable elder statesman Senator George W. Norris of Nebraska had put it aptly when he said "it is time for another Roosevelt in the White House." Names carry weight in politics.

My personal admiration for Franklin D. Roosevelt was born at the Chicago convention—and not for anything he did.

I had known little of him before. The two occasions on which I had heard him nominate Al Smith had impressed me favorably. During the months before his nomination at Chicago, the air was filled with whispered propaganda that Roosevelt was a weakling, that he was wishy-washy. When I got to Chicago I heard this repeated on every side. But it nearly always came from persons, some of them friends, now employed by big corporate interests; and my conclusion was that if these people were afraid of him, if they did not want his nomination, then he must be all right. I began to admire him for his enemies.

This was clinched the night at Al Smith's headquarters, before the convention, when we were handed a statement issued in the name of Mayor Frank Hague of Jersey City, the boss of northern New Jersey and also vice chairman of the Democratic National Committee. This was the opening blast of the campaign by Smith. Roosevelt was described by the New Jersey boss as "the weakest" of the candidates before the convention "in the eyes of the rank and file." (That seems ironical now.) "The Democratic Party has a golden opportunity, a fact which every man and woman interested in democracy knows, but for the party at this time to select the weakest man before the people, cannot bring the party to success nor alleviate through such a candidate the conditions from which our people are suffering," the Hague statement said.

Again the "weak" characterization.

That aroused my suspicions.

But, beyond that, I knew something about Frank Hague. I had gone to Sea Girt, N.J., in 1928 with Al Smith for the mammoth celebration that Frank Hague had staged for him. While there I sat on the front porch of the Monmouth Hotel one whole morning and listened to a newspaper friend of mine tell all about Frank Hague and how he operated. This reporter, whom I had known when he was assigned in Washington, now was with a New Jersey paper and had investigated Mr. Hague's career very carefully. So when Hague took up the crusade against Roosevelt it elevated the candidate in my eyes. Hague, I knew, merely was the spokesman for Smith.

Al Smith had very bitter personal feelings for Frank Roosevelt. I was impressed with this when I talked to him in his office high up in the Empire State Building on my way to Chicago in 1932. It appeared to be a deep, personal grudge. I have heard his attitude explained in various ways. I have heard that when Roosevelt became governor, Smith still tried to guide him, that he looked upon Roosevelt as a protégé and acted accordingly; and that Roosevelt let him know that he was going to be governor in his own right. This was said to be responsible for the rift. I have no authoritative information, but I always have suspected that it was the bitterness of an older man toward a younger man, a protégé, who comes along and begins to occupy the limelight and who proves himself a more popular figure. Al Smith had lost New York in 1928 as a Presidential candidate. Roosevelt had carried it for governor by a small margin. Al Smith had lost the Presidency. Now the signs pointed strongly to Roosevelt's nomination and election to the White House. Smith was determined to do all in his power to prevent it. That always has seemed to me the simple explanation. It is fundamental human psychology.

Once again I was witness to the bitterness which fermented in the soul of Al Smith. It was a few days later during the convention.

I was standing in the runway which admitted to the convention floor. Overhead was the platform. Some orator was delivering a seconding speech for Roosevelt and he was doing it up with lavish and extravagant phrases. Al Smith came bustling, in his erect and brisk manner, along the passageway. He was dressed in evening clothes. He stood beside me and inclined his ear upward toward the platform. I can see him now. He heard the name—Franklin Delano Roosevelt. His face twisted into ugly lines. He turned on his heel and stamped away snarling.

"I can go back to the hotel and listen to that over the rad-dio."

He was gone.

In this controversy my sympathies lay with Roosevelt. I had been at the State Democratic Convention at Rochester the night that Al Smith had begged Roosevelt over long distance telephone to accept the nomination as governor to run on the ticket with him. We stopped at Rochester on the way back from that first western trip which I have described. Smith's word was awaited on the gubernatorial nominee. He had addressed the convention and later gathered with the leaders. Several names were offered. But Smith wanted Roosevelt. He thought Roosevelt would give the ticket strength and help him carry the state. He called Roosevelt at Warm Springs, Ga. (Mrs. Roosevelt, who was at the Rochester convention as a delegate, first had opposed Smith's plan, then had acquiesced.) Roosevelt balked. He thought his health hadn't recovered sufficiently for him to make the race. Smith pleaded. Finally he won his way. Frank Roosevelt, as Al called him, made the sacrifice.

Three times Roosevelt had placed the name of Smith before Democratic national conventions. Smith had had his opportunity and failed.

Now he was coming to wreak his vengeance, if possible, on the younger man who seemed about to get the prize denied him.

He arrived in Chicago in the breezy Smith manner. A crowd was at the station to welcome him at a very early hour in the morning.

Later we gathered about him at a press conference which, like some of those on the 1928 campaign trip, looked more like a mass meeting. Also the conference was opened by George Morris, veteran political writer of the New York *World Telegram,* with a facetious question in mockery of some of the questions of local correspondents on that famous 1928 trip on which George and I had been bunk-mates.

"What did you have for breakfast?"

"Ham and eggs," Smith shot back.

He was the brusque Smith of old. He grinned and rolled his cigar in his mouth, biting his words.

Asked what he thought the party should do to assure victory, he threw back unhesitatingly:

"Write an honest, concise, clear platform and nominate me."

He was told that it was being reported he was merely part of a "Stop Roosevelt" movement. He growled:

"Nothing to it. I'm combating a 'stop Smith' movement that commenced a year and a half ago."

He said later he had no second choice.

"I'm for myself alone," he added bluntly.

A formal statement was handed around by one of his attachés declaring for unconditional repeal of the Eighteenth Amendment and revision of the Volstead Act to permit "the sale of beverages of reasonable alcoholic content."

Smith's arrival gave the "Stop Roosevelt" movement life and vigor and dramatic quality. Emissaries of the various candidates began their rounds of the headquarters of the other candidates. Wisps of gossip blew about the lobbies and corridors, fugitive clouds that congealed into fact or evaporated into thin air. Newspapermen grabbed at them, examined them casually, talked them into balloons. For anything can be true at political conventions. Standing by the hour, shifting from one foot to another, in front of rooms where conferences are held, in tiled hotel lobbies, brings on that disease known as "convention feet." The soles begin to ache and the only surcease is that relief which comes at last when they are laid to rest on cool sheets and there's nothing to do until early morning.

By the hour, before the convention had assembled, in those preliminary days which are the most fun because everything then is uncertain and anything is possible, we idled up and down the corridor in the Congress Hotel about the headquarters of the candidates, the public headquarters, gaily decked with placards proclaiming the virtues of the aspirants. We called it "Presidential Row." Leaflets were set out neatly on tables for the stragglers who wandered in curiously. About the room circulated young men and women, employed for the occasion, who made it a point to be excessively cordial to visitors. Flowers and potted palms in corners revealed an effort to achieve a homelikeness.

In some respects this row was like the side show in a circus, chiefly perhaps because of "Alfalfa Bill" Murray of Oklahoma, the frontier statesman who concealed his really wide erudition behind the mask of a cow hand. He was a raw-boned gentleman with weathered face and seedy mustachios which curled down across his sunken cheeks. Most any time you passed his lair you would see him sitting there, his thin legs draped over one corner of his desk, his lean body slumped in a chair reared back perilously, talking with visitors in his high-pitched drawl. A section of bare, hairy shank showed below his pants, for he did not wear garters— an affectation that he decried.

"Alfalfa Bill" was a candidate for President in his own right he would tell you. He did not care at all for Governor Roosevelt. In this row, too, were the headquarters of Al Smith and ex-Senator Jim Reed of Missouri and Speaker of the House Jack Garner. Reed was here for the convention, amiable enough in his sardonic way, punctuating his discourse with those hoarse chuckles that coursed up from way down. He had little hope except to be in on the trading. Garner was not at Chicago. Nor was Newton D. Baker, the highly rated "dark horse" behind whom it was said at that time the "Stop Roosevelt" allies eventually would concentrate. Governor Albert C. Ritchie of Maryland, one of the shining knights of the repeal crusade, was very much in evidence, but not here. He had an elaborate room on a mezzanine floor where pretty young girls from Maryland pinned a button in your lapel before you could get across the threshhold. (One of our young men achieved eighteen Ritchie buttons in one day. The girls *were* pretty.) The handsome Maryland governor arrived in Chicago in a whirlwind of band music which preceded him along Michigan Boulevard and shook the hotel when the bandsmen stormed right in and through the lobby and up the steps. Ritchie looked somehow like a wax figure in a show window. His dress was elegant, as always. He was pleasantly reserved, seeming to hold himself in for fear he might disturb that bland equanimity which was his public self. His face was constantly alight with a beneficent smile that never became openly joyous. His chuckle often was strained and artificial. He just wouldn't let himself go. He wouldn't emerge from the campaign photograph.

William G. McAdoo, looking just as vital and energetic as he had at Madison Square Garden in 1924, darted about like an elongated hummingbird, lighting for a moment, then flitting away. He was nursing the Garner candidacy which was promoted by William Randolph Hearst and had the backing here of the Texas and California delegations. Serious and earnest Representative Sam Rayburn of Texas was the Garner manager.

The conferences brewed and bubbled through Chicago's hotels. McAdoo created a mild sensation by calling upon Al Smith and swiftly the report spread that the bitter foes of Madison Square Garden were joining common cause against Roosevelt. But then McAdoo called at Roosevelt headquarters and rumors cropped up of a possible trade to give Garner second place on the ticket. The lank and lithe Californian was all over the place, enjoying his mystery rôle tremendously. He beamed and shook hands and slapped backs and was hailed everywhere as "Mac."

James M. Cox of Ohio, to whom Frank Roosevelt had played second fiddle as Vice Presidential candidate in 1920, occupied a penthouse where the "Stop Roosevelt" forces were supposed to do their plotting. But Kenneth Watson, then with the Scripps-Howard newspapers, sat outside the suite for two or three days on guard and saw no signs of activity and finally gave up his watch. That should have been the tip-off to the later collapse of the "Stop Roosevelt" campaign. There were too many prima donnas.

In those gruelling days and nights at Chicago, before the Roosevelt nomination, I came to know big Jim Farley. I liked and admired him then. I have come to like and admire him more with seven years association and acquaintance. Jim was all over the place, his bald head towering above the mob. He chewed his gum and reiterated his absolute confidence of Roosevelt's nomination, though he had to drop the "first ballot" promise. Jim did not know everything about national politics then. He knew that the first thing to do is to go out and gather delegates and this he had done so effectively that Roosevelt entered the convention with a majority though not the necessary two-thirds. But he did not know that you can't always depend on state political leaders, or professed leaders, to "deliver" as they are sure they can. He was led into the fight to abolish the two-thirds rule by a canvass that indicated he could win. He thought these fellows knew. When one of his ward leaders or county leaders in New York told him he could "deliver" then Farley knew he could stop worrying. But not so here, as he found out. He had to give up his fight to abolish the two-thirds rule. But he was triumphant in an important test when Senator Thomas J. Walsh of Montana was elected permanent chairman against Jouett Shouse, candidate of the Smith-Raskob forces, and likewise was successful in seating the Louisiana delegation headed by Huey Long, then a strong Roosevelt ally, and a Minnesota delegation favorable to Roosevelt. Farley had decided to raise the issue with the Smith forces in the election of a permanent chairman before he came to Chicago. I went to see him in New York on the way to Chicago at the same time I called upon Smith. He fixed the appointment at 8 o'clock in the morning, which seemed an ungodly hour to me. But he was there, already at work, when I got to the office. I found him frank and straightforward. He told me he was going to stand behind Tom Walsh and I wrote the story several days ahead of the fight in the convention.

Farley had his anxious hours, but no worry could disturb his outward optimism. He kept smiling and chewing his gum.

Through three ballots the allies held their lines against him. Weak places began to appear along the Roosevelt front on the third ballot which was taken early in the morning. Farley had kept the convention in session all night with the hope he would put the nomination over. I watched Huey Long as he dashed about, here, there and everywhere. Sweat poured down his face. His pongee suit was wilting about him and its starchless tails flapped only halfheartedly as he charged upon delegations that were weakening in their support of Roosevelt. I stood near him as he lectured the Mississippi delegation in his inimitable way. He threatened all sorts of dire punishment if they didn't stay in line. Then, presto, he was off the floor and upstairs into the smoking room where Jim Farley had his headquarters and was receiving his reports, conferring with his lieutenants, and mapping his strategy. Senator Wheeler of Montana and Dill of Washington and National Committeeman Bruce Kremer of Montana were among those with Farley when Huey dashed in that night to deliver his report and express his opinions. In a few minutes he came from the conference room, stopped to buy himself an orange drink at a nearby stand, and buttonholed Senator Byrd of Virginia who strolled past. He was a busy fellow.

The Iowa delegation was in a stew and I went over to see what was happening there. Some of the delegates wanted to switch to Newton Baker. I asked one of them how it was that Iowa had pledged itself to Roosevelt in the first place.

"Well," he said, "Jim Farley came out and asked us and nobody else did."

There's a wealth of practical political wisdom there.

I began to see that this man Farley did not overlook much and I had faith, when the Roosevelt leaders forced an adjournment a few minutes later, that somehow he would find a way to nominate his man. It was broad day outside. The convention recessed at 9 o'clock.

I was in our workroom at the convention hall late the next afternoon waiting for opening of the night session when the flash came on our wire from the main office downtown that California and Texas had voted to switch from Garner to Roosevelt. That meant Roosevelt's nomination—at the cost of Jack Garner's selection as Vice Presidential candidate.

I strolled outside in the lobby which ran around the building and came upon Frank Hague. He was standing alone by a door, leaning on his cane. I took a particular delight in telling him the news. He frowned and dismissed my information with a wave of his hand.

"Aw," he grunted, "that's just a newspaper report."

"It happens to be true," I retorted.

Hague found out not long afterward. The convention was alive with the news when the delegates swarmed in to take their seats. The clerk began to call the roll. When California was reached, McAdoo was recognized and made his way to the platform. The delegates knew what was coming. The suave Californian stepped to the front of the platform, before the microphone, and the mobs in the galleries howled and hooted and hissed. Here, as at Madison Square Garden eight years before, the galleries were for Al Smith. Mayor Tony Cermak had to go to the rescue and demand order from his Chicagoans. It proved a difficult task. McAdoo didn't seem to mind, in fact seemed to relish the uproar. A sly smile sneaked across his face, gradually uncovering his teeth. My impression was of a cat advancing craftily upon its prey. This was his hour of vengeance. For eight years he had waited for it. Now he would pay back Al Smith. His smile said all that. Finally the tumult was stilled and he made his announcement that California was voting for Roosevelt.

Not long afterward it was all over and now we heard "Happy Days Are Here Again" in confident blasts and madness captured the delegates. Democrats seem to be night owls by nature. They deliberated and celebrated until early morning. Again I crawled wearily into my bed. But not for long. The telephone jangled cruelly. It was Bob Bender. He wanted me to come over to the workroom and write a story about all the feuds which had come to a head in this convention for the early afternoon wire. Somewhat groggy I sat down before a typewriter in the early morning and pounded it out.

Al Smith had been cut down in the feuding. He could not take defeat gracefully. He deserted the convention and went home.

Sixty-seven of New York's delegates still stood staunchly by him to the end. One of these was Jimmy Walker, who had no reason to feel kindly toward Roosevelt. On one ballot, Walker was hustled into the convention hall, a coat thrown over his pajamas, just before his name was called in a poll of the New York delegation. He stood up and shouted defiantly:

"Alfred E. Smith."

323

Walker had nominated Roosevelt for governor of New York at the 1928 state convention. But he did not like the job overmuch. He got his first intimation of his task when he stepped off the train at Rochester coming from New York.

"What!" he exclaimed, "he will destroy Tammany."

It was not long thereafter that Roosevelt destroyed him. The dapper darling of New York was prophetic. Tammany was broken later, but for that most credit must go to Fiorello LaGuardia and a younger man named Thomas E. Dewey.

The knight errant of modern American politics descended from the heavens upon the convention, literally like a smiling Jove from another planet. Beginning a career of precedent-breaking, he flew from Albany to address the delegates who had just nominated him and gave the campaign its captivating phrase "a new deal."

Roosevelt the crusader was unveiled before the enraptured delegates and before a reporter who has his emotional sprees and still a few heroes in spite of many disappointments. America had long waited for a hero. So had I. There he stood. Roosevelt on the stump still stirs me as he stirred me that day when he appeared before the Chicago convention. Then I first knew that characteristic toss of the head. Then I first knew that confidential look with the upraised eyebrow he gives his audience when he has delivered a thrust, succeeded by the slow grin as the audience catches it and tosses it around in laughter. Then I first knew the mockery which he touched off by popping his mouth open suddenly in the shape of an O. Then I first knew the tone of his voice as it drips with scorn. Then I first knew the emphatic rage as he lambasts his enemies. Many, many times since have I watched him and heard him, from the back platforms of trains, from the stage in packed halls and auditoriums, from the rostrum of the House of Representatives. Still he stirs me with his wizardry and his magic.

I can see the tricks now, the tricks of gesture and of rhetoric, the tricks he plays with facts and figures often. Still I love to watch it.

The paradox of that 1936 Democratic Presidential campaign was Jack Garner, the Vice Presidential candidate.

"Roosevelt's all right—but this man Garner! Why he's a radical!"

It all seems funny now. It seemed funny to me then. I had lived close to Jack Garner for years about the Capitol, watched his sham-battling with his crony, the elegant Nick Longworth of Ohio, and never had he impressed me as a radical. He won this reputation because of his sponsorship of the $1,200,000,000 public buildings bill in the Hoover administration which so aroused the President then in the White House and horrified orthodox Republicans and some Democrats. He had a rambunctious Texas steer manner on the floor of the House often. He had ridiculed "Uncle Andy," as he called Secretary of Treasury Mellon, but had never hurt the Treasury head noticeably. His Republican colleagues never feared him except as a sort of gadfly with whom they had to contend.

He and Nick Longworth would joust viciously with each other on the floor and then, the session over, go arm in arm to the office of the one or the other for a sociable hour. Being a Southerner, I could see the real Garner under the camouflage of "radicalism" that his enemies of those days threw about him. In the Senate we had the same sort of spectacle in Jim Watson of Indiana and Pat Harrison of Mississippi. They were boon companions. I have seen them tear into each other on the Senate floor, then leave the chamber grinning, arm in arm.

They understood each other, and so did Nick and Jack.

I had seen the Garner Presidential candidacy as it was nursed by William Randolph Hearst and the pap was a sales tax. Hearst wanted a sales tax. This would help relieve the income tax burden that he seemed to feel so keenly. When the depression struck and more revenue was needed, the House Democratic leadership became responsible for producing a tax bill, since the party was in control there. The Ways and Means Committee approved a manufacturer's sales tax. Garner was cagey. I asked him about his position and his answer indicated very clearly that he favored this form of tax. Without his admission, of course, it was obvious that he approved of the tax since he was Speaker and director of policy and would not let the Democrats on the committee bring in a tax bill that did not meet with his approval. But he tried to remain in the background on the issue. I was covering the House as my regular assignment in those days and I noticed numerous private conferences between the Speaker and Hearst representatives. In time the alliance came out into the open. Garner was the Hearst candidate for President.

But he couldn't put the sales tax over. Soon after the bill was drafted and made public the outcry started. Leaders of the revolt were LaGuardia of New York and Doughton of North Carolina, the latter a Democrat and a member of the Ways and Means Committee. LaGuardia was never more effective in organizing a countermovement. The stocky little New Yorker and the tall, gawky, somber North Carolinian were constantly together plotting their strategy and buttonholing members and stirring up opposition. The revolt swept through the Southern Democrats. Most of their states had enacted sales taxes to meet dwindling revenues and the voters were complaining.

When the vote was taken the Southern Democrats deserted in droves, and the sales tax was badly beaten. Most

326

of its support was from Republicans. The tax was fought as a big business device to stave off higher income taxes on them. It was presented as an unfair tax that discriminated against the little fellow.

Garner did not go on the floor when the revolt broke. I was in the lobby during the fight and saw him walking up and down with Representative Isaac Bachrach of New Jersey, a Republican friend. Bachrach had his arm about Garner's shoulder and was admonishing him not to take it so hard. It was a terrific defeat for a Speaker of the House.

But the next day, having recovered himself, Garner took the floor. He said he had never favored a sales tax anyway and he called upon the House to adopt a substitute program that would meet the revenue needs.

Garner of the sales tax fight was no "radical." The "radical" element was on the other side in that fight.

But now, in 1932, Garner was a "radical." He was even called "that wild man."

Democrats kept him under strict surveillance. Charles S. Hand, formerly a reporter for the old New York *World*, was assigned to go to Uvalde, Tex., Garner's home and sit with the Vice Presidential candidate as an advisor. They didn't want Garner to be throwing any monkey wrenches into the machinery. They kept him under cover. He didn't want to make any speeches, so they didn't need to worry. A great deal of persuasion was necessary to get him to make his one address during the campaign.

Roosevelt, the "conservative," carried the ball for the Democrats in the campaign.

It's funny to look back on it now, since Garner has become the symbol of conservatism against Roosevelt's "radicalism." That, of course, is due to the undercover fight against some New Deal objectives which the Vice President has been conducting since early 1937. He never comes out in the open. He works through his Southern lieutenants. He has proved an effective sniper.

The 1932 Democratic triumph never was in doubt.

Only one look at the doleful delegates who assembled for the Republican Convention at Chicago, in this same stadium, a few days earlier, was all I needed. They came from all over the country, as delegates do, and they reflected the political pessimism back home.

Outside the convention hall, as they assembled for the opening session, Communist orators were haranguing the crowds from soap boxes. They had moved right in upon the citadels of Republicanism. They threatened for a time to invade the hall, but Chicago's stoutest coppers were marshalled about the door and they thought better of it and dispersed peacefully.

Inside were all the usual trappings. Flags hung from the rafters in appropriate folds. The galleries were well filled. The state banners were in place. The press boxes on each side of the main platform were white with shirt-sleeved newspapermen. Photographers exploded their flashlights.

But something was missing.

Senator Lester J. Dickinson of Iowa, he who once had been leader of the House farm bloc, once had been a mild symbol of revolt, but who was now a staunch champion of Herbert Hoover and all Hoover stood for, tried to supply it. He was the keynote speaker. He gestured and he shouted and he emphasized. He worked very, very hard. But he couldn't stir up this crowd. They knew they were beaten already. They *had* to renominate Hoover. Why, then, let's do it quickly and go back home. That was the attitude.

But their leaders put them through all the necessary motions and routine as if this convention really were important. From Washington, over long distance telephone, Herbert

Hoover directed the affair. They sweated over the platform, as politicians will, as if a platform would matter this year. They resolved in the usual thousands of words that conceal meaning.

One slowly dying issue almost exhausted their patience. This was prohibition. After much straining with language, they came out with a proposal to resubmit the Eighteenth Amendment to the states. A wet minority led by Senator Bingham of Connecticut presented a brief plank for outright repeal. It was overwhelmingly voted down. That was a three-day newspaper story, and that was all.

The only other fight—and it had its humorous aspects—was over an attempt to substitute Charles G. Dawes, Vice President under Coolidge, for Vice President Charles Curtis as the Vice Presidential candidate—as if this would matter either. But we covered this minor engagement as if it were the battle of the century. I read back over my stories of that day to find one headline writer interpreting my remarks about Dawes as a "stampede" that "stirs delegates." The cry of the delegates, I observe from my copy, was for a "rip-snorting, hell-raising" Vice Presidential candidate. The fight was hot for a few hours, that is, until the Vice President's sister moved into action with all banners flying and scattered those who were trying to oust her brother. This was the indomitable Dolly Curtis Gann. Alice Roosevelt could have told the delegates something about Dolly. They had tossed a few teacups at each other in a Washington social war over precedence at the dinner table that enlivened the newspapers for several weeks and Dolly had triumphed.

With the same pertinacity, she now got her brother back on the ticket.

It was just as well. Dawes would have been a more vulnerable candidate. He had resigned as president of the Reconstruction Finance Corporation shortly before the Republican convention. The reason, it came out some time later, was in

329

order that the RFC could grant a loan of $90,000,000 to the Central Republic Bank and Trust Company of Chicago known as the Dawes bank.

Between Republican and Democratic conventions I had a train meeting assignment. I met Dawes one morning when he returned to Chicago after his resignation. He did not look like the rip-snorting, hell-raising figure whom some of the Republicans had wanted to nominate for Vice President. He was a dejected, dispirited man. In his hands he carried a typewritten statement which he passed around to newspapermen. It predicted business improvement. That's all he had to say. He was manifestly uneasy and nervous, not the hail fellow, the "Hell and Maria" I had known about Washington for several years. I wondered at the time what was wrong. A few days later rumors began to circulate about the shaky banking situation in Chicago. Later the loan was revealed.

The house was falling down about Hoover's head even as he was renominated.

All the fuss over the party's prohibition stand, all the toil over the rest of the platform, was so useless.

Democrats a few days later in their convention did it up neat. They wrote a short, straightforward platform. They advocated outright repeal of the Eighteenth Amendment and spoke concisely on other subjects. A dry minority fought in vain for a plank merely advocating resubmission, like the Republican, without a declaration one way or the other. Al Smith led the successful fight for the majority repeal plank and received a tremendous personal ovation which I have always thought he interpreted as a call from the convention. From that moment, it has seemed to me, his became a lone fight for his own nomination, rather than a concerted fight with others to defeat Roosevelt.

That is the way of ambition.

330

26

AS I look back across just a few years I see Hoover standing on the east front of the Capitol on March 4 in the rôle of a scapegoat.

The simile is not exact or accurate, but it is suggestive to me. We chose him to bear the sins of omission and commission of a generation which was ignorant sometimes, blind sometimes, consciously selfish and arrogant sometimes. There were those who saw it as in a mirror darkly and tried to tell us. No one could see clearly for we are only human and we are in the grip of a multitude of forces outside and beyond us which we cannot understand. Nor am I suddenly assuming the toga of a mystic.

These forces are very real and very realistic. They seethe out of the machine and machine civilization. We still are struggling to adapt these forces to a way of life that will give us food and clothing and shelter and that thing we call liberty.

It has all happened in my time.

In my time has come the automobile, the airplane, the radio and a vast new network of communication between men and nations so that we can know a few minutes later what happened on the other side of the world. There has developed an intricate and complex industrial structure to house the machine and smart men have invented financial devices that permit control of our lives to lodge in the hands of a few. In my time lately has come want in a land of plenty, all growing from the complexity of our new modes of living and a yet faulty system of distribution.

Life in my early years, from my vantage point, seemed fairly simple and yet I know now, when I saw poverty and misery among the people who worked in a woollen mill, that the claws of a heartless, factory-regimented civilization were closing about the lives of those who did not know how to take care of themselves and owners who did not see that they had a responsibility to those who toiled for them. In college I still found ignorance and the desire to nourish it, coming, not from the professors, but from those who controlled the college. They did not see their responsibility either. They did not know what was happening in the world about them and to the world about them.

I saw a President of the United States who accepted the system that he found and acquiesced in its management by those who created it and was willing to consider them as big brothers and neighbors without asking any questions. "Radicals" of that day, as they were called, raised their voices to protect the rights of the cogs in this system, but no one would hear. Government was in the hands of the lords of the economic system. This persisted through the rule of another man who became President, who was too canny to think of the lords as big-hearted neighbors, for he was shrewd about human nature, but who accepted them nevertheless because they seemed to be clever men since they had gathered so much of the world's goods to themselves.

I had seen the system collapse, at least temporarily, about a man who was far more intelligent than either of these two, but who was as blind as they because he never had probed very deeply below the glossy surface to learn what was going on underneath and why. He had been among the ruling economic clique and his vision necessarily was distorted.

Now came a man who was curious at least.

I see him now, standing there, as one who stood between the past and a future that is uncertain. I see him as the link between that other age and a new age and as an instrument of the changes which must come. Drawing lines in this manner is very dangerous, I know, and I may be entirely

332

wrong in attempting it. But that is the way I see it from this position within the hurricane.

Stretching away from that man on the front of the Capitol on March 4, 1933, was a battlefield strewn with wreckage. I see it now. Haggard people crawled along hopelessly in bread lines, the wounded and the casuals. Sympathetic Americans tried to give them sustenance and aid. The field was strewn with broken banks and factories with vacant eyes and boarded up buildings along Main Street where business once had flourished. City people evicted from their homes and tenant farmers who had no work were in the sorrowful procession which, in the mind's eye, one now can see winding away from the Capitol.

The system was in ruins for the moment. The cracked and broken beams and girders stood bare and gaunt before the eye. And, rising there as the man talked, I see a giant crucible into which the broken parts were dumped to burn out the impurities, with the hope of bringing from the molten metal a new structure to meet the needs of today.

It is not easy.

The crucible still sends forth its smoke.

Ignorant and faithless stewardship, both economic and political, lay back of this catastrophe.

As a reporter and an observer I saw the curtain torn away.

What took place in two rooms, one in a temporary wooden war building, the other at the Capitol, is a necessary prelude to the Roosevelt régime. It is necessary to an understanding of what had happened to lift Franklin D. Roosevelt to that platform in front of the Capitol, of his own harsh words about driving the money-changers from the temple, and of some of the things he did after he left that platform, rolled up his sleeves, and went to work.

There are two outstanding figures in the drama which was played out in the two rooms, one in the Federal Trade Commission down near the Tidal Basin, the other a caucus room in the Senate Office Building with marble floors and big windows and crystal chandeliers.

The driving force of the investigation into what we came to call "the power trust" was a somber faced Vermonter, lean and dour, Robert E. Healey, chief counsel of the Federal Trade Commission. Energizing the Senate Banking Committee's investigation into financial practices of the boom era was Ferdinand Pecora, now a New York state supreme court judge, a vigorous, persistent lawyer who had been born in Sicily, brought to this country when he was five years old, and struggled his way upward in New York City.

Healey's fortuitous entry into the power investigation is one of those paradoxes that make Washington constantly intriguing. He was a conservative lawyer representing banking and industrial interests. He was appointed by President Coolidge upon recommendation of Attorney General John Garibaldi Sargent whom I have already described as not in any way inclined to challenge the status quo. Nor was Healey what the conservatives label "a trouble-maker." He was rugged and honest. When the Senate ordered an investigation of the power industry he began to inquire into the subject in a careful, methodical way. What he found there amazed him. It was a stench in his nostrils. Slowly, carefully, unemotionally he dug out the facts. One thing led to another and before he was through he had spent years rather than months at the job and had put down coldly in the record a clear, documented record of financial shenanigans such as the country had not suspected could ever exist. It was one of the most thorough and most effective investigations ever conducted in Washington.

Healey got into it by a rare chance. The power interests brought every pressure possible to ward off an investigation. Their constant irritants were Senator Norris of Nebraska, that tireless old warrior who still carried on his battle for cheaper power, and Senator Walsh of Montana, still the foe of special privilege, who sent chills of fear through the entrenched power industry with a resolution for a Senate investigation. Everybody knew now what a Walsh investigation meant.

Representatives of the power trust, realizing they were unable to head off the investigation, thought they saw a way to temper the blow by diverting the inquiry to the Federal Trade Commission, then a lifeless agency enjoying the quietude which existed in that time in other quarters of government. The Trade Commission, they figured, would let the industry's sleeping dogs lie and not be very curious about this segment of big business then so well protected in Washington. They thought, in brief that they would be "whitewashed." Senator Walter F. George of Georgia, my own native state, where power exercised a strong influence in politics, became their intermediary and proposed an amendment to the Norris resolution which would send the investigation to the Trade Commission. A representative of the Georgia Power Company spent much time about Senator George's office during the Senate fight.

George won—so he and the power interests thought. They did not know about Healey. They did not know that, once he learned the real nature of his quarry, he would hang on like a bulldog, despite very little support from the Commission itself. Ironically, it is doubtful that the Senate would have done a job anywhere approaching that of Healey. A Senate Committee probably would have hit the high spots, created a few stories in the newspapers, and then dropped the subject. It is safe to say that the complete, detailed picture

335

of the power holding company superstructure drawn by Healey and his assistants never would have come from a Senate investigation.

For the exposure of the financial racketeering and the power industry's pervasive influence in politics and government, the American people are indebted to Healey and his corps of able assistants, headed by Colonel W. T. Chantland who later became counsel succeeding Healey in charge of the investigation. For getting the facts before the public credit is due to Ruth Finney of the Scripps-Howard newspapers and Marion L. Ramsay, then with the Hearst newspapers, now with the Rural Electrification Administration. They followed the maze of financial intricacies day by day and translated them into clear and concise stories that the average reader could understand. Theirs was a notable public service.

In an interesting and fascinating book, *Pyramids of Power*, Ramsay has told the whole story of the struggle over electric power, economic and political, and graphically portrayed the part played by Senator Norris, President Roosevelt, Frank R. McNinch, for a long time chairman of the Federal Power Commission, and others in public power development.

The Federal Trade Commission investigation fills volumes and it is a familiar story now—inflated valuations as a base for high rates; erection of a pyramided holding company structure as a means of centering control in the hands of a few and to pile up profits through all sorts of intercompany manipulation; high-powered propaganda which reached into the schoolroom through influence over text-books and fees paid to teachers; purchase of political protection to ward off regulation by campaign contributions and, in at least one case in New York state, regular annual payments to a member of the legislature.

The country learned how low some of the idols of the golden era of prosperity, the supposed Big Men of America, could stoop in their mad chase for profits. It learned how proper development and expansion of the electrical industry had been sacrificed to profits for a few. It learned what a toll it was paying to the electrical magnates. It learned how lightly its supposed Big Men regarded corruption of politics to achieve their ends.

This was the stewardship which had broken faith, which had shirked the responsibility that economic power should entail.

These were among the rulers of America!

This investigation had started in the Hoover administration. The ground was well broken for Roosevelt, when he took office, to attempt to correct some of the abuses. He moved on a broad front. He brought to fruition the dream of Senator Norris. The actuality was even bigger than the dream in the Tennessee Valley project which is bringing manifold blessings in the way of cheaper electricity, and widespread use of electrical appliances, flood control, navigation, reforestation in Tennessee and the southeast. Private companies in the area, while still fighting the vast government project, were forced to reduce their rates and found as a result that their revenues grew bigger than ever. Tennessee's big private company finally sold out to the TVA and Tennessee municipalities.

The Roosevelt administration program envisages extension of electricity to the farms through the Rural Electrification Administration. It is opening up new areas for settlement in the west, with provision for cheap electricity, irrigation, reclamation at Bonneville in Oregon, Grand Coulee in Washington, Caspar Alcova in Wyoming, Fort Peck in Montana.

The power interests fought back stubbornly and still fight back.

One of the bitterest legislative battles I have witnessed in my two decades in Washington was that over the public utility holding company act of 1935 sponsored by President Roosevelt to break up the holding company superstructure, reorganize power control and distribution on a geographical basis and bring power companies under federal regulation by the Securities and Exchange Commission.

President Roosevelt here was attacking a corporate giant that had many allies and almost unlimited resources. It was, perhaps, when his whole administration is assessed, the hardest battle of a Presidential career that saw so many hard battles. The electric industry, though now lacking some of the prestige and power it once had enjoyed because of the revelations of the Federal Trade Commission, still was able through the expenditure of money on propaganda and in politics to exert itself mightily. Legislators had become accustomed to do its bidding. It had made itself feared by politicians because of the money it was able to dump into campaigns back home. Always available wherever there was danger was a huge war chest. Many politicians found it expedient to hedge and compromise if they wanted to stay in state legislatures or Congress. In its employ were skilled publicity men. They harped upon the ogres of Communism and Socialism. They capitalized upon the widespread investment in the industry and told the investors that the savings they had put into power companies now were being jeopardized. They made much of what we came to know facetiously as "the widows and orphans" argument. They inaugurated chain letters and chain telegraph messages which showered upon Congress from their constituents back home. The administration found it necessary to expose the lobby and its methods to combat the potent foe. The public forgets easily and the Federal Trade Commission's investigation was a thing of the past now. For this task the administration chose the alert, able and industrious Senator Hugo

Black of Alabama. The special committee which he headed showed the big money that was being spilled in the campaign of propaganda. It disclosed the intricate interlacing of the power industry with other major industries through interlocking directorates, through financial tie-ups. It revealed, in short, that the administration was not only fighting the power industry but all other big industry. This was a common battle of the big corporate interests. They were joined in a united front. Franklin Roosevelt faced not one giant, but many.

One phase of the investigation gave the power company crusade a ludicrous and ridiculous turn. This had to do with an Associated Gas and Electric Company official in Pennsylvania who devised a very original scheme for the telegraph barrage upon Congressmen, in particular one Congressman who came from that district. He merely got hold of a city directory, went into the Western Union office at Warren, Pa., and dictated telegrams, warning this Congressman of all the dire things that would happen to the world if the public utility holding company bill should pass. Then he would sign names from the city directory, without any authority whatever. But the Congressman was not naïve. He discovered telegrams from very close friends who he was sure would not be wiring him about the Wheeler-Rayburn bill. He checked with them and found they had not wired him. He also discovered that all the telegrams were signed with names beginning with A, B, C, and D.

He advised the Black lobby committee and they rounded up a cast of characters which enlivened proceedings for several days. Especially amusing was the nineteen-year-old messenger boy, Elmer Danielson, who was studying for the ministry. Elmer was one of the messenger boys who had been paid three cents apiece for all the signatures he could get for the telegrams of protest against the bill. Elmer got only six. Some of the others did a better business. Telegraph and Associated Gas and Electric employees appeared before the committee. When the Congressman got hot on the trail in his personal investigations, the telegrams were taken into the basement of the Western Union office and burned, though a federal law requires that all telegrams must be kept a year before being destroyed.

Washington chuckled for days about Elmer the Western Union messenger. He became a national character overnight. Most amusing was his description of the arguments he used against the Wheeler-Rayburn bill in soliciting the telegrams of protest. He convinced his mother and a few friends, or else they wanted to be helpful. He wasn't quite sure whether the bill would take the power business from the Big Men or turn it over to the Big Men. He became confused under cross-examination. He was asked how he stood now on the controversial measure. He was very sure about this. He quickly replied without cracking a smile: "Neutral."

This incident served to make a joke out of the telegraph barrage and to ease the tension on Congressmen. They discovered identical form messages of protests in both letters and telegrams. A touch of stark realism was supplied in letters scrawled on scratch paper with pencil, to make it appear that the masses, the common people, were terribly aroused over this bill. The power companies overplayed their hands. The joke was turned back on them.

Perhaps the most comic character of those times was Howard C. Hopson, big mogul of the Associated Gas and Electric Company, chiefly because of his adventures as the nation's leading missing witness. Twice he was at large with Congressional Committees looking for him. He was one of the principal directors of the power company lobby.

I first saw him during the Senate Banking Committee investigation in the early days of the New Deal.

340

One night I was sitting with Ferdinand Pecora in his hotel suite. The telephone rang. I heard Pecora say:

"Well—you'd better deliver him. You know he's had four or five lawyers already and none of them has been able to get him before the committee."

I had learned earlier that evening that Hopson had been dodging the committee. Pecora's men had been trying for six weeks to find him and serve a subpoena. His New York office explained that he was on an automobile trip somewhere for his health and claimed not to know his whereabouts.

Pecora turned from the telephone grinning. The caller was Pat Hurley, Secretary of War in the Hoover administration. He was talking from his estate at Leesburg, Va., where he had settled himself and his family for the practice of law in Washington. He now had become Hopson's lawyer. Hopson, he said, was ready to appear before the committee. Hurley promised to produce him. He delivered the power magnate the next morning before the committee and, with him, several trunks full of documents. There was quite a lively controversy about those documents. Pecora insisted he had instructed Hopson to have them sent to the committee's New York office where his experts were working with records and files. But Hopson had them shipped from his New York office to Washington. His delivery of the documents was a fine ironical gesture. He smiled as they were loaded into the room and piled up in view of the committee. After much wrangling the power official consented to have them reshipped to New York. That was done subsequently. But he sent the bill to the committee.

Hopson was a round, dumpy little man with a round face. He had a big mouth that seemed to stretch from ear to ear and altogether, had the look of a bullfrog. His manner was aloof and hostile. He became a familiar figure in Congressional hearings.

Several months later he turned up "missing" again. This time not one, but two, committees were trying to locate him. One was the Black lobby investigating committee, the other a special House Lobby Committee headed by Representative John J. O'Connor, Democratic chairman of the Rules Committee. Finally it was discovered that Hopson was at a Washington hotel. This time he had been automobiling in Virginia and West Virginia. The House Committee got hold of him first and refused to release him, even while he was not testifying, to the Black Committee. There was quite a wrangle about that for awhile. O'Connor was accused of trying to shelter the power magnate. It turned out that O'Connor's brother, Basil O'Connor of New York, was representing Hopson for a $25,000 fee. This came out when he finally was taken before the Senate Committee where he told about his propaganda campaign.

Hopson I remember well because of his wanderings, his successive rôles as missing witness, his financial operations which the Federal Trade Commission had disclosed, and because of the pressure some of his lawyers tried to put on our paper in New York, the *World Telegram.*

One day I got a call from Lee Wood, executive editor of the *World Telegram.* He told me that several Associated Gas and Electric Company lawyers had descended upon him and were complaining bitterly about a cartoon drawn by Rollin Kirby. I was involved because the cartoon was based on a story I had written. My story was based on an official release of the Federal Trade Commission. The complaint was a strange one. The lawyers admitted that the story had correctly interpreted the release, but challenged the facts in the release. Lee Wood directed me to look up the citations in the record on which it was based. I spent several hours at it, going through two large volumes. I marked the citations and shipped both of them to New York. I heard no more of that.

This incident was indicative of the tactics of this company and, I might add, of others. I learned it had become a common practice to watch the newspapers and then deploy a skirmish line of lawyers upon an editor. They quibbled repeatedly over newspaper stories, the effort apparently being to overawe an editor so that thereafter he would be constantly conscious of stories involving the company, and thus might become wary and timid.

It didn't work that way with Lee Wood.

Our papers covered closely the running battle on the Wheeler-Rayburn bill as it moved from House to Senate, with Ruth Finney writing the stories. Representative O'Connor tried to prevent a record vote on the "death sentence" as it was called in the House. Many members did not want to be recorded publicly. They did not want either the power companies or their constituents to know how they had voted. O'Connor refused to provide a rule for a record vote on the "death sentence" provision. The vote instead was to be a "teller" vote. In such a vote members march into the well of the House and pass back up the main aisle between two "tellers" one representing each side, who keep the count. They surge down in a drove and it is hard to identify them. It is all done very quickly.

Lee Miller, managing editor of the Scripps-Howard Newspaper Alliance, suggested that our staff attempt to compile a voting record from the press gallery. We located ourselves about the gallery and did make a record. The roll call was published in our newspapers, including our Washington paper, the *Daily News*. Many members were annoyed, including Representative O'Connor who had ducked the vote. Most credit for the success of this stunt goes to Charter Heslep, reporter on the *News*. Though he had been covering the House for only nine months he had learned every one of the 435 members by sight, which is a rare accomplishment.

343

He spotted the bulk of them. Herbert Little, a member of our staff then, and I sat on either side of Charter taking down the names alternately as he called them out in rapid-fire order.

The public utility holding company battle was a fascinating one because it brought into play all the forces which come into head-on conflict when great economic issues are involved. The power giant, flanked by its other big business allies, moved into position with its money and resources and its influence. On the other side, President Roosevelt sought to rally public support. Caught between were members of Congress, the very human instruments of legislation.

President Roosevelt's eventual victory is a tribute to his pertinacity. It is a tribute also to those who directed the battle at the Capitol, Senator Wheeler and Representative Sam Rayburn of Texas and their able lieutenants. They were on the firing line. Nor can two young men be overlooked, Benjamin V. Cohen, New Deal legal aide who drafted the bill which has stood the test of the courts, and Thomas G. Corcoran, the resourceful young Irishman, who plotted the strategy and the propaganda campaign from the administration side. The team of Corcoran and Cohen, active from the early days of the New Deal, began to move more into the spotlight with this successful adventure.

27

PRACTICE of the unscrupulous money-changers
stand indicted in the court of public opinion, rejected by the hearts and minds of men. . . . The
money-changers have fled from their high seats
in the temple of our civilization. We may now restore
that temple to the ancient truths. The measure of the restoration lies in the extent to which we apply social values more
noble than monetary profits."

That's what Roosevelt had said standing at the East Front
of the Capitol.

Day after day, week after week, month after month, I saw
the money-changers on the rack.

The scene became a familiar one. For a time the Senate
Banking Committee sat in its own committee room. Then,
when the show became too popular, it was moved to the
hippodrome at the front of the Senate Office Building on the
third floor, the huge Senate Caucus Room.

The Caucus Room was a setting for a drama in the grand
manner—and we had one in this investigation of the frantic
and fanciful manipulation of the stock market, the frenzied
finance of what we now choose to dismiss briefly as the
"boom era." It had that vacant, hollow, boxlike quality of
Westminster Hall where King Charles I was condemned
to die and Warren Hastings was tried, but it is a much more
cheerful place. Long windows which reach from ceiling to
floor let in a cold light in the winter and the sunshine and
a vagrant breeze in the spring and summer. Overhead are
the crystal chandeliers which have reflected both heat and
light, in their time, for many famous controversies have
echoed in this room. Underfoot is a marble floor which has
resounded to the tap, tap, tap of curious thousands who have

345

come here through the years to sit by the hour and observe one or another inquisition of Democracy.

Most any day, between the hours of ten and one and two and five, you could find amusement here over a period of months, high comedy, satire, frequently farce and always and forever the undertone of tragedy if you were concerned and fearful of your country's welfare, as so many of us were in those days.

There might be several Senators present. There might be only one or two about the long table placed lengthwise in the front half of the room where the "court" held its sessions. The rear half was reserved for spectators. But the man always at the head of the table would hold your attention— a comfortable, Santa Claus sort of gentleman, without the customary whiskers; with round, ruddy face, a globular kind of nose, cleanly cropped mustache, a fringe of white hair about a bald top, nose glasses perched perilously.

His eyes might be closed as the swarthy man with the protuberant jaw at his side pushed questions at a gentleman sitting across the table. Then, all at once, open pop the eyes. Out comes, easily and casually, a penetrating inquiry. If the answer didn't satisfy—a gruff:

"Well, I can't see—"

That gentleman was Senator Duncan U. Fletcher of Florida, chairman of the Senate Banking Committee. He was seventy-five years old then. He is dead now. You imagined that he would grace a rocking chair, on a sunny porch, with a soft hat lying across his lap.

But he was not that kind. He was tough and of hard fiber. He kept the investigation going when those who would squelch it brought pressure wherever they could. He stood steadfast, a gray, moss-covered rock.

The swarthy man at his side would be Ferdinand Pecora, the persistent and indefatigable. His gray-sprinkled pompadour was belligerent. His stubby finger pointed accusingly as he gesticulated with his cigar. Pecora was flanked by a group of bright and eager young men, who whispered suggested questions, furnished a letter, a record, including David Saperstein, who later became head of the important Trading Division of the Securities and Exchange Commission, and Max Lowenthal, who worked tirelessly for reforms in railroad finance. Both were lawyers.

The man in the witness chair might be, according to the time one happened to wander into the big room, J. P. Morgan, fondling the heavy gold chain that crawled across his paunch like a glittering oversized caterpillar; the lean and accommodating Clarence Dillon, suave and friendly; Albert H. Wiggin, mouthing his answers hesitantly, with a protest, his big jowls hanging loosely, his eyes indicating that he disliked all this; commanding Charles E. Mitchell, the super-salesman banker; Winthrop W. Aldrich, with his very proper manner, his incisive mode of speech; the sleek Richard F. Whitney, president of the New York Stock Exchange, cutting the air with his broad A's, objecting so frequently:

"Oh, no, Mr. Pecora."

It was somehow appropriate to the history and tradition of America that Pecora, who had come from Sicily, should become the public prosecutor of men whose heritage—for most of them—reached far deeper into American soil. The levelling process was never better exemplified.

He was short and solid and squarish like so many of his kind who, through the centuries, had cultivated their fertile little acres, had followed Caesar into Gaul, had trooped after Spartacus and his gladiators in a futile attempt to throw off their yoke, had forced Roman civilization, by the sword, upon so much of Europe, had been engulfed by hardier men from the North, only to rise again and again and, in one blazing era, create the Renaissance. One of them had found

347

a new land in the West and millions of his kind had come flocking to the new land later, to dig its ditches and lay its railroads and do its myriad odd jobs and some to rise to places of influence and trust, as had Ferdinand Pecora.

This was Democracy triumphantly arousing itself in one of its periodic bursts of energy to save itself and restore itself.

Now the words would bite and crackle across the table. Now there would be a monotonous flow of questions and answers like the mumbling of bees pecking at the flowers in a summer garden on a sultry afternoon. Then Senator Fletcher would nod. There would, on occasion, be a buzzing gadfly in the committee room in the person of Senator James Couzens of Michigan, who would peck and pull at a witness who proved reluctant. He was merciless in his judgments and caustic of tongue.

Often, too, the audience heard the raspy voice of Senator Carter Glass of Virginia. The Virginia Senator sought to protect the House of Morgan from the insinuations and imputations of Pecora. John W. Davis, counsel for the Morgans, was his old and dear friend. Glass resented any aspersions upon John Davis. Likewise another of the Morgan clan, Rufus Leffingwell, was a friend and protégé. Leffingwell had served under Glass as an Assistant Secretary of Treasury when the Virginian had been Secretary of Treasury in the Wilson administration.

Frequently Pecora and Glass engaged in heated verbal spats. Once they carried on a running debate across the table. The audience took sides and as now one, now the other, drove home a thrust, exultant hand clapping echoed about the big chamber.

One by one, the Rulers of America were brought before the bar.

There was the afternoon that Pecora asked J. P. Morgan if he had paid any income tax in 1930. The question silenced the room, as if Pecora suddenly had squirted asphyxiating gas upon everyone present. Anyone near the financier could hear his big gold watch ticking off the seconds. We at the press table sat forward in our chairs, tense and strained.

Morgan didn't know.

Pecora then proceeded to show that he had paid no tax, and out of the agitated scratching of pencils at the press table flew the flashes to the public at large. Further questioning quickly developed that neither J. P. Morgan nor any of the J. P. Morgan partners had paid any income tax for 1930 or 1931 and very little for 1932.

"I really do not know anything whatever about the income tax statements of the office," Morgan protested, fingering his gold chain.

It was all perfectly legal, of course, accomplished by a revaluation of stock incident to a rearrangement of partnership relationships. It was within the law, and John W. Davis was very indignant over the insinuations about his clients—he who once had led the Democratic forces.

We learned, too, how the great banking firm was held in awe by agents of the Internal Revenue Bureau. Pecora showed that tax agents spent only one day in going over the partnership return of J. P. Morgan and Company and Drexel and Company, the Philadelphia branch. He also showed that a return merely prepared in the J. P. Morgan office, even of an outsider, was given special consideration. Pecora read the comment of one revenue agent on such a return: "Returned without examination for the reason that the return was prepared in the office of J. P. Morgan and Company and it has been our experience that any schedule made by that office is correct."

Then there were the "bargain" or "preferred" lists that Pecora laid down on the table of the Senate Banking Committee. They carried the names of distinguished persons in the business, financial and political world who had been "let in" by J. P. Morgan and Company on stock issues at a low price as a special favor. Calvin Coolidge was on one of the lists. So was Owen J. Roberts, now as Associate Justice of the Supreme Court, and Secretary of Treasury William H. Woodin in the Roosevelt Cabinet, and Newton D. Baker, and General Pershing, and Charles A. Lindbergh, and a number of others. John J. Raskob, former chairman of the Democratic National Committee, also was among the favored who were offered stock in Morgan holding companies at a cut rate. There was some tittering about the table when Pecora read the letter Raskob wrote to George Whitney, J. P. Morgan partner, thanking him for the stock. It is worth printing again. It came from Palm Beach and reads:

"Dear George:

"Many thanks for your trouble and for so kindly remembering me. My check for $40,000 is enclosed herewith in payment for the Alleghany stock. . . . I appreciate deeply the many courtesies shown me by you and your partners, and sincerely hope the future holds opportunities for me to reciprocate. The weather is fine and I am thoroughly enjoying golf and sunshine.

"Best regards and good luck.

"John."

All one happy family.

The income tax story naturally attracted most public attention because it was easily comprehensible to the average man who paid his taxes regularly, did not know about the legal dodges of clever lawyers, and could not, of course, himself afford the clever lawyers.

It shocked the public consciousness.

But there were other revelations, day by day, which were even more significant fundamentally. Gradually, by constant delving, Pecora disclosed the power which the small group of partners in J. P. Morgan and Company—and, in the end, one man, J. P. Morgan, himself, for he had the final word—exercised over the business and industry of the United States through their financing operations and through direct influence as members of boards of directors of the nation's great industrial enterprises. Likewise, the subsequent investigation of a special Senate Committee into the munitions trade showed the influence of the great banking house in foreign affairs and hinted at its part in taking the United States into the World War.

These were the real rulers of America, not the politicians who sat in Washington.

The psychology among the masters of finance that they were privileged men, that it was their right to do what they saw fit, that the public had no right to question them or their motives or their stewardship was only too clearly shown by Pecora as he probed into the other big New York banks and financial institutions to compile a record that went into volumes which he subsequently boiled down in a very illuminating book, *Wall Street Under Oath*.

We saw and heard much of Albert H. Wiggin. He was led through a story of his stewardship of the great Chase National Bank. Wiggin proceeded on the theory that it was the privilege of himself and some of the other top officials of the bank to speculate for their profit from the favored positions which they occupied.

The opportunity was offered by utilizing, in the boom days, the investment and securities affiliate which had been formed in 1917, the Chase Securities Corporation and which, from 1917 to 1933, netted a profit of over $41,000,000. Each holder of Chase Bank stock held also an equal number of shares in the Chase Securities Corporation, but knew little or nothing of operations of the latter with his money.

The Chase Securities Corporation, however, was but the basic speculating medium. Wiggin and a few of his close associates operated also through a subsidiary known as the Metpotan Corporation and six personal holding companies of Wiggin, himself, three of which were organized in Canada with the hope of reducing the income tax of him and members of his family.

From his salary and bonuses Wiggin received enough to provide far more than the necessities of life. The bank's board was more than generous. His straight salary was $175,000 in 1928 and the same in 1929; $218,750 in 1930, and $250,000 in 1931. It thus increased, as Pecora points out, as depression gripped the rest of the country. He took a cut in 1932—and received only $220,300! His bonuses, lavishly voted by his board, were in addition.

But this was a mere fraction of the huge income which he received. The bulk he derived from trading in the stock of his own bank. His operations were intricate and it was quite a job for Pecora and his brilliant young assistants to unravel them. Altogether the Chase Securities Corporation, of itself, or through the Metpotan Corporation, operated eight pools in the bank's stock between 1927 and 1931. Wiggin shared in these operations. When the Chase Securities Corporation had a "good thing" in the way of a security it cut in Wiggin through one or the other of his private and personal companies. That was part of the game. But his heavy profits came from his own operations through these personal companies in stock of the bank. None of the profits went back to the bank. They all went to the companies owned lock, stock and barrel by Wiggin and members of his family.

In the period 1928-1932, the cash profit to Wiggin and his personal companies was $10,425,000. He did much better than the Metpotan Corporation which, though operating in pools involving some $860,000,000 in the same period, came out in the end, due to losses, with the slight profit of only $159,000.

His regular salary and bonuses were thus a negligible part of his operations. His combined salary and bonus for 1928 of $275,000, for instance, was far short of paying his income tax on the profits in 1928 of the personal companies controlled by himself and his family. The profits for that year were $6,800,000, and his income tax was $962,000.

A sizable part of his four-year $10,425,000 profit from his personal companies—$4,008,538—was made in the brief period between September 19, 1929, and December 11 that year while the stock market was crashing, Pecora points out, and that was accomplished by selling the stock of his own bank short! It was during these days that the giants of American finance were loudly exhorting: "Don't sell America short." And, irony of ironies, Wiggin paid no income tax whatever on this 1929 profit. It was all legal. It was done by manipulation of income through his various personal companies.

During the crash and resultant depression Chase National Bank stock catapulted downward with great losses to other shareholders and to the public which was investing in the bank stock. The stock had been swept to higher and higher levels by the operations of the "insiders." But Wiggin suffered no losses.

The big banker had lost the confidence of his own kind even before the Senate investigation. He had gone too far. So he was gently eased from the seat of power and retired— on a pension of $100,000 a year. When his operations became public property through Pecora's inquiry he gave up the pension. It was a bit too brazen.

Wiggin's retirement was nicely managed with the appropriate gesture which Wall Street makes toward its own, bowing graciously if sorrowfully even when one of its own is caught. Pecora produced before the Senate Committee an extract from the "complimentary minute" of the bank's executive committee when it accepted Wiggin's resignation as chairman of the board of directors and elevated Winthrop W. Aldrich, son-in-law of the late John D. Rockefeller, Sr., to his place. Aldrich sat with the executive committee when it approved the "complimentary minute" which contains these sentences:

"The services of Mr. Wiggins not only to this institution, but to banking throughout the world, have been of a pre-eminent character. The Chase National Bank is in no small measure a monument to his energy, wisdom, vision and character."

During the depression, while he was piling up his millions, Wiggin joined other giants of industry and finance in stressing the necessity of reducing wages for the average man. He denounced the theory that high wages produce prosperity and said that business "may reasonably ask labor to accept a moderate reduction in wages, designed to reduce costs and to increase both employment and the buying power of labor." This was in a report to the stockholders of the bank.

We heard another big New York "banker," under close questioning by Pecora, finally confess grudgingly that perhaps "on the backlook," as he put it, the participation of a bank in joint stock-market accounts—which Pecora bluntly called "pools"—was "unfortunate, and I would not do it again."

This was Charles E. Mitchell, president of the National City Bank and the National City Company, its investment affiliate, whom Senator Glass of Virginia had so roundly denounced back in the delirious days when Mitchell refused to stop dumping surplus bank funds in the stock-market vortex.

354

"As a matter of fact, I would rather look to the time when we would be completely out of that sort of thing. I do not believe that it is a thing that we should be doing, Mr. Pecora."

He told the Senate Banking Committee this in 1933.

Mr. Mitchell's operations were the most amazing and spectacular of all, chiefly because he ran his bank's affiliate, the National City Company, as a stock-jobbing concern, spreading his salesmen far and wide across the country hawking all sorts of stocks. They were high-pressure men of the most daring variety. Constantly they were spurred on from the home office by contests, just as if they had been selling soap or vacuum cleaners or some new type of breakfast food.

"Charlie" Mitchell was a symbol for the go-getter in high finance. The National City Company stepped ahead of all others as a purveyor of stocks and bonds. The salesmen received frequent "flashes" as they were called to cheer them on. In the end, when the duped investor saw the stocks he had bought under the inspiration of these "flashes" go tumbling down and his savings wiped out, he had hot and cold "flashes."

Comparable to the Metpotan Corporation through which the Chase Securities Corporation operated and the various personal holding companies through which Wiggin scraped off the cream for himself, were the "management funds" through which Mitchell and his executives in the National City Company operated in the stock market. He considered these executives as privileged men who should be permitted an opportunity to make more than the mere $25,000 a year salaries that they received. They were, he explained, "the equivalents of the partners in a private banking or investment firm." He aped the structure of the House of Morgan.

The National City Company itself which had been set up back in 1911 was a closed corporation. Its operations were

355

secret. Stockholders of the bank, as in the case of Chase National, held also interest in stock of the affiliate, the National City Company, but, as Pecora put it, it was only a "beneficial interest."

Pecora showed how a self-perpetuating board of three trustees chosen from the "insiders" held legal title to the stock of the National City Company. This board did not render an account of its operations. Nor did it keep any minutes or make any reports. While the Bank, in its annual report, gave some information about the Company, it was very sketchy, Pecora brought out. Before 1931 there was no statement of earnings and no balance sheet.

The "management fund" was a treasury of millions of dollars. It was set up by withdrawing a fifth of the total net operating profits of the year, after a deduction of 8 per cent on the capital stock, surplus and undivided profits. This meant, as Pecora explained, that for every $5 the Company earned, the management levied a toll of $1—after the first charge of 8 per cent on capital.

During 1926, 1928, and 1929, Mitchell had received a total of $4,418,732 from the "management fund" and of this he got $1,108,000 in 1929, a year when the National City Company suffered heavy losses in the stock market. But were the profits of the "management fund" returned when the company entailed losses? Not at all. This money was considered the property of the insiders, though in the face of the 1929 losses, Mitchell said this money should be considered "an advance" which would be deducted from future profits in the "management fund." But there were no future profits, in fact, no "management fund." So no restoration ever was made.

Mitchell saw that the bank was helpful to the higher-ups when the depression struck, we learned. A "morale loan fund" was set up from which officers of the bank could borrow, with or without collateral, and with no interest, to bolster up "the morale of the organization," as Mitchell phrased it. A total of $2,400,000 of stockholder money was passed out in such loans of which, Pecora discovered, only 5 per cent had been paid back when the Senate Banking Committee investigated the bank's affairs in early 1933.

Employees of the bank received no such special treatment.

They could buy stock, yes. After the 1929 crash, the lower employees were allowed to buy stock under a plan that first was established in 1927 for officers and higher ranks of employees. It was an installment plan. The purchase price was deducted from their salaries, so much a month, over a four-year period. They paid $200 and $220 a share for stock, of which the book value never was over $70. It declined to $100, then gradually down to $25 at one time. It stood at $40 a share at the time of the Senate Committee hearings. Once committed, an employee could escape this obligation only by resigning—and nobody was resigning in those days.

Among the National City Company offerings were foreign bonds, Peruvian and Brazilian, which were sold to the public when the public would buy anything, even though private confidential reports to the National City Company very clearly showed the financial condition of the political units to which the loans were to go and bank experts in the field had warned against any such offerings.

"Anything goes" was the motto in the high-rolling days.

These bonds and others like them similarly "bad" from the outset turned up in the vaults of banks all over the country when the collapse came and contributed to the piles of "frozen assets" unearthed by harried bank examiners.

We heard Clarence Dillon, of Dillon, Read and Company, as he poured out his story, with frequent bitter comments from Senator Couzens. Dillon disclosed, under careful questioning, how he had set up investment companies on a small outlay which gave his company control of vast sums of other people's money. He was accused of "rotten ethics" by the outspoken Senator Couzens who denounced his operations as "reprehensible."

Then we were led through the dizzy operations whereby the late Van Sweringen brothers of Cleveland, starting with $1,000,000, secured control gradually, by successive sales of stock and successive holding company creations, of a $2,000,000,000 dollar transportation network which stretched across the country. This railroad empire was virtually "in hock" to J. P. Morgan and Company when the Senate Banking Committee conducted its investigations. The two men from Cleveland appeared to the Morgan Company to have a good thing and they cut in on it, much to their discomfiture in the end. Subsequently the collateral was sold on the auction block and the railroad passed into other hands virtually for a song. The Van Sweringen transactions came under investigation by the Senate Interstate Commerce Committee again during the Roosevelt administration preparatory to further legislation to eliminate financial abuses in the railroads.

I had seen the two Van Sweringens, Otis P. and Mantis J., as they began their dizzy upward climb, back in the Coolidge administration. They were before the Interstate Commerce Commission with an application for consolidation of their holdings into one system. I heard an impassioned plea on their behalf by Newton D. Baker, their lawyer. Baker was at his emotional best, drawing a picture of the two boys in knickerbockers as they sold newspapers on the streets of Cleveland. He dramatized a Horatio Alger success story. The commission was not moved by his rhetoric and turned down the application.

358

But the Van Sweringens went on and up until the final collapse, another success story with a very sad ending.

They learned a lot of tricks, but not enough.

They were casuals of the delirious decade, along with Samuel Insull and so many others.

Newton Baker, one-time fighting civic crusader in Cleveland under Mayor Tom Johnson when young men made that a model city, one-time flaming idealist of the "New Freedom" of Woodrow Wilson, went on to become a spokesman for big corporations, and was allied with the power interests against the Roosevelt New Deal.

The times had swept past him.

Of all the Wall Street figures who paraded before the Senate Banking Committee in 1933 and 1934, the two of whom I have the most vivid recollections are the two Whitneys, Richard F., called "Dick" by his friends, then president of the New York Stock Exchange, and George, a partner of J. P. Morgan and Company. Both were arrogant and supercilious. During the investigation of the House of Morgan, George was the constant prompter, the ever ready fountain who bubbled the necessary facts and figures. He always sat near the committee table, eternally alert. He was a symbol of the competent clerk. He was slender and ever immaculate. When the witness would grope for a figure, the date of a transaction, a whisper would go about among the satellites of the House of Morgan:

"Ask George."

They would ask George.

He seemed always to know. He was the detail man.

Dick Whitney, of the lordly presence, the gradually increasing girth, was the more self-righteous, the more condescending. His face was hard and set. He seldom smiled. He looked down his big nose with a sneer at the puny mortals of Congress. The stock market could mind its own business. It could regulate itself. This he emphasized over and over as he appeared before House and Senate Committees, which were drafting regulatory legislation. The stock market, he said, was "a perfect institution." Its members were high-minded men, its officers were vigilant men. It had adequate rules.

Dick and several associates rented a whole house in Washington when the stock-market bill was before Congress.

They inspired statements, poured out propaganda, lobbied with members.

We found out what the man who stood on the East Front of the Capitol that March 4 meant by "the money-changers."

28

ONE night in that early, hectic, breathless era of the New Deal which my friend Ernest K. Lindley has called "The First Hundred Days," a group of us kept our vigil in front of the White House, waiting for one of the innumerable conferences to break up. They came in dizzy succession, those meetings in which the President, his Cabinet and his experts drafted plans, first to salvage the banks and get the nation's financial system back into some sort of order, and later for other legislative measures to patch up the weakened structure of the American economy and to reform some of the abuses revealed.

It began to rain and, by the grace of a kindly police officer, we herded ourselves on the front portico. Marvin McIntyre, one of the President's secretaries whom we all had known for many years about Washington as a newspaperman, came out and joined us. Mac is never so happy as when he is "harmonizing." He loves to assemble a quick quartet. It is as important to him in his leisure moments—and he had very few in those days and the years afterward—to harmonize a bit as it was for those baseball players whom Ring Lardner has left us as merry minstrels of the washroom on the train as they went from one city to another. Mac drew us about him and we struck up the White House favorite "Home on the Range." Rich and strong and slightly raucous, it filled the rain-drenched air as we huddled together, arms across each other's shoulders, on the front porch of the White House. We finished. Then, suddenly, we all looked at each other and laughed.

"Imagine doing this in the Hoover administration!" someone said.

He spoke the thought of all of us.

That scene is typical to me of the carefree bravado of those days. The gloom, the tenseness, the fear of the closing months of the Hoover administration had vanished. It seemed for a time that the country had gone to hell. But, what the hell, said we, we are going to build it over again! We were so confident and cocksure.

So, too, were the young men who descended upon Washington from college cloisters and lawyers' offices and quickly found themselves places behind hundreds of desks and began to explore every cranny of the national economy, to probe its faults and to draw diagrams and blueprints of a new world. They were going to make the world over. We talked then of a planned economy. We learned new nomenclature. In time there were agencies with initials which gave the whole task the aspects of revolution. We spoke of "The Roosevelt Revolution."

They were exciting, exhilarating days. It was one of the most joyous periods of my life. We came alive, we were eager.

We were infected with a gay spirit of adventure, for something concrete and constructive finally was being done about the chaos which confronted the nation. The buoyancy and informality of the New Deal, the roll-up-your-sleeves and go-to-it attitude, percolated out from the conferences at the White House, from conferences in other government buildings, from conferences at the Capitol where Congressmen were caught up in the enthusiasm.

We achieved a national unity that was glorious to see. A little sadly I look back upon it. It was good that we were able to get together in that time, for otherwise we might have lost our democracy. But it is good, too, I suppose, that when we acquired a certain health again we began to quarrel and question, for otherwise we might have lost the resiliency necessary for democracy and might have set up a system that later would have been available for something other than democracy. Franklin D. Roosevelt, however, never would have been party to anything else than democracy. Of that I am convinced.

I think Mrs. Roosevelt expressed most aptly the feeling of many of us on that dark March 4, 1933, in an interview after the inauguration and the parade when she and her husband were back in the White House.

"It was," she said, "very, very solemn and a little terrifying. The crowds were so tremendous and you felt that they would do anything if only someone would tell them what to do. I felt that particularly because when Franklin got to that part of his speech in which he said it might become necessary for him to assume powers ordinarily granted to a President in war time, he received his biggest demonstration.

"One has a feeling of going it blindly, because we're in a tremendous stream and none of us knows where we're going to land."

(It was good to have in the White House a First Lady who spoke of her husband as "Franklin," who had a feeling for the average, struggling American, who had a strong social consciousness, who was intelligent and who was not afraid to speak out in her own right. Mrs. Roosevelt has been a force in these years. I have often commented, and I think it is true, that when all is said and done, perhaps the quiet, pervasive influence of Mrs. Roosevelt with the American people through women and the home probably will outweigh, in the long run, that of her husband. It is an unconscious sort of force.)

Yes, the great throng before the Capitol thundered its approval when the President declared that if Congress did not take measures necessary to meet the national emergency "I shall ask the Congress for the one remaining instrument to meet the crisis—broad Executive power to wage a war

363

against the emergency, as great as the power that would be given to me if we were in fact invaded by a foreign foe." The people were ready to cast their woes on his shoulders, give him the power, and let him proceed to clear out the débris and refashion our democracy.

Nor was it the masses alone who reacted that way. In a continuous line in those days the great in American business, industry and finance came to Washington to pledge their allegiance, and to beg that he assume extraordinary powers. They wanted someone to save their skins. They had thrown up their hands. They wanted to preserve what they had. He proved to be their best friend, the best friend of the capitalistic system. But there came a time when they could not see it that way. When they were saved they changed their minds. For when they were saved they also gained new strength. They did not want to yield any of their power.

In a trip through the country in late 1935 and early 1936, I sat one bitter, wintry day, when it was 28 below zero outside, warming myself at the magnetism of young Governor Phil LaFollette of Wisconsin in his office at the Capitol at Madison. He and I chatted about this and that as the wintry blasts roared about the Capitol outside. He was a sparkling, radiant pigmy behind the huge desk. We talked about the vengeful reaction that was sweeping up against the Roosevelt program from the big interests.

Phil then used a simile—the first time I had heard it put that way—to illustrate the psychology of the business, industrial and financial leaders. It was, he said, like the drunk you pick up from the gutter. Ever afterward he bears resentment toward you for you saw him in that degrading position. Roosevelt figuratively had seen America's Big Men in the gutter and had picked them up, dusted them off and set them on their feet. They could not bear to think they had been so helpless and so submissive to "that man in the White House," as they now were beginning to call him.

Yes, Roosevelt could have become a dictator in 1933. He did not. We were fortunate that it happened to be he who was chosen to assume command at that particular time. I have never doubted Roosevelt's fundamental democracy, his determination to preserve and restore democracy despite the daring nature of some of his ventures, the instinct and greed for power of some of those around him and, in these latter days, the self-righteousness assumed by himself and some of his satellites, that theirs is the only right way and that everyone who differs becomes, automatically, a "Tory" or something else equally as odious.

His first job was to do something, and do it quickly to save the nation's banking structure. The banks were cracking all about us on that March 4. One of his objectives throughout his administration has been to harness financial power, to move the financial capital from New York to Washington, to turn the control of money and credit back to the people through their elected representatives. This he could have accomplished in one bold stroke by taking over the banks at the time and nationalizing them. But he did not take this way, though he was urged to. Instead he turned the banks back to their owners and operators and tried to realize his ends by the slow process of reform of the system through law. How hard that has been, how it was resisted, I myself can testify; for I covered the tedious course through Congress of the securities act, the stock market act, and the banking acts of the administration designed to give Washington regulatory powers over the operations of private finance.

Roosevelt in those early days was the confident commander, blithe of spirit, resourceful.

One night I walked away from one of the general legislative conferences with a Republican leader. We strolled along the White House driveway.

"My, that man is refreshing after Hoover!" he said.

"Like a nice, cool highball after drinking stale, flat beer. It is interesting, too, to watch him operate. I sat there tonight, sort of back in a corner—after all, I'm a Republican, you know."

He smiled.

"He was courteous. He deferred here and there. He was good-humored. But all the way through he kept a straight line toward what he wanted. When it was all over, he had got his way. He's smart!"

In his voice was the admiration of one politician for another.

Roosevelt's calm and optimism carried us through those trying days, so that we could joke about our individual plights as he closed the banks. That was ordered in a proclamation issued at the White House at one o'clock in the morning of Monday, March 6, less than two days after he had been in the White House. Most of the banks were shut down already. The bank holiday he proclaimed stopped all financial transactions. Working day and night, he and his experts drew up a plan for their reopening. He called in the heads of the press associations and explained the plan to them. Ray Clapper represented us, the United Press. I was on the night service at that time. I was in the office standing by, ready at the telephone to take the story when Ray called. His voice had a tense quality and he sounded far away. He explained he was calling from within the White House. He dictated his lead, which was pulled from my typewriter and rushed to the wire. Take by take the story went out.

The next night the President talked to the people in their homes about the radio in the first of his "fireside chats." He explained the banking dilemma in simple language and told what was being done about it. It was a masterpiece of exposition. His voice inspired confidence. The effect was just as if he were sitting in the room with the family. He displayed in that talk the insight into public psychology which made him the idol of the masses.

He won the newspapermen of Washington by casting aside the bars reared by Harding and maintained through the Coolidge and Hoover eras—the requirement of written questions handed in ahead of press conferences. He abolished the written questions and installed the open, free, oral conference. We flocked to the White House in those days to shoot questions at him about the complicated and technical plans for the banks. We found him frank and informative. The doubters among us—and I was one of them—predicted that the free and open conference would last a few weeks and then would be abandoned. But it has extended down to this day as I write. He still submits to any questions. He does not, however, answer all of them. Some he cannot, for various reasons. To some he replies that he cannot discuss such and such a matter yet. Some he parries cleverly. But we are free to ask what we please—and sometimes the questions are not what would be called "polite." He encourages frankness—and we often get it back. It is no minor ordeal to face a group of newspaper reporters twice a week, year in and year out. He takes it easily and seems to relish it.

He has always been good copy.

He was from the very start.

He had no time to waste, and he wasted none. He closed the banks promptly. He had the governors of the states assembled about him at the White House a few hours later. They voted their cooperation in the emergency. He called Congress into extra session, and it convened on Thursday,

367

March 9, before he had been President a week. In the flash of an eye, almost, Congress passed the banking bill providing for reorganization and reopening of the banks. The bill was completed only half an hour before Congress met, and copies were not available for the members. But they took the measure on faith. Republicans had worked with Democrats in drafting the plan. Ogden L. Mills, Hoover's Secretary of the Treasury, Arthur Ballantine, Assistant Secretary, and others of the Republican régime, had remained behind to assist. It was a common, patriotic venture.

The plan for salvaging the banks having been put into effect, Roosevelt then inaugurated that series of measures directed at weaknesses along the entire façade of the economic structure which have gone on throughout his occupancy of the White House, dizzily at first, more slowly as new forces he released stirred up conflicts and beat back upon Congress. It was an era of reform such as the nation never had witnessed before in so short a time.

In those early days there was the AAA, the crop production control and subsidy plan to meet the surplus problem and provide purchasing power for that long famished segment of the American economy; the NRA, planned economy for industry to increase wages and shorten hours and reemploy the idle; the TVA, Roosevelt's first invasion along the electric power front; the HOLC to pare down mortgage indebtedness on homes and save thousands on the edge of foreclosure; the farm mortgage act to do the same for rural homes— some purely salvage measures, some combined salvage and reform. Roosevelt was breaking new ground swiftly.

But this is not to be a history of those measures. Whole books have been written about some of them. Roosevelt's own public papers and messages to Congress and speeches fill four full volumes and will call for more. Some of the hasty structure has been torn down already, some of it revised. A major part of it remains, possibly subject to future alteration and revision, to supplements and additions.

My endeavor is to recapture the fine frenzy of that period, to recapture my own enthusiasm and zest. For it had an important influence upon my thinking. New hope filled me. I saw that something could be done about lots of things. Those who had been so long in the minority, crying in the wilderness, now became a militant majority. A new period of education began for me. I went back to school. We reporters all went back to school—we have commented on it often since. We had to in order to turn out our daily copy, for the administration was probing into the whole economic structure. The classrooms were government offices, headquarters for the new agencies which sprang up over night in Washington.

We began to learn about our country.

I had suspected before. Now I came to know.

As I look back upon myself in those days I see that I was pretty naïve in some respects. I was so eager, so hopeful. I don't regret it. I regret none of my enthusiasms. Some of them died away, but I still retain others. Some heroes developed bad cases of clay feet. Some have worn well. I am glad that I could have faith again in something.

I learned to know my country, then, and I learned to love it, and I knew that it could be saved.

The battle still goes on. Some experiments have failed. But there is a way and we will find it.

Nothing in those days was so exciting and so much fun, day in and day out, as that venture known as NRA.

I covered the creation of it in Congress and lived with it for months as it spread itself through the land under the symbol of the "Blue Eagle." Its germ was in the thirty-hour week bill sponsored by Senator Hugo Black which the

369

Senate had passed. Later, Secretary of Labor Perkins enlarged upon this in a suggested bill permitting agreements to raise wages and reduce working hours. Business, through the United States Chamber of Commerce and the National Manufacturers Association, demanded that it be included in concessions in the nature of fair trade practices to protect honest business against chisellers and in price agreements so that it could absorb the wage increases and the employment of additional people under the reduction of hours. The NRA was the result.

In it we saw, then, briefly, the solution of most of the ills of our industrial economy. We were ecstatic in those days about planned economy. Across the skies there flashed, saber in hand, that salty and virile and versatile cavalry officer, General Hugh S. Johnson, and we followed him about as he tried to bring industry into a cooperative system. He was alive and earnest and he was fun. The NRA was set up in that vast monument left by Herbert Hoover, the Commerce Department Building, and day and night we patrolled its corridors watching the intricate machinery function. Up and down, in and out of the myriad rooms, paraded the big men of business and industry and labor leaders who now were given new opportunities under famous Section 7-a guaranteeing the right of collective bargaining. They trooped in to haggle over the codes which were set up for various industries.

After one long night vigil we got in the wee small hours the plan for the Presidential agreements, the blanket codes to which business and industry were asked to subscribe voluntarily until the regular codes authorized under the act could be formulated. Business and industry did cooperate splendidly in the first flush of the NRA. It began to bog down later as the agreements among industries sent prices up and caused discord among the farmers who saw their gains in the AAA nullified, as the codes were stretched too far to cover a multitude of small businesses which set up a reaction politically powerful. The cry of "monopoly" was raised. We saw the whole structure collapse finally under Supreme Court fiat.

But it was a glorious adventure. During those days I became very fond of the swashbuckling General Johnson. He was a dynamo and a foghorn. He resorted boldly to direct action. One day he took an army airplane, flew to Harrisburg, Pa., brought Governor Pinchot and representatives of coal operators and coal labor leaders to Washington, locked them in a room and, finally, late at night, emerged with an agreement settling an industrial controversy. We scrambled up from a card game and spread the story to the country.

Johnson and the administration felt the power of the empires of coal and steel and automobile which now began to fight back against the new dispensation for labor. They won compromises in their code agreements covering labor.

Labor got its first real opportunity under NRA. The smarter union leaders capitalized upon it, especially John L. Lewis, who headed then only a straggling army in his United Mine Workers, their ranks thinned and broken by the depression, and Sidney Hillman, head of the Amalgamated Clothing Workers. They moved right in and seized their advantage, becoming members of the labor advisory board. Lewis built his organization up again and became an outstanding leader in industrial unionism. Hillman helped the general cause of labor by his wisdom in those days. They opened the way for a general forward movement of labor later under the Wagner National Labor Relations Act.

I saw the paternalism of my South rise up again.

Its symbol was William D. Anderson, president of the Bibb Manufacturing Company which has several mills in Georgia. He fought the NRA scheme. I heard him the day he appeared in the Commerce Department auditorium during consideration of the code for the textile industry. He described his paternalistic system—the company stores, the company houses, the company church—defending it. He painted an idyllic picture of contentment. He told proudly how many bouquets of flowers his workers had distributed among themselves the year before. It was something over 5,000 as I remember it. He had it down to the last bud. He told of the Maypole dance every year and waxed almost poetic. A survey had disclosed to a Congressional Committee some time previously what meager wages his workers were paid. I was chagrined—for my South and for him. I had known him personally. He was a fine, handsome figure of a man, a power in church and state. His son was my roommate and close friend in college.

Mr. Anderson was a sincere paternalist. I have no doubt of that. He looked upon the system as normal. His viewpoint was the same as that, for instance, of Andrew W. Mellon. I learned more about that system some time later, and saw its influence exert itself through the Southern wing of the Democratic Party to shackle the new progressive movement that Roosevelt had aroused.

Here in NRA I saw the conflict begin to sputter which grew more bitter with time. Labor was revived and began to try its strength. Such men as Anderson threw out their ultimatums and the battle was joined. Labor found itself arrayed against giants, for industry now was brought together in great monopolies, prepared for joint action where labor was concerned. I saw the war also of business against business, of small business against large business, of big business against big business. I saw the fight to get monopolistic agreements that would permit the fixing of prices to freeze out competition. I learned how complicated the structure has become, how delicate are its adjustments.

The brew in the crucible bubbled and sent forth noxious fumes.

Paradoxically, Roosevelt's most vigorous fight with Congress in those early days was to push through the "economy bill," a measure which granted him power to cut down government salaries and various forms of compensation, including war veterans benefits. He had bitterly denounced the expenditures of the Hoover administration, the failure of Hoover to balance the budget, most notably in his Pittsburgh speech, which in recent years has been thrown up to him so often. In his message to Congress urging the economy bill, he had said:

"Too often in recent history liberal governments have been wrecked on rocks of loose fiscal policy. We must avoid that danger."

How he fought to put this bill over! The Senate balked. The House was backing him up. Back and forth the bill was thrown as he tried to get the Senate to yield. He won finally after compromise. The bone of contention was the cut in veterans' compensation. This was a touchy political issue for members of Congress. He had to work furiously even to get the bill through with a compromise. I was about the Senate that night. Roosevelt needed seven votes changed in that body. He sat on the telephone at the White House and called one Senator after another. He won eight men over and the bill was passed.

He even called Senator Charles McNary, the Republican leader. McNary told me about it. It was a gesture that pleased him. When he called McNary, he told him that he had signed that day a bill in which McNary was interested, a local measure for Oregon, and he inquired if Charlie, as he called him, wouldn't go along on the economy bill. McNary told him no. He chuckled as he told the story. He liked Roosevelt for going all the way to the top in the Republican Party in his effort to win his way.

I remember also the dilemma that night of Senator George Norris. He was conscientiously opposed to the economy bill because of the reduction in compensation for war veterans. But Roosevelt had thrown his support behind Norris's long-cherished dream, the TVA bill which had expanded from Norris's own measure for government operation of the Muscle Shoals plants. Norris did not want to desert the President. He walked disconsolately about the corridors outside the Senate chamber that night, battling with his conscience. Finally, when the roll was called he was absent. He had ducked the vote. I imagine it was the only time in his life that he ever had evaded an issue. I could forgive the old warrior for that.

The New Deal remedies in those early days comprised a strange hybrid of orthodox measures and startling departures. At the outset, as during his campaign, the new President put large emphasis on reduction of government expenditures and balancing the budget, borrowing from the Hoover-Ogden Mills philosophy, which fitted in with the most conservative views. In his extemporaneous address to the governors of states immediately after he entered the White House he stressed the necessity of localities and states taking care of the relief problem as far as possible in words that were reminiscent of Herbert Hoover.

"The federal government, of course, does have to prevent anybody from starving, but the federal government should not be called upon to exercise that duty until other agencies fail. The primary duty is that of the locality, the city, county, town. If they fail and cannot raise enough to meet the needs, the next responsibility is on the states and they have to do all they can. If it is proven that they cannot do any more and that the funds are still insufficient, it is the duty of the federal government to step in."

He continued the Reconstruction Finance Corporation and broadened its lending activities. The measures to assist the city and farm home owner, to pare down the load of debt so people could save their homes, followed the Hoover pattern. The AAA was unorthodox only in that this particular form of farm relief had not been tried, though it and other artificial measures like it long had been advocated. It was no more radical than the McNary-Haugen bill which such conservatives as Charles G. Dawes, the ex-Vice President and banker, and Frank O. Lowden, ex-Governor of Illinois and man of large property, had championed.

The most radical departure of all was NRA, which was of the essence of planned economy so bitterly attacked subsequently in other forms by business which hugged it to its bosom at first. Business, especially big business, saw a way to strengthen itself in NRA and saw nothing unorthodox in it when it was formulated. It cooled off when it could not realize the price-fixing it had envisioned.

Therefore, it seems a little strange now, after the fact, when critics of some of the later stages of the New Deal point back glowingly to the early New Deal and give it their unqualified blessing. In NRA were the germs of all later developments on the New Deal front, the Wagner Labor Relations Act which business fought so bitterly; the wage-hour bill which was so stoutly resisted; regulation of business practices which, when sought in other directions, has ruffled the back of business. NRA contained all the basic assumptions of business regulation. If the principle was good in that complicated and unwieldy instrument, the only logical conclusion is that the principle was good if carried out subsequently in a different manner.

So some of the criticism seems a little weak and illogical. More consistent are those of progressive bent, such as Senator Borah of Idaho, who attacked NRA as fostering monopoly and saw the ultimate consequences of this form of business planning, and yet who continue to demand some means of regulating business that will go to the root of the evils inherent in our present system.

Moments of high drama stand out in memory, moments surrounding the announcement of new departures in that pulsating period of quick evolution. I watched in wonder and amazement as President Roosevelt broke new paths, shattered precedents. The show was replete with constant surprises, unexpected dénouements, and intriguing lines that hardly had died away before the startled audience, breathless and fascinated, watched another of the continuous and successive acts put on by the man in the White House, himself a consummate actor.

There was the day that negotiations were announced preliminary to recognition of Soviet Russia. Looking back upon it now it doesn't seem so shocking as it did then. The reader must take himself back and remember that Russia had been the forbidden, the international outlaw, the abhorred of Secretary of State Hughes and his successors. Again, under Stalin, she became to Americans five years later an even more forbidding figure.

The President broke the news at a press conference in October 1934. Reports from Russia earlier in the day forecast some announcement. The word spread swiftly through Washington. At the appointed hour of four o'clock in the afternoon the lobby of the executive offices was crammed with newspapermen and women, the largest press conference thus far held in the Roosevelt administration.

Nervously we waited, smoked and jabbered.

Finally, the noise was hushed at the signal from Pat McKenna, veteran doorkeeper, and the now subdued throng squeezed itself through the door into the President's office. The President sat behind his desk, smiling, as we gathered about in a semicircle. It took what seemed a very long time for all the correspondents to get inside and take their places. Every inch of space was occupied in what ordinarily appears a very roomy office.

"All in," came from Bill Donaldson, superintendent of the House Press Gallery, who always functions at these conferences, standing at the door to see that only accredited correspondents are admitted.

A hush fell over the assemblage. The tick of the ancient little clock on the mantelpiece sounded noisy.

"Shut the door!" commanded the President.

This meant something important. It was an occasional precaution taken so that no one in the rear would slip out ahead with the news in advance of those helplessly jammed about his desk.

The President then held up two documents. They were, he explained, two letters which told the whole story. One was his letter to Mikhail Kalinin, of the All-Union Central Executive Committee, U.S.S.R. He read that, prefacing his reading with the statement that this was the first direct communication with Moscow in sixteen years.

Thus the gap was bridged, not by the Secretary of State, not through regular diplomatic channels, but in a personal letter from the President of the United States, himself, a friendly letter, almost an informal letter.

The President then read the reply from Kalinin.

"Who'll he talk with?" some one asked after the Kalinin letter revealed that M. M. Litvinov, Soviet Foreign Commissar, would come to Washington for negotiations.

"With me," came the prompt answer.

Someone wanted to know whether this meant recognition of Russia. The President explained, emphatically, that it did not, that the letters spoke for themselves.

"Can we say it is a forerunner of negotiations?" another voice asked from the rear.

The crowd laughed. The President threw up his hands and joined in. But everybody knew what it meant.

There was another time, five years later, when President Roosevelt wrote another personal note to President Kalinin, on behalf of Finland and Esthonia. But things had changed.

Then there was the day, in the same office, five months later, that he announced devaluation of the dollar.

That should not have been surprising either. We had gone through some strange money motions already. Professor George F. Warren of Cornell had convinced the administration of the price-raising efficacy of his scheme to buy gold in the world market at a gradually increasing price. So, for a time, we made little jokes about the meetings in the Treasury when he and Henry A. Morgenthau, then acting Secretary in the absence of Secretary Woodin, who was ill, and big, bluff Jesse Jones, chairman of the RFC, would assemble daily and fix the price of gold. This seemed a peculiar sort of mesmerism. Then we had seen the President authorize the purchase by the Treasury of all domestically mined silver at 64.5 cents an ounce, 19 cents above its price at that time, a sop to the inflationists led by the redoubtable Senator Elmer Thomas, Oklahoma Democrat. Thomas had pushed through the amendment to the AAA bill early in the administration giving the President the broad monetary powers that enabled him to do this and to buy gold in the world market and to perform all those tricks with gold and silver—including devaluation of the dollar and the later nationalization of silver, the series of acts which brought gold streaming to our shores to be buried at Fort Knox, Ky., later and a flood of silver that was put in a hole in the ground at West Point.

No, there should have been nothing startling about devaluation of the dollar, even though it came suddenly, without warning.

But I had an eerie feeling, a feeling of existing somehow in the fourth dimension, when I stood with the crowd of my colleagues about the big desk and listened to the President's announcement and his explanation of the new trick.

Suddenly traditions crumbled. A strange new world seemed to open ahead of us. Gone, figuratively was the world symbolized in the prints about the wall showing quiet scenes along the Hudson River with paddle wheel boats sedately moving along the Palisades and little settlements at the foot of the steep rock walls.

Money is sacred to an American and now something queer had been done to money.

The last stronghold of an old world had fallen.

It was, for a moment, unbelievable, though ordained for weeks.

The dollar bill cut nearly in half!

The President prefaced his discussion by explaining that he wanted the news to get out quickly to American gold markets which would be open until 5:30, so they would receive it before foreign markets which would not open until morning. So he would be brief and to the point. He was.

He told the essential facts for a news story. Press association reporters broke away, shoving through the crowd, finally free and away, with a clatter and a dash, down the corridors to their telephones. A mad echo of disturbance reverberated for a moment and then again quiet. The news was being flashed to all parts of the world.

Some one then asked why the particular figure of 59.06 cents was selected for the value of the dollar. It was explained that this involved the realm of higher mathematics, that it was desirable to get a fraction between 59 and 60 that would make the price of gold a round number—$35 an ounce being the result.

Casually the President talked.

Stirring and exciting days those were.

29

I STOOD in the station at Kansas City one night in February 1936, and had a vision of our empire.

(I was on a trip about the country. In sub-zero weather I had been wandering through the Middle West and central Northwest, writing as I went, through Indiana and Illinois and Wisconsin and Minnesota and Nebraska and Iowa and Kansas and was taking off for the Far West now.)

Whirling train wheels speed you through a desert of tarnished snow across which wagon wheels moved a nation into a new empire of the West.

You walk under the vaulted roof of Kansas City's great Union Station and see, one after another, the gates that lead away to this vast land. You feel that you stand at the threshold of great adventure. The people who sit here in twos and threes waiting for their trains seem likewise affected. They speak in undertones beneath the high vault that recalls a great cathedral.

Romantic names blaze above the gates—Ranger, Missionary, Apache, Night Hawk, Golden State, Oil Special and

Sunnyland—and again the pages of your story book fly open before your eyes and you're a youngster lying prone before a kindly fire.

Pioneers in wagon trains; LaSalle paddling his canoe in still virgin waters; George Rogers Clark; General Custer and Sitting Bull, and Major Reno riding swiftly but too late; the sudden attack from the circling red men, the guns poking through the spokes of the wagons; thousands of eager people surging about a line to rush, at the crack of a pistol, into new lands—the Dakotas, Oklahoma; the craze for gold and oil; and now the ancients craving for a sunny spot in California for reclining days.

The puny quarrels of little men sink into insignificance.

After all—here is an empire that our fathers built and left to us.

I was out to see this empire at close hand.

I learned that our fathers, while building, also had ravaged and that we had ravaged after them.

My eyes were opened to the way we had spoiled a glorious heritage.

My eyes saw also how we might begin to restore it, for we were beginning. It would take a long time and much care and much love.

I think Franklin D. Roosevelt's chief service has been to show America to itself, to open its eyes. That is the beginning of our wisdom, if we will see it.

One day the sky over Washington was covered with a dingy pall. The wind had brought it in from the West. For the first time we became really conscious of the "Dust Bowl." At a press conference President Roosevelt had talked in simple language about the phenomenon and explained it. He told how two-dollar wheat in World War days had led to the feverish ploughing up of great tracts to plant wheat, wheat, wheat. Greedy men had ripped off the buffalo grass cover which held the land together. Now, stripped of its cover, the dirt became the whim of wind and weather. We had exported our wheat to Europe during the war. At the same time we were, in effect, exporting our rich topsoil. He put it vividly. The dust hovering over Washington told us the price we were paying.

When I went out now to see the country and its people I began, for the first time, really to see it and them.

I had learned in the laboratory at Washington. Now I moved from the laboratory to the field.

Back and forth, going and coming, I crossed the Dust Bowl area in Kansas and Colorado. The first time it was covered by snow. Three heavy snowfalls in some parts of the Dust Bowl had helped some, and when I talked to Governor Alfred M. Landon, who later was to become the Republican Presidential nominee, he spoke encouragingly of this moisture.

When I returned across the Colorado and Kansas Dust Bowl area the snow was gone. Miles and miles of brown land lay exposed, with a dry sort of grass growth in some places, others scooped bare, and, very rarely, a pale green carpet of struggling grass. I passed through towns which a few months before had been nearly inundated by sand.

It was a desolate spectacle.

The day I left Norman, Okla., where I had been visiting friends at the University, the sky was overcast with dust blowing up from the Oklahoma and Texas Panhandle. Sand dunes as high as the barns dotted the land about Guymon, I was told. At Norman I had met and talked to Dr. Paul Sears who had portrayed the problem in his book, *Deserts on the March*. He had just returned from an inspection of the Guymon area.

382

I had asked him about a solution. His reply was that the land should be turned back to grass for a period of from ten to fifty years.

"That's hardly a political solution, is it?" I asked.

He smiled and agreed that perhaps it wasn't a political solution, but it was the real solution. He thought it would take a long time and careful planning. I discovered in my association with Dr. Sears that, when he went travelling, he saw things in the landscape to which I had never paid any attention. I did not even know how to look at the country.

Secretary of Agriculture Wallace and his experts already had begun to work at the Dust Bowl problem and also, on a broad front, to tackle the general problem of erosion of our soil in our whole agricultural region. At last we had begun to see and to act.

Again I saw the tragedy of our ruthless exploitation of our land in another section—the Northwest.

There the Resettlement Administration directed by Dr. Rexford G. Tugwell was engaged on a land rehabilitation program on a large scale. It had begun to acquire depleted forest lands and arid grazing lands in Washington, Oregon and Idaho, with eventual acquisition of 638,000 acres planned for reclaiming. Erosion caused by rapid exploitation of timber resources, by over-grazing, and by over-cultivation had turned this once fertile land into a desert area similar to the Dust Bowls in parts of Kansas, Nebraska, Colorado, Wyoming and Oklahoma.

Oregon and Washington also had had their dust storms— as sailors fifty miles at sea had discovered. Many farmers were forced to leave land that they could no longer cultivate with profit. Others still remained in the new wilderness, derelicts, struggling to eke out an existence, and failing year by year. Their homes had degenerated into tumble-down

383

shacks. A bent old man with long beard, John C. Rush, was still living in a hovel at Lamonte, Ore., when I was in that country—the only inhabitant left, and told how he had founded the town thirty years ago, and how it once had flourished. It was now only a desolate wilderness, like Tyre or Sidon.

The Resettlement Administration then was working out a program which called for purchase of the worn-out land and for moving the farmers elsewhere. The purchase price, if insufficient to start the farmer in another locality, was supplemented by loans. At that time the Resettlement Administration already had aided between 6,000 and 7,000 farmers. In some cases of absolute destitution, outright grants were made with accompanying loans for the purchase of necessary new equipment, seed, supplies and the like.

Rex Tugwell, who had been one of the major philosophers and planners of the New Deal, especially in its rehabilitation and reclamation aspects, was then very much of a bogeyman with businessmen throughout the country. He was scathingly denounced as a Socialist or a Communist, whatever label came quickest to the tongue.

But I found that he was looked upon as a benefactor in that country.

Especially was this true in one spot, one of the "satellite cities," as he named them, at Longview, Wash.

I walked about and inspected the colony and talked to the inhabitants. It was in a neat little valley. Each of the small houses was of different design, with attractive colored roofs, and with a couple of acres behind for flowers, vegetables, a cow and chickens.

Conditions were suitable for this experiment. The colony was about two miles from Longview, itself a model planned city laid out in 1923 about several big lumber mills along the Columbia River. The men of the families which lived in the colony all had jobs in the lumber and pulp mills, their yearly earnings varying from $500 to $1200. They were on a five-day week, leaving them Saturday and Sunday to tend their gardens and keep things in repair. All had automobiles, most of them of not so recent vintage, but sufficiently reliable to take them to and from work and on week-end outings. A garage was connected with each house.

The people I talked to were all enthusiastic about having these little homes of their own.

The cost varied from $2,400 to $3,650, with an average of $2,700. No down payment was required. Each family was paying from $13.50 to $16.75 a month which would amortize the obligation over a long period. No one was behind in his payments when I was there. The sixty families occupying the houses had been carefully selected from four hundred applicants.

I was piloted about the colony by a Republican editor and representatives of the local Chamber of Commerce, who not only approved this New Deal venture but were at that time trying to get the colony enlarged.

Here I found what I often discovered elsewhere, that is, that people who lived in the locality and saw such experiments were for them, where they were practical and on a sound basis—and for very practical reasons. They took care of an underprivileged group, put them on their feet, made them self-supporting so they could be good citizens and send their children to school, and, to the benefit of businessmen, afforded purchasing power for their profit.

Some of the Tugwell experiments elsewhere were ill-planned and were failures. There is no question about that. Republicans let the country know about that, and with exaggerated emphasis. But experimentation is always accompanied at the outset by mistakes, necessarily so. Sometimes proper account is not taken of the human equation.

But little by little, in meeting the manifold problems that encompass us in the way of stranded populations which cannot exist, we will be required to embark upon experiments if we are to repair our economy and remake our country.

Our democracy cannot survive otherwise.

There was another area of distress where Tugwell was regarded as a benefactor.

That was in the North and South Dakota drought areas through which I travelled with President Roosevelt a few months later in the late summer of 1936. Back and forth we rode across desolate country scorched and burned by the relentless sun.

As usual on such trips, the President inspected the area closely, talked to the people about their problems. Frequently he left the train and took automobile trips into the countryside.

The train would roll to a stop in one of the North or South Dakota towns. A crowd always was gathered, from far and near. The President would appear on the rear platform, and a cheer would swell up to surround him. He would leave the train, get into an automobile and make a tour through the countryside. When he would return he would still find the crowd there.

Then he talked to them. He told them they looked cheerful despite their plight. He told them to keep their chins up and they echoed back that they would. He told them that the government was going to help them. He told them they were not going to be moved from the land.

(This last assurance was to mollify resentment aroused by reports that the plan for restoration of this country might require that some of the people be moved. Some of the administration advisers regarded this as necessary for they saw no prospect of farmers in some of the sections ever being able to make ends meet.)

As the President talked, you could feel his good nature, his promise of help, all offered with his amiable and encouraging informality, pervade the crowds which listened to him. They talked among themselves about what he was saying, how he looked.

At Pierre, S.D., after the President had spoken and re-entered the train, the crowd wanted more. Then the strange troupe which accompanied him—officials, "brain-trusters," and members of his family, took their places on the stage into which the back platform had been transformed.

Franklin Roosevelt, Jr., acted as master of ceremonies. He introduced the visiting dignitaries—Secretary of Agriculture Wallace, Harry L. Hopkins, then WPA administrator, accompanying Senators and Congressmen, Colonel Edwin M. Watson, the big genial military aide, all of whom spoke a few words, and—

"We want Tugwell! We want Tugwell!"

He was in the crowd, not on the platform. As the demand was repeated, he hoisted himself up with athletic agility to the rear platform, climbed over the rail and stood there, an Eastern fashion plate, the typical "dude" type to these people.

But he was not the evil genius that he was among Eastern businessmen. He was the handsome and well mannered giver of gifts as Resettlement Administrator. They now cheered him as he appeared and again after he made a brief talk. It was not thus two years before, I learned, when he had come out to this country to make speeches. They didn't like his scholarly manner, the "high-brow" tone of his addresses. But lately he had spent much time among these people, and now he was a benefactor.

That was an interesting experience—that tour through the drought country.

Still ringing in my ears, as if yesterday, is the constantly reiterated line of Governor Tom Berry of South Dakota—the

387

professional barker for the troupe as it wandered through his state—when he introduced the President. He would stand on the back platform, a squat, plain-looking fellow with a greasy, droopy felt hat—and always he would say:

"When he says 'my friends' he means 'my friends.' "

We always waited to hear it—and it always came forth in a high-pitched drawl, almost a sing-song.

We reporters had another little joke among ourselves on that trip.

We called the President "Roosevelt the rainmaker."

He did bring the rain, not much rain, but yet rain.

I joined the Roosevelt special train at Bismarck, N.D., from which point the President began his swing through the drought area. I had been travelling on the campaign train of Alf M. Landon then on his first eastern tour, when I got instructions at Buffalo suddenly to join Roosevelt for the drought tour. (During that campaign I switched back and forth from Roosevelt to Landon to get the complete picture.) Franklyn Waltman, then with the Washington *Post,* received similar instructions. We got off the Landon train early in the morning in a downpour of rain in the Chicago yards and went to the airport where we got a plane.

The rain had extended to Minnesota and eastern North Dakota, we discovered. But it had not reached into the area of severe drought. Below us, as we flew, we could see the cruel handiwork of the sun. There was no green in the neat pattern below—only the seared yellow and brown of blasted wheat and corn.

At the Bismarck airport was a deputy sheriff.

"It looked like we were going to get it—but it never came," he said, disconsolately.

We arrived at the train and found the compartment reserved for us. The President was away at the time, making the first of his automobile tours. He returned to find a large

388

crowd waiting. He made a short speech, outlining the administration's plans for meeting the drought emergency. He held out hope. He told the people he knew they would stay in this country and would lick the drought. After his speech he went back to his private car.

An hour later the rain came—not much, as I said, but it was rain, and a good omen. (Frank and I had been sending our wives messages as we flew across the country signed "The Rainmakers." They are resentful to this day that the President got the credit!)

This rolling empire of the Dakotas, now pock-marked with drought, was not so many years ago part of the old frontier.

Now it had become, along with other states in the Great Plains area, part of a new frontier in the eyes of the Roosevelt administration, a frontier of barren and burned fields to be reconquered and reconstructed.

Science was to be used in restoring the new frontier under a comprehensive plan being developed by President Roosevelt and his expert advisers as he toured several hundred miles back and forth across North and South Dakota and saw with his own eyes the destruction wrought by a burning sun, with no surcease of nourishing rain.

The scene was not an unfamiliar one to the people who lived there. They had seen their crops burned, their cattle suffer and die from lack of water in other years—only so recently as 1934. They were hopeful—to the wonder of us visiting Easterners who, following the trail of drought with the President by train and automobile caravan, saw miles and miles of sickly, stubble-like broomstraw cut near the ground which we were told was wheat that never matured; miles and miles of corn that reached slightly higher, never bore an ear, and now drooped its helpless head and leaves like an army of disconsolate midget scarecrows.

Where there should be grass for pasture there were only dried blades and clumps of Russian thistle. Here and there, but rarely, were green spots where the cattle of some fortunate rancher fed. Frequently, along the road, we saw men and women and boys tending a few cows which they shepherded from place to place in search of feed. Thousands and thousands of head of cattle had been shipped from the state.

Along the roads were groups of farmers with pick and shovel, doing odd jobs of road improvement. They were part of the 33,000 farmers who had been put on WPA at $40 a month at any sort of work, so they could feed their families. Nearby in the field their cars were parked—for not so long ago they were fairly prosperous and a car was needed to move about in this land of magnificent distances and far horizons.

President Roosevelt talked to a typical farmer who was working on a dam, big Steve Brown, in overalls. Once he had a fine house. He had been a homesteader for fifty-one years. Now he was broke.

People here were like people elsewhere. When they had a good year or two some lived up to it, spending their profits. When the desolation of drought came, they had nothing. Others were thrifty, like handsome young Stanley Ripley who sat astride a spirited horse, decked out in chaps and flaming bandana, to wave at the President as the car passed— behind and about him a fine herd of Herefords which he had brought out proudly for the President to see. In his fields were great stacks of hay brought from the Red River Valley. But, they told us, if he couldn't carry his herd through the winter it would be just too bad. (He was such a blithe, debonair spirit. I hope he pulled through.)

This was an up-and-down country, lucky today, unlucky tomorrow, and always in the back of the mind was the big year not long ago, just as the prospector recalls the big strike and keeps panning the gravel.

This was not Dust Bowl country. The soil was rich and still deep and black. What it needed, partly, was rain. But rain had been shy this year, and it was shy in 1934. This couldn't go on.

The story was essentially the same as that of the Dust Bowl to the south—overdevelopment for quick profits and cultivation on too small a scale to pay out. It was the tragedy of 160-acres-and-a-mule economy growing from the Homestead Act of long ago.

They plowed up land which should have been left for grazing. They ravished it. They cultivated it on too small a scale—160 acres was not enough to make a living, when you must figure on a drought every so often.

Thus the tragedy which a series of bad years had brought.

The Roosevelt plan contemplated, first, emergency relief for the present and the winter, and, for the long time pull, a program of soil conservation, proper land use, dams for storing water for cattle and reclamation, crop insurance, cultivation on a larger scale, and, in some cases, removal of families to better areas in the river beds and return of their worn-out holdings to grass and recuperation.

These people did not want to leave the Dakotas. And President Roosevelt assured them that the administration did not want them to leave, but to work out their own salvation with the help of the federal government, the state and themselves, pioneers of the new frontier. They loved this land which reached away, almost forever, it seemed.

On another western trip a year later, again with President Roosevelt, I saw the beginnings of restoration.

We journeyed into the Pacific Northwest, a land at that time alive with the movements of people, migrants fleeing with their goods strapped to their shaky automobiles, fleeing from their impoverished farms in the Dust Bowl.

Some of them were settling in Idaho. We rode for miles and miles one day through new lands opened to reclamation. One of the local government officials who accompanied us explained that many of the Dust Bowl refugees were taking lands here. On one side we would see flourishing production, apples, alfalfa, wheat. Just across the road was an ocean of sagebrush. The land now under cultivation had looked just like that once. All it needed was clearing the sagebrush and water.

This reclamation is not new. It started long ago. The New Deal carried it forward.

In Washington and Oregon we saw brave and bold new ventures inaugurated by the Roosevelt administration. These were the giant power and reclamation projects embodied in the Bonneville Dam along the Columbia River in Oregon and the Grand Coulee Dam in Washington. We visited both of them.

Grand Coulee literally took my breath. Other works of man which I have seen are dwarfs in comparison.

A stocky gentleman of fifty-nine, a man with a story, got on the Presidential special train at Tacoma to ride to the next stop at Ephrata, where we were to get off for the automobile trip to Grand Coulee Dam. He was Rufus Woods, editor of the Wenatchee, Wash., *Daily World*.

The editor carried several copies of his paper in which was reprinted an article he had written nineteen years before. The headline over the nineteen-year-old article read "Formulate Brand New Idea for Irrigation Grant, Adams, Franklin Counties, Covering Million Acres or More; Last and Newest and Most Ambitious Idea Contemplates Turning of Columbia River Back Into Its Old Bed in Grand Coulee, the Development of a Water Plant Equal to Niagara and the Construction of the Greatest Irrigation Project in the World— First Conceived by William Clapp of Ephrata, Wash."

Beside this reprint was a box, captioned "The First Article Ever Written on Grand Coulee Dam," which recited these circumstances:

"On July 18, 1918, appeared the first article ever written on the Grand Coulee Dam. The Wenatchee *World* editor had gone to Ephrata, where he met W. Gale Matthews. Gale said, 'Come with me. Let's go over to Bill Clapp's office. He has a story for you.'"

Rufus Woods got the story. Excitedly he dashed back to his office and wrote it.

Some newspaper stories never come true. Some take years. Rufus Woods' story was coming true after nineteen years for what he outlined is exactly what was being done by thousands of men working on the biggest concrete dam in the world. It would overawe the pyramids of Egypt.

The editor told in the paper which he distributed through the train that day how he had been derided for his dream. When Judge P. S. Steiner of the Superior Court read his original story, he wrote to his friend:

"You are proposing damming the Columbia. Verily, Baron Munchausen, thou art a piker."

But, in 1922, General George Goethals, builder of the Panama Canal, inspected the site and said the dream was practical. Subsequently Calvin Coolidge and Herbert Hoover said it should be done. But they did nothing. Now it was being done by the Roosevelt administration.

In a caravan of automobiles, more than a mile long, our party moved into the forbidding and deserted gorge where, in the ice age, the mighty Columbia poured its waters and carved its course. The ice pack had diverted the course of the river. When the glacier retreated, the Columbia turned back into its original course.

For fifty miles we rode through the old gorge. On each side rose dark cliffs, ranging from 500 to 1,000 feet. Sagebrush covered the floor of the valley. An occasional lake broke the monotony. Here and there a deserted farmhouse told the story of settlers who had come here forty years ago when the land was opened and had to give up for lack of water.

I had a feeling of being transported back into primeval days as we rode through the gorge. Here once flowed the Columbia. At one point a great sheer cliff, stretching across the chasm, marked a waterfall beside which Niagara would be puny. Man now was going to turn the Columbia back into this ancient gorge to form a reservoir fifty miles long, from which water will be pumped over the hills to more than a million acres of rich land which needs only moisture. In addition to forming this mammoth reservoir, the dam will back up the Columbia along its present course for one hundred and fifty miles into Canada, creating a lake along whose shores President Roosevelt, in a speech that day, envisioned at some future day a new civilization.

Emerging from the gorge, we came upon the dam.

I stood high above and looked down upon the incompleted wall of concrete which, when it is finished, will be 550 feet high and three-quarters of a mile across. A third this size now, the prospect staggered the imagination. Thousands of men crawled around far below at their little jobs, like so many ants. Giant machines, looking small from where I stood, swung tons of concrete across the river bed. Doll-houses, so they seemed, clustered about the monument of cement.

In his paper, Rufus Woods told about the migration to a new frontier, a man-made frontier in the Northwest, where millions of acres will be opened to cultivation and electricity will be furnished for light, power, heating, cooking and other services from Bonneville in Oregon, Grand Coulee in Washington, and, eventually, eight other dams to be constructed along the Columbia River.

President Roosevelt saw this development in terms of new homes for Dust Bowl families.

People in the Northwest are eagerly watching. Politicians know how the wind blows. Republicans join Democrats on the water and power issue in the Northwest. That is settled. They quarrel over other issues. One cry is dinned into the politician's ear:

"Water and power."

I talked to a leading businessman in Seattle who found much fault with Franklin D. Roosevelt on many measures. But he was 100 per cent for Grand Coulee Dam. He saw it as a home for thousands of families who were being driven from impoverished farm lands in his own state. There was nothing radical to him in moving people from areas where they could not exist to new homes provided by government help. He saw that this makes for sound citizenship and for local prosperity.

We are told that these ventures are costly.

So is disease that springs from lack of nourishment, from squalor, in our rural districts as well as in the slums of our cities. So is crime that breeds among the alleys, that is nurtured by lack of decent surroundings, by lack of education, by lack of jobs for our boys growing into manhood. So is insanity that comes from inbreeding in our backward communities.

Another year—that was in 1938—I was again in the West with Roosevelt.

In California I learned at first hand of the migration to that state from the barren acres of the Dust Bowl and of the South. Day by day they had been crossing the border in their ramshackle automobiles, seeking a land of milk and honey and finding only abject poverty in filthy camps, fighting to get a day's work at a starvation wage.

The trail of this new problem led me back beyond the Dust Bowl to my own South, to tenant farmers who were being driven from the land, to tenant farmers who knew no other

395

occupation and who knew only one recourse—to fly toward the west.

I visited some of the camps and talked to the people and later wrote about them and their problem. I found them good American stock, anxious to work and to provide for their families. They were the casuals of the long exploitation of our natural human resources. The system could not find places for them and they came boiling, suddenly, up into our consciousness. They had been our bearers of water and our hewers of wood. They had degenerated through the years into slavery and peonage. They knew only how to scratch the land and provide for themselves from day to day. Now they could not do that.

The causes are not simple, or entirely of yesterday or the day before. They go a long way back. They go far afield. They go to a new nationalism which has endeavored to make each nation self-contained, so that there is no longer the demand for our agricultural products in other countries which once bought from us. They go to our own attempts to solve this problem by reducing our acreage so surpluses won't pile up and depress prices, which, in turn, reduces the necessary man-power on farms. I talked to relief directors in the South, some time before my trip to California, who told me of their increasing rural problem due to the reduction of acreage.

"These big farmers are just businessmen, like businessmen in the city," one relief director told me. "They are not philanthropists. So, when their acreage is reduced, they let their tenants go, just as the factory owner does when the demand for his products go down."

The causes go, too, to the replacement of men by machines on the farm, a swiftly developing problem which has been overshadowed by the replacement of men by machines in our industrial structure.

They go, also, to a lack of education for years. We are only beginning to educate for farming.

Roosevelt has seen the problem, and made a beginning. The cure is not easy, if there is one, nor can it be quick.

My own eyes have been opened.

This is my own land and these are my countrymen.

30

THE masses are in rebellion.

The masses are on the march in America.

They are leaving ancient habitats where they can no longer make enough to live from day to day and they go streaming, like lost souls, to some other place on a far horizon which must be greener. From worn-out and dust-blown lands in Kansas and Nebraska and Wyoming and Colorado and Oklahoma they fly northwestward to Idaho and Washington and Oregon and they fly westward to California, the El Dorado of old. To California they fly also from Georgia and Alabama and Mississippi and Arkansas, from my South.

They are on the loose.

They are pioneers looking for a new frontier, and there is no new frontier, except such a frontier as we may create by consciously reclaiming the country we have mutilated. Backward in the years, their great-great-grandfathers and their great-grandfathers and their grandfathers moved, too, as they are moving, first from ancient homelands across the seas in small and stinking little boats to a new America, and, in time, from the cities which grew up along the Eastern coast, further west, and always further west. Smart men moved forever ahead of them and with them, ready to exploit them. They needed railroads to open up the new country and clever men wheedled vast tracts of land, fertile land, land beneath which coal and oil and gold were hid, from legislators with whom money and blocks of stock were persuasive arguments and they built the railroads. They used the railroads for rich, quick profits through stock-market speculation. They bought and sold railroads like so many baubles, getting richer and richer. They acquired vast tracts of land from the government, and they acquired other vast areas by the fraud of dummy settlers whom they hired to take out title to the land, and they acquired other vast areas by tricking the Indians. They got an empire within their grasp, and they squeezed it. They became "empire builders" and we made heroes and great men of them. We set up our own American dynasty, a dynasty in which we glorified the strong and the acquisitive and the scheming. We created our own aristocracy of money and cupidity.

When the industrial system grew up around our cities, our dynasty of wealth and power got their hands on that. Fewer and fewer men seized bigger and bigger portions and tied it together by legalistic devices into modern industrial baronies on the feudal pattern, with power over the lives of many men, women and children, just like the feudal barons of old. I had learned how arrogant and selfish and thoughtless this dynasty was in our own day.

Now the serfs in this modern feudal system are beginning to find out something about all this.

It is almost too late.

But, once awake, they are demanding their share. They are organizing in labor unions to get it in small bits and peaceably. They are organizing as farmers and farm tenants and share-croppers to get a few acres or the right to till a few acres. In the city and the country they are organizing as consumers to protect themselves from the too heavy toll taken by the great monopolies.

But some would get their heritage back more quickly in larger shares and care not for orderly procedure. In desperation and ignorance they follow after false gods. That cannot be helped. So, in the years of depression and desolation when so many lost all hope, they rallied about other leaders than their elected leader in the White House, who himself, was trying to release them from some of their bonds but in a more orthodox way.

Hence the phenomena of Huey Long of Louisiana and old Dr. Francis E. Townsend who once carried a little satchel as a country doctor in North Dakota, and all that crop of smaller messiahs who sprang up about them, among whom was the priest, Father Charles E. Coughlin, who, in these latter days, stirs up racial hatred in a land dedicated to freedom of race and religion.

In Huey Long was a potential American Hitler. I say that advisedly. I knew the man. I knew the land from which he sprang. I knew his abilities and I knew the desperation to which he appealed.

In 1934, when he was at the height of his power, I went to Louisiana and spent some time there studying the dictatorship which he had erected in that one state. Huey then was in the United States Senate, but he still kept his pudgy hands on Louisiana. As a matter of fact just at that time he had taken the final steps which made his power in Louisiana absolute by a series of measures which he had jammed through a supine legislature. He was now The State.

Huey Long had in himself and in conditions in Louisiana among his own people the perfect combination for dictatorship. He rose from the people. He knew them. He knew the way to their hearts and their minds. He saw in them the way to power.

They provided fertile ground, and now I speak of the common masses back in the hinterlands of Louisiana and the common people in New Orleans. Little had been done for them by the successive governors of Louisiana. For the most part, government in Louisiana, what little there was, was dictated by what they like to call "the better element," that is, the élite economically and socially, those who had and saw government only as a means of keeping what they had.

It did not matter if such government was corrupt, if it paid dividends for those who occupied its offices, just so long as it did not interfere too much with the privileges of those who enjoyed economic and social prestige and power.

This sort of government had never worried about the half-starved peasants in Louisiana's backlands, those who picked the cotton and harvested the sugar cane and waded about in the rice fields, who trapped the marshes and fished in the bayous and the lakes and the Gulf, who slaved in the lumber camps and in the factories in the towns, and, in these latter days, worked about the oil fields.

I once spent a whole Sunday listening to a newspaperman who had seen in the young and resourceful Huey Long the instrument by which he and others of like mind who deplored the old political machine could break its power and try to get progressive government for Louisiana. Now, as he walked up and down his sun porch which overlooked the Gulf, he was berating himself and berating the Frankenstein's monster into which Huey had developed. For they had selected Huey, groomed him, pinned their hopes upon him, and now look at him! Huey had just finished winding the chains about the state, and the paper that day had tallied up the new laws by which Louisiana's dictator now controlled the elections in every city, town and village of the state, dominated the courts, held business and industry in thrall. He had levied a tax upon newspapers in the effort to throttle a hostile press; and newspapermen, who had helped to make him, such as my friend, looked in alarm upon the political champion they had raised up.

They had showed him the common people—and there he saw, among the kind he knew, his way to power.

He called to them, and they responded. He promised them a decent way of life, and they rallied about him. He gave them something in the way of bright new roads, and a moratorium for their heavy-hanging mortgages, and tax exemption on their small homes, and free schoolbooks for their children, and a collection of fine buildings for their University, his University it became. But above all, he gave them a champion who knew how to talk their language, who knew how to make them laugh, who knew how to bully them and make them like it. Huey Long was a vivid flash of color against the drab existence in the backwoods. He brought them his own zest for life. He was a one-man vaudeville show so that, days after he had passed that way, they would say to each other, chuckling with fond remembrance:

"Did you hear what old Huey said?"

He also gave them hate, which is as necessary to life as love. He created their enemies for them. He curled his tongue about the names of big corporations, about those who rolled in wealth. He taught them to despise—through bitter envy— those who enjoyed life leisurely in the pleasant ways of New Orleans. He set the "state," as Louisiana beyond New Orleans is called, against the city which is New Orleans.

He taught them to believe only him. He taught them to mistrust the newspapers.

"Don't believe those lying newspapers," he would shout. "Wait till I tell you the truth."

In time he assured them the ballot, and him their votes, by repealing the poll tax law which kept so many of them from the polls, for cash money was scarce among them. Then, finally, he gave them a cause—"Share-the-Wealth." It was vague. He, himself, could never tell how it would be achieved. But he promised them $5,000 and a car and a radio and, in their hunger for some of the pleasant things of life, they believed him, because they wanted so to believe him.

Consequently they voted to strengthen his hands, to give him whatever he wanted in the way of laws, for if he was strong—so he had convinced them—then he could give them all the things he had promised them. To the common people he offered a millennium. To shrewder politicians he offered juicy bits of graft. He became a dictator, and they didn't care.

The deliverer which the down-trodden in Louisiana envisioned in Huey, other down-trodden also saw in him, as he spread from his own state and began to preach "Share-the-Wealth" and to prance before the nation. He became a national character with a following, how great no one ever knew or ever had an opportunity to find out. He had his eyes on the White House. There's no doubt about that. From the best sources I learned that he had plotted with Father Coughlin and Dr. Townsend to put a third party in the field in 1936. He did not expect to carry the election. He hoped to carry eight or nine states and to throw the election to the Republicans and defeat President Roosevelt. He saw his own chance in 1940.

Then the assassin's gun struck him down one night in the corridor of the state capitol outside the governor's office where once he had ruled and which his brother later was to occupy after him. That removed a complicating factor in our politics, at least, if not a real danger to American democracy.

In the long run he gave the poor people of Louisiana little that was lasting. He did not achieve any fundamental reforms. Peonage still existed. He did nothing to lift the slaves from their low estate. He left upon the state a load of debt. He left also the machinery of exploitation and the psychology of dictatorship. To those who succeeded him, those faithful lieutenants whom he had picked to be about him, he left a theory of government which was that the state belonged to them as their personal property and they could do with it as they pleased. They could plunder and steal. And how they did!

The relief with which Louisiana, that is, the average intelligent citizen of Louisiana, saw Huey pass from their midst was somewhat similar to that with which the nation at large welcomed the end of the World War and the loosing of restrictions and the sudden dissipation of the exacting requirements of a tense and anxious patriotism.

No longer could Huey descend upon them, the swashbuckling dictator, and line up his troops about the City Hall in New Orleans. No longer would his henchmen take command of the ballot boxes and make their voting a futile gesture. No longer would his rowdy bodyguards elbow honest citizens roughly from the path of the half-mad clown whose silly grin concealed a ruthless heart.

Louisiana and New Orleans relaxed and sought forgetfulness as the nation had after the World War.

Never had they been greatly concerned about government. They became conscious of it under Huey because, toward the end, it pinched their pocketbooks and disturbed their easy way of life. No one knows how long they would have tolerated him. After all, they did not vote him out of office. They never would have complained much about Huey—I mean the intelligent, vocal citizenry—had he contented himself, as other rulers of the state had, with the ordinary graft that Louisiana expects, and had taken it quietly and not rudely intruded himself upon them to remind them what weaklings they were and how he could do with them about as he wished.

403

His successors promised a return to quiet ways, and no Huey Long appeared among them. They repealed the repressive election laws, retaining such measures as appealed to the masses, and Louisiana lapsed into a gentle slumber once more.

The Roosevelt administration, which had been at war with Huey, effected a "truce," as it was politely called, and once again government money was allotted to Louisiana. It had been withheld in Huey's time.

Suddenly the government dropped income tax indictments against a number of Huey's henchmen—and this was said to be part of the "truce." Westbrook Pegler called it by a name which has stuck ever since and is a part now of everyday Louisiana vernacular—"the Second Louisiana Purchase." These indictments were the outgrowth of a long and careful investigation by a corps of internal revenue agents who began their work first in the Hoover administration. The grand jury had sat for nine months studying the evidence. One of the Long gang, a minor member, had been convicted and sent to the Atlanta penitentiary. Another had been acquitted. Then the rest of the indictments were quashed.

This incensed Secretary of Treasury Morgenthau and Elmer Irey, chief of the Intelligence Unit, who had directed the lengthy investigation. But their resentment availed nothing.

Suspicious circumstances surrounded the quashing of the income tax indictments. Immediately afterward, Louisiana's political leaders announced they were for Roosevelt's renomination. Some fear had existed that a block of Southern state delegations would be broken off from Roosevelt at the convention and later in the election. Governor Eugene Talmadge of Georgia had allied himself with Huey before the latter's death. Gene Talmadge was noisy and active. This threat never seemed serious to me, and certainly not after

Huey's death. Talmadge was not a Huey Long. I knew something of Gene Talmadge. But politicians take no chances. They want to be very sure. Louisiana fell in line at the 1936 Philadelphia convention. It was rather ludicrous to see Seymour Weiss, one of the Long leaders, struggling about the hall in the parade after the renomination of Roosevelt under a big banner "I am for Roosevelt." One of the income tax indictments which had been dropped was against Seymour Weiss.

Nine members of the grand jury which had voted the indictments sent a blistering protest to Attorney General Homer S. Cummings, saying "we, as members of the grand jury have every cause to feel aggrieved and outraged." They said "if the evidence revealed in the grand jury rooms under the guidance of the assistants of the U.S. Attorney General's office was sufficient to indict, then we fail to understand under what proper theory consistent with the integrity and sacredness of the proper administration of justice how this identical evidence has now become so weakened as to warrant the dismissal of criminal charges.

"It seems to us, Mr. Attorney General," the letter concluded, "that such procedure cannot fail to bring the administration of justice into disrepute and dishonor in the minds and judgment of the people."

So thought many others who were shocked at this strange procedure.

The letter from the grand jury opened the way for a quizzing of the Attorney General at a press conference. He had no satisfactory answer, at least so far as I was concerned, and I asked him many questions. He considered all the "hullaballoo," as he called it, to be "synthetic." He regarded the whole incident as a routine matter. The cases, he said, "are as dead as Julius Caesar." Pointing out that the government had won its first case and lost the second, he said "the question

405

arose whether the available evidence might reasonably be expected to result in convictions. It was concluded to leave the decision entirely to the judgment and discretion of United States Attorney Viosca who, upon review of the matter, concluded that convictions could not be obtained and that the only proper course was to dismiss the cases. His motion to dismiss was granted by Judge Borah. The Department of Justice has full confidence in Mr. Viosca, upon whom the burden of these prosecutions would rest, and feels that there is no just ground for criticizing his action."

It developed that Seymour Weiss was in Washington the day before it was announced that the cases were being dismissed. Cummings said he did not see Weiss. Postmaster General James A. Farley said he had not seen him either. Somebody did!

Cummings, at one point during the press conference, said: "All these things are very practical."

So it seemed.

I was in Louisiana in the spring of 1938 and, from information gleaned from newspapermen there at the time, I wrote that "the boys Huey Long left behind him are doing very nicely." They were, I wrote, making politics pay. Plenty of people in Louisiana knew what was going on. In that story I predicted that there would be an explosion some day. I am claiming no credit as a prophet. I merely reported what I had learned.

The explosion did come—a year later. The federal government moved its investigators into Louisiana on a wide front. Caught in the net of indictments for alleged graft were Seymour Weiss, Richard W. Leche, the governor, who had resigned when a scandal broke about the University of Louisiana; Dr. James Monroe Smith, president of the University, who fled to Canada when it was discovered that he had been speculating in the grain market with funds misappropriated from the University; Abraham L. Shushan, who had been one of Huey's lieutenants. Crookedness reached into the highest places of the state. The big fellows were aped by the smaller fry all down the line. They took less. Many of them were caught, too, in the fine fish net flung over the state by the government.

The saturnalia of graft and corruption was fantastic and almost unbelievable.

When Weiss was indicted, it was revealed that only a short time before he had paid a judgment on income taxes under a civil suit for the very same offense covered by the previous criminal suit which had been dropped in 1936. Not only that, but one of the new indictments covered an alleged transaction which occurred only four months after the government had dropped the original income tax indictments.

They were brazen in their operations.

We express fears for our democracy. Democracy is nourished at the roots in local government. The roots had been poisoned in Louisiana so as to produce a rank and noisome growth. The roots were fed from the dank and putrid soil of dictatorship. This dictatorship was possible because local government had not looked after its people, so that its people went chasing off after a demagogue.

So poisoned was the structure that, in the end, the federal government had to come in with its indirect weapons and round up crooks on income tax and mail fraud charges. It is lucky that the federal government has developed these weapons, but it is a sad commentary that it has had to take over the responsibility which citizens of the state had shirked and which they must assume themselves if we are to retain our democracy.

Louisiana offers morals which are quite obvious.

Our democracy cannot survive if we do not provide for our citizenry.

Millions of citizens went chasing after another demagogue and his will-o'-the-wisp—Dr. Townsend and his Old Age Pension scheme.

In 1936, in my tour of the country, I came upon Los Angeles, and there saw the disastrous effects of the impact of depression upon a city built by the promoter, and found the reason for many other things I had observed elsewhere, among them, the fanatical cult of the old folks whose god was Dr. Townsend.

I ran into a newspaperman whom I had known for a time when he had been stationed in Washington. Some time before—prior to the depression—he had made an analysis of Los Angeles for the Commerce Department which told something of the city and explained the distressing condition in which it now found itself, with virtually every third person on relief. This analysis showed less industry than any of the other dozen big cities of the nation; more married women working. The latter largely were employed in the headquarters of promoters. Los Angeles was the mecca of promoters. They sold oil stock, gold stock, real estate and real estate paper. Glittering Hollywood on its edges also was a speculative venture in some respects.

When the depression fell it descended with added force. For the promoters, those who had something to sell to people who had a little money for a venture, who wanted to take a flyer, a risk, found their business suddenly stopped. Stocks and bonds and mortgages went tumbling in value. Investments of all sorts went bad. When I was there I discovered that 50 per cent of those on relief were white-collar workers, the highest proportion of any similar city in the country. Eight thousand men were working on WPA community garden projects, many of them ex-brokers, ex-salesmen of stocks and bonds and the like. There were 10,000 women on sewing projects, many of them formerly employed as secretaries, stenographers, clerks in promotional offices.

Symbolized in the city was all the mad fever of the reckless era and its aftermath when depression descended. Still, despite the wreck and ruin of the gold-brick business and the refuse it had piled up at relief stations and on relief projects, those who had money carried on gaily. Moving picture idols were making theirs—and spending it. I went to the race track at Santa Anita one afternoon, and the totalizer showed $50,000 and $60,000 being bet on every race and, back in the city, destitute people were thankful for a little handout from Uncle Sam.

When the depression hit, it cut deeply into little nest eggs of the thousands and thousands of old people who had come out to sit in the sun in the twilight of life. They represented another migration. This was the end of a trail which led back fifteen and twenty years to Iowa, Kansas, Nebraska and other Midwest states when war prices drove up the value of farm lands and lots of older people sold out and retired, or left their farms to their children to operate and came west to California. Thousands of others who had annuities and investments on which they could live comfortably swelled the exodus.

They helped to increase the population of Los Angeles which had jumped from 102,000 in 1900 to well over a million in 1930 and now was in the top rank of American cities.

Along came the depression. One big building and loan association had crumpled and carried away the savings of thousands. All sorts of investments depreciated. Some were wiped out, leaving only worthless paper. Payments on the farm back home that had been sold were stopped. Children who had been sending funds along could do so no longer.

The old people—and the young, too—were ripe for saviors. Upton Sinclair was first with his EPIC—End Poverty in Cali-

409

fornia—plan of production for use, which very nearly sent him to the governor's chair. Then came the benign old man, Dr. Townsend, the Pied Piper who was going to give all the old folks $200 a month, and started that long parade which began to wind outward from southern California and gradually moved over the Rockies and across the plains and prairies to terrify the citadels of capital in the East.

In the heart of San Francisco, along that street where the trolley car climbs on its cable toward the sky, I listened to the new gospel according to St. Francis Townsend which had gripped the Pacific Coast in a crusade of the old folks.

About sixty or seventy elderly persons were gathered in the weekly meeting of a Townsend Club—one of thousands along the Pacific Coast—in a hall adjoining headquarters of the Northern California Area of "OARP"—Old Age Revolving Pensions, Inc.

Most were fairly well dressed. A few of the women wore fur coats, some of which had seen several seasons. On the back row several old men talked animatedly before the meeting began.

In front of them sat an old woman, scrawny and rawboned, who opened a paper bag on her lap and began to eat. When the chairman called the meeting to order and asked for "My Country 'Tis of Thee," she munched and sang at the same time.

After the song they recited in unison the pledge to the flag, with their hands on their hearts.

The speaker of the evening was introduced, a lean gentleman of Chautauqua bearing, with hair plastered closely and a heavy gold chain across his front, who explained that he once had been a newspaper man. Before long his listeners learned that he spoke regularly to Townsend Clubs, that he was a Democrat of Tennessee extraction and his wife a Republican from the North, but that both are now Town-sendites first and Democratic or Republican second.

The old woman extracted another morsel from her bag and prepared to enjoy herself.

The speaker described the Townsend Plan—and as simply and effectively as I've ever heard it described—with homely examples and then in mock surprise, added:

"And some people don't know yet that it will end the depression!"

"The idea," he continued, "is to stop the depression. Our administration in Washington is trying to stop it and they've done a pretty good job—but it's not functioning as well as it ought."

You got the idea as he went along that his Tennessee democracy was hard to shake out of his system.

He told his hearers that they were to be the "distributing agents of prosperity under the Townsend Plan." He liked the phrase and repeated it.

"I bet when you start you'll be able to spend that two hundred all right—and be sitting around waiting for the next check."

The old lady cackled and took another bite.

"Senator Borah told the people up in Idaho he was for our plan," the speaker said. "But then he went to New York and forgot about it.

"I thought President Roosevelt might be for it. You know Jim Farley went up to Oregon and told those folks up there that either the Townsend Plan or something like it would fit into the President's recovery program. But then they said the President didn't say that.

"But I still believe President Roosevelt's a man of enough sense to come along with us."

Such meetings as this were going on nightly along the Pacific Coast and further east. I found Townsendism a powerful force in Idaho, so that even Senator Borah was giving it a mild nod to protect his Senate seat from the ambitious Governor Ben C. Ross who was making gestures to the old folks. It was a religion in Washington and Oregon. Newspaper editors were afraid to criticize it. The least word of criticism brought boycotts! One editor in a town in Washington told me he dared not breathe a word against Townsendism. It held his town tightly in its grasp, even though there were only two people there who were sixty years old. Many young people espoused Townsendism because it would help their aged and dependent parents and lift that much of the burden of depression from them.

"I know it's not courageous and all that for a newspaper editor to dodge this issue," the editor explained to me, "but after all I've got to live, too, you know. If I went out after the Townsend Plan they'd ruin me."

Many other editors found themselves in the same dilemma.

Much of the pension pressure in Oregon and Washington, I learned, led back to the desolation of vast tracts of land by erosion caused by ruthless cutting of the forests, of which I have spoken previously. The younger people could leave and seek work elsewhere. The older folks were left behind without any means of sustenance. Townsendism seemed a way of salvation to them.

All the tragedy and pity of the old folks and the cheap chicanery of the politicians who exploited and deluded them for their own ends was concentrated and driven home to me at the Townsend convention in Cleveland in mid-July 1936.

From the press section along the front of the stage I looked upon some 10,000 elderly people who had gathered to renew their faith and to rekindle their enthusiasm. Here, in this same great auditorium with its resonant pipe organ, Calvin Coolidge had been renominated . How little we thought then of the wrath to come which now was overspreading our land, though we had been warned of this that same year in Cleveland, but in another auditorium, by the less prosperous, less sleek, and more penetrating crowd which had assembled, with a sort of religious fervor to nominate Senator Robert M. LaFollette for President. Here, only a few weeks before the Townsend convention, I had watched the Republicans nominate a hitherto little-known governor from Kansas, and had seen them embark on a campaign still oblivious to the realities of this day, still pinning their faith on a return to what they called yet "the good old days," some sort of golden era when the stock market bubbled and frothed, and the rich got richer, and the poor somehow could be hypnotized into accepting their lot and liking it, though I'll say that their candidate, whom I came to know well, was not so deceived. The candidate had no such illusions.

These aged people here were filled with illusions.

Among them were stout, comfortable men and women, patient and untroubled and believing. Among them, too, and these were more numerous, were weazened, hard-bitten men and women, their burned faces creased with worry of hot winds which seared their fields, floods which swept away their crops, debts perpetually due.

The men, for the most part, went about coatless. In and out of the auditorium, in and out of Cleveland's hotels, they strolled in their shirt sleeves. They and their women gathered in groups before and after the sessions and talked of the circumstances of their uneventful lives, of the land from which they had come, of their children and grandchildren.

In convention assembled, however, they were crusaders incarnate, they were transformed into disciples of a cause, and with sublime faith they looked to their patron saint before them. Dr. Townsend sat on the platform constantly, the symbol, enveloped in the arms of a regal chair. His face was a mask of patient solemnity. Perhaps he saw himself in the rôle of Abraham Lincoln whose name was so often mentioned here, or perhaps as a modern Moses leading his people from Egypt into the promised land. Moses spoke through the old spiritual from a mammoth banner over his head which proclaimed:

"I am tired of overlords and poverty. God said: 'My people shall be free.'"

Every so often he would rise with a majestic air and his disciples would vow their allegiance in cheers.

"Now listen, my children," he would say in his deep voice.

On either side of the shepherd sat his apostles, some of them shrewd and scheming men. They were politicians and orators of the fullfledged demagogue type, men who knew the trickery of words with which to weave a spell about the old folks who sat there before them.

I pitied the old people and hated those who deluded them. It was tragedy of a sort.

There was a camp-meeting, revival spirit about the convention. All the trappings were provided. The old tunes were played to warm the blood, to recall better days, days of young manhood and young womanhood. Again they were individuals in their own right engaged in a common cause. They were somebody, not just old folks cast aside and treated with feigned sympathy by sons and daughters and relatives who tolerated them.

There were the old tunes with Townsend Plan words. They followed the words in leaflets distributed among them and lifted their quavering voices to the old tunes—"The Battle Hymn of the Republic," "Tramp, Tramp, Tramp, the Boys Are Marching," "Onward Christian Soldiers," "Marching Through Georgia," martial airs and, now and again, the old sentimental favorites—"Coming Through the Rye,"

"Auld Lang Syne," "Love's Old Sweet Song," "I Was Seeing Nellie Home."

Cowbells clanged. American flags were waved.

They were joyous and serious by turn.

An assorted lot of evangelists sweated through their performances on the stage, some of the best rabble-rousers offered by the stump and the pulpit of that day. Disgust turned to pity as I watched the old folks drink in the cheap and artful outpourings.

It was served up literally in a pitcher by the Rev. Gerald L. K. Smith, the one-time preacher who had elevated himself, by an oratorical manner akin to the late Huey Long's, to a place beside the Louisiana dictator, and, when he aligned himself with the losing element in the mad scramble for power after Huey's death, had jumped easily across the short span from "Share-the-Wealth" as proclaimed by Long to the doctrine espoused by Dr. Townsend. In his frequent speeches before the Townsend convention, he would drink from the pitcher on the stand before him, eschewing the glass. After one of his flights of words, he would throw back his head with a smile of triumph, raise his fist and swing it toward the old folks, and shout:

"Give that a hand."

And they would, a deafening roar as he drank deep from the pitcher.

Gerald Smith enjoyed in the Townsend Plan a new meal ticket for a season. He horned himself close into the councils. At press conferences with the Doctor, he would sit by the old man's side and intrude answers to questions, much to our annoyance, finally outspoken. It seemed, for a time, that he was winning his way with the Doctor and I, for one, predicted during that convention that he was on the verge of virtually taking over the old-age pension movement for himself. But he eventually was edged out of this movement, too, and flitted on to preach other doctrines for a price.

Gerald Smith had one saving grace. In groups where only newspapermen were present, he did not assume the high-and-mighty attitude of others of his kind, but recognized that we knew he was much of a mountebank and grinned as we kidded him about his trade and its tricks. It was a living for him, as writing about such as he was a living for us.

He took the newspapers to task frequently from the platform. He would hold up copies of a newspaper and decry the stories there about the convention and, resorting to the trick that Huey had used so effectively, would shout and tear his hair about "these lying newspapers." He looked down one day during one of these fits of assumed rage at us in the press section. His words were taken more seriously by the crowd. Several of the old folks in the front rows were fired up by his remarks and, rising to his words, glowered threateningly at us. Some of them actually wanted to take measures. But nothing occurred more than bitter tirades.

Gerald Smith revealed the basic danger of the religious-flag-waving-appeal to passion and prejudice approach which was his and had been Huey's. I don't like to use labels. They have been worn out and have become meaningless. But this was, for want of a better term, what we call fascist in the original mode.

He spoke of God and country. They were honest God-fearing Americans. They didn't want any foreign isms. His insinuations were against labor unions. He linked up such things with foreigners and atheism. He tried to instil in his hearers contentment with their lot, obedience to authority, which meant the authority of the existing rulers of the economic system—and it was only natural that his next jump, after Townsendism, was to form an organization of businessmen for which he preached the same gospel.

Gerald Smith met his match in another Smith—Gomer Smith, the roaring orator from Oklahoma who later went to Congress for a term and tried unsuccessfully for the United States Senate. The two Smiths engaged in a rough-and-tumble debate from the platform that keyed up the old folks to a fine frenzy and they howled in high glee. Gomer Smith objected to the anti-Rooseveltism of the preacher and the apparent attempt to make the Townsend Plan a unified movement against the President in the 1936 campaign. The two orators sweated and raged from the platform. This rift in the high command, also noted among the rank and file, was taken into a secret session of the leaders one night when an ouster drive against Gomer Smith developed. Late in the evening, as we waited along the corridors, the two Smiths emerged from the hotel room where the conference was held, arm in arm, and went downstairs together. Gerald said his would be orange juice as the two went by together, laughing.

In his opening speech, Dr. Townsend bitterly arraigned President Roosevelt and the New Deal. He still was smarting from the investigation of his organization by a special House Committee which, when he walked out in a huff and refused to testify, had started legal proceedings against him for contempt. He called the investigation "an inquisition" and blamed the administration for it. He accused President Roosevelt of a "deliberate, Machiavellian, planned attempt to discredit and wreck the American principle of government." Gerald Smith was even stronger in his tirade against the administration. He breathed the venom of Huey against Jim Farley and saw the hand of Moscow in the New Deal. He, who had been one of Huey's tools, charged President Roosevelt with aiming at a dictatorship.

Representative Martin M. Smith, a Democrat from the state of Washington, nervously listened to these attacks on

417

the administration. As temporary chairman, he had insisted that the Townsend Plan must not be capitalized by any party or any persons. He could see the intent of Dr. Townsend and Gerald Smith. He was up for reelection. He had organized the first Roosevelt Club in his state in 1932, and he had to keep his alliance with the Democratic organization. Sheridan Downey from California, who had been candidate for lieutenant governor on the Upton Sinclair EPIC plan ticket, who now espoused Townsendism and who later became its champion in the Senate, also used his influence to thwart those who would make the Townsend Plan a vehicle against President Roosevelt.

One of the many paradoxes of the strange meeting at Cleveland was the gentle treatment of Governor Landon, the Republican Presidential candidate, who not only had denounced Townsendism in no uncertain terms but also was critical of the old-age pension plan already enacted by initiation of President Roosevelt.

Father Coughlin was invited to the convention as a guest speaker and, tearing off his coat and jerking off his clerical collar, he delivered one of his philippics against President Roosevelt and the New Deal.

But the outstanding performance of all was saved for the final day of the convention when Norman Thomas, the Socialist, appeared. He ridiculed the Townsend Plan and literally tore it to tatters. He rebuked Gerald Smith and Father Coughlin because they had not mentioned it in their speeches, accusing them of trying to use the elderly people for their own political ends. He was almost mobbed. Several times he was forced to stop by the vengeful "boos" which thundered up at him. Dr. Townsend had to quiet his people, repeatedly, before Thomas could proceed. But he proceeded, right to the end, and had his say. The angry chorus followed him from the convention hall when he had finished. He left smiling and triumphant.

There must have been a few twinges of conscience among the cheap politicians when they examined their own intentions later, though perhaps cheap politicians have few touches of conscience. Norman Thomas had showed them up for what they really were. Such fantasies as the Townsend Plan, he argued, did not meet the problem which the country and the old folks faced. He urged a more basic approach.

Dr. Townsend's desire to swing his followers in a united bloc against President Roosevelt was not realized. Extravagant claims by the Townsend leaders that the loose alliance of their forces, those of Father Coughlin, and the third-party movement, the Union Party, led by Representative William Lemke of North Dakota, would damage President Roosevelt were punctured by the election.

Huey Long, Dr. Townsend and Father Coughlin, however, were effective in their attack from the left flank.

Huey's "Share-the-Wealth" crusade was responsible for what the newspapers called the "Soak-the-Rich" tax bill of the Roosevelt administration which boosted surtaxes on the very wealthy to their all-time peak.

Father Coughlin's advocacy of complete centralization of credit control in the federal government had its influence in further strengthening of the Federal Reserve System's authority.

The popularity of the Townsend Plan, its potency as a political issue, advanced the passage of a social security program by the administration. When Townsendism reared its head again, the Roosevelt administration again moved in 1939 to meet the attack on the left flank by revision of the social security act—to liberalize the old-age pension system by blanketing in many old people previously ineligible, by increasing the benefits, and, in a new departure, to provide real social insurance by authorizing benefits for widows and orphans of workers eligible under the system, whenever they might die.

The messiahs gradually shoved President Roosevelt toward the left.

31

AS Huey Long and Dr. Townsend and Father Coughlin gently pushed President Roosevelt toward the left, the President and his New Deal, still manifestly popular with a great section of the electorate, edged the Republican Party in 1936 slightly off its traditional base.

Its appeal was to the middle classes and, of course, the rich froth at the top which furnished financial assistance but not a great many votes. But these classes, its leaders realized, were not sufficient to win an election. It must dig down into the mass of farmers and laborers, the millions on relief, the millions of others who had been assisted by New Deal measures, and who now were being organized by the Democrats into political units conscious of their power. This organization of beneficiaries of the New Deal created a new political force of which we do not yet know the full potentialities. We will see its impact on elections still in the future.

Republicans, in 1936, did not appreciate the significance of this new political consciousness and organization. They did not realize its fixed and stationary nature—fixed, that is, to President Roosevelt, and standing stationary against all appeals. Roosevelt was their faith.

So Republicans resorted to window-dressing here and there, to some modest compromises and some more radical departures, chiefly as affected the farmers and labor, with the result that their program as enunciated by their candidate was a crazy-quilt pattern designed to catch groups all along the line, but, as a whole, satisfactory to nobody. There was a middle-class revolt against New Dealism, a protest vote. It was substantial, but it was no longer enough to win an election.

American politics had undergone a transformation, little realized at the time.

The middle class, growing smaller and less influential, no longer dominated the nation's life or its politics.

Astute Eastern Republican leaders had little hope of breaking through the Roosevelt front. Such hope as there was, they saw, was to nominate a Westerner in an effort to recapture some of that Middle Western agricultural belt once so strongly Republican. The West nurtured the mildly progressive wing of the party to which, in challenging Roosevelt, some gesture now was necessary. The West had been demanding recognition and a candidate of its own. Hoover was born in the agricultural Middle West and had lived in California, but he was not a Westerner in political thought or philosophy. The West did not regard him as one of its own. He was identified, perhaps because of his international and cosmopolitan background, with the East, with big business and industry and finance.

So now, the Eastern party leaders agreed, we'll make a gesture to the West. It's the only hope. It probably will fail. If it succeeds, well and good. If it fails, then the East again can assume its rightful place in the party. We will have graciously yielded the West its chance.

The cue was given as soon as the Eastern leaders arrived in Cleveland for the Republican convention. J. Henry Roraback, the bulky National Committeeman from Connecticut, who for years had been a power in the party not at all comparable with the size and influence of the state from which he came, announced himself for Governor Alfred M. Landon of Kansas soon after he got to Cleveland. Another potent Eastern leader, National Committeeman Daniel S. Pomeroy of New Jersey, physically a dapper midget alongside his colleague Roraback, a polished Feist to the Connecticut mastiff, headed a delegation pledged to the Kansas governor.

These two men and Charles D. Hilles, the taciturn, thin-lipped National Committeeman from New York with the cold eye and the austerity of a Methodist steward passing the collection plate, composed the triumvirate which ruled the Eastern G.O.P. frontier and, for that reason, very nearly ruled the party of prestige and privilege for so long a period. Mr. Hilles was characteristically cautious and noncommittal, but it was easy to see that he was ready to fall in line with his two associates, since there seemed no other way.

Significant, too, was the support of Governor Landon by C. Bascom Slemp of Virginia, formerly National Committeeman, the wily politician who for years had dealt out the Southern delegations like so many black-and-tan packages of coffee across the counter.

"This is a rank-and-file convention," unctiously quoth Slemp, his pop eyes pools of innocence.

And he did not even smile when he said it, though he must have tittered in that nervous way of his when he talked with his cronies afterward.

"The rank and file of delegates are for Landon. As the former Secretary of Calvin Coolidge, I regard Governor Landon as the nearest approach to the Coolidge ideals."

Velvety Walter F. Brown of Toledo, a smart Ohio political operator who had been drafted by Herbert Hoover to coax delegates for the 1928 convention and, successful at that, had become chief patronage dispenser as Postmaster General in the Hoover Cabinet, took the cue early in the 1936 convention in an effort to save himself from a gang in Ohio which was determined to shear him of his place and power. Interviewed when he arrived, he intoned in his nasal, high-pitched voice that "there's a very general sentiment for Landon among the delegates throughout the country." Walter Brown, to me, always was the antithesis of the political leader, and yet for years he had been one of the most skilful in Ohio, which is tribute enough, and had wielded large influence nationally in the Hoover years. He was almost effeminate in appearance with soft, white hands and a gentleness that belied the tough-fibred realist he was underneath. Now he was being shoved from the scene. Ohio rejected him later as National Committeeman at this convention.

Significant, too, was the word from the Mellon barony of Pennsylvania. The cadaverous ex-Senator David A. Reed saw much sentiment for Governor Landon in his state delegation when he arrived for the convention.

Everybody knew, well before the convention even met, that it was Landon.

The testimony of these leaders was proof enough.

I first saw Governor Landon at Topeka late in January 1936.

When I arrived at the governor's mansion, a big, rambling, typical Middle Western home like those to be found in the best residential districts of cities in that area, I was ushered into the governor's study by the maid who had answered the door. A fire was burning in the grate. Kansas was cold and bleak and snow covered the ground.

I sat waiting for the governor. Suddenly I was conscious of a sound, and I turned. There he stood in the door. I got to my feet. I saw a small figure. The first impression was disappointing—for a Presidential candidate. He struck me as an exact symbol of the average man. We shook hands. He had a pleasant smile.

We sat down and I asked questions and he talked, now with his head resting against the back of his chair, now—as he became emphatic—leaning forward alertly. Occasionally he got up and roved about the room—not with the nervous pacing of some of the public men I had interviewed, but in an easy stroll. The most definite impression of the man was an air of casualness which extended to his dress. He was a comfortable sort of fellow.

As he answered my questions and talked he built up the pattern of a political philosophy compounded of bits of stern conservatism and bits of what some call liberalism. His emphasis on economy was instinctive and inherent. It was predominant in his personal life and in his political creed. (He had kept a personal budget in college—and much was made of that later.) He had a close interest in the farmer, living with him as he did in Kansas. He had accepted the AAA while it was alive and, now that the Supreme Court had nullified this form of farm relief (which had happened only a few weeks before), he saw eye to eye with Roosevelt on a long-time soil conservation program whereby worn-out land would be withdrawn from cultivation for a cash rental. Farm relief, he held, must not be made a political issue. That was hardly possible between him and the President, considering their common views.

He accepted some New Deal objectives in other directions as they related to spreading benefits of government on a wider basis, but he criticized the administration of New Deal reforms. He accepted the fact of a changing and complex society which necessitated new departures in government.

He bespoke the antipathy of the farmer and small business-man in his region to what he called "the great industrial plutocracy" which had been built up in the country and which, he held, intensified the depression. He was for social security, for assistance to the unemployed but not, he insisted, as a privilege or a vested right, not as charity, but as a common obligation.

What tantalized me at the time, and I wrote as much in my story, was how he would have economy of the sort of which he talked and, at the same time, provide for farm subsidies and relief costs on the scale he advocated. I saw that conflict rise to plague him later and to transform his campaign into a confusion of paradoxes from which it was impossible for him to extricate himself.

I left with the conviction that he would not be the nominee of the convention a few months hence.

As I went further west and talked with people I heard very little mention of him. Senator Borah of Idaho, shop-worn politically as he was, was most frequently mentioned. But, even while I travelled further west, William Randolph Hearst and his clever phrase-makers descended upon Topeka and took over the mild-mannered governor and began to organize a propaganda campaign that blossomed forth soon into newspapers and magazines. Overnight Alf Landon became a figure and a character, so that, by the time I returned to the East several weeks later, the Kansas governor stood at the top of the polls and Republican politicians were talking about him.

It was another one of those masterly jobs of creative journalism such as I had first seen, over a decade before, when the timid and cautious Calvin Coolidge had stepped into the White House at the death of Warren G. Harding and become, almost in the flash of an eye, the strong, silent man.

It can be done only in America, but how well it can be done in America! I still marvel.

425

America hypnotizes itself and creates its heroes quickly—as quickly as it destroys them.

But that came later.

I arrived at Cleveland to find the legend full-blown, the legend of "Alf," the plain fellow from Kansas, just as, years before, it had been "Cal" the plain fellow from Vermont who kept his mouth shut and tended to his business.

It was clever and effective publicity. The idea was to offset the glamorous, dramatic figure in the White House who had some people a little dizzy with his lightning reforms and his legerdemain; to encourage a current tendency of Americans to retreat from reality, to retire mentally to former days when life and its problems seemed simple, at least in retrospect from this depressing and confusing time—a tendency even then reflected in the literature of the day, in the drama and moving pictures which delved back into the past and recaptured a primitive simplicity. President Roosevelt had held the "horse-and-buggy" days up to ridicule. Now the Republicans would glorify them.

Very apt was the choice of the Landon campaign song; the lilting "Oh, Susanna," the song of the Oregon trail.

One day wandering through one of Cleveland's hotels before the convention opened I ran into an old friend who worked for the Hearst newspapers, the late John Lambert. John told me of the selection of this song. He invited me to go by the room where the group of Kansas newspaper editors who were "brain-trusting" and nurturing the Landon campaign were gathered.

They were discussing informally the trappings of their campaign to put Landon over at the convention. They had their song and now someone suggested that they ought to hire a band. Good idea, agreed the others. They lolled about upon the beds and chairs and tables. One was for a twenty-piece band. Another thought that wasn't big enough and suggested forty pieces. There ought to be a lot of brass, put in another. How much would it cost? They began to figure. Finally they decided upon a twenty-piece band. After all, it shouldn't be too elaborate.

The Kansans, thinking and acting along ordinary lines common to Kansas, were far shrewder in their appraisal of how to present their candidate than would have been a crew of high-priced publicity men.

So we heard the band and saw the pictures of smiling "Alf." "Oh, Susanna." It caught on. The band played through the streets and paused for a serenade before the hotels where delegates stood gossiping in the tiled lobbies, shifting from one tired foot to the other. A trio, two accordions and a fiddle, wandered, minstrel-like, through dining rooms and into noisy cocktail bars.

Everybody smiled and clapped and thought of the old home town. The sights and sounds and smells which were Cleveland faded away and a pleasant reverie lulled the senses—

An old man who dozes before the country store suddenly pushes his head against the friendly post where it reclines, jimmies his chair forward, spews a stream of tobacco juice into the road and settles back to meditation.

A casual boy, with straw hat shoved back across his freckled face carelessly, flaps his bare feet along an unpaved road and squeezes the gray powder comfortably through his toes.

"Horse-and-buggy days."

"Alf" Landon of Kansas.

He grinned from the posters, just one of the folks. You felt you could call him "Alf," and it would be all right.

And one hilarious night he grinned from scores of banners as the bands played "Oh, Susanna" and the wild procession streamed giddily about Cleveland's convention hall,

427

and "Alf" Landon was the Republican nominee for President.

It happened on the first ballot. John Hamilton of Kansas and Roy Roberts, managing editor of the Kansas City *Star*, who had been one of us as a Washington correspondent a few years before, had done their work well. The boom for Frank Knox, the Chicago publisher, had faded away and he had taken second place on the ticket. The cagey Senator Vandenberg of Michigan had gambled with the fates and decided to save himself for four years later when he figured that a Republican ticket would do better.

There was just one hitch before the nomination of the Kansas governor and, when I think of that, I think of the tiny line of worry on the face of John Hamilton as he stopped for a moment in the milling, excited throng in the aisle in front of the press section. He rested his arm on the rail. I asked him how it looked.

"Everything's all right," he replied. "This is just a personal tribute."

"This" to which he referred was the chant "We want Hoover" which was sweeping the convention hall.

Herbert Hoover was gone now. He had stood there on the platform above us, looking out over the crowd, timidly venturing a half smile, raising his hand now and then in that hesitant incomplete gesture that I had known so well eight years before. He had finished the address which the convention had asked him to deliver—as its standard bearer in two campaigns, its President in the White House in desperate years. A tumult shook the hall. State banners began to bob about in a merry parade. Hoover would start from the platform, get a few feet and then, when the crescendo of personal tribute would rise again, would return to the front of the platform. Finally he left the platform and the hall and returned to his hotel. I think he had expected someone to jump up and nominate him and stampede the convention, hoping against hope. But no one had. So he had left.

But the crowd now was whipped up to a fine frenzy. Someone started the chant "We want Hoover" and it was taken up all over the convention. It was too bad that Herbert Hoover had left—except that he would not have known how to take it. He would have been very, very uncomfortable.

I'm quite sure John Hamilton was uncomfortable despite his protestations to me. But his lines held firm.

Landon was nominated the next night and John Hamilton breathed easy once more.

Alf M. Landon had been a Teddy Roosevelt Bull-Mooser in 1912, as had the Kansas editor, one of his sponsors now, William Allen White, that perpetually amusing, delightful, and sagacious figure of our national life.

A rash of Kansas progressivism broke out over Alf Landon, back home in Kansas, during the Cleveland convention, much to the annoyance of some of his Eastern backers. The Supreme Court, in the backward trail which had knocked down some of the Rooseveltian reforms, penetrated even deeper into the foggy wilderness of American jurisprudence and bowled over New York state's minimum wage law for women. This decision, another of the 5-to-4 fiats, had shaken even conservatives, and had intensified the clamor, now growing more general, to "do something about the Supreme Court." Republicans would not dare attack that sacred institution directly. But Landon thought the party should express itself in some manner, and he and his representatives in Cleveland sought a plank in the party platform endorsing a constitutional amendment empowering the states to draft laws regulating wages, hours and working conditions. This was begging the question somewhat, but it was strong medicine for orthodox Republicans and the platform-makers refused such a plank. So he sent a message to the convention after it had adopted the platform—but before it nominated him—"interpreting" the platform for himself to include advocacy of such a constitutional amendment, and also eventual return to the gold standard as well as extension of the Civil Service to cover all positions below the rank of assistant secretaries in all departments and including the entire Post Office Department and postal services—two other planks which he and his friends sought in vain from the platform committee.

Twice before had nominees taken issue with the party's platform, both Democrats—Alton B. Parker in 1904 proclaiming his adherence to the gold standard against the Bryan silverites, and Al Smith in 1928 refusing to abide by the platform on prohibition. Those two candidates had spoken after being nominated. Landon took his position in advance, giving the delegates an opportunity to reject him if they desired. It was a bold stroke that raised his stock in the country, for the moment.

There's a humorous little sidelight on the Landon "telegram" to the convention, expressing his views.

As is often the case there was no "telegram."

Landon was in constant touch with William Allen White, Roy Roberts, Hamilton and others by telephone. He outlined his views on the subjects previously mentioned and through consultations the message was drafted and worked out. But no telegram ever was sent.

The draft was completed only a short time before it was to be read to the convention. Then suddenly Roy Roberts, himself a newspaperman, realized that while this was supposed to be a telegram from Landon, there was nothing to indicate that—and he knew newspapermen would be curious. (As it turned out, they were not very curious.) So, at the last minute, he and Hamilton dashed away to a Western Union stand in the lobby which circled the hall outside. Roy

430

procured a blank and laboriously using the well known newspaper two-finger "hunt and punch" system started to make a copy of the "telegram" from a copy on white paper which Hamilton had.

He hardly had begun when, over the loud-speaker, came an announcement by Representative Bertrand H. Snell of New York, permanent chairman of the convention, that John Hamilton would be recognized to read a message from Governor Landon. Hamilton dashed away with his copy, made his way to the platform from the rear, and read it to the convention. When he finished, Lyle Wilson of the United Press, sitting on the front row of the press section, shouted up at him:

"Give me that, John."

John complied, confused, forgetting that he had but this one copy.

Wilson snatched it and had the operator at his side send it. Other newspapermen began to howl and shout for copies. John had none. Wilson thus got a beat on one of the big stories of the convention. The others had to wait until his operator had transmitted it.

The battle within the secret sessions of the Resolutions Committee over the three planks which Landon added to his platform at his own initiative demonstrated the division within the Republican Party over political, economic and social philosophy and approach, a division which has continued, which occasionally has broken into the open in recent months, and which becomes more manifest as the party seeks to formulate a program for the 1940 campaign. Division within the Democratic Party has taken the spotlight since it is the party in power responsible for policy and program.

Landon became aware, even before he was nominated, of the several wild horses that he would have to ride in the campaign, though he could not foresee that, before it was over, the spectacle would become a public circus that would be so highly amusing to so large a part of the American audience.

In the end he was a confused little jockey with the horses struggling to dash off in every direction.

He got one vote for his proposed constitutional amendment plank in the drafting subcommittee of the Resolutions Committee. That came from William Allen White. Another Kansan, Henry J. Allen, ex-governor and ex-Senator, went before the committee with a personal plea for the amendment plank on behalf of Landon, but nobody would pay any attention. Ex-Senator Reed, spokesman of the Mellon interests, led the fight against it, demonstrating that big business still had a powerful voice in the Republican Party. Landon would not back down. He suggested that the plank be carried to the floor for a fight. John Hamilton advised against this, and it was decided to use the message to the convention instead.

In his proposed Civil Service reform plank the Kansas governor ran up against the practical politicians who argued —and successfully—that it was folly to lop off Post Office patronage, the sustenance of political organization. This was particularly efficacious in the South where it was the basis of the Southern political machines, about all, in fact, that the Republican Party had in the South. Southern Republican bosses clung desperately to these sinews of their organizations. In this way they had built up their power. Thus they were able, every four years, to trade their support to ambitious Republican Presidential aspirants for a price, to sell their black-and-tan delegations to the highest bidder. How often I had watched that process.

No, Mr. Landon, no funny idealism from you. Thus, in effect, spoke up the hard-boiled politicians.

In demanding a plank advocating an eventual return to the gold standard, the Kansas governor took his stand with the Eastern, hard-money conservatives against the Western inflationists whose chief spokesman at the convention was

Senator Borah. But the conservatives on the Resolutions Committee preferred to yield on this point, and refused to back the governor, as a gesture to the West where they needed support if they were to win.

Senator Borah was, to me, a disappointing figure at this Republican convention. He was, again, the eternal Prodigal Son of the Republican Party. He arrived, the familiar shambling figure, but less fiery, still, however, with a hint of the old power, a power emanating somehow from his leonine head, his spiritual placidity, his casual air of humility that derives from inner confidence. He was bearing a handful of delegates, an antipathy to the midget Kansas governor, a few ideas about the platform, including some out-of-date thoughts about monopoly, and his perpetual idealistic allegiance to a Republican Party which never existed. This allegiance so often before, in the end, had weakened his resistance to the more realistic powers that be. He still was able to draw a crowd. A press conference was set for a morning hour, was postponed from time to time, and finally, at four o'clock, we waited in a small room where we almost were sitting upon each other. It was necessary to move the conference to a big dining room. It was a veritable mass meeting. The ample Senator sat himself down on one of those spindly-legged gold chairs (which seemed hardly capable of supporting his weight) in the middle of the polished floor, like an exhibit, and we gathered about in a giant circle. He warmed up to his rôle of Chief Thorn-in-the-Flesh as a dozen photographers snapped his picture with a pyrotechnic display of flashbulbs and, when that was over, as we began to shoot questions at him. Smilingly he answered.

He was interested in a strong plank condemning monopoly and pledging enforcement of the antitrust laws and this gave him an opportunity for an aside to the effect that one of the candidates at this convention—and we did not have to guess very hard—was being supported by oil men. He was joining no alliance with anybody against anybody else. He wanted a foreign affairs plank that would pledge the party against any entangling alliances abroad, by which he renewed his isolationism. He did not want any mention of the gold standard in the platform. He wanted the party to endorse the administration's silver policy. He did not see any point in advocating a constitutional amendment to let states regulate wages, hours and conditions of labor, for he was sure the states already had this power and that the Supreme Court, once presented with a properly drafted state law, would so declare.

They did not make him a member of the Resolutions Committee. He sat on the outside and met his emissaries from time to time with news of the progress of his ideas. He expressed himself as satisfied, when the platform was completed, with its treatment of the subjects in which he was interested, picked up his hand satchel and left Cleveland before the convention really got down to business. They invited him to address the convention. He refused.

He went away, a spent warrior with no fight left. He had asked little. He did arouse himself when he heard, on his way back to Washington, about Landon's gold-standard position as enunciated in the message to the convention. That seemed to anger him. He kept party leaders on tenterhooks wondering what he would do, whether he would support Landon, whether he would bolt. He enjoyed their suspense and gave them a tantalizing nibble from time to time. In the end he went back home to Idaho and bothered only about his own reelection. He remained completely aloof from the national campaign, just as if there were none. John Hamilton worried his red head for a time about getting Landon and Borah together, and then gave it up and forgot about it. Borah knew John was piloting a sinking ship and he did not care to get aboard.

Landon should have known his well-nigh impossible task by the time the convention was over.

He couldn't satisfy Borah. Nobody ever did—and that would not have been so bad; except that Borah did represent a large body of Western opinion. He could not satisfy the Eastern conservative leaders. But all the diverse groups pulled and hauled at him anyhow.

I liked the man and I felt sorry for him as I saw him go to work. He did have good instincts and a refreshing viewpoint—for a Republican.

I galloped about the country with him, off and on, sandwiching myself in between him and President Roosevelt during the campaign, now with one, now the other. Always he had about him the group of Kansas newspapermen and editors who were like so many guardian angels. They realized early, as did all of us who travelled with him, that he was perhaps one of the worst public speakers who ever ran for President, and that his radio voice lacked most of the necessary qualities. A radio voice, we realized for the first time in 1936, was an essential now in politics. Roosevelt had made it so. Landon had a course of instruction on radio speaking. As the campaign progressed he improved some—but not much.

But his little group of guardian angels was ever hopeful. I can see them now, and hear them, as they sat around together after a public meeting, trying to see improvement.

"I believe he was better tonight," one would suggest.

"Yes, I believe he was," was the assurance from another. It was almost like the mother who had heard her child "speak a piece" at the school exercises.

435

His manner of speaking was one problem. What he said in his speeches was another.

It probably would have been better had he confined himself throughout to the meaningless platitudes of his first few speeches such as the one he delivered at West Middlesex, Pa., his birthplace, where he essayed that priceless line: "Wherever I have gone in this country I have found Americans." He could not have gotten into so much trouble, and he got into plenty through his inconsistencies.

At first he said little and contented himself with creation of an atmosphere. I travelled with him on that trip from West Middlesex through the Pennsylvania of his early boyhood and into western New York. There he employed what I labelled "the lavender-and-old-lace technique." It was a sentimental journey. It brought the little red schoolhouse and the ivy-mantled church back into politics. He attended Sunday services in a neat brick church in West Middlesex and all the townfolk who could not get into the church crowded the walks outside to see a Presidential candidate. We newspapermen, of course, trooped into church behind him and properly took notes of the sermon and joined, self-consciously, in singing the hymns we had known long ago.

We might have been campaigning with William McKinley —though McKinley, of course, had done his campaigning from a front porch. There was something of that turn-of-the-century aloofness in this journey through the little towns. It was late August. The feel of autumn was in the air. The sun sifted through the trees in a mellow haze and dappled the streets and the middle-class homes with beneficent tawny lights and shadows. There was coolness in the breeze which rustled the leaves and was driving the summer slowly before it into retreat for another year. We might have been living in a world of long ago, for all the peaceful surface of things

436

in the small towns and for all the things of which Landon spoke in that Pennsylvania journey. Only occasionally did we glimpse the dingy factory which had raised so many of the problems which confronted us in this day. Not until we got to Buffalo did we rub up against the plain people of the big city, and know that we were back into a today that was a thousand years from the yesterday through which we had been travelling.

Not once in that sentimental journey, though it was along the very fringes of the industrial East, did Governor Landon say a word about labor, about wages and working conditions, about social security. The philosophy which emanated from him, not in words but in his actions, was built about the roseate thought that America was once a happy land and that perhaps it would be a happy land again.

Other days were the happy days.

So the genial candidate, who knew something of the psychology of the average man, pointed back to other days by recalling his own experience in the western Pennsylvania and New York of the late 'nineties. Everywhere he went he dug up an old association.

At Sharon he recalled how he used to fish along the towpath of the old canal. Conneautville, where he went to school for a year, brought back memories of the racket store where he spent his pennies and nickels, the foundry where he used to play, the first storm door he ever saw, and Dr. Sloan's horse and buggy in which he once rode. He grinned when he spoke of the horse and buggy—and the audience got the point. Then he spotted in the crowd the two "girls" he used to know "looking just as pretty as they ever did."

And the band played "Oh, Susanna."

Grant Flynn, who still ran the racket store as he had for forty-five years, stood out in front, an old man now, and allowed that though he was a Democrat maybe he'd vote for

437

"Alf" Landon this year. Children were in and out of the store, as Alf once was, eyeing enviously the knickknacks on the gloomy shelves.

The hero of the day, the boy who had made good in the West, stood on the steps of the old frame hotel, rubbing elbows with his friends, and talked in his neighborly, slightly halting, impromptu manner to the townspeople and visitors in for the day who were jammed about the sunny square. His manner was just a bit self-conscious.

Conneautville supplied, fortuitously, one of those exciting episodes of the small town on a holiday. There was a flurry of excitement about the front of the hotel where Landon stood, a commotion in the crowd, and shouts of "stop him." A pickpocket had been plying his trade. Down a side street men and boys dashed madly in pursuit. Just before we left, a deputy sheriff brought his quarry to the train siding and we took down the name of the frightened and dishevelled young man. He had been handled very roughly. (He had picked the wrong town, the wrong occasion and the wrong pocket.) The deputy sheriff wanted us to know he was not of Conneautville, not one of theirs. He came from somewhere else.

Nor was Alf Landon a stranger, we discovered, in Erie. The train was stopped on a bridge which crossed above the streets and the crowd was gathered below. It responded with a merry laugh when he told them that he once thought the Reed House was "the grandest hotel in the world." He had an uncle, he said, who used to run a locomotive on the Bessemer many years ago. And then, delving into family history, he related how his great-great-grandfather raised a regiment in this section and marched it through the woods to Admiral Perry's base in Erie in the War of 1812.

The Republican candidate was at his best in these informal little talks on that trip. He seemed to have an appreciative audience, at least, here amid the scenes of his early life. He never recaptured the informal manner and approach afterward. People in the West, among whom I travelled with him later, were disturbed and were not so receptive to what I might call this small talk. And, when he declaimed seriously later about major issues before great throngs, he appeared a futile, ineffectual little man who lost his audience completely by the time he was half through his speech. Here, in his brief excursions into a world of the past, he had a charm. He won the sympathy of his audience by his friendliness and by his lack of oratorical finesse. He had to grope occasionally for words, often stumbled and left his sentences in mid-air. He had a hesitant manner, half embarrassed, saved by a grin, a duck of the head, and a wave of the hand, characteristic of the late Will Rogers. The crowd saw itself in him.

He reached out and boldly took hold of an issue affecting civil liberties in his speech at Chautauqua, N.Y. There he condemned the New York law—also duplicated in a few other states—requiring schoolteachers to take an oath of allegiance. In thus giving expression for the first time to the Kansas liberalism which had discomfited some of his orthodox G.O.P. backers at the Cleveland convention he stepped on the toes of William Randolph Hearst, his chief newspaper sponsor and promoter, whose New York papers had campaigned for the act, as well as such organizations as the American Legion, the Daughters of the American Revolution, not to mention leaders of his own party in New York state. A Republican had introduced the bill. The Democratic Governor, Herbert H. Lehman, had signed it, so the Democrats had some responsibility. Landon was, for the moment, like the small boy who suddenly kicks his father in the shins. His Chautauqua speech was a one-day sensation. Mild liberals who were supporting him turned it over in their hands proudly and held it up for all to see with: "Look! We told you."

On that occasion, I witnessed for the first time that spectacle known as "The Chautauqua Salute," when, at the appropriate time, everyone in the audience waves his handkerchief, like a great flutter of white pigeons loosed upon the air. It is quite remarkable.

At Buffalo, the Republican candidate stepped back into character as a regular Republican with a denunciation of the undistributed profits tax which President Roosevelt's New Dealers had devised to force the disgorging of hidden surpluses of great corporations. He pledged repeal of the law. In his discussion of taxes, he went out of his way to crack William Randolph Hearst on the shins again by condemning the sales tax principle as an invisible tax which bears too heavily upon the wage earner, the salaried worker, the small businessman and the farmer.

He spoke in the baseball park at Buffalo. A raw, cold wind whistled across the field. Altogether it was a gloomy prospect and those who had gathered to take a look at the man who was trying to unseat Franklin D. Roosevelt shuffled about in the night wind, trying to keep warm. A speech on taxation meant little to most of them and interest waned. His hearers began to straggle away before he had completed his speech.

But there were some who rose to it—the dignified proper businessmen and party leaders who sat on the platform. Ogden L. Mills, former Secretary of the Treasury, and Representative James W. Wadsworth, two conservative leaders, clapped their hands enthusiastically when he denounced New Deal "soak-the-rich" tax plans, and seemed, for the moment, to forget the weather.

Always these old-line party leaders, some so discredited by this time, managed to group themselves about the Kansas candidate on the platform when he spoke. So it had been at West Middlesex, Pa., when Joe Grundy, the high-tariff advocate, the collector of campaign funds from his state's big interests, the foe of social and child labor legislation, emerged from an oblivion to which the New Deal temporarily had consigned him, and beamed and smiled from the platform, shaking hands around with others of his ilk who had been invited—much against the counsel of some of the newer party leaders in Pennsylvania. Joseph N. Pew, the oil magnate who began, in 1936, to buy an interest in the Republican Party and since then has acquired a rather heavy mortgage on its Pennsylvania principality, was present. So, too, was ex-Senator Reed—representing the Mellons.

They could stand a few "liberal" gestures from Alf Landon. They thought they would be able to manage him and keep him in line if he ever got in the White House, of which, of course, they were not very hopeful.

Later, however, as the campaign developed, they began to have doubts about their candidate—and they lost interest.

The cause célèbre was the farm speech he delivered at Des Moines. Here, in a desperate gesture to the agricultural Middle West, he virtually promised to open all spigots of the Treasury at Washington and pour out to the farmers to their satiety. They had asked almost nothing that he wouldn't deliver—according to his speech.

The scene was well laid for this drama of beneficence, what I termed at the time Landon's "Me, too," act. The meeting was at the race track and we looked back, from the press section, upon an expectant mob in the grandstands. Many farmers had driven in from the surrounding countryside to see what the Republican candidate had to offer them. Suddenly, as we waited and watched the crowd, there was a commotion down the race track at the turn into the homestretch. Sirens howled and an automobile procession appeared, preceded by policemen on motorcycles. The crowd began to roar. Standing up in an automobile, waving his hat to the crowd, was the smiling "Alf."

"Paul Revere," someone near me in the press section mumbled.

Paul Revere was a silversmith. His modern prototype dealt, this evening, in gold, great handfuls of it. You could almost see the yellow flood rolling like so much lava from the Treasury as the little man promised and promised and promised. Republican criticism of the rain of farm checks from the New Deal of which we had heard so much for so long, was drowned in the lava flow of gold this night.

He used the term "cash benefits" four times. He would pay the farmers, if elected, all checks that were due them under New Deal obligations. He would use the full power of the government to relieve distress arising from the drought. This, he said, meant continuation of relief checks. It meant also, he said, continuation of seed loans "and other necessary assistance in order that the farmer may get started again." He approved the AAA, now killed by the Supreme Court, as an emergency measure but claimed in its later stages it had sought permanent control of agriculture from Washington. To supplant the AAA, he was for a soil conservation program, with benefits even to those who were not able actually to practice conservation. (The New Deal already was embarked upon a soil conservation program.) He was for crop insurance, though apparently on a private insurance basis, rather than the scheme for payment in kind proposed by Secretary of Agriculture Wallace. He was for Wallace's "ever normal granary" plan for storing surplus crops on the farm. He was for government aid to help tenant farmers acquire their own lands, already advocated by the administration. Then, on top of all of that, he advanced a plan for equalizing the industrial tariff for the farmers which he did not explain, but only quoted the Republican platform—"To

442

provide, in case of agricultural products of which there are exportable surpluses, the payment of reasonable benefits upon the domestically consumed portions of such crops, in order to make the tariff effective." Landon declined afterward to tell newspaper correspondents how this scheme would be worked out, but it appeared to be along the lines of the Export Bounty plan or McNary-Haugen bill, both long advocated in Congress, with subsidies paid on the part of the crop domestically consumed and the surplus to be dumped at world prices.

Landon conceded realistically in his Des Moines speech that the foreign market virtually had disappeared, agreeing with Secretary Wallace. This was a shift from the previous Republican attitude. Farm editors who had met with him at Topeka a few days before had been responsible for the switch. They also had told the Republican candidate that the crop curtailment program would have to be continued, but he would not accept this view.

Landon's lavish promises to the farmers at Des Moines were provoked by Republican questionnaires in the Middle Western agricultural area showing concern over the candidate's emphasis upon economy. Yet, in his Des Moines speech, he had continued to stress his determination to cut out extravagances and reduce the tax burden!

A few months after the election I was talking with one of the campaign managers and I spoke of the Des Moines "Me, too" speech and the inconsistencies. He could afford to be philosophical now and to smile, though still with an ironic curl of the corners of his mouth.

"Well—a lot of other people saw the inconsistency of that speech—and promptly. You know some of the fat cats who had been contributing stopped right then. They told me 'We know what Roosevelt will do—but this fellow Landon—.' They just refused to give any more."

Nor was the conflict between manifold farm benefits and economy the only inconsistency in that performance.

The program he outlined at Des Moines was national planning for agriculture of the most expansive sort and brought an exultant editorial outburst from the Des Moines *Register* which was supporting the Kansas governor but which, hitherto, had found little over which to wax enthusiastic.

"Governor Landon," it said, "has dumped 'laissez-faire' ideology clear out of the window. He has plumped for a broad fine policy of national planning in the sense that our national founders themselves did not shrink from."

Ten days before the Des Moines speech, speaking at Portland, Me., with an appeal for "free enterprise" tuned to business and financial ears, the Republican candidate had pointedly condemned the philosophy of national planning as applied to economic problems.

"Planned economy," he said, "is incompatible with the democratic form of government. It must lead to ever increasing executive authority."

He also said: "Do we want the government forever forbidding us to plant what we want to plant in our own fields?" and yet, at Des Moines, he had espoused the soil conservation idea which was to withdraw worn-out acreage from cultivation and to plant soil-restoring crops—all at the behest of a national government which would pay farmers for doing this, and would not pay them if they failed to comply.

Landon might have been able to live down his inconsistencies had he been campaigning in "the horse-and-buggydays" before political speeches were spread to every part of the country by radio and newspapers—and had he not been up against an opponent who quickly picked up his inconsistencies and held them up to ridicule.

He jumped from one bed of hot coals to another as he headed north from Des Moines on this journey which some of us among the accompanying newspaper correspondents labeled "the cheese trip."

The "cheese" incident arose from his speech at Minneapolis on the reciprocal trade treaties, negotiated by the administration. Seeking to win favor with the dairy interests he pointed out that, in the first four months of the reciprocal trade treaty with Canada, the price of cheese had dropped from 17 to 12½ cents a pound. He neglected to point out what all the dairy people knew, that, at the time he spoke, the price of cheese was 17½ cents a pound, the peak since 1929. Secretary Wallace did not neglect to point it out—and as soon as he learned of the Republican candidate's "bull." I don't think it was premeditated on Landon's part. His researchers had failed him, or someone who had prepared this section of his speech foolishly thought the discrepancy would not be noted. The candidate remained silent when confronted with the facts.

His own supporters were seriously split over his Minneapolis speech. Henry Haskell, editor of the Kansas City *Star,* one of his principal backers, sought to dissuade him from attacking the reciprocal trade treaties negotiated by Secretary of State Hull which was one phase of administration policy approved by the *Star.* Landon executed a typical straddle. He approved the principle of tariff negotiations, but condemned the treaties negotiated on the ground they were bad bargains. The trade treaties were very unpopular among the cattle and dairy interests of the West. They were, however, thoroughly in line with the views of many leading Eastern Republicans identified with business interests of all sorts which were looking for foreign markets. Ogden L. Mills had fought in the Resolutions Committee at the Cleveland convention against a declaration for repeal of the President's power to negotiate trade treaties, as had William Allen White, but in vain.

I remember also the sour look on the face of ex-Secretary of State Frank B. Kellogg when Landon was denouncing the Hull treaties at Minneapolis. Kellogg sat on the platform, on the front row. He kept his hands folded forbiddingly when others applauded. He looked at the party's candidate for President as if he did not care so much for him.

Landon's stock was fairly high immediately after his nomination and before he opened his mouth and went about showing himself.

I think it began to hit its real down-grade on that "cheese" trip, and it went down and down and down, as the results on election day a few weeks later so clearly revealed. In the big meetings he bravely struggled ahead with his manuscript, but, after people had taken a good look at him and satisfied their curiosity, their interest wandered. There was a noticeable drop. The applause came further and further apart. When he had finished, and everybody knew the ordeal was over, they would rise in great relief and clap loudly and shout—and then depart for their homes.

Similarly, this was true of the brief back-platform appearances through Iowa and Minnesota and Wisconsin on that trip, I observed. The candidate would receive a noisy and cordial welcome when he stepped from the door of his private car to the back platform. The people would be interested for a minute or two as he spoke. Then there was a letdown so noticeable you could actually feel it. They would wave from what appeared to be motives of good sportsmanship, in a friendly but noncommittal way, as the train pulled out.

The little man from Kansas fought valiantly ahead, tugged this way and that by the conflicting groups within his party, so that, if he appeared at some time, before some large audience, with his tie pulled awry and his head tousled and a couple of husky tacklers about his knees, it would have been exactly in keeping. That was the impression I had of him.

Yet, I am told, his spirits rose high toward the end, after one of those monster demonstrations in Madison Square Garden that either party can stage for a candidate. He felt then that he might win. Twenty thousand respectable Republicans crowded into the Garden can make a lot of noise on a night off.

I had seen it when Herbert Hoover spoke there in 1932.

But this election was not being decided by the respectable middle-class folk. The decision was in the hands of millions on the East Sides and tenement districts of the nation, the millions of farmers and tenant farmers who were getting a living or a handout for the first time in several years.

They knew who their benefactor was.

32

WE had come rolling down the Rockies from Colorado—our farthest point west—with President Roosevelt on his triumphal campaign tour in 1936. The train literally waded through oceans of people wherever we stopped—and we stopped very often.

Eager, happy, smiling seas of humanity swept about the rear platform.

There was such a crowd at Colorado Springs. Several little boys carried signs thanking the President for various local projects. A little fellow was weighted under one which, to me, was symbolic of this whole new mass movement in American politics.

"Thanks for the sewage plant, Roosevelt," it read.

Like a conquering hero the President paraded the next day, all day, through Kansas, the home state of his rival for the Presidency. Jim Farley, in an unguarded moment, had called Landon, "a typical governor of a typical prairie state" and Republicans had advertised this far and wide as a slight upon the great state of Kansas and its governor by a New Yorker.

The people didn't seem to mind, at least the thousands who came out to welcome the President.

They included William Allen White, a friend of the President's who, by this time, had been gently eased from the Landon campaign along with other liberals of his stamp.

Concluding a little talk from the back platform at Emporia, where White edits his famous *Emporia Gazette,* the President had said, as an afterthought, it seemed:

"If I come back, it may be in one of those three-and-a-half year periods when Bill White is with me."

Someone spotted the editor in the crowd.

"Please make way for Mr. White—the man with the gray hat," shouted a radio announcer from the platform.

A lane was opened and the rotund newspaperman was helped aboard the platform.

"Two great Americans are now shaking hands," boomed the announcer.

"Hello, Bill," welcomed the President. "I won't talk about that other six months, now."

(The editor grinned amiably—if sheepishly.)

Politicians who boarded the train brought word—and they were cocksure about it—that the President would carry Kansas.

The Kansas crowds seemed to be saying that, too, but it was hard to believe.

. There came a time, though, as this journey turned back toward the East, when we were overwhelmed and jabbed in the sides and very nearly suffocated in the tumultuous throngs, when we would believe most anything. We knew it would be a landslide but few of us could go all the way with Jim Farley who, when we got back to New York, was claiming everything but Maine and Vermont. (There were two in the newspaper corps who went along with him—our own George Morris of the New York *World Telegram,* who has been uncannily correct on politics through a long career, and another good friend, Bob Allen of the *Washington Merry-Go-Round.* They, too, gave Landon two states—and he got exactly those. Being conservative I gave him a minimum of eight and a maximum of eleven.)

The President had one theme on this campaign tour.

"Four Years Ago and Now" was the text.

"You look happier today than you did four years ago."

They shouted back at him exultantly in proof—the multitude we had seen—about the back of the train in the smaller towns where we paused only a few moments; in the cities where they stood three and four deep for miles—in Minneapolis, St. Paul, Omaha, Denver, Kansas City, St. Louis on the way out and turning east again; in auditoriums, open air stadiums, and city squares where they were packed like sardines to hear the President.

Then we came, at Chicago, to the greatest political spectacle I have seen, and I have seen many with Franklin D. Roosevelt.

Our cars burrowed, like so many moles, through the solidly packed earth of humanity down Chicago's streets to the auditorium and there, so great was the mob, we newspapermen literally had to fight to get inside. As the automobiles in which we rode struggled slowly through the human mass, there were menacing cries of anger against the Chicago *Tribune* and the Hearst papers in Chicago which were fight-

449

ing Roosevelt so bitterly. These people no longer had any respect for the press or confidence in it. The press finally had overreached itself, we discovered, and was losing its influence.

I learned the secret of this tremendous outpouring in Chicago, the rainfall of 50,000 balloons, the air armada, the splash of fireworks above Michigan Boulevard and the Loop. Pat Nash, the elder National Committeeman and State Democratic boss, and Mayor Ed Kelly of Chicago, the boss of the city, were trying to outdo another boss further east, Mayor Frank Hague of Jersey City, who had turned out 250,000 people and 70,000 school children to welcome the President two weeks before.

I had ridden in that procession which wound slowly through Jersey City—but it was in the middle of the day and not at night. Mayor Frank Hague had his political minions out and organized, down to the smallest tot in the first grade who, like all the others in the first grade and the second grade and on up, clutched American flags and waved them at the word from their teachers, when President Roosevelt passed.

Hague could be proud of his organization and the people over whom he had ruled for so long.

There I witnesed the irony of politics, which is not unusual because it is so frequent, when President Roosevelt and Frank Hague stood, side by side, in front of the mammoth new hospital which Hague had built for Jersey City with the help of PWA. As Hague introduced the President and praised him, I thought again of the night in 1932 when he had issued that statement calling Franklin D. Roosevelt "the weakest candidate before the people." Hague had been long on the bandwagon now. In 1934, ahead of anyone else, he had come out for Roosevelt for 1936 and, later, when the government was threatening the iron-handed régime of

Jersey City, where Hague had ruthlessly persecuted labor organizers and virtually suspended civil liberties, the boss declared for a third term for Roosevelt.

Big city bosses long had been potent satraps in the Democratic Party, as I had observed at national conventions where we had loitered patiently about their headquarters, notably those of Tammany, to try to pry a word, a gesture, from close-mouthed men usually flashy and overdressed. Always I had thought undue importance was attached to Tammany, that this organization had been overpublicized. (Foes of the Democratic Party had done much of this. The cartoons of Thomas Nast so long ago depicting the noisome Tiger had created a symbol of big city corruption which always could be capitalized to advantage in the small towns and the farms of the Middle and Far West.) Tammany's enmity had been in reality a favorable augury, for the three Democratic Presidents since the Civil War had been nominated over its opposition—Cleveland, Wilson and Roosevelt.

Now, in our time, the power of the big city machines was waning. They were weakened when the federal government's relief agency, the WPA, moved in to supply food and shelter and jobs, once furnished by the big city bosses to build up their organizations. The occasional scuttle of coal and basket of groceries and the temporary job for the boy which had won for the local boss the hearts of the city's unfortunate in the tenement districts no longer could match the more adequate and more regular relief of the federal government.

The late Charlie Murphy, had he stood now at his lamppost on Fourteenth Street outside the Tammany Wigwam where he was wont nightly to receive requests for favors, would have kept a lonely vigil.

Thus deprived of the perquisites which had nourished their organizations, the big city bosses were easier victims of re-

451

form movements. Tammany fell before Fiorello LaGuardia and Tom Dewey. The Democratic administration, itself, invaded Kansas City and put its overlord, the aging Tom Pendergast, behind the bars. For years he had ruled and his empire seemed impregnable. Frank Hague's influence was reduced as the federal government encouraged the public outburst against his suppression of civil liberties, and as the courts took steps to circumscribe the authority he arrogated to himself over the civil rights of workers in his domain.

No little credit for the administration's attack upon its own bosses must be given to Tom Dewey. The New York City district attorney had frightened Democratic political captains by the widespread public applause for his war on Tammany and New York rackets allied with Tammany. It almost had won him the governor's chair in a contest with New York's most successful Democratic vote-getter, Herbert H. Lehman. He was mentioned for the Republican Presidential nomination. Accordingly, there began at Washington, under Attorney General Frank Murphy, that assault on bossdom which moved not only upon Kansas City, but also into Louisiana, and which was popularly known as the New Deal crusade to "out-Dewey Dewey."

So Democratic bosses, their preserves threatened, began to make their obeisances before Roosevelt.

That takes me back to that giant demonstration in Chicago, from which I have digressed.

Its bosses outdid themselves.

In Detroit 300,000 were massed at night in Cadillac Square and their hallelujahs could be heard for blocks.

The Roosevelt train moved slowly into the East like the chair of a Roman Emperor borne on the shoulders of the mob.

Rain did not frighten away the millions in Ohio's industrial belt. It was pouring as we rode through Cincinnati's streets, but a clear, sunshiny day could not have brought out more than stood for miles to welcome the caravan as it proceeded to the open-air stadium where the President spoke. There thousands more were assembled under a roof of umbrellas. This was staid Cincinnati, a Republican stronghold— nor given to exuberance even over Republicans.

At Columbus, where we stopped briefly, there was a freight train on the adjoining track. It blocked the crowd off on that side. But a score of venturesome souls who wanted to see the President did not let that deter them. They lay on their stomachs under the cars, peering up at the Chief Executive. One woman had her baby with her.

That scene comes back vividly, as did the welcome accorded Mrs. Roosevelt by the women at Columbus. I was in the diner having lunch as the train rolled slowly to a stop through the crowds on each side of the track. Mrs. Roosevelt was having her lunch with a family party at the front of the car. She looked out the window. As women would recognize her their faces would blossom in smiles and up went their hands in salutes, almost an automatic gesture. This salute moved down the front of the crowd as if it had been rehearsed.

Victory rode with the Roosevelt train. It was in the air. Consequently, the journey from Washington to the West and back again was like a gay party. Laughter and merriment echoed up and down the compartment cars. Meals were joyous affairs, with much bantering back and forth between the tables.

It was a contrast with the more serious atmosphere aboard the Landon train, where doubt and uncertainty sobered the Republican candidate and his escort. There was little joking with the Landon party. It was all a serious matter.

We had our jokes and fun on the Roosevelt train. We newspapermen cataloged his speeches by number—Number One

"National Unity," Number Two "Water and Power," and so on. In order that we would not have to get off the train at the numerous stops—which was virtually an open invitation, with the huge crowds, to get left behind—a loudspeaker was set up in the dining car and, at every stop, we would rush into the dining car, find a seat, take out our pencils or portable typewriters, and get the gist of the speech as the President talked from the back platform.

One day we were thus assembled on the first leg of the trip west. Back in a corner, unnoticed, sat the widow of the late Senator Gilbert N. Hitchcock of Nebraska. The paper in Omaha in which the Hitchcock family still owned an interest had endorsed Governor Landon. Mrs. Hitchcock had been invited to go along on this trip so that the people of her home state would know that she was for President Roosevelt, in an effort to offset the effect of the paper's endorsement of the Republican candidate.

From the back platform, through the loudspeaker, came the voice of the President engaged in delivering Number One "National Unity," according to our catalog. He spoke the sentence we had heard so often in ridicule of the inconsistency his foe had displayed, most notably in the Portland, Me., and Des Moines speeches, in which Landon had come out, now against, now for national planning.

"I don't make one speech in the East and another in the West—"

"No—it's the same old bull everywhere," blurted out one of the newspaper correspondents, who had not seen Mrs. Hitchcock.

His wisecrack provoked a laugh through the car, and she joined in. She thought it was so good that she told the President about it later in the Roosevelt family's private car. The President laughed uproariously.

Then there was the time, on the return trip, that we stopped at Bloomington, Ill. We sat, pencils poised, typewriters ready, for the President's speech. There came booming through the loudspeaker:

"I am glad to come to Bloomingburgh."

In the collection of his public papers and speeches, President Roosevelt left this error just as it occurred and in a footnote explained:

"It will be noticed that in my foregoing remarks at Bloomington, Ill., I referred to the city as Bloomingburgh. The mistake caused much amusement among the members of the press and of my party on the campaign train.

"The reason for the error was that I had received a telegram that very morning stating that my old friend, former Assemblyman John K. Evans of Bloomingburgh, N.Y., was very ill. In fact, he died in 1937. He was a former close associate of mine during the senatorial contest in the 1911 legislature in Albany; and I was thinking of him and our past association, as I proceeded to the rear platform of the train to speak. The 'slip' was caused by the tenor of my thoughts at the time; and I did not realize the mistake until the train was again under way and it was laughingly brought to my attention."

That tells something of the man. Herbert Hoover would have corrected it, I'm sure.

Roosevelt is the consummate politician on these trips. He refers to local legends and local characters. He refers to the crops of the neighborhood and is always sure, when he does, whether they are good or bad. He knows whether they've had enough rain. He always finds out, and, one day, we learned as innocent eavesdroppers, how he did it. The train had stopped once, then had moved on a few hundred feet further so that the crowd could hear him better. When the train stopped the first time the loudspeaker was turned on. Over it came the voice of the President talking in a subdued conversational tone to one of the local politicians. He was on the back platform.

"What do you raise around here?"
He was told.
"Have you had rain lately?"
"Yes, we had a good one the other day."
And so on.
The train stopped.
The crowd shouted its welcome. The President began to speak—
"Well, I'm glad you've had enough rain here—"
And so on.

Roosevelt began openly in the 1936 campaign his attempt to realize a long-cherished dream—realignment of the nation's political forces into two definite parties, a liberal and a conservative—which he projected later to its second stage in 1938 in the ill-fated "purge," as the newspapers chose to call it, when he sought actively to defeat some Democrats he regarded as "conservative" in the primaries.

He sounded his clarion call for the support of independents and progressive Republicans in a speech at Omaha, Neb., where he asked for the reelection of Senator George W. Norris, who was running in 1936 as an independent in a three-cornered race. The President turned his back on the regular Democratic nominee, the rabble-rousing Terry Carpenter, a diminutive and mild form of Huey Long. Norris was a staunch Roosevelt follower, but he had, for years, been Republican by party label, though irregularly Republican.

This was the first time that President Roosevelt had publicly ignored party lines in a campaign, though he had boasted often how he, himself, had crossed his party line in his voting, notably to cast his ballot for his fifth cousin, the redoubtable T. R.; and it was significant that, in the 1936 campaign, he had studiously avoided mention of the Democratic Party. The omission was intentional and noticeable.

Old-line Democrats even then, in 1936, were beginning to desert him. He welcomed their defection and capitalized upon it. This was made easy, for the anti-Roosevelt Democrats had set up a very vulnerable straw man in the American Liberty League, and it was an even better target because of the leadership of the League by two Democrats in whom the rank and file long ago had lost confidence—Al Smith and John W. Davis, the lawyer for J. P. Morgan. Nor was the Liberty League made any more palatable with the masses by the membership of conservative Republicans, among whom were lawyers for great corporations, including United States Steel. The League actually became a joke in the West.

But President Roosevelt went further in 1936 than to declare for George Norris.

In Minnesota, where Republicans seemed to offer a real threat, he intervened directly to form an alliance with the Farmer-Labor Party which then controlled that state. He induced Democratic candidates for the United States Senate and governor to withdraw when he was in Minnesota in 1936 only a few weeks before the election, in a deal to insure victory for Farmer-Labor candidates for these posts and to carry the state for him for President. One Democratic faction in the state already was allied with the Farmer-Labor Party. But leaders of the regular Democratic faction, which bitterly opposed the Farmer-Labor Party, was very resentful. They could, of course, do nothing about it.

In Wisconsin, the President had a tacit alliance with the LaFollettes, though he kept out of that state in 1936. Phil LaFollette, seeking a third term as governor, did not need his help, and there was no reason to offend Democrats. Phil, anyhow, never was as closely identified with the New Deal, politically or in sympathy, as was his brother, Senator Bob, which was revealed two years later when Phil launched the new independent party, the NPA, National Progressives of America, and accompanied this futile gesture with criticism of the New Deal. It had not, he held, effectively met the nation's problems.

The common people were not voting party labels in 1936 as religiously as before.

They were voting a man.

To me, the whole political story of the country was epitomized in the jubilant night meeting for President Roosevelt in the baseball park, Forbes Field, at Pittsburgh on an eastern campaign swing just before his triumphal tour of the West.

As I picked my way through the mad throng which filled the grandstand and the field an hour before the President was due to arrive, I saw a plump little old woman, nearly as broad as long, run cackling and screeching merrily through the crowd. She was just buoyant with animal spirits. All by herself she was having one magnificent time.

Crushed on her head, a bit onesided in a gesture of bravado, was a red, white and blue hat. It did not stand up properly and erect, like the other souvenir hats you spotted here and there in the jostling, merry crowd. (Across the front of the hats was a picture of the President.) It looked for all the world like the tricolored cockade which other women wore once so many years ago. Gaily and nonchalantly she dashed away and was lost in the crowd.

She was the crowd.

Before the President arrived, before the convoy of motorcycle policemen put-putted slowly through a gate in the far corner of the park, before the deliverer appeared in his open car to wave his hat and set off a great burst of human joy and delirium that swept across the field and thundered back from the grandstand—they had their Danton, one of their own.

State Senator Warren R. Roberts he was, a stern-faced, square sort of fellow, who knew the common touch.

458

He gave them their enemies and they spat out their names
—Andy Mellon (poor, poor Andy, he said, and they tittered); Textile Joe Grundy, Pew (the oil man), Rockefeller
(the still bigger oil man).

"Boo" came the swelling chorus after each name to smite
their champion pleasantly in the face. He smiled with grim
satisfaction. (You could almost hear the swish of the guillotine blade as it fell.)

Then, cleverly, he began to set the poor off against the rich.

"The President," he said, "has decreed that your children
shall enjoy equal opportunity with the sons of the rich." He
spoke of "the smug complacence of pseudo-aristocracy." He
recalled how the sons of the poor and the sons of the rich
shared tins of bully beef, fought side by side, died together, in
the World War. But since then, he said, something had
happened.

A Mirabeau appeared in the handsome presence of their
governor, George H. Earle, a son of wealth who had taken
up the cause of the common people. He, too, gave them their
enemies:

"There are the Mellons, who have grown fabulously
wealthy from the toil of the men of iron and steel, the men
whose brain and brawn have made this great city; Grundy,
whose sweatshop operators have been the shame and disgrace
of Pennsylvania for a generation; Pew, who strives to build
a political and economic empire with himself as dictator; the
duPonts, whose dollars were earned with the blood of American soldiers; Morgan, financier of war."

Between each name he was forced to pause as the crowd
vented its scorn on its enemies, like the whine of the hurricane before it strikes. He stood, smiling and confident, enjoying the tempest he had produced. (Again, you could almost
hear the swish of the guillotine blade as it fell.)

The mob was whipped into a frenzy ready for the deliverer.

He entered in an open car. It might have been the chariot of a Roman Emperor.

They drowned him with paeans of joy.

It was at Pittsburgh, in 1932, that President Roosevelt had so bitterly excoriated Herbert Hoover for his failure to balance the budget—that speech which had been thrown back into his teeth so often by the Republicans. Tonight he referred to that, told the people why he could not balance the budget.

"To balance the budget in 1933 or 1934 or 1935 would have been a crime against the American people," he declared.

"To do so we should either have had to make a capital levy that would have been confiscatory, or we should have had to set our face against human suffering with callous indifference. When Americans suffered, we refused to pass by on the other side."

And, later, he said:

"I ask you the simple question: Has it not been a sounder investment for us during these past three years to spend eight billion dollars for American industry, American farms, American homes and the care of American citizens?"

They roared their "yes."

He did not need to explain to these people who listened to him tonight.

The federal budget was something far away from their lives. They had been helped—that's all that concerned them.

President Roosevelt spoke that night to 60,000 people in the ball park, more people, as one of the earlier speakers had pointed out, than ever had gathered in the city of Pittsburgh before to listen to a Democrat.

Frank Knox, the Republican Vice Presidential candidate, spoke also that night in Pittsburgh—at Duquesne Gardens. He had an audience of 10,000. Again he tried to explain away his earlier insinuation that the Roosevelt administration program had made life insurance policies insecure, a campaign utterance which the Democrats seized and exploited to the full.

But he only got in deeper when he tried to explain.

My story the next day was about the little old woman and the Dantons and Mirabeaus who gave the mob its enemies.

There was the story of the new mass movement in American politics.

I said in my story that the revolution was over.

In that I was wrong.

I sat in the rain across from the White House and watched the inauguration parade go by.

The elegant cadets of the Military Academy swung past, their lines true, marching as one man with a single gun. In their steps followed the splendid young men of the Naval Academy, trained to a fine edge.

Then came the boys of the CCC, the Civilian Conservation Corps, the boys who had been rescued from the streets, the pool rooms, the tenements, and sent into the woods and into the farm sections to help remake the country and themselves, to conserve the forests and the soil and human bodies and human spirits.

From a distance they were a drab blur against the rain. They came nearer out of the mist, but not with the precision of West Point or Annapolis. They appeared as individuals rather than a machinelike unit.

Long and short, fat and lean, helter-skelter.

The vanguard, the little group in front corresponding to the outpost of commanding officers in the military and naval units, was a sight to behold. But the laugh was choked back in your throat.

All sizes they were, ranging from a stocky youngster under five feet to a gawky, raw-boned fellow who looked as if he would be at home with a squirrel gun in Tennessee's mountains.

Then the solid column of companies paraded by.

They tried to keep step, and were fairly successful. Their shoulders lacked that squareness of the cadets and midshipmen. Their hands swung loosely. But the spirit was there. They marched proudly, if not skilfully. There was a recognition of this when somebody said:

"They march better than all the rest."

For they didn't.

There was a company of Negroes, all sizes. As it swung past the President, eyes right, a half-pint Negro in the rear rank poked out his chest and gave the situation everything he had of military bearing.

Here was the real meaning of that inauguration.

33

I WAS sitting by the radio at home the night President Roosevelt delivered his final speech of the 1936 campaign at Madison Square Garden. I could see it all clearly. My imagination was stimulated by the cheers which splashed against the radio in a deafening wave. Then I was caught suddenly by his voice. Had I heard aright?

"I should like to have it said of my first Administration that in it the forces of selfishness and of lust for power met their match. I should like to have it said of my second Administration that in it these forces met their master."

It jarred. A tiny pain of suspicion curled about in my brain. I didn't like it. The pain lingered. The next day I looked up the speech in the newspapers. Yes, there it was. It was true. He had said it all right.

Nor was it altogether what he said. There was a vengeful-ness in his voice when he said it.

I'll grant he had provocation for anger that night. He was striking back at the last-minute campaign against the social security law. Employers were inserting slips in the pay en-velopes of the workers telling them that their wages would be reduced by the tax they had to pay to the government. It was an organized campaign. He labelled it "deceit" and that's what it was, in that it was a distortion and not the whole story. His speech that night was one of his most effec-tive—and it rings still on quiet reading today.

But I didn't like that sentence about "their master."

Of course he was reelected. We knew he would be, we who had been out in the country during the campaign.

That sentence did not hurt him. Nothing could have hurt him then. He deserved to win.

But I wondered.

The election triumph was far beyond the expectation of most political prophets, including the President himself.

It *was* a heady draught for any man. Especially this man.

Three months later we gathered one morning for a regu-lar press conference. As we entered the President's office, Democratic congressional leaders were leaving it. (Senate Leader Joe Robinson of Arkansas remained behind to attend the press conference.) The President evidently had an impor-tant announcement. He had some mimeographed sheets on the desk before him. He said the best way for him to tell the story was to read a message he was sending to Congress at noon. He began to read. As he continued you could feel the tension increase among the correspondents in the room. What a story!

What he read was his plan to "pack" the Supreme Court, as it came to be called later, a devious scheme to reorganize the Court with justices friendly to New Deal reforms. It provided that a new member of the Court would be appointed for every sitting member over seventy who did not voluntarily retire from the Court. If none of the six over seventy should retire, then a Supreme Court of fifteen members would be the result. Whatever happened, the President could get a Court to his own liking—should the bill become law.

The President's target was the four conservatives who were standing pat against his New Deal philosophy—Justices Mc-Reynolds, Butler, Van Devanter and Sutherland. If his proposal were enacted, and those over seventy—six in all—did not elect to retire, then they would find beside them on the bench six new and younger men hand-picked by the President. Chief Justice Hughes and Justice Brandeis, the great liberal who was a god-father and father confessor to so many of the young intellectuals in the New Deal, also would be caught in the scheme, since both were over seventy. The President was willing to sacrifice Brandeis to blast the four who were antagonistic, and bitterly so, to his program and philosophy.

The "packing" plan was a surprise to the country and a jolt to many members of President Roosevelt's own party, particularly the leaders upon whom responsibility would fall for pushing it through Congress. They were not consulted. The first any of them, except Senator Robinson, knew of it was when President Roosevelt called them to the White House at nine o'clock in the morning, read them his message, and announced he was sending it to Congress that day. Senator Robinson had been called over the telephone the night before, too late to do anything.

I found later at the Capitol much resentment among the Congressional leaders over the President's failure to take them into his confidence, to advise with them. This was the beginning of discord which broke like a battery of thunder when long-repressed resentments among his followers, provoked by quick legislative sorties without congressional consultation, crackled forth from alienated groups here and there. On occasion, enough of them deserted to create an anti-Administration majority with Republicans.

From February 5, 1937, dated a slow ebb in the Roosevelt fortune—with temporary recoveries, to be sure, from time to time—which was not checked until the outbreak of war in Europe created one of those emergency situations in which, through all our history, the President becomes the commanding figure by the very nature of things.

I was for the Court plan when the President announced it and for some time thereafter.

I was for it because I saw the opportunity for the country to learn, in the debate which must necessarily follow it—and which did boil up into one of the greatest debates in our history—that the Supreme Court was composed, after all, of nine human beings and not nine gods; nine men who were controlled, as the rest of us are, by prejudices and predilections; nine men who were political appointees and who would be chosen by the President who happened to be in power because their views on social and economic questions coincided with his general philosophy. I saw an opportunity for the country to learn that such a group, chosen as they were, really were in a position to rule the country through the veto power they exercised over legislation, and to make the legislative power a joke—as they had on numerous occasions. They were not elected by the people. They were not responsible to the people. They could not be removed by the people—except by the power of impeachment and this required a showing of actual misdeeds and did not go to the secret, inner springs of a man's philosophy.

The curtain was torn aside from the holy of holies in the process of debate, and eyes were opened.

Mine were opened wider. The projection of the plan started me off again into the history of the Supreme Court.

I learned, of course, that other Presidents had "packed" the Supreme Court, that the Court had been an instrument so many times for maintaining and building up the power of the economic oligarchy which now had fastened its talons, in real earnest, upon the country. I was glad to see this particular Supreme Court—that is, its conservative majority—given a good wallop. And it was a good thing for the country to have its curiosity aroused.

I was for the President's Court plan because at the time it happened to be the plan advanced through which the Court would be called to account. This was the plan espoused by an administration which had enough public support so that the attack would be effective. So, since this was the vehicle, I was for it—at the time and for the purposes for which it was put forward.

My personal preference was then, and still is, for going the whole way and shearing the Supreme Court of its power to pass on constitutional questions, so we would have a more flexible democracy. If the people, through Congress, make their mistakes, then let the people, through Congress, correct them, even if it causes temporary ills. Practically, I know this might have its drawbacks for a time, until we began to choose better men for Congress, for we have leaned upon the Supreme Court as a backstop to check Congress.

As time went on, as the debate continued, I came to the conclusion that the President's plan was a makeshift, a purely temporary remedy of a political nature, which, if accomplished, would set a precedent for the constant "packing" and overturning of the Court. Sometime it might prove dangerous. I was glad, in the end, to see the plan defeated. I was glad, also, to see that our people still speak out, that our Democratic pendulum still is able to swing back—even if it swings back too far and in a direction that I personally would disapprove. It is good for the people to rise up and check their rulers on occasion. They had checked their economic rulers under Roosevelt. Now they were checking him, their political ruler.

The final result seemed to me a satisfactory result under our system of checks and balances. The Court was swung back into line and vacancies opened the way, in time, for President Roosevelt to remodel the Court through the appointment of five judges, so that he had his own majority in the end. Again the Court began in effect to "follow the iliction returns," as Mr. Dooley put it.

From the press conference where the President announced his Court plan, I returned to the office.

There, thumbing through the United Press story about the plan, I found an old friend of mine and of our Scripps-Howard staff, a veteran labor organizer and crusader, a big figure of a man who had come from a wealthy family and had given his life to helping the under-dog. He was a fighter, yet cultured, profound and erudite.

I stopped to chat with him. He was rubbing his chin, a habit he has when puzzled.

"I don't like it," he said.

He was sixty-eight years old.

But you couldn't tell him he should retire. He was still husky and vigorous and his mind was active and fresh.

He wanted to do something to check the power of the Court. He would have been for direct action, even. But he didn't like this method. He accepted it, however, and fought for it, a soldier enlisted with Roosevelt.

I thought the reaction of the Supreme Court would make a good story—that is, such reaction as I could get from watching the justices on the bench. Of course their spoken reaction would have made a tremendous story. But, unfortunately, the members of the Supreme Court do not lower themselves to the common realm of newspaper interviews.

So I hurried to the Court and watched.

It looked just like another day of arguments.

The nine men were at their places on the massive, elevated bench which stretches across one end of the Court room, somberly outlined in their black robes against the heavy red curtain behind. The Court room was about half filled with spectators. A New Jersey lawyer was talking to the Justices from below the bench, looking upward as he argued, as even the best of lawyers must do. The New Jersey lawyer's voice rose and fell, hardly disturbing the serene calm which hung, like a constitutional benediction, in the sanctified atmosphere.

He did not know, none of the spectators knew, of the momentous events impending. For the President's message had not been made public when the Court met. It was just at this time being read to Congress across the square.

In the concentration on his argument, the lawyer perhaps did not notice the mimeographed sheets which Chief Justice Hughes was reading, his eyes intent as he flipped over the pages. The Chief Justice read a page with but a glance. I knew what he was reading. It was that message I already had heard, which had some not very pleasant words about Supreme Court justices who were growing old and suggested that, if they did not retire, younger men should be appointed to sit with them and help them with their work.

The lawyer talked on and on about the New Jersey Teachers Tenure Act.

The Chief Justice was concerned now about his own tenure.

468

The copy of the President's message had been handed to him by Elmore Cropley, the clerk of the Court. After glancing through a few pages he broke into the lawyer's argument, returning with his Baptist conscientiousness to his business, and asked some questions about a teacher who was getting $2,300 a year.

"I want to get this thing straight in my mind," he said to the lawyer.

Then he returned to his reading.

Meanwhile an attendant had handed a copy of the message to Justice Owen J. Roberts, one of the three judges who were under seventy. The handsome Pennsylvanian thumbed rapidly through the pages, then stopped to study one passage intently, stroking his chin with his long fingers.

Presently the Chief Justice finished reading his copy. He moved about restlessly in his chair. Then he handed the copy to Justice Willis Van Devanter, at his right, who was on the Roosevelt proscribed list. Expressionless, this consistent opponent of the New Deal read the message.

The lawyer talked on.

Chief Justice Hughes appeared to fix his attention upon him, but I could imagine that his mind was elsewhere. He picked up a brief lying on his desk, absently, and turned through that.

A Court messenger appeared through the curtains noiselessly and distributed copies of the message to the justices who had not seen it. Justice Pierce Butler, who sat next to Justice Roberts at one end of the bench, hunched his big shoulders over the document. He was seventy—and no friend of the New Deal.

Next to him sat Justice Louis D. Brandeis, then eighty, who had stood by the Roosevelt program. He glanced at the mimeographed sheets, switched on the desk light in front of him and began to read intently. His finely chiselled features were silhouetted by the light.

Justice Butler meanwhile had finished reading and turned to talk with Justice Roberts. The portly Butler began to chuckle. He and Roberts seemed to enjoy the situation. From time to time, for quite a while, one would turn to the other and converse in low tones.

Justice Brandeis finally concluded reading the message and settled back, his full head of hair a bristling crown against the back of the tall chair. Thus he sat, in contemplation, for a few minutes. Then he picked up the message and reread it, occasionally fingering his ear.

Meanwhile, Justice James Clark McReynolds, a bitter New Deal foe, Justice George Sutherland, also anti-New Deal, and the two other justices who were, with Roberts, under seventy, Harlan Fiske Stone and Benjamin N. Cardozo, had read the President's words. The latter two had been friendly to the President's objectives.

The Chief Justice talked with Justice Van Devanter. Both looked grave. Justice Van Devanter was actually grim. He smiled once or twice, but it was a sardonic smile that twisted the corners of his mouth and poked up his eyebrows.

The reading was completed all up and down the line. Two or three of the justices interrupted the lawyer discussing the New Jersey Teachers Tenure Act. Routine had returned to the Court.

But a pall seemed to have dropped down along the bench.

Words hung in the air, words from those printed pages:

"This brings forward the question of aged or infirm judges—a subject of delicacy and yet one which requires frank discussion. . . . Perform their duties to the very edge of the grave. . . . In exceptional cases, of course, judges, like other men, retain to an advanced age full mental and physical vigor. Those not so fortunate are often unable to perceive their own infirmity."

Six men beyond seventy.

I wondered what they thought.

Not in recent years had a President of the United States spoken so lightly of the august Supreme Court of the United States, though Theodore Roosevelt in a speech at Harvard, once had described a member of the Court in that day as "an old fuzzy-wuzzy with sweetbread brains," and, in his Bull Moose campaign in 1912, he had advocated recall of judicial decisions in lower courts. He had been critical of the Supreme Court, too.

Abraham Lincoln had arraigned the Supreme Court for the Dred Scott decision.

To get a parallel for President Roosevelt's rough frontal assault on the Court, however, one has to go back to Andrew Jackson. In fact, a thorough understanding of Andy Jackson is necessary to a thorough understanding of Franklin D. Roosevelt. Jackson is perhaps the second Roosevelt's chief model. Their careers parallel in many respects.

The Supreme Court was challenged.

Chief Justice Hughes was challenged.

So there began that mighty duel up and down Pennsylvania Avenue across the mile between the White House and the Supreme Court on Capitol Hill which is one of the most dramatic political battles of our period, none the less so because it was all done quietly and off-stage after the President had delivered his blow.

Two skilful antagonists were Roosevelt and Hughes.

The Chief Justice was fighting for the prestige of the Supreme Court. Had the President put over his bill, the Court would have gone under a shadow from which it would not have emerged for years. Hughes could not fight openly. That would have lowered the dignity of the Chief Justice and the

Court. He could not descend into the arena. Others must—and did—fight the open battle for the Court.

The President's bill started out apparently with good prospects of success. There was a time when it seemed that the bill eventually would pass. Hughes could not permit that. His only recourse to save the Court was to trim its sails to the wind. This deft operation was accomplished by swinging Owen Roberts to his side when the Washington minimum wage law for women came before the Court. The Court upheld this statute by a 5 to 4 vote, and the pressure was relieved. The Court, so the public saw, was coming to its senses.

It had been the Court's invalidation of the New York minimum wage law which had so shocked the country, even to the extent of pushing Alfred M. Landon into advocacy of a constitutional amendment which would guarantee to states the rights to pass such legislation. Roberts had voted against the New York law. Now he switched, only nine months later, to support the Washington law. I have listened to technical legal arguments by lawyers in which they seek to draw a distinction between the two laws so far as constitutionality goes, to justify Roberts's switch, but to a layman, at least to this layman, it all seems shadow-boxing with the issue. Both involved the right of the state to prescribe a minimum wage for women. That's all I can see in it, if the technicians will pardon me. Also, it was constantly said about Washington at the time that Hughes had induced Roberts to change his position—and that it was pure political expediency on the part of the Chief Justice.

He became a politician, himself, and a skilful one.

In essence this was a great political battle. Roosevelt played politics, and Hughes played politics. I followed that titanic struggle closely throughout. No one can ever again, as far as I am concerned, argue with any effect that the Supreme Court is above politics. It is inextricably woven into the political pattern.

472

The swing toward a more modern philosophy, started by the Washington minimum wage law decision, was carried on in the decision upholding the Wagner Labor Relations Act. This stretched the federal power to lengths that would have been impossible a few months before and probably would not have occurred without the impact of public opinion which President Roosevelt brought upon the Court. Hughes was directing a masterly retreat that, in the end, saved the Court. In the Wagner Act decision, the Court even brought a pants factory in Richmond, Va., within the purview of federal regulation and Roosevelt could have asked no more.

The Court bill was relegated to the shelf through the combined effect of the Court's change of attitude, itself forced by public opinion which swelled up behind the President, and by the attack in public, press and Congress upon the theory of the proposed bill, itself supported by another large block of public opinion.

More effective in bringing about the death of the Court bill than the noisy word battle which went on out in front were the quiet moves behind the scene such as the Chief Justice's delicate job of steering his colleague Roberts into line for a more liberal approach toward federal regulation.

Very influential also were the prolonged public hearings by the Senate Judiciary Committee, and I speak now not of the arguments, but of the delay which gave the opposition time to marshal its forces and rally public opinion. Senator Henry F. Ashurst of Arizona, the courtly Senate philosopher and wit, chairman of the committee, decreed that the bill must have full and proper consideration. No one could take exception to this, for the Court reform bill was, after all, perhaps the most far-reaching measure presented to Congress in modern times.

Ashurst posed throughout as the friend of the bill, even though he had ridiculed rumors that the administration would ever propose such a measure only a short time before it was submitted by President Roosevelt and entrusted to his committee. He, himself, was for a constitutional amendment. But he accepted publicly the proposed solution, swallowing his words with accustomed grace. As the hearings dragged on, however, some New Dealers became very suspicious of him. They professed to see in the delay a very definite bit of strategy. Ashurst insisted that extended hearings would help the administration bill.

In those days, when we newspapermen hinted the New Deal suspicions to him, he solemnly and stoutly maintained his innocence of any guile.

Loyally he voted for the bill in committee. Never once, during the hearings, or anywhere else, did he publicly reveal any misgivings about the measure or say anything that might be construed as even an intimation that he did not approve of it.

The day it was sent back to the committee by the Senate, which meant the end of it, he walked cheerily from the chamber with a wise smile on his face and, when we encountered him in the lobby outside, he said with a merry laugh:

"My head is bowed, but unbloody."

He performed one of the most difficult skating feats ever seen in the Senate, but was at all times the master of his skates—by which I refer to his own remark a few years ago in a Senate speech:

"Politics is like being on roller skates. Sometimes you go where you want to go and sometimes you go where the skates take you."

Many politicians could learn much from Ashurst.

He has always been, to me, one of the most delightful and interesting figures in public life.

President Roosevelt, I am convinced, never expected to get the Court bill through as it was written. The best he hoped for, I imagine, was some sort of compromise that would have added one or two judges to the Court. A compromise of this sort was in the wind for a time. The opportunity, if seized, might have won such a compromise, though I am inclined to doubt it, in view of the lagging interest of the measure's supporters when the Chief Justice yielded to the storm and directed the Court in a different direction, and the delay of the bill in committee.

Sometimes I have wondered if President Roosevelt ever expected anything else than just what he got—a torrential public debate that educated the rank and file on the Court and its place and power in the federal set-up, and the resultant retreat of Chief Justice Hughes that modified the Court's attitude toward his program.

Quietly, without much ado, the President did see Congress enact a minor yet important part of his Court program. One law speeded up final action on cases involving constitutionality of acts of Congress by providing direct appeal from federal district courts to the Supreme Court, without the intermediary and often tedious course through Circuit Courts of Appeal. Another provided for creation of a panel of three judges in the federal district courts to sit on cases involving constitutionality of acts of Congress, instead of the one judge of the district, which was a means of offsetting the influence of a known hostile judge. The efficacy of this procedure was demonstrated in the TVA cases where a judge known to be unsympathetic to TVA found his views counteracted by two other judges who were assigned to sit with him. Also, Congress enacted a statute permitting retirement of Supreme Court judges at seventy on full pay.

Roosevelt's Court plan struck like a bolt of lightning on a clear summer day.

There had been much talk of "an era of good feeling," by which those who promoted it, largely the interests whom the President had irritated and annoyed with his reforms, meant an era from which reform would be missing. They hoped that his overwhelming victory would give him compassion—for them.

No one who knew the President would put much credence in that, nor would anyone who had followed the clues which he had dropped along the road from time to time in the last year. The inevitable end of the chase in this game of hare and hounds was a big signpost labelled "Something must be done about the Supreme Court," though the manner of the doing was a real surprise, that is, to most of us. Two members of our staff, Herbert Little, who had covered the Supreme Court for years, and George Morris, correspondent for our Memphis *Commercial Appeal,* had written stories about a month before the plan actually was promulgated suggesting that this was the method which was being considered. But the plan most often discussed publicly had been a constitutional amendment giving Congress power to legislate on matters affecting social and economic welfare, though we knew that several of the most skilful lawyers had sat down, with pencil and paper, and tried to draft such an amendment, and found themselves in a dilemma.

But to anyone who had followed the clues, only the method should have been surprising.

I had stood outside the Supreme Court the day that august body handed down its decision killing NRA, its blue eagle and all the eggs that the bird had laid—some of which had spoiled and emitted a bad smell. The Court was still meeting then in that tiny little room in the Capitol, that room once large enough for the Senate of the United States. I did not regularly cover the Supreme Court, so I could not get a seat. Outside I waited and got the news of that decision from Herb Little.

It looked as if the Supreme Court was getting ready to tear down the New Deal.

President Roosevelt was not ready at the first press conference after the NRA decision. He merely raised the manifold questions growing out of the confusion which the Court left in the wake of its decision. The story for us, he said, was the actual spot news of what happened in the country the next few days as the codes went out of existence and employers began to lengthen hours and reduce wages.

He put the country—and especially the workers who had enjoyed shorter hours and better wages under NRA—on guard.

Two days later, at the next press conference, he was ready to speak—and he spoke at length. That was the now famous "horse-and-buggy" press conference, in which he accused the Supreme Court of taking the country back to the horse-and-buggy age, of taking its interpretation of the Constitution back fifty years.

"We have," he said, "been relegated to the horse-and-buggy definition of interstate commerce."

In the Schechter case nullifying NRA, the President said, the Supreme Court "has gone back to the old Knight case in 1885, which in fact limited any application of interstate commerce to goods in transit—nothing else."

"Since 1885," he continued, "the Court in various decisions has enlarged upon the definition of interstate commerce— railroad cases, coal cases and so forth and so on. It was clearly the opinion of the Congress before this decision and the opinion of various attorneys-general, regardless of party, that the words 'interstate commerce' applied not only to an actual shipment of goods but also to a great many other things that affected interstate commerce."

He pointed out the close interrelation of modern life which requires national treatment of economic and social problems.

477

"The prosperity of the farmer does have an effect today on the manufacturer in Pittsburgh. The prosperity of the clothing worker in the city of New York has an effect on the prosperity of the farmer in Wisconsin, and so it goes. We are interdependent—we are tied in together. And the hope has been that we could, through a period of years, interpret the interstate commerce clause of the Constitution in the light of these new things that have come to the country. It had been our hope that under the interstate commerce clause we could recognize by legislation and by judicial decision that a harmful practice in one section of the country could be prevented on the theory that it was doing harm to another section of the country.

"That was why the Congress for a good many years, and most lawyers, have had the thought that in drafting legislation we could depend on an interpretation that would enlarge the constitutional meaning of interstate commerce to include not only those matters of direct interstate commerce, but also those matters which indirectly affect interstate commerce."

He built up his case step by step. The informal talk at that press conference, for which, of course, he had prepared carefully, is still today a masterly argument when read, page after page, in his collected papers. He kept us gathered about his desk for nearly two hours. It was a memorable occasion. We who heard it could be sure that something was coming later.

But he only posed the problem that day and left the remedy to some future day. He wanted to start the country thinking.

The issue, as he boiled it down, was this:

"Is the United States going to decide, are the people of this country going to decide that their federal government shall in the future have no right under any implied power or any court-approved power to enter into a solution of a national

478

economic problem, but that that national economic problem must be decided only by the states?"

"And so," he said later, "we are facing a very, very great national non-partisan issue. We have got to decide one way or the other. I don't mean this summer or winter or next fall, but over a period, perhaps, of five years or ten years we have got to decide: whether we are going to relegate to the forty-eight states practically all control over economic conditions—not only state economic conditions but national economic conditions; and along with that whether we are going to relegate to the states all control over social and working conditions throughout the country regardless of whether those conditions have a very definite significance and effect in other states outside of the individual states.

"That is one side of the picture.

"The other side of the picture is whether in some way we are going to turn over or restore to—whichever way you choose to put it—turn over or restore to the federal government the powers which exist in the national governments of every other nation in the world to enact and administer laws that have a bearing on, and general control over, national economic problems and national social problems.

"That actually is the biggest question that has come before this country outside of time of war, and it has to be decided. And, as I say, it may take five years or ten years."

He said five or ten years. He seemed embarked upon a solution that would take time, perhaps a constitutional amendment.

I rushed back to the office and wrote a story forecasting a constitutional amendment.

He had given the country an intriguing phrase that summed up his whole argument—"horse-and-buggy age."

He had planted a seed that began soon to sprout in discussion all over the country.

In his press conference, he had said, among other things, that the Court had put its veto on legislation regulating coal mining and agriculture in its NRA decision. How prophetic he was!

I sat in the Court, now moved into its resplendent new building across the square from the Capitol, the day that it nullified the AAA in that tortuous, involved, devious decision by Justice Owen J. Roberts. Never did a judge kill a legislative creature with more elegance and soft grace. The strangling was tedious, but very, very thorough. Justice Roberts delivers his decisions from memory. His handsome face and powerful figure is enhanced by the black robe of his high office. He looks out over the Court with practised calm and pronounces his death sentence with the gentle suavity of a Shakespearean actor of the old school.

In wonder I listened that day. It amazed me how he could wander so many, many times around the barn, like a stray horse with a bad eye on the wrong side, before he could find the door, but it amazed me more how he could have memorized that mumbo-jumbo of legalistic argument.

But he had—and we poor, puny mortals in the Court room sat mutely, in absolute silence, waiting to find where he would arrive. He got there finally, triumphantly, and settled back in judicial magnificence.

I was wrapped up in the Roosevelt economic and social program. I took it all personally. When Justice Roberts had rendered his wordy masterpiece I suffered an acute sense of depression. It seemed that the whole structure was coming down about our ears.

One incident was like the long run on the gridiron that does not win the game but is beautiful to watch.

That was the tart lecture delivered to the Court itself by Justice Stone. There was no elegance or fine elocution with his dissenting opinion. He read it. But it was appropriately sharp and pungent, like a breeze off the sea through the

pine trees. He told the Court—in effect, that is, the majority—
that it was getting too high and mighty, that it was setting
itself up on a pinnacle, that it was arrogating legislative
power to itself and, in doing this, it was torturing the Constitution. There is that one pithy sentence he uttered:

"While unconstitutional exercise of power by the executive
and legislative bodies is subject to judicial restraint, the only
check on our exercise of power is our own sense of self-
restraint."

Touché, Justice Stone!

That decision was by a 6-to-3 vote. The story was—and I
don't doubt it—that Chief Justice Hughes agreed with the
minority but cast his vote with the majority so there would
not be another 5-to-4 decision. The public was getting a little
sick of those hairline decisions. They were hurting the Court.
The Chief Justice perhaps knew that Franklin D. Roosevelt
had something up his sleeve. That "horse-and-buggy age"
phrase was percolating out through the country.

In the tour of the country in late 1935 and early 1936 of
which I have spoken previously, one of my tasks was to check
up on reaction to the Supreme Court's attitude on the New
Deal program, particularly on the AAA decision in the
farm states, to determine how the people would regard a
proposed constitutional amendment enlarging Congressional
powers in economic and social legislation. I found, incidentally, that the farmers were stunned and confused by the
killing of their farm program, but I found also an underlying respect for the Supreme Court, and so reported.

One night I went to a neighborhood rally of the Johnson
County, Ind., Farm Bureau not far from Indianapolis. Outside the schoolhouse, we picked our way between rows of
automobiles—reminders of the good times the farmer had
been enjoying. These symbols of better times were thrown
into sharp relief by the lights from the schoolhouse. In a bare

combination gymnasium and auditorium the farmers, their wives and their children were assembled.

A rather phlegmatic, solemn lot, they nodded appreciatively when the young county agent, who represented the Agriculture Department, smiled and said:

"I know what you people are thinking about: 'Are we going to get our checks or not?'

"I don't know. That's up to Congress. Everything that can be done will be done. Of course it will take some time because of the Supreme Court decision. But as soon as the wreckage is cleared away they'll do something about it."

The chief speaker of the evening was Hassil Schenck, vice-president of the Indiana Farm Bureau Federation, a big, broad fellow who himself owned 140 acres to the north. He spiced his talk with stories, stressing his points with quick ironical darts, and, as he warmed up, reached at times the fervent tone of the itinerant evangelist.

"We thought we'd won," he said, "until the Supreme Court came along and unwon us."

This provoked a chuckling grunt.

"I felt pretty bad at first—but I feel better now."

His eyes twinkling, he continued:

"I'm not going to criticize the Supreme Court. It's not thought the right thing to do. But I know people who criticize their neighbors. I've done it. So have you. You criticize your Congressman and sometimes even the President."

An appreciative titter fluttered through his audience.

"If you got up right close to those Supreme Court judges and put your hands on them"—he thrust his big hand out gingerly and drew it back quickly—"I wonder if they'd be real people. When they put on their robes do they become different?

"I'm not going to criticize them. But I think, if we look down through history, that opinion of Justice Stone will become a milestone. Look at the records of those who voted against Triple A. They all used to be corporation lawyers. I heard over the radio that Chief Justice Hughes switched over at the last minute. It might have been one of those 5-to-4 decisions—just one man deciding this great question."

He recalled then that the Constitution already had been amended twenty-one times. He described the various amendments, finally reminding his hearers:

"And then they took away our booze with an amendment, and then they gave it back again."

The audience chortled.

But still they gave no indication of their attitude toward amending the Constitution. When the meeting ended, crates of apples were set out along the front edge of the stage. They helped themselves, and the low soft mumble of neighborhood gossip was punctuated with the clean, crisp sound of the biting of apples. Then they wandered gradually, by twos and threes, into the night and off home.

I found confusion and a mixed reaction to the Triple A death sentence in the Middle West. I was impressed by one underlying theme. That was that if Congress did not provide a substitute, then the farmers would make a noise in Washington. This ran through the diverse reception of the Supreme Court decision which reflected occasional anger at the Supreme Court, but generally a sorrowful acquiescence, and, very rarely, criticism of President Roosevelt and Secretary of Agriculture Wallace for devising a scheme that would not stand the Court test. But, for the most part, farmers seemed to be convinced that Congress would be able to find a way around the decision and write an act that would be constitutional. They were very determined that they should have a program. They knew now that it was politically possible to enjoy federal assistance. That had been proved. They had won recognition after a long fight. They were insistent upon keeping it.

Some of President Roosevelt's supporters whom I consulted on the Supreme Court issue, politicians in the Middle West, expressed the opinion that a constitutional amendment—which then was the solution most generally proposed—would not take well generally in that section, even among the farmers who now had felt the sting of a Supreme Court spanking.

This judgment turned out later to be sound when the President projected his reform plan.

Republicans were hopeful of a Supreme Court issue in 1936, but the Supreme Court itself fortuitously worked for the Democrats when, on the eve of the Republican convention, it threw out the New York minimum wage law so that the party's candidate himself could not accept such doctrine passively. They could only insinuate that Roosevelt had indicated, by his challenge of the Court's dicta, that he was prepared to do something about the Court. But the President eluded them and gave no inkling of his intentions, though throughout the campaign he sought to lay the groundwork, to prepare the public mind by emphasizing the necessity of national handling of problems that affected the whole people, as he had in his "horse-and-buggy" press conference.

When he sprang his reform plan upon the country after the election, Republicans capitalized his failure to tell the voters of his plans beforehand, during the campaign, and this had some effect. He had misled the public, Republicans claimed, by his silence during the campaign.

The President's refusal to drag the Supreme Court issue into the campaign, especially when he did not have then an exact idea of how it should be handled, seemed to me nothing more than a course of political expediency to which leaders often resort. Both parties frequently were guilty of such tactics. It is to be expected in politics, and of politicians. Roosevelt certainly had left no doubt about his feelings on the Court. Because of the numerous issues of that 1936 campaign, it was impossible to get what might be termed a "mandate" upon an issue such as the Supreme Court and the Constitution. Congress, receptive as it is to public opinion, properly can adjudge such issues after careful consideration, and this it did later.

Likewise, at a subsequent election, the people can speak out—as they did; and a President can have his test—as he did.

34

AND now came the Avenging Angels.

What had been hopefully proclaimed as "an era of good feeling" after the sweeping 1936 victory was to last only briefly. It was slowly transformed during the bitter fight over President Roosevelt's Supreme Court reform bill into an "era of vengeance"— within the Democratic Party.

It split the party wide open, though, in reality, it served only to bring into the open once again the unamalgamable elements within that party which is so strangely compounded and which rises to power occasionally and hangs together for a short span only by grace of the lethargy into which the Republican Party must always fall in time as a result of overeating at the expense of the great masses of people.

President Roosevelt had the better of the Court fight though the bill he proposed was buried in a Senate committee pigeonhole. He lost the battle, but won the war. He got what he wanted, which was a change in the attitude of the Court toward his reform program. During the battle the fires of vengeance were set to burning. Members of his party said unkind things of him, publicly and privately. What is often called his "Dutch stubbornness" asserted itself, and he ordered the battle to go on—against hopeless odds, we who were covering the engagement could see—long after he had achieved his ends.

He did not know when he had won.

He pressed forward to spoil his victory and sow the seeds of rebellion within his party.

Franklin D. Roosevelt, like many strong and masterful characters, becomes bitter in defeat. There is in him, as there was in Woodrow Wilson, a hard strain of vindictiveness. This was nurtured and encouraged now by the amateur parlor politicians, the younger men mostly, who long had whispered at his side. They had done his errands well and had risen to places in the sun, young men full of zeal who saw only in intense blacks and whites. They could not see, as Jim Farley the practical politician saw so well, that men in politics cannot be divided into white knights and black knights, that it is best to take them over the long pull, placate them and win their support when you can, let them stray occasionally if they must—always remembering that there is another day and another battle when they will be needed.

But the President now gently eased aside both Jim Farley and his policy of leniency.

In his place emerged the young men in white robes with flaming swords to seize the reins, to urge on the now aroused gladiator.

Chief among them were WPA Administrator Harry L. Hopkins, able and resourceful, a brilliant practical administrator, now turned crusader; Tom Corcoran, the tireless man-at-arms with an instinct for power never suspected from his round, innocent face; the quiet, studious and lovable Ben Cohen, of the penetrating and philosophical mind who is the best legal draftsman of the New Deal; and a vigorous and outspoken elder, Secretary of Interior Harold L. Ickes. There were others also who contributed their counsel and their services, among them the brainy Robert H. Jackson, perhaps the most effective spokesman of New Deal philosophy. These men, long in the inner councils, now assumed more influence and prominence as the "era of vengeance" opened. It is an exaggeration to place upon his counsellors the responsibility for the vengeful crusade upon which Franklin D. Roosevelt embarked to punish those who had dared to oppose him on the Court program. The President acts upon his own inner impulses. But zealous men of the type he now chose to be about him, lacking in practical political judgment as most of them were, only spurred him on in his course. They were incapable of sound political advice. What he wanted they urged him on to do, unmindful of the consequences.

There was a certain impractical, blithe, debonair spirit about the program of vengeance, of which Franklin Roosevelt is capable at times when he casts off the reins of astute political advisers and steps out on his own abetted by "yes-men" of idealistic temperament akin to his.

His foes chose a bitter name for his adventure. They called it "the purge," stealing the term from the dictators of Europe.

Opposition newspapers blazoned the term to the public.

The "purge" was not a sudden, overnight development. It flowered slowly from the rank and poisonous hatred generated as passions were aroused by the fight over the Supreme Court. As the struggle developed I saw the poison slowly spreading. Some within the New Deal began to use names in speaking of those who did not see eye to eye with the President on the Court reform program. They damned their opponents in the short ugly words of the saloon and the men's room. They cried vengeance upon them—and the opportunity for vengeance was at hand in the 1938 Congressional elections when a number of Senators who took issue with the President were up for reelection.

Long before this I had heard of the desire of New Dealers to root out, at the first opportunity, those whom they considered not entirely consecrated members of the church. They wanted to draw the line, separate enemies from friends —and enemies were those who did not agree 100 per cent with every New Deal measure—and thereupon build a new Democratic Party along New Deal lines. This fitted in with Franklin D. Roosevelt's desire to create a new party.

So we got the "purge."

I was honestly in favor of President Roosevelt's aim to create, if possible, a new liberal party. I was chiefly interested in his attempt to root out the reactionary members of the old bourbon machine in the South—men who gave the New Deal lip-service but awaited the time when they could knife it. I never considered that most of the representatives in the South—in House and Senate—really represented the masses of Southern farmers and workers. Later I will tell why. With the President's attempt to give a voice in the South to the people I was in entire accord. I am still, whoever shoulders this task—and it is almost superhuman, I'll agree.

He had, in my opinion, every right to draw the line, provided the issues were real—and in the South they were real. He sized up the situation there very accurately. Woodrow Wilson had attempted a "purge" among Democrats over the issue of United States participation in the World War. He had sought to defeat those who had opposed his policies. His cause was flimsy, to my mind, when compared to that which was ripe for Franklin D. Roosevelt in the South, for the issue in the South was whether the people should rule their own destinies, or whether they should be represented forever in the halls of Congress by representatives of mill-owners, corporations, banks who had kept them in virtual peonage for generations. This was something that had to do with their daily lives, not the righteousness or uprighteousness of a war fought on European battlefields over the vague and illusory cry "Make the world safe for democracy." Franklin Roosevelt was trying to make the South safe for democracy, which, to my way of thinking, is much more to the point.

I think it still is to the point, for I know something of the illusion of democracy in my South.

That phase of the Roosevelt crusade I favored 100 per cent.

But the Roosevelt 1938 crusade to eliminate reactionary forces in the Democratic Party was both confusing and mismanaged. It proceeded in the first place from vengeance over defeat of the Court bill. Roosevelt chose to make this the issue. It was ill chosen. Men might be most liberal and progressive in their political philosophy and yet be utterly unable to agree that the Roosevelt plan to "pack" the Supreme Court was the way to meet that issue. Many honest progressives did disagree—and I speak of those with long records of earnest and honest service.

I could choose one of the accepted of the New Deal, Felix Frankfurter, whom the New Dealers themselves would agree is one of their very own. He later was appointed to the Supreme Court by President Roosevelt. He did not approve of the "packing" plan. He declined to endorse it publicly. He refused to appear before the Senate Judiciary Committee in its behalf.

I prefer, however, to take a man who for years had been on the firing line for progressive government. I speak of Senator Burton K. Wheeler of Montana, whom I have known for a long time and whom I have watched in the forefront of progressivism for a long time. Burt Wheeler always has feared the possibility of tyranny of government. Once he was the victim of a plot by a government official who had him indicted in the effort to squelch an investigation of his department. That was Harry M. Daugherty, Attorney General of Warren G. Harding. I have told that story. In the Roosevelt Court-"packing" plan Senator Wheeler saw the possibility of political control of the Supreme Court which might, in the end, endanger civil liberties. The Supreme Court, in notable cases in its history, has been a bulwark for the protection of civil liberties. Wheeler had been approached months before the Court plan was advanced and had stated plainly that he could not approve any such solution of the problem. He only remained consistent when the proposal was submitted to Congress after the election.

Yet Wheeler was vilified privately by the New Dealers, some of whom were not dry behind the ears when the Montana Senator was active in the fight for progressive government—and active at a time when it was costly. He went to the front when it was not popular. It struck me as peculiarly ironical that young men who had come into power with Roosevelt should dare to assume the right of saying who was liberal and who was conservative, who was friend and who was foe of real liberalism in government, and should set themselves up to judge a man who had been on the firing line for years before they came along. Nor could I forget that when Burt Wheeler was campaigning with the late Bob LaFollette of Wisconsin, deserting his party and endangering his own political future, Franklin D. Roosevelt was out stumping the country for John W. Davis, the J. P. Morgan lawyer, and attacking the Wisconsin Senator.

It was therefore rather amazing to hear some of the criticism of Wheeler, private to be true, by the young New Dealers. He had helped win one of the hardest battles of the whole New Deal era, enactment of the public utility holding company act. In those days they had thanked God for Burt Wheeler. Now they were calling him names.

Wheeler was not up for reelection in 1938, so they could not seek his downfall.

But there were others, and in various and sundry ways, none of them politically well managed, the crusaders sought to execute judgment.

An interesting case was that of Senator Guy Gillette of Iowa. Gillette could not go along on the "packing" plan. His idea of a solution was to require seven out of nine judges to declare an act of Congress unconstitutional. This was also the proposal of the veteran progressive, Senator George W. Norris of Nebraska. Nobody could challenge the sincerity of George W. Norris. Yet Gillette, too, was marked for the slaughter, and here it was that Harry Hopkins assumed a political rôle and provoked a storm of criticism because Hopkins was also the federal dispenser of relief money. Hopkins had been born in Iowa and had gone to college there. But he had been long out of the state. He announced that if he were voting in Iowa—which he could not do— that he would vote for Otha D. Wearin, a House member, who was Gillette's opponent in the Democratic primary. This proxy appeal fell flat. Gillette was renominated. He was elected, but by only a slim margin, after a campaign in which his opponent, ex-Senator Lester J. Dickinson, had accused him of trying to wreck the Supreme Court by his proposal that the vote of seven out of nine judges be required to declare an act of Congress unconstitutional!

The cases of Gillette and Wheeler demonstrate the inconsistency of trying to draw a line between sheep and goats by taking the single yardstick of the Supreme Court issue in the form in which President Roosevelt submitted it. There were other cases, as, for instance, the President's support of Senator Robert J. Bulkley in Ohio against another Democrat, former Governor George White, contrasted with his open and avowed campaign to defeat Senator Walter F. George of Georgia; for the latter's record on New Deal measures up to the time of the 1938 election was much better than that of Senator Bulkley. Fundamentally, Senator George is conservative by inclination and representative of the industrial and financial oligarchy which rules his state, and there was a definite issue there; but the inconsistency of the "purge" campaign was glaringly apparent when George and Bulkley's records were compared, and Bulkley likewise appeared to cling to some principles which the New Dealers abhorred, though he had given his support to the Court plan.

This streak of inconsistency ran through the whole crusade.

Nine Senators who were up for reelection in 1938 had taken a position against the Court plan and presumably were marked for some sort of punishment. But President Roosevelt did not attempt to molest some of these, at least publicly, though the New Deal amateur politicoes had sought privately to encourage opposition. They found themselves against too heavy odds in the case of men such as Senators Clark of Missouri, Adams of Colorado, McCarran of Nevada, all of whom easily triumphed.

The vengeance crusade lacked consistency, but, most of all, it lacked political finesse, management and preparation, and its political deficiencies may be traced largely to the failure of Jim Farley to participate. As an experienced political general Farley could not see the wisdom of the venture. He did not play politics that way. He sympathized only in the effort to defeat Senator Millard F. Tydings of Maryland, and that on the ground of loyalty, which makes sense to the practical politician. Jim had bestowed many political favors upon Tydings, or so he felt, and he thought the Maryland Senator had not reciprocated properly in support of the administration. But Jim did not like the way the anti-Tydings campaign was handled, and does not like to think of that episode.

An interesting adventure it was when President Roosevelt swept across the country in the summer of 1938, picking and choosing among Democrats.

We rode first to the little town of Marietta, Ohio, and there, in an idyllic setting, from a pavilion among the trees with the river flowing in the background, President Roosevelt bestowed his blessing upon Senator Bulkley in the course of a speech in celebration of the sesquicentennial of the opening of the Northwest Territory. The rejected Democrat, former Governor White, had to perform the embarrassing task of introducing the President who was, he knew, to ignore him. Governor White looked glum and dour. The burden of his chagrin was the heavier because this was his home town, and these people to whom the President talked were his neighbors. Bulkley grinned amiably in the Cheshire cat manner familiar to habitués of the Senate.

From Marietta, we went to Cincinnati and across into Kentucky. At the Latonia racetrack, under a broiling sun, the President asked the people to send his Senate Democratic leader—"Dear Alben" Barkley—back to Washington, rather than nominate Governor "Happy" Chandler. But "Happy," the consummate cheerful sophomore nearly stole the show. Nobody could squelch him. Before the President spoke he rose from a front seat in the judges' stand, held his hands clasped over his head in the gesture of the prize ring. His adherents in the grandstand bellowed back "Hi, Happy!" He smiled when the speech began. He smiled throughout. And he came up smiling when it was all over.

"Dear Alben" was overshadowed on this occasion by the more youthful political showman. He was having his troubles as Senate leader and now here he was with more trouble in a hard campaign to get back to the Senate. His election as Senate leader by his fellow Democrats—by the narrow margin of one vote over the veteran Senator Pat Harrison—intensified the factional feud within Senate Democratic ranks between New Dealers and conservatives. President Roosevelt had poked up the fires by taking sides in the Senate-leadership contest in a letter, addressed to "Dear Alben," which was the cue to his personal preference.

Southward from Kentucky we headed toward Oklahoma and there, under another day's broiling sun, before another grandstand crowded with sweltering humanity just outside of Oklahoma City, President Roosevelt went to the rescue of Senator Elmer Thomas who was being hard pressed by the wild Indian orator, Gomer Smith, whom I had seen in furious encounter with the Reverend Gerald Smith at the Cleveland Townsend convention two years before. Elmer Thomas had been a constant irritant to the administration and especially Secretary of the Treasury Morgenthau earlier in the New Deal with his constant pressure for inflationary measures; but of late he had followed the administration faithfully and now was winning his reward.

As the train hurried across Nevada, we got reports from the Oklahoma primary election. Thomas had been saved from the noisy Smith. The reports, incidentally, came by long distance telephone to the President on his special train from Harry Hopkins in Washington who now was operating as a full-fledged politician. The state WPA had been active in Oklahoma on behalf of Senator Thomas and a candidate for governor, William Keys, who had been WPA director.

From Oklahoma we turned into Texas and there, for three days, local Congressmen played tag with President Roosevelt's coattails all the way across that state. They boarded the train and prayerfully hoped for a word from the President. As one of them remarked, "If the President would only just say 'my friend Congressman Blank,'—that's all, just mention my name." My good friend Maury Maverick had come all the way from San Antonio to join the train and get a blessing. He had an anxious wait. Finally, at Amarillo in the Panhandle—many days' journey from San Antonio, or so it seemed in that vast state—the President mentioned his

494

name, just barely within the state borders. Maury lost in a very close race and later was elected Mayor of San Antonio. We miss him about Washington.

In Colorado, Senator Adams joined the Presidential party on the train, and in Nevada, Senator McCarran got aboard. While neither received even a nod publicly from the President, each was photographed with the Chief Executive, and the "purge" as far as they were concerned did not materialize. In California there was a veritable galaxy of ambitious political talent seeking a Presidential pat, candidates for the United States Senate and the governorship.

The now elderly but still virile McAdoo, the incumbent seeking reelection, had always been friendly with the President, but he had one especially binding claim upon the man in the White House. He still traded on his part in throwing the California and Texas delegations to Roosevelt at Chicago in 1932 which clinched the Roosevelt nomination. But Mc-Adoo took no chances. He, and the young wife he had taken unto himself only shortly before in a third marriage, met the Presidential train at Stockton, outside San Francisco, rode with the President in that joyful and triumphal tour through the city, and accompanied the party in its visit of Yosemite National Park. McAdoo never let the President get out of his sight. It was funny, almost ludicrous. We stopped for lunch at a lodge in the middle of the Park. The President slipped off to have lunch by himself with a few Secret Service men among the giant trees. But he could not elude the vigilant Senator. McAdoo hunted him out and intruded into this privacy. Finally he won his reward in a brief mention as the train arrived at Los Angeles in the home territory of McAdoo's opponent, Sheridan Downey, who was stirring up a political cyclone as a champion not only of the Townsend old-age pension plan, but also of the newly evolved "Thirty Dollars Every Thursday" movement which was a new

495

religion in California and was sweeping in a mad frenzy through that always impressionable state. Everybody who should know told us that McAdoo would win despite this new hysteria, and I for one was surprised when Downey defeated the Senator, though I should have known better, being familiar with California and its taste for panaceas.

President Roosevelt went off on a fishing cruise which would take him through the Panama Canal and land him in Florida many days later. I returned to Washington by slow stages up the Pacific Coast and across the North and Middle West. I stopped here and there to take soundings. Temporarily the "purge" was forgotten, and it looked to some as if this episode might have ended. We soon found how wrong was this deduction.

The cue came as Harry Hopkins set off to join the President when he landed in Florida for his trip through Georgia and South Carolina. Harry was now close in the President's political councils and we learned, from newspaper reports that came through, that he was whispering in the President's ear, saying "Go ahead, Mr. President." The President laid the ground in his speech at the University where he sketched the general philosophy of his crusade for a new liberal party. He followed this up specifically at Barnesville the next day by asking boldly for the defeat of Senator George and the election of the district attorney at Atlanta, Lawrence Camp, whom the administration political group had induced to seek the Senate seat. Nor did the President overlook Gene Talmadge, again howling for a return to power in Georgia politics. He spoke vaguely of those of demagogic tendency and promoters of panaceas—and everybody knew he meant Gene of the red suspenders and the cornfield wisecrack.

In South Carolina later the President let it be known that he wanted Senator "Cotton Ed" Smith eliminated from the Senate.

But I discovered, likewise, that the President was combatting an old prejudice that still simmers, and that only needs provocation to blow up into a consuming fire. This was local pride and local sovereignty, for want of a better description. Georgia, I was convinced, was overwhelmingly in favor of the President. But many resented his presuming to tell them for whom they should vote in their own state. Let him handle his job in Washington. They liked the way he was doing that. They did not want him to interfere in their affairs. It was hard for them to realize that their representatives and those from other Southern states and a few others could coalesce into a bloc in Congress that would be able to checkmate the President. They elected a man and usually did not pay a great deal of attention to him. After all, Washington and what happened there was something far off and a little mysterious. They could not see that it had much to do with them. And when he came back home and told them how he had voted for their interests—well, they took him on faith, more or less, having no way to find out what really happened. It was very difficult to draw the issue as the President was trying to draw it.

The economic lords of the state encouraged this local prejudice. They were influential with the newspapers and with the corporations, large and small, for which the masses worked. They whipped up this fever of provincialism, although I must say that they found they were not so powerful as they thought they were.

I saw something of the George campaign. It was indignant state pride asserting itself. The Senator assumed the martyr rôle and carried it off very well. I sat in the auditorium at Macon and witnessed one of the bits of showmanship. A Georgia politician by the name of Edgar Dunlap, a big, genial sort of fellow from an old family, was one of the managers of the George campaign. He had a federal job as state counsel for the RFC. He was ousted suddenly from this post because of his political activity on behalf of Senator George. The meeting in Macon was in the afternoon. In order to help fill the hall, employees of the Bibb Manufacturing Company, of which I have spoken previously in discussing the paternalistic system of the South, had been excused from their work so they might attend the political rally. Soon after the meeting started one of the speakers told of the Dunlap incident and then shouted, dramatically:

"Stand up, Edgar Dunlap!"

The American Legion Band played "Dixie." Dunlap stood up. His was a surprise appearance. He was about halfway back in the auditorium. He was asked to come forward and he bounced along the aisle and up the side steps to the platform. There he stood until the band finished the Southern anthem. He is a member of the Legion. When the uproar subsided, he made a little speech in which he capitalized his martyrdom. Then the Senator himself was called upon and he capitalized *his* martyrdom. He spoke of communism in Washington and the attempt of young communists in the brain trust to seize the government and eradicate such statesmen as himself.

It was all very neat—and, to me, very funny, though more than a little nauseous.

It fooled many people—but not all, I am glad to say.

I was overjoyed to see a new consciousness of political interest on the part of the workers of Georgia, an interest that was not large enough in 1938 to turn the tide but may become a really important factor in time. Their political consciousness and their organization were offset by the prejudice expressed in two ways—in behalf of local pride and independence, and in the votes cast for Gene Talmadge among the backwoods farmers, chiefly, and by some of the rank and file of the cities who just naturally like his barnyard type of politician, an amusing demagogue. The irony of that primary election was that Gene Talmadge gave Senator George an awful scare. He ran second. Early reports on election night indicated he would win, but, as the boxes reported from the respectable small towns with their tight political machines, the tide was turned in the Senator's favor.

President Roosevelt's candidate, Lawrence Camp, ran third. He was an ineffectual campaigner and had no organization and little money. His last-minute entry into the race was an example of the amateur, bungling way in which the New Dealers—bereft of Jim Farley's counsel—had handled the whole campaign of rooting out anti-New Deal figures from Congress. His showing was good in view of the many handicaps he faced, not least of which was his own shortcoming as a stump campaigner. That counts a great deal still in my state, where people like a show with their politics.

I became aware of the Talmadge strength very soon after I drove across the Tugaloo River bridge which separates South Carolina and Georgia. I stopped at Toccoa and chatted with some of the people gathered about the courthouse. They were country folks in for the day, men in overalls who chewed tobacco and were discouragingly uncommunicative. I gathered, after some leading questions, that most of them were going to vote for "Old Gene" Talmadge, as they called him.

As I travelled down the road to Atlanta, stopping here and there, I found that Talmadge was going to be a real factor in the race.

Always, when I cross the state line and get back into my native Georgia, I get a thrill. I thought it was gone, but in 1938 it came back with the old force and as I recalled this and that incident of my childhood and school days I realized that, at bottom, I always would be a Georgian.

I guess it's in the blood.

But I have come to see some things through the stranger's eyes.

Certainly, a few years before I would not have felt a keen personal interest in an attempt such as this of Roosevelt's to start a political revolution in Georgia. Now I did. I saw, when I came back to my own people and to my own state, the need for such a revolution, the need for a restoration of democracy in Georgia, the need for taking power from those who had held it so long and had so misused it.

35

I WAS, as I have said, glad to see Franklin D. Roosevelt strike at entrenched bourbonism in the South. Though he lost his immediate objective in Georgia and South Carolina, he did start, as in the Supreme Court fight, a healthy if bitter debate that forced the two Senators to take the defensive and try to explain themselves. This was an accomplishment and a step toward restoration of democracy in the South. The Senators' explanations failed to satisfy great numbers of voters, as the results showed. But they were sufficiently successful in beclouding the real issues by appeals to state and local pride against interference from outside, by raising the racial issue which "Cotton Ed" Smith in his clownish, bucolic way made his dominant theme, by prating about communism and claiming that the "brain trust" in Washington was permeated with it.

President Roosevelt's political prestige suffered, at least temporarily, from his defeats in Georgia and South Carolina. Similarly it was dimmed still further by his adventure in "the old free state of Maryland!" I was among the newspapermen who trooped along in what the local newspapers called the "invasion" of Maryland. The President took a two-day automobile tour through the state with the avowed purpose of rousing the populace to unseat Senator Millard E. Tydings and, in his stead, send to Washington the diminutive philosopher and able progressive, Representative David J. Lewis.

The missionary work was largely in the famous Eastern Shore region, that isolated, flat and lush truck garden for the big city market, where people are provincial, independent and very resentful of outside interference, whether it be by a Henry L. Mencken who lectures them with his acid words for a lynching episode, by labor organizers who try to raise the pay of workers in a few runaway mills, or by Franklin D. Roosevelt trying to tell them how they should vote.

They detested Mencken. They detested John L. Lewis. And they were cold and insulting to Franklin D. Roosevelt.

They expressed their feelings in signs, stretched here and there across the road, which played in various ways on the "invasion" idea. Yet publicly and outwardly, aside from these signs, there was no untoward incident. Those who disapproved did not come out to hoot. They either stayed away, or kept quiet if they joined the crowds which gathered in the little towns through which the President and his party travelled. There were crowds of people but little enthusiasm.

The Tydings lieutenants had paved with their hostile intentions the road over which the President rode. From hundreds of trees the thin-faced Tydings looked upon the "invasion." It was as if the woods were full of Tydings. And you got the impression, as you rode with the President, that this was another Tydings, a big, statesmanlike figure, a new and powerful character, not the rather inoffensive member of Congress who was never taken very seriously, who was known rather for the way he boldly proclaimed positions and then retreated from them the following day. President Roosevelt had created this martyr over whom Maryland's newspapers, particularly the *Sun* papers of Baltimore, dripped great tears as if he were about to spill his last drop of blood for liberty, as if he were on the verge of giving his all to save the land from the heel of a cruel tyrant. Tydings had been heroic only in a single-handed campaign to balance the budget. He was going to cut 10 per cent off government expenditures. But the next day he thought better of this crusade, as he had thought better of other crusades. His chief charm to one who had to spend his days about the Capitol was an occasional humorous speech. He sometimes achieved a light touch that was a relief in a wilderness of dull solemnity.

Yet a new Tydings emerged, and, lo and behold, some of his friends started a Presidential boom for him.

The Eastern Shore political situation was tersely summed up by the Negro porter of a Salisbury hotel on query by Eddie Folliard of the *Washington Post*:

"Some says Tydings and some says Lewis but mo' says Tydings."

Perhaps the most regrettable reflex from the "purge" campaign was the creation of martyrs—that, and the fact that those whom the President had sought unsuccessfully to drive from public office now returned to Washington, smarting from the "purge" adventure, to work out their spleen by solidifying the hitherto loosely organized conservative bloc, largely made up of fellow Southerners, plotting actively now against the President and his New Deal.

President Roosevelt did not liberalize the Democratic Party. He only ripped it wider apart.

Why, then, did he undertake the "purge"?

Washington is full of theories and explanations on this point as on all others, so I may as well contribute my own. Basically, one cannot forget that Franklin D. Roosevelt's consuming desire is to build a new liberal party. He was convinced, undoubtedly, by himself and perhaps by the exhortations of counsellors who shared this ideal that 1938 was the time to strike—the last time, in fact, while he was President; for I am convinced, whatever may be the ultimate outcome, that he did not, in 1938, intend to seek a third nomination. I think the whole crusade was a bit impulsive in inspiration as well as execution, which explains its stops and starts and misfires. The desertion of many Democrats on his Court plan stirred up his anger. Advisers of the sort I have described poured on the flames the fuel of their hero worship and of their own ambition. Most of them, I think, were sincere, if impracticable, in desiring to perpetuate the Roosevelt dynasty which, of course, included them. They had come to believe their own solution of the nation's problems was the right and proper one, and anyone who tried to offer other solutions or tried to check their projects must be classed as an open enemy.

This combination of impulses produced the "purge."

I have always thought, however, that President Roosevelt had a long-time objective that looked beyond any successes or failures in the specific 1938 campaign. I think, as in the Court plan, that he hoped to raise the issue, start a public debate, and provoke the voters themselves to inquire more closely into what the men they elected to office actually did when they got to Washington. This certainly was the effect in Georgia, South Carolina and Maryland. He piqued the curiosity of the voters. Furthermore, I think he envisaged definite political results for the future, 1940 in particular, and this in two ways.

First, as I see it, he hoped by backing a particular candidate whom he considered "liberal" to attract a nucleus of voters who would be the basis of a future political organization. I think that in some instances he saw here a way to get New Deal delegations to the 1940 convention. In the second place, I think he wanted to put those who had opposed his policies on the "spot," to read their records to the voters, so that in 1940 he could point back to their records since their reelection and say "I told you so. I told you about these men. Are they the sort you want to dictate the nomination of a candidate for President in 1940?" For the men whom he saw fit to mark and brand as his enemies and those who are like-minded, particularly in the Senate, are the leaders who wield great influence at national conventions. He wanted to discredit them to diminish their influence.

This is the way I analyze it, and the "purge" still may bear unexpected fruit in time. Its dismal failure in its practical, immediate purpose, that is, to drive certain men from office, may have checked any valuable long-time gains and certainly it deepened the schism within the party.

There is no question that the President shook the party to its roots and made it extremely sensitive to its conflicting philosophies.

Only in one case did the Roosevelt "purge" work. That was the defeat of Representative John J. O'Connor of New York. O'Connor had been chairman of the Rules Committee, the final bottleneck through which bills must move to the floor of the House. The administration thought he had not been properly cooperative in getting House consideration for some important New Deal bills. The committee was a hard-boiled group with the conservative inclinations of men long in public office. It was overloaded with Southerners. O'Connor naturally had his troubles. The administration was particularly peeved over the committee's pocketing of the wage-hour bill for months. Five Southerners threw up a blockade and refused to budge. With support of Republican members, they were able to keep the bill from the floor.

The O'Connor defeat served to dramatize again the long fight over the wage-hour bill, a measure requiring an eventual maximum work week of forty hours and 40 cents an hour wage in industries which it covered—and there were great gaps in its coverage. It served, too, to reveal the Southern economic and social philosophy which, when it asserted itself as it now was doing, threw a blight over the new liberalism advocated by Roosevelt, retarded the progressive march of the Democratic Party, and offered the real explanation of the party split.

Southern Democracy was the ball and chain which hobbled the party's forward movement.

It was this which Roosevelt was fighting when he boldly demanded defeat of Senators George and Smith. Both had voted against the bill. He was striking through them at the Southern system represented by them and others in House and Senate who voted against the bill. They spoke for the mill-owners and dominant economic interests to whose advantage it had been to keep the Southern worker on a low wage.

For a longer time than anyone who knew the South, as I did, would have expected, Franklin D. Roosevelt had kept the Southerners in Congress in line because of the popularity throughout the country of his reform program. He held the whip over them. They had to go along. But as the Roosevelt reform program opened out to include measures such as the Wagner Labor Relations Act and the wage-hour bill which endangered the Southern system, then the Southerners began to balk. For their real masters now called them to account.

505

These real masters were the business, financial and industrial interests which had fattened on the low-wage economy—both in the mill and on the farm—and who, over the years, continued to control the political machines. They spoke with a loud voice and their automatons in Congress responded.

Though numerically in a minority among Democrats in Congress for the larger part of the Roosevelt era, because of the landslides which had poured Democrats into Congress from East and West, the Southerners exercised power far beyond their numerical strength because they controlled key places. They were represented out of all proportion, for instance, on the Rules Committee, the tight little oligarchy which says what bills shall come before the House and under what sort of procedure. The Vice President who presided over the Senate and who, because of his long legislative career in the House, carried weight far beyond his nominal post, was a Southerner. So were the Speaker of the House and the party leader. Southerners held the lion's share of important committee chairmanships. All this disproportionate representation in strategic positions was a result of the fact that these places are allotted on the basis of priority of service, and Southern Democrats are able to get elected year after year, thus gradually moving upward by the grace of the seniority rule. This has, at times, brought men of small caliber and ability to important positions.

As Roosevelt struck at the privileged rulers of the Southern system, this machine began to function, though not as a whole, for such leaders as Speaker Bankhead of Alabama and Democratic Leader Sam Rayburn of Texas remained loyal. But, on one occasion or another, a key figure of a committee group would adopt obstructive or dilatory tactics. It is so often difficult to fix direct responsibility in a legislative assembly because so much is done by indirection. Any number of examples might be cited, but illustrative were the sniping tactics of Vice President Garner behind the scenes, aimed chiefly at New Deal labor and spending policies; the blockade against the wage-hour bill by the five Southerners on the Rules Committee; the speech by Representative Hatton Sumners, Texas chairman of the Judiciary Committee, condemning the President's Supreme Court reform plan; the investigation of un-American activities, so-called, by Representative Martin Dies of Texas, which was turned against New Deal labor policies.

Jack Garner never operated publicly, but through suggestions to Southern senatorial friends. He was a valuable counsellor on strategy because of his long experience. There was no real occasion for Hatton Sumners' speech on the Court bill. The measure was not before the House. But Sumners is a man of wide influence in the House and his speech was made with this in mind. It was effective.

Individual Southern Democrats became bolder in their desertions from the administration, both in House and Senate, as the President's prestige was lowered—in Congress and country—by his Court bill crusade, and some of them revolted openly after the "purge" campaign and the defeat of progressive Democrats in the East and West in the 1938 elections. The tide was turning, and they began to move with it. Their defection now endangered the Roosevelt program because Republicans had enlarged their forces, especially in the House, in the 1938 elections, and this tacit alliance of the opposition elements created anti-administration majorities on some issues.

With misgivings I saw the Southerners begin to clutch their strangling hands about the neck of the Democratic Party again.

I knew something of the Southern system. I had been born into it. I had learned much about it through the years. I had learned more about it in a trip through the South in late 1936 on an assignment to investigate a new migration of small, sweatshop type of industry into Southern small towns —an industrial carpetbag movement.

36

I FOLLOWED the trail of this migration through Tennessee and Mississippi and Alabama and Georgia, where it was at that time most widely spread, and in looking into this new type of exploitation of my South I learned many other things about its social structure and its politics.

From New York and New Jersey and Pennsylvania and Indiana and other states many small manufacturers—and, in some few cases, large operators—were fleeing from labor laws and unions, which required them to pay decent wages, to the poverty-stricken small towns of the South which welcomed them with open arms, in fact, in many cases invited them.

The nullification of NRA by the Supreme Court swelled this tide of migration, for it abolished the compulsory wage of $12 a week—the minimum which in the South generally became the maximum—and Southern labor laws were so inadequate and unions so few and far between and the low-wage system so fixed by custom and so enforced by the economic rulers that no other compulsions existed. It was, for the most part, a land free of any sort of restrictions.

The South offered a surplus of white, Anglo-Saxon labor, as its little Chambers of Commerce advertised, which meant compliant and unquestioning labor; but it now was offering a great deal more. It gave free buildings, free power, free water, tax exemptions for a period of years. It was a land of industrial promise, a land of milk and honey. Come and get it, the South called.

They were coming, exultantly.

I discovered various schemes of inducement. In Tennessee a plan used effectively by many towns was to provide a building for the migrating company and to pay for it by deducting 5 or 6 per cent from the wages of the workers. These wage deductions were turned over to the city. In at least one case, at Manchester, Tenn., the wages were paid and the deductions taken out by the city clerk—until the state labor department put a stop to this practice. When I was in Tennessee the labor department records showed that twenty-one towns had brought in new factories by some special inducement.

Mississippi, when I was there, had just inaugurated the plan to "balance agriculture with industry" as Governor Hugh White, its sponsor, called it. He put through a law which permitted cities, subject to approval by a local election, to bond themselves to finance buildings for new industries and to grant five-year tax exemption. Previously, several towns had built plants by public subscription with the proviso that the building would be deeded to the migrant corporation if it made a stated payroll within a specified time. Governor White, himself, had promoted such a venture for his home town of Columbia before he became governor and, when he returned home after negotiating successfully, he was met at the station by a parade of citizens and a band!

Variations on the Tennessee and Mississippi schemes were found in Alabama and Georgia.

Governor White's welcome home with a contract for a factory—in which Mississippi citizens lavishly financed the migrant—was more tragic than comic. It spoke expressively of the hunger of the South for industries to provide payrolls for its people. The agricultural economy had broken down, what with the loss of markets for the South's staple for so long—cotton. In Mississippi this was complicated by the dying out of the lumber industry also which had been a revenue and work producer. Governor White posed the problem for me in a long discussion in his office at the capitol at Jackson. He cited statistics showing that the value of all industrial enterprises in the state amounted to only $35 per capita, whereas the average for all other Southern states— and some of them were poor enough—was four times that; that the average farm income in Mississippi was only $180 a year; and that the average annual income of all the people in the state was $212, against a national average of $636.

I recognized the distressing condition that he pictured.

But I told him that I thought Mississippi was selling out too cheap; that the low wage offered by the invading industries was no compensation for the advantages which the state gave in exchange; that this sort of starvation income would not help his state. The companies were sending their profits back east and they were shipping the products which they manufactured for such low cost into other markets to compete with industries which were paying decent wages.

The human angle struck me forcefully. Wages were unbelievably low, not only in Mississippi, but in similar runaway plants in other states which I covered in my investigation. The exploitation of my own people made my blood boil. The invaders were capitalizing upon the surplus of labor piled up by the languishing cotton economy. Wages ran $5, $6, $7 and $8 a week, mostly in the small garment and shoe factories. A Mississippi storekeeper in a town in the southern part of the state showed me one day a check for 97 cents which had been paid a girl for two weeks' work. She had worked every day, but in the whole two weeks had been given credit for only 3.24 standard hours, as they are called. The rest of her work was disallowed, as far as compensation was concerned, on the excuse that it did not come up to specification. The storekeeper knew her and said she was an intelligent and capable person. She quit her job at the end of the two weeks.

"She came to me and showed me the check and said she wanted to tear it up and throw it in the face of the boss," he explained. "I told her not to do that, to let me cash it, and I could keep it as a souvenir."

The storekeeper disclaimed any philanthropy or idealism in his interest in better pay for the workers—though after talking with him awhile I was convinced that he had such impulses.

"It's just business with me. If these girls got bigger checks I'd get a bigger share of them. So would other business. This sort of thing is not helping our town."

The incident of the 97-cent check, while extreme, is illustrative of the various ruses used to chisel down even the low wage scale. Quota systems of various sorts were in effect in many places which I visited. The apprentice system also was widely exploited. The learner's period was dragged out for weeks in some cases. The pay was negligible and, in a few cases, nothing. There were cases where the apprentice was dismissed on one excuse or another at the end of the period and another "apprentice" taken on, so that a continuing stream of help was available for virtually no cost. This was made possible by the surplus labor on the farms. In Mississippi I found numerous instances where girls and women were coming from as far as twenty miles away to work in the factories. Often a neighbor operated a sort of jitney service, picking the girls up in the morning and returning them at night for a certain amount a week.

As abhorrent to me as the cheap shysters who were exploiting the helpless and ignorant Southern people were those who permitted it, nay encouraged it. As I went about from place to place, I became aware of the Southern paternalistic system exemplified in a communion of interest of the haves against the have-nots, of the master element against the slaves whom they dismiss as "poor white trash" and who are to be left in their state of servitude and ignorance. This communion of interest includes the Chambers of Commerce and the churches which throw the protecting cloak of business and religion about the established order.

It expressed itself in open warfare against labor unions and labor organizers. I know labor organizers in the South who have been driven out of town, some who have been beaten and shot. In some towns they hardly dared show themselves, though this now has been changed considerably by the guarantees of the Wagner Labor Relations Act.

Governor White, in my conference with him, revealed the predilections and the antagonisms characteristic of the Southern paternalistic system and, before we got through our conversation, we were both verging on bitterness. Each failed to see the viewpoint of the other.

I had been attracted by a portion of his message to the legislature proposing the "balance agriculture with industry plan" in which he had said: "Our high percentage of native Anglo-Saxon citizenship, with an absence of the disturbing elements so common to larger industrial centers, offers a great attraction for those looking for new fields in which to establish their factories."

I asked him about his attitude toward labor unions.

"I haven't anything to say," he replied.

"What would be your attitude if labor unions came into the state to organize in these factories?" I inquired.

"I haven't anything to say on that subject," was his answer.

"Do you believe in collective bargaining as a principle?"

"I couldn't discuss that."

Wages, he said, are a matter for local communities. He claimed that no industry which had come into the state was paying low wages. I explained that data I had gathered showed wages around $5, $6, $7, and $8 a week. He said he thought wages had been increased somewhat recently.

"I think the average wage today is $10," he interjected.

I pointed out the NRA minimum was $12.

He was for NRA, he said, and was sorry to see it annulled. It would be all right with him if something like NRA should be restored, he added.

"I'm in favor of people having an income to maintain a decent standard of living."

I asked him if he thought the present wage scale would permit a decent standard of living.

"Only fair," he answered. "That's been true. I'd like to see high wages—we all would. But we've got to have a condition to bring them about. We've got to have a demand for our labor."

In Tennessee I visited, among other places, the small town which was said to be the first to offer "open house" to outside industries. Dickson, Tenn., is pleasantly situated in a farming region about forty miles west of Nashville. When I got there the plant which had been invited into Dickson was embroiled in a political legal controversy which had the citizens disturbed and workers in the factory agitated. In the middle of the controversy was portly Mayor Dan E. Beasley who ran a hardware store on the main street. He had sponsored the agreement three years before with a garment plant which operated formerly in Pennsylvania. Under the agreement, the plant was financed by a bond issue and the workers bound themselves to a 6 per cent weekly deduction to retire the bonds. The company was given a five-year tax exemption, free power, light and water, and was charged $1 a year for rent. Subsequently the company wanted an addition and the city agreed to continue the wage deductions to finance that. This had provoked some grumbling among the workers who wondered how long this sort of thing would go on. In the few months before I visited the town a number of disturbing incidents had occurred.

Fifty-three workers refused one week to pay their 6 per cent which, under the agreement, it was the town's responsibility to collect. Mayor Beasley and his friends claimed that the company had spread a rumor among the workers that they did not have to pay. The company's object, it was charged, was to break the agreement so it could buy the plant, title to which was in the Dickson Development Corporation, an agency of the town. Subsequently, some of the workers joined in a suit seeking an accounting from the mayor of $24,000 they had paid into the liquidation fund and asking a ruling as to the city's right to own and lease the factory building. Mayor Beasley struck back and ordered collection of taxes from the company, and the county followed suit on behalf of county taxes. The company retaliated by seeking an injunction against the collection of taxes.

It was all mixed up. I only sketch these various legal steps to show the complications that could arise, when men resort to such strange subterfuges.

I found Mayor Beasley puzzled and confused, weary of the whole business, when I visited him in a warehouse back of his hardware store.

"I want 'em out," he said of the company, adding, "I would never enter an agreement like that again."

The company, he said, paid low wages.

"I was against NRA," he commented, "but when I see things like this I think maybe it would be a good thing to have some sort of control."

Explaining why he had negotiated the agreement for the factory in the first place, he said that agriculture was depressed, there was little money in the community, and the relief load was heavy. He thought it would be a good idea to get the factory and bring some money into the town.

"I've lived here for thirty years," he said. "I wanted to do something for these people."

It was turning out very badly. I don't know what has happened since.

An interesting commentary on the type of management which existed at the Dickson plant I found in the records of the state labor department at Nashville. In its report to the department, the company said that $12 a week was the average wage for 460 female and 71 male employees. An investigator for the department who inspected the payroll reported 382 employees getting $5.55 a week. Foremen, cutters, floor managers and other supervisory and specialized employees had been included to get the higher average. The NRA minimum, I again remark, was $12.

The state labor department faced a difficult task. It had only five inspectors to cover the whole state, and officials admitted that reports necessarily might contain misleading information such as that discovered by the inspector at Dickson. The state's report for the year 1935 showed that 50 per cent of women employed in manufacturing industries in Tennessee got less than $12 a week.

Lewisburg, Tenn., had an interesting story. It built a municipal hall, used it for one meeting, and then turned it over to the General Shoe Corporation for a factory. The building was paid for with $30,000 from the city and $30,000 from the employees through a 5 per cent wage deduction weekly. In store windows all about town the city posted signs warning merchants to deduct 5 per cent from pay checks presented to be cashed; otherwise the bank would make the deduction and the merchants would stand the loss. If an employee demanded the full amount of the check from the bank—and he could under the law—he would get a letter warning him that this was not good practice.

The Labor Department brought a case against the city and the company for alleged violation of banking laws.

"When I went to Lewisburg on that case," an inspector said, "they told me, 'It looks like you fellows are down here to start trouble.' I asked them whether they thought the city could secede from the Union."

Once established in a town, a plant could exert pressure because of the city's desire for it to remain. The General Shoe Corporation had a plant in an old building at Gallatin, Tenn. It received offers from five other towns to build a new plant for it. Faced with loss of the plant, Gallatin voted a $45,000 bond issue to erect a new plant and hold the company there. The competition was keen.

Typical of the contract which workers signed with the city to get jobs in the invading plants is that used at Manchester which reads:

"I the undersigned hereby make application for employment at the garment factory erected by the town of Manchester, Tenn., and agree with the said town of Manchester, Tenn., that in the event I am given employment at the said factory for and in consideration of the said town of Manchester, Tenn., securing employment for me with the operator of said factory, that I will pay to the said town of Manchester, Tenn., 6 per cent of my weekly salary or wage, to be paid as directed by the aforesaid town."

A committee from the city council passed on all applications to make sure that the "right" type of employee was hired.

In Mississippi I found that the federal government—both the WPA and the United States Office of Education—had been duped by a scheme concocted by Mississippi towns and Chambers of Commerce to use federal funds to build plants and, ostensibly, train workers for private garment manufacturers who had migrated from the North, East and Middle West.

The scheme, stopped by order of then WPA Administrator Harry L. Hopkins when he discovered it, affords an insight into the psychology of some civic leaders in Mississippi and explains a lot about its public figures and its politicians and businessmen.

Five Mississippi towns submitted projects to WPA for "industrial training schools." The money was allocated and used to build factories which were turned over to migrating companies. Money advanced by the Office of Education, presumably for teachers in vocational training schools, was paid instead to foremen in these plants. "Student" workers received no pay at all for a long time, though they were turning out goods, and subsequently were paid very low wages, in some cases $4 a week, for a further period as "learners."

The five towns where this clever scheme was tried were Philadelphia, Lumberton, Columbia, Brookhaven and Ellisville.

In his office at WPA headquarters in Jackson, R. B. Wall, deputy administrator for Mississippi and also mayor of Brookhaven, related with engaging frankness the whole story behind the "vocational schools."

All of them, he said, were intended at the outset for factories.

In the case of Brookhaven, he explained, he already had picked out the company to use the plant before the project for an "industrial training school" was submitted to WPA in Washington.

"I might as well be frank—it was a camouflage," he said. "Other places had been getting away with things. I didn't see why we couldn't try it."

He explained that the specifications were "shot in" during the rush in the last two days before a WPA deadline in the hope that in the hurry and confusion they would be approved. He called in an architect, he said, to draw plans for a factory. The architect first said that he could not draw such plans in the short time specified, but then recalled that he had some plans for a garment factory at McComb, Miss., which could be adapted. This was done.

The original project approved by WPA called for $45,466 from the government and $16,281 from the city. When Hopkins ordered the project stopped, the city provided funds to complete the plant. The government put in altogether between $35,000 and $40,000, and the city about $50,000.

"I'll show you the specifications submitted to Washington," the mayor offered and pushed a buzzer.

The proposition was thus stated:

"The sponsor proposes a project for the erection and completion of an Industrial Training School for the City of Brookhaven as set forth herein and in accordance with plans and specifications for same."

The justification was as follows:

"A development of this type will greatly expedite the industrial expansion of Brookhaven and vicinity as well as stimulate industry by the introduction of qualified craftsmen."

"That's a pretty good blanket, isn't it?" he asked with a twinkle.

It certainly said nothing about a factory.

I told the WPA deputy administrator-mayor that I would like to see the plant at Brookhaven. He assured me that I could do so, and added that if any question was raised I should have the manager call him. So on my journey through central and southern Mississippi I stopped at Brookhaven.

It was a commodious modern, light and airy building. I introduced myself to the manager and told him I would like to see the plant. This company had migrated from Terre Haute, Ind.

"We don't allow anyone to go through the plant."

"What's your reason?" I asked.

He explained that it was an old custom in garment factories not to let visitors in because they might steal methods. I assured him that I knew nothing whatever about methods, and told him what the mayor had said, but he persisted.

I then asked what wages he paid. He said the average worker could make up to $11 or $12 a week. I asked what the average was. He replied that he'd have to go through the books and that would take a lot of time—a lot more, I saw at once, than he intended to give to me.

The girls were leaving the building for the lunch period. Outside I stopped a group of them and asked what was the average pay. I was told about $7 a week. I asked if any of them ever made as much as $11 or $12 a week.

"Not since the first two weeks," one of them replied.

My request to see the plant at Brookhaven and the reason advanced for refusing permission, have a little side history.

Previously I had visited a plant at Crystal Springs further north. Because I like to get a first-hand view of things I write, I merely wanted to see what the inside of a garment factory looked like, see the machines, see what the operators have to do, and the like. It was merely the reporter's instinct.

The factory at Crystal Springs was on the edge of that little town in the middle of the tomato belt. It also was a light, airy modern building. I pushed open the door and entered an office at the right. There I found a slender young man standing near the radiator, and a girl at a typewriter—apparently the managerial and office staff of the small plant.

I identified myself and asked the young man if I might look through the plant.

"No one is permitted to go through the plant."

"Why?" I inquired.

"Because it might distract the girls and cause some one to injure herself with the machine."

I had never affected girls that way before—but maybe I looked better than I always had thought.

"Any other reason?"

He only smiled.

I asked what his wage scale was, explaining that I had obtained information elsewhere and in fairness, wanted to check with him.

"I can't tell you that. We are just getting started, you know."

The plant had been operating six months.

"This is a ———— factory, isn't it?" I asked, naming a concern in Pennsylvania which was moving its plants from that state.

"No," he replied.

"Whose is it, then?"

"Mine."

"Who are you?"

"I can't tell you that."

"Who is the foreman?"

"I am."

Balked, I said: "It's a case of from me to me with love, huh?"

He smiled, his secretary laughed, and I departed.

Later I learned from the mayor, R. S. Brent, who also was station agent, that the factory was the property of the Pennsylvania company I had named and that the young man was one of the family and was operating it. From the mayor and citizens I talked to I also learned how the plant came to be there, and it was an interesting story of the part power companies were playing in luring new industries to the South as markets for electricity.

The Mississippi Power Company wanted to buy the city's municipal power plant and the town wanted a factory. A three-way deal was worked out. The mayor explained that the plan envisaged getting enough from the power company for the plant to put up a garment factory, but that the provision for a garment plant could not legally be included in the sale of the city power plant, nor could the city itself, under state law, enter into a contract with a private corporation.

The Chamber of Commerce came to the rescue and set up a corporation which received $30,000 from the power company to build the garment plant. Under the contract, the plant was to go to the garment company if its payroll for ten years reached $500,000; otherwise, it would revert to the power company. The city received $302,000 for the power plant. The mayor insisted this was a good price, though this was challenged by others who said the price included vague considerations and that the city only got about $160,000. The mayor said the garment company had to pay good wages, but he had no idea what wages were being paid.

A drugstore owner, G. A. Thaxton, who sought to stop the whole funny transaction, said new girls at the plant worked for a month for nothing. The average wage, according to checks he handled and reports from the workers, was about $5 a week. He saw one check, he said, for $10.40. The garment plant had promised, as had happened in so many other cases, to pay $12 to $18 a week.

The druggist had filed a taxpayer's suit to enjoin sale of the power plant on the ground that the minutes of the

521

board of aldermen had been changed in a secret, illegal session; but he withdrew the suit, he explained, when he saw that the town was going to approve the sale in an election, in order to leave the way clear for such action later.

"This is the craziest thing I ever saw, for a bunch of sensible people to give away a power plant," he ejaculated. "People all around here who had had anything to do with the power company advised against it."

Thaxton and W. C. Scott, another citizen, explained that the city power plant had made an average of $19,000 a year for the last five years and that the city owed only $60,000 on it. The rates were not low, they explained, but the plant had helped to finance the city and eventually the city would have owned it outright.

"We've got a bad thing here," commented Scott, shaking his head sadly.

Through a December rain we drove out to the mill town of Clinton, Tenn., nineteen miles from Knoxville.

A meeting of the new union, we were told, was being held in Volunteer Hall, whatever that might be. On the outskirts of the town my escort, a union organizer (incidentally he is a former Union Theological student, trained for the ministry), inquired at a garage where the hall was. No one seemed to know. We drove into the town and began to inquire. As we were asking directions of another inhabitant, a young man came up and said, in a low voice, that if we were going to the union meeting we could follow his car. We did. His approach was in the hush-hush manner then associated with unionism in the South. It was the grapevine system.

A mile out of town he turned off and led us along a slippery mud road through the woods. Suddenly we came upon a barn-like structure. It was a chicken-fighting club. Permission to use the school or the courthouse had been denied. The cock-fighting club was more hospitable.

Through the rain we approached the frame building. There was a peephole in the door, but no one stood on guard there. The meeting was in progress. Through the peephole came the sound of a pronounced Scottish accent, deep-burred. We pushed open the door and entered to behold a strange scene.

Standing in the middle of the arena, a man was addressing a group of men and women who perched like so many chickens, on a tier of benches leading up toward the roof. I counted them. There were eighty. They occupied less than a third of the circular grandstand. Some of the men wore overalls. The women were dressed, one imagined, as they would dress for church. The benches had no backs and some of the listeners were hunched over, elbows on knees, faces cupped in hands. They were a receptive and serious group.

Occasionally, as the rain hammered noisily at the roof in a fresh and furious onslaught, they hung over more closely to catch the words of the speaker who at such moments raised his voice above the tumult overhead.

The speaker was a Presbyterian minister, I learned, Dr. T. B. Cowan, "Scotty" Cowan they called him, whose charge was a church in Chattanooga. He was one of the few ministers in the South who raised their voices in behalf of organized labor against the established order. He had driven the 120 miles from Chattanooga through the rain for this meeting, and had to drive back immediately afterward for a service in Chattanooga.

There was a reason for his being here. At least three of the ministers in this mill town had been preaching against unionism, telling their flocks that it was wrong to belong to a labor union. Three or four of the workers said that one of them had gone further than preaching from the pulpit and was visiting members of his congregation to talk from house to house and family to family against union organization.

So "Scotty" had come here for a very definite purpose.

He was an alert, aggressive fellow of medium build who planted himself four-square when he emphasized a point, throwing his head back. His manner was earnest and persuasive. He had a flashing sense of humor. His face was nearly round and was mellow with kindliness.

As he talked he walked up and down the edge of the arena, like a gladiator challenging a foe. Over his head there turned round and round in the wind which swept into the bleak structure, a sign with the legend:

"No drunkenness, no profane language."

Even a cock-fighting club has its standards.

As his text, Scotty had chosen:

"A man is worth more than a machine."

Plain and understandable to these people.

He spoke of democracy in government, and added:

"We haven't quite got democracy in the church yet. Some ministers have a habit of kowtowing to the powers that be."

Then he told them that the Bible and the Constitution approved organization of workers into unions.

So does the church, he continued. Taking from his pocket a dog-eared pamphlet prepared by the International Council of Religious Education, he read quotations from the Federal Council of Churches and from declarations of numerous individual church organizations of all denominations approving union organization.

The quotations seemed to be convincing. He appeared to have smashed the dogma of the neighborhood ministers, at least for those gathered here, for they heartily applauded as he took his seat. When the meeting was over, I asked some of the workers about conditions in the mill and there was one unanimous complaint:

"The Bedeaux system."

This system was just then being introduced into the South. Breathlessly they interrupted each other as they tried to tell how it affected them. The general atmosphere was one of bewilderment. They told of threats that they would be fired if they didn't make their quotas. Ten workers, some of them old hands, were let out a few weeks before, they said, but were taken back when the others protested.

Their bosses, they said, put pressure on them because there was a bonus for the bosses whose crews turned out a certain quota.

"They tell us that under this system we can make more money—but we don't seem able to do it," was the general comment.

Still grumbling excitedly about the Bedeaux system they flocked from the cockpit into the rain.

In a sordid slum district on the outskirts of a southern city, I visited a day nursery for children of women workers in the factories which stuck up their smudgy faces below. The big frame house squatted on a slight eminence. The wages of the women whose children were kept here during the day ranged from $5 to $10 a week, more often $5 than $10.

From the front porch one looked across a dump heap toward the factories and the city beyond. Behind and to the right and left were the meager frame houses, some virtually hovels, where these mothers lived. In charge of the children was an efficient, attractive young woman, a graduate nurse from one of the South's leading university training schools who became interested in this home as a student and selected it for her career.

She sat in the front room, a cheerful body, and, rocking in an old chair as she talked, told about the people who lived in the neighborhood, the parents of the children whom she watched. Child noises drifted in through the doors. Forty-two children were enrolled in the home.

There was not a lot she could do except to care for the children and advise the mothers.

They made so little—and at least a third of the fathers, she said, were indolent and idle most of the time, another third had deserted their wives or were in and out, while the other third were fairly reliable when they could get work. It was a sort of matriarchal segment of what we call civilization. But the family income, even when fathers helped, was pitiable.

The nursery superintendent had formed a club of the women and got them together once a week to show them how to make their pittance go as far as possible. She helped them make budgets. She showed them how to save pennies in what they bought.

"How do they live?" I asked.

"They don't," she replied. "They exist."

Her aim was to inject, as far as possible with the material at hand, some sort of reliance in the mothers who struggled from day to day. When she went into the nursery she found that some of the mothers had acquired an attitude that the home owed them what they got. So she required them to pay a mite each week toward the upkeep of their children.

"Even as little as a nickel," she said.

The home was supported by the United Charities and by a contribution from the county of $2 a month for each child. She had a trained social worker to assist at one time, but this now had become impossible. The appropriation was too little.

There were some discouraging cases—discouraging to everybody but this cheerful young woman who stood by and did her best.

There was one mother of seven children whose husband refused to work. She made $9 a week. That was the sole support of the family, except for such help as that supplied by the nursery home. Her seventh child arrived a few months before.

There was the spinster whose family lived in the country outside. They could support her, but she insisted on being independent. A four-year-old nephew lived with her and stayed in the school during the day. She was very proud of him and took excellent care of him. She also was proud of her $7 a week job in the factory where she worked from seven in the morning to four-thirty in the afternoon, with half an hour off for lunch, standing before a machine putting biscuits in a box, working a treadle with her foot and keeping both hands busy.

"She wanted me to see her factory and see her job," the superintendent said. "She's proud of herself. She insisted so that I went one day. She showed me how she operated her machine. She introduced me to her boss."

Then there was the young woman who had three illegitimate children, with a fourth coming. The men just sort of come and go, helping with the expenses while the light of love shines.

"I can't blame her much," the young superintendent said. "You get broad-minded in a job like this. She's got to live. What can you do?"

These families had lived in this same spot, most of them, for generations. They might move across the street, or to the next block, when they couldn't pay their rent, but they never moved away. They were inert, acquiescent. They lacked education. Most have not been beyond the fourth or fifth grade.

Occasionally, the superintendent said, they would talk about how nice it would be to make better wages, but they were not resentful. They didn't blame anybody. They didn't know about collective bargaining. She had about given them up except to help them make what they got go as far as possible. It was the children in whom she put hope.

"I want them to go to high school, to get an education, to know something better."

There was yearning in her voice, and her eyes shone.

She glanced at her watch.

"It's time for lunch—would you like to see them?"

We stood at the steps leading to the dining room downstairs and watched them file down, the very tiny ones ranging in age from two to four. Their faces were bright. They chattered gaily. In the dining room they were remarkably handy with forks and spoons for boys and girls so young. When they finished they took their plates to the kitchen. When lunch was over, they returned to the nursery, a pleasant room with modern equipment, for their naps.

The next age group filed down to the dining room.

The light was not so bright in their eyes. They had that pinched look. They were beginning to enter the prison house, I thought, recalling that line of Wordsworth's. Young as they were they seemed to sense it somehow.

Six blocks from the home is a factory owned by one of the city's wealthy families. In 1928, when times were prosperous, it was paying good wages, just as high as in the East. It was a union plant. When the depression came it cut wages. There was a strike. The plant left the city and moved to a smaller town where there were no unions and labor was cheap. Recently the city plant was reopened and now it paid the women from $8 to $10 a week. In 1928 they got from $25 to $40.

That's what was happening in my South.

This trip was a revelation.

It made me bitter.

I had come up from this South. Now I saw it again first-hand.

It was alien, and yet it was very familiar.

No longer was I of it, though its suns and its rivers run through my blood—and always will. I will know forever the sight of its cotton-fields stretching away, white and lovely, to the far woods, the sweet smell of its pine forests, the blue haze across its mountains; but I will want to forget, though I know I cannot, its dirty little towns and its shacks in the country and the farm tools rusting in the rain, and the people who work in its mills and till acres which grow more barren and sit listlessly on the unpainted front porches in the evening and look forward to a dreary tomorrow and tomorrow and tomorrow.

Roosevelt was trying to do something about all this, and I exulted as he spoke bitterly of the South's feudalism.

The system struck back at him through its elected representatives—by and large the chosen of the dominant social and economic interests. These interests ruled politics still through their money and their influence. When a champion of the people arose he usually was a demagogue who fooled the masses with his clever tricks and his glittering, false promises and did little for them. Of such was Huey Long and others who have come and gone through the years.

Democracy still does not exist in the South. Thousands and thousands are disfranchised by the poll tax, an archaic toll. It is not much, but cash money is scarce and precious, so people neglect their voting privilege. Eight of the nine states which still impose the poll tax are in the South. Such laws should be repealed.

But a change is working in the South.

Roosevelt started it, not only in strong and truthful words, but in such legislative acts as the wage-hour bill, which he finally got through Congress—compromised much in form, it is true, after a long fight—and the Wagner Labor Relations Act, which guaranteed workers the right to organize into unions to protect themselves, in assistance to farmers and sharecroppers.

I have been much in the South since I wandered along the trail of the new industrial carpetbaggers.

There are signs of a renascence. I saw it on a resettlement project of the Agriculture Department in Arkansas where young married couples, once sharecroppers, are starting out anew, full of hope. I saw it in union meetings where workers gathered to claim their rights now protected. They are beginning—but slowly, of course—to shed that slave complex. There is much hope for the future of the South. It is a bountiful land if properly cultivated. It can be also a great industrial empire serving its own manifold needs and those of the rest of the country. It must serve itself and not be a slave market for exploitation by others. It must furnish its own brains, its own money, and not depend upon other brains and financial markets far away. That will take time, education.

I saw the South that I had known as a child, that dark and brooding evil spirit of the South, rise up to hamper and impede the most hopeful era of reform in my time. My trail started deep in the South. It goes back now to the South. For the South tries to bind its chains again about the hopeful limbs of a national progressivism and slows down the march.

But the chains will be thrown off.

And we will march again.

I am sure of that.

530

The aristocracy now is becoming more of an economic aristocracy. It expects the same homage that the old plantation owner expected from his slaves, but it is less kindly as a whole. It looks down upon people who work in its cotton mills. It looks down upon the tenants who toil on its farms.

The South still has the slave-holding instinct.

That's the way it looks to me, who have been long away, when I go back and look at it and then come away and think of it.

I know I don't look upon many things as the Southerner does any more.

What has caused this change has been my story.

Things that happened to me as a boy and a young man in the South disturbed me and aroused my suspicions. I have told of them. Still as a young man I arrived in Washington to see the high idealism of the World War days turned to dust and ashes in a period of heinous corruption when brazen politicians looted the sanctuary of the people. My sympathies joined then with those who were trying to cast out the crooked, cast out the grabbing and the selfish, and turn the government back to the people. For long they fought in vain. The economic lords and masters tightened their hold upon the instruments of government. Finally they over-reached themselves and the house fell about them, taking down with it a President who tried to preserve the system that had nurtured him, but could not stay the sure retribution.

I watched the people rise in their wrath under another President who gave them hope and courage and bread and meat and clothing and shelter.

He began to remake the system that he found, and we still are in the midst of that process.

I exulted with the new dispensation, after all the sorry, hopeless years. I became wrapped up in this experiment which we call the New Deal.

Then disillusion came when it, too, overreached itself; and I learned still another truth which is that idealists, themselves, once they have tasted power, may come to see power as an end and abuse it also. They become convinced that they only are right and can use their power as they see fit to promote that right. I discovered that power, even of the virtuous, tends in time to overreach itself and that a democracy, to succeed and survive, must experience a constant battle for power among opposing forces, for that is the check that we have and the only check that we have.

That check began to operate in the 1938 congressional elections which saw a surprising upsurge that may be attributed to many factors and influences. Among them, I am convinced, was a reaction against a cast of mind which has developed in Washington, a zealous and intemperate sort of righteousness which brooks no questioning of its motives or its acts.

This was manifest in an arbitrariness in administration of reforms.

What we have come to know in the international field as "power politics" began to appear.

Of this I had a personal experience.

I'm sorry that it had to happen. For it spoiled some illusions. But I am wiser for it.

In the late spring of 1938 reports began to come from Kentucky that the WPA there was being built into a political organization on behalf of Senator Alben W. Barkley, whom the President and the national administration were supporting for reelection against Governor "Happy" Chandler, and that workers were being coerced, intimidated and levied upon for campaign contributions from the meager wages paid by the federal government. Likewise, it was reported that Governor Chandler's managers, on their side, were exploiting the state employees and using every sort of pressure to line them up behind the governor.

I went to Kentucky to investigate these reports.

For two weeks I travelled through the length and breadth of the state, talking to politicians on both sides, WPA directors, WPA workers, state officials and employees. When I had completed my investigation I wrote a series of eight stories in which I reported what I had found, which was that the WPA was deep in politics on behalf of Senator Barkley and that Chandler's state political leaders were using state employees in every possible way and levying upon their salaries. I called it "a grand political racket in which the taxpayer is the victim."

To me it was another job of reporting, one that I did not particularly relish when I discovered the facts, for it was a keen disappointment to find that the WPA was being exploited for politics and to ponder the ultimate effects to our Democracy if such a large group, dependent upon the administration in power, should be hereafter utilized and organized politically. Personally my sympathies lay with Senator Barkley in the Kentucky primary election, and with the President and the New Deal. I could not, however, condone such tactics. A much bigger and broader question was involved here than the mere election of a United States Senator.

My expectation was that the disclosures of politics in WPA in Kentucky would bring a prompt reaction from Washington in some sort of disciplinary action by WPA Administrator Harry L. Hopkins. Nothing happened immediately. Meanwhile, the stories—published locally in the *Washington News*—created interest in the Senate. That body, a few days before their publication, had defeated by a narrow margin a bill by Senator Carl A. Hatch, Democrat of New Mexico, prohibiting the use of WPA in politics. During debate, Sen-

535

ator Barkley had protested against tying up the WPA when state candidates had state machines which they would use.

Harry Hopkins finally acted. In a fifteen-page statement (based on an investigation by WPA investigators) he denounced me and the Scripps-Howard newspapers and impugned my integrity as a reporter. The press release was handed to me in the office of Aubrey Williams, deputy WPA Administrator. A group of us had gone to see him to check on an impromptu speech he had made before representatives of the Workers Alliance in which he had urged them to "keep your friends in power." I handed him a transcript of the speech which had been taken down by stenographers employed by the Workers Alliance and he said he had been properly quoted. The speech had created quite a sensation, coming, as it did, on top of numerous allegations about the political activity of WPA. While we were talking to Williams, a press relations representative brought in copies of the Hopkins statement about my stories. Williams said:

"We've got you, now, Tom!"

In my stories I had selected a number of incidents sworn to in affidavits about WPA political activity, illustrating the various types of pressure and intimidation. I had collected others, but I made a selection. Harry Hopkins counted these up and found twenty-two charges. He denied all but two.

In view of my disclosures and the Hopkins denial, the Senate Campaign Fund Investigating Committee, created every two years, dispatched an investigator to Kentucky. Altogether he spent several weeks in the state. His initial findings led the committee, headed by Senator Sheppard of Texas, to issue a statement describing the situation in Kentucky as "deplorable" and saying "these facts should arouse the conscience of the country. They imperil the right of the people to a free and unpolluted ballot." Thereafter the investigation was continued with even more devastating disclosures about the state WPA political activities under direction of Barkley campaign managers.

The final report revealed a far more extensive political use of WPA than I had disclosed, including collection of several thousand dollars from WPA employees, and it showed that the Chandler forces had collected some $70,000 from state highway employees and from state employees of federal and joint federal-state agencies, among them social security, old-age assistance, unemployment compensation, for the governor's campaign fund.

Congressional attention was directed anew to a curb on such political activities, and, after a long fight, the Hatch bill was passed prohibiting politics in WPA and otherwise restricting political activity of federal officeholders. There still is need to extend the ban into state politics to protect the state officeholder, as well as the taxpayer, from such exploitation as that by the Chandler forces in Kentucky which was, as a matter of fact, just another example of the tactics employed by many state machines.

This bare and sketchy outline of the Kentucky episode gives no inkling whatever of the emotional turmoil through which I went in those days when friends within the New Deal turned upon me. I was an outlaw, a pariah. Nor did I enjoy the blandishments of those opposed fundamentally to the New Deal.

I was unable to understand the attitude of those with whom I had worked, whose social and economic objectives I had shared. They sought refuge in the seductive philosophy that the end justifies the means and, under this philosophy, they condoned the political organization of relief workers. It was vain to point out that relief is likely to continue for a long time, and that it might become a force which could be regimented politically in threatening directions.

The psychology that had developed seemed to me to be dangerous.

I think I know how it had happened. It had evolved from zealous and unflagging idealism which finally, out of bitterness over the tactics of New Deal foes, was seeking a defense. It was a defensive attitude first, protective, then it came to be positive and aggressive. In defending itself, it came to harden itself about its own ideas and objectives. They were right, and, in time, came to be supremely right. To protect them, it must perpetuate itself and, in the end, anything necessary to perpetuate itself was justified.

To me it was a sad and disappointing climax to a magnificent and glorious adventure. The fine frenzy and comradery of the early days of the New Deal were disappearing and were being supplanted by austerity and bitterness, like that of the blooming young girl who turns into the sour old maid.

I want to pause a minute to recall that first, fine careless rapture. I want to pay my tribute to the young men and the middle-aged men and the older men who came flocking into Washington with the Roosevelt Revolution. They supplied brains and ideas and enthusiasm. They represented, perhaps, the finest collection of intelligence that any American administration had ever gathered together. They were refreshing after the orthodox politicians of the old school with whom we had to deal for so many years. The country owes them much.

We are in a confusing period.

The New Deal, as an instrument of domestic reform, has been checkmated and weakened. Going on within the Democratic Party is a struggle for ascendency between the ardent New Dealers and the conservative elements, exemplified largely in the Southern wing which had capitalized the very dissatisfaction which the New Dealers helped to create with the misuse of their powers.

Likewise the Republican Party is split over policy and method of approach to major problems. It, too, has its liberal and conservative wings. It, too, has its lunatic fringe which goes chasing off after the Townsend old-age pension plan, a strange contrast to the solemn brethren who know only one remedy and chant it unceasingly:

"Balance the budget."

The crucible still smokes.

Its fires still crackle with the strange fuels which have been poured into it, representing new forces released by the Roosevelt administration. Socialization, which has been going on slowly in the country for a long time, has been quickened. Private investment has languished, and the government begins to move in to supply the need, here and there. Periodically we hear the cry about "breathing spells" and "business appeasement" and talk about whether Roosevelt is going to stop his reforms and let business alone, whether he will define how far he is going. If we would be sensible we would see that this is all so much wasted breath, for Roosevelt is in the midst of a tide and cannot very well give assurances today when circumstances might require him to advance yet another step six months hence—and perhaps in a direction no one even suspected. Nor will whatever President who follows him in the White House. This is a changing economy.

In my opinion we will be in a state of turmoil for years to come until we have oriented ourselves to a new sort of world.

We have suddenly, in a short span, set up new agencies to look after manifold interests of the people. This has produced a top-heavy bureaucratic structure in Washington. I think we have got to decentralize administration of many of our new bureaus which will require careful selection of personnel to be in charge of local administration. They must be able persons who can be trusted to administer without interference from Washington. They must be given responsibility and must exercise it.

In this way, too, we will supply something now missing in centralized control from Washington. This is an intimate knowledge of conditions in various parts of the country. We still have our local differences, despite the radio and the automobile and other modern inventions. Some parts of the country are less advanced than others, less able to move swiftly with reforms and new modes of doing things. What is good in New York, what can be done in New York, is perhaps not good for Wyoming, nor can it be done the same way in Wyoming. What is good for Chicago may not be good for southern Georgia. We must realize that. A local administrator who knows conditions and people in his particular region can trim the cloth to fit those conditions and those people and can slowly popularize innovations which otherwise might be resisted. A spirit of tolerance and understanding is essential. That frequently has been absent in Washington.

There are many able and understanding administrators now, as you can find if you go about the country, as I do. There are also some of the other kind.

That will give us a more resilient and effective democracy.

One dangerous tendency has developed as the federal government has moved to supply new needs. This is the "gimme" philosophy. By fulfilling needs, we encourage new demands. This is to be expected. It is only human. The danger of it is that the cheap politician—and there are many of him—capitalizes it. In some cases he goes so far as to create new needs by suggesting them and holding out the temptation. An example that runs through the years of our political history is the capitalizing of the war veterans. But many new ones have come along of late. They represent real needs, but the politician lures them on to more than they need. There are the farmers, the pension-seekers, the relief clients, among others. The threat lies in the coalition of representatives of such groups in Congress in logrolling, the familiar process we have seen often in the tariff. We saw some of this in the 1939 regular session.

Businessmen who shout for balancing the budget and cutting down expenses, as members of Chambers of Commerce and Republicans, turn around, as citizens, and demand from Washington all sorts of appropriations for local projects, or for their own interests, and never seem to see the inconsistency. (So do Congressmen.) They never seem to realize that it is the sum total of all these local expenditures which they demand that make up the total expenditures which they deplore.

I have seen this so often as I travel about the country—and as I walk the corridors of Washington.

We have moved far in the last seven years.

We must move much farther.

Of one thing I am sure. The basic reforms of the Roosevelt New Deal are securely fixed in the law of the land. We are not going to discard our social security program, our guarantees to labor, the reforms of our banking and financial system, nor the principle of federal assistance to the unemployed, the farmer, the home owner. All these things have been established, and many more.

Much remains to be done by somebody coming after.

We have the unemployed with us still. We have a huge load of debt. Basic problems still are unsolved.

But we have stirred from our lethargy. We have become curious and alert. We do not hesitate to experiment. Our democracy is a very live, if confused, animal. It is the hope of democracy everywhere, and the hope of a disordered world.

Only one threat to it I now see.

That is war.

As I write this final chapter the alarums of war are sounding in Europe. Nations again are fighting one another. Our whole attention is on war. For the moment our domestic affairs have been shoved into the background. The fight between the New Dealers and the anti-New Dealers subsided, temporarily. Strange new alignments appeared over foreign policy.

Issues are confused. Bitter passions are aroused.

The current rulers of Europe are again at their old chess game, moving the pieces about, and we sit on this side of the Atlantic and watch, fascinated, like naïve children. Some of us remember our experience in the last chess game, and how we were duped. We want none of it. Some of us remember, but still are lured by grandiose dreams of some vague sort of American destiny, and see ourselves as the monitor of European affairs. Some of us are stagestruck. The young, who will have to fight a war, do not know about the last one.

I pray, for the sake of our democracy, that we can stay out of it.

Otherwise I don't think our democracy will survive in the way we would like to see it and live in it.

I think this is paramount.

I have seen, as I came along the road, the people I would like to fight for. They are my own.

They live in a great country that can become still greater. They live in my South, and in the great cities of the East, and in the Middle West and in the far reaches of the West clear to the Pacific.

Again, as in a mist, I see them.

542

INDEX

Index

547

Boyden, Roland W., 112-13
Brandeis, Justice, 464, 469, 470
Brandon, Governor W. W., 188
Brazilian, bonds, 357
Brookhart, Senator Smith Wildman, 153, 170, 298
Brookhaven, Miss., migrating industry in, 517-19
Brown, Walter F., 423
Brucker, Governor Wilbur, 304
Bryan, William Jennings, 71; crusade against evolution theory, 122, 123, 274; at 1924 Democratic convention, 185, 186, 189, 193, 194, 274
Buenos Aires, 251
Buffalo, N.Y., Landon speech at, 440
Bulkley, Senator Robert J., 491, 492, 493
Bureau of Standards, 217
Burke, James Francis, 244
Burton, Theodore, 195
Butler, Justice, 464, 469, 470
Butler, Nicholas Murray, 229
Butte, Mont., Smith at, 239
Byrd, Admiral Richard E., 214, 215

Camp, Lawrence, 496, 499
Candler, Asa, 28, 29, 30
Caraway, Senator Thaddeus, tariff lobby investigation, 268, 269, 270; see investigations, tariff
Cardoza, Justice, 470
Carpenter, Terry, 456
carpetbaggers, industrial, 508-30; see industry, migration of
CCC (Civilian Conservation Corps), 461, 542
Central America, 218, 247, 248
Central Republic Bank and Trust Co., gets $90,000,000 from RFC, 329, 330; see Dawes, Charles G.
Cermak, Tony, 323
chain gang, 14
chambers of commerce, 6, 33, 509, 512, 541; U.S., 370
Chandler, Governor "Happy" A. B., Roosevelt opposes in 1938 campaign, 493, 494; state machine activities, 534, 537

Chantland, W. T., power investigation, 336
Charleston, 7
Chase Securities Corporation, 351, 352
Chautauqua, N.Y., Landon speech at, 439
Chiang Kai-Shek, 215
Christian, George, 95, 100, 101, 130, 131, 132, 133, 134
Cincinnati, welcome to Roosevelt, 452, 453
Clapper, Raymond, 70, 71, 366
Clark, Senator Bennett Champ, 492
Clark, Champ, Speaker of House, death of, 76
Clark, Mrs., 76
Clarksburg, W.Va., John W. Davis notification ceremonies, 202
coal, strike, 95-105
Cohen, Benjamin V., 344, 486, 487
Coli, 214
Colorado Springs, Roosevelt visit, 447
Columbia, Miss., migrating industry at, 517
Columbus, Ohio, Roosevelt welcome, 453
communism, 116
companionate marriage, 119
Confederacy, influence on University, 30-3
Confederate flag, 8; Memorial Day, 21
Conneautville, Pa., Landon at, 438
Constitution, Atlanta, newspaper, 16, 55
conventions, 1924 Democratic, 181-94; LaFollette Progressive, 195-201; 1928 Republican, 223-31; 1928 Democratic, 231-4; 1932 Democratic, 312-28; 1932 Republican, 328-30; Townsend (1936), 412-20; 1936 Republican, 420-3, 426-34
Coolidge, Calvin, welcomes President and Mrs. Harding, 76; impressions of, 135-41; takes oath, 135; nomination as Vice President, 136, 137; his philosophy, 137, 179, 180, 199; boom, 137; economy, 138; created into myth, 139; faces Harding administration scandals, 141; forces Daugherty out, 155, 156, 163, 169,

George, Senator Walter F., sponsors power investigation by Federal Trade Commission instead of Senate, 335, 336; Roosevelt's attempt to defeat, 491, 492, 496-9; how he campaigned, 497-501

Georgia Power Company, 335

Georgia, University of, 30-42; Roosevelt speech at, 496

Germany, 107, 112, 296

Gillette, Senator Guy, 491

Glass, Senator Carter, 67, 237, 262, 348

Goethals, General George, 393

Gompers, Samuel, 103, 136

Grady, Henry W., 70

Gran Chaco, 250

Grand Coulee Dam, 392, 393, 394

Greene, Ward, 121

Greenwich Village, 119

Hague, Mayor Frank, criticizes Roosevelt as weak, 314; career, 314; 1936 celebration for Roosevelt, 450-2

Hamilton, John, 428-31, 434

Hamon, Jake, 270

Hand, Charles S., 327

Harding, President Warren G., 69; first reaction to, 71; inauguration, 72-6; takes oath, 73; on government interference in business, tariffs, golden rule, ideals for America, 73, 74; arrival in Washington, 76; farewell at Marion, Ohio, 76; dinner with "Ohio Gang," 76, 77; opens White House gates, 84; farewell speech, Marion, quote from, 84; views on politicians, 87; fires Bureau of Engraving and Printing employees, 87; entertains financiers at White House, 91, 92; decides on tariff ahead of tax legislation, 94; proclaims "cooperation" between President and Congress, 94; coal and railway strikes, 95-105; labor attitude, 98-100; trip to Alaska, speeches, 123-6; death and funeral, 127-34; meets Forbes, 145; denounces Forbes, asks resignation, 145; mentioned, 161, 163, 255, 259, 263, 278, 310

Harding, Mrs., 128-34

Harris, Joel Chandler, 13

Harrison, Senator Pat, 183, 189, 190, 493, 494

Haskell, Henry, 445

Hatch, Senator Carl, sponsors bill forbidding WPA political activity, 535, 536

Haupert, Pete, 101

Hawley, Representative Willis C., 310

Hays, Will H., 87, 88

Haynes, Roy A., 118

Healey, Robert E., conducts Federal Trade Power investigation, 334-6; see investigations

Hearst, William Randolph, 15, 326, 425, 439, 440, 449

Heflin, Senator Tom, 237

Heney, Francis J., 175

Herrin County, Ill., 97

Heslep, Charter, 343, 344

Hilles, Charles D., 422

Hillman, Sidney, 371

Hitchcock, Senator Gilbert N., 454

Hitchcock, Mrs., 454

Hitler, Adolf, 36, 116

hoarding, 83, 84

HOLC, 368

Holmes, George R., 111

Hood, General John B., 9

Hoover, Herbert, at Harding inauguration, 75; his rôle in Harding administration, 80, 81; on tariffs, foreign loans, 91; at White House financial conference, 91; directs unemployment conference, 96, 97; to Alaska with Harding, 127; mentioned, 163, 166, 209; Mississippi flood relief, 220; nominated, 223; Mellon's permission necessary, 224; farm issue at convention, 227; prohibition, 228, 229; what he typified, 234, 235, 239; 1928 campaign, 243-7; pressures, 244; on Muscle Shoals, 244; his timidity before crowds, 245, 246; election-night scene, 246, 247; South American trip, 247-51; in Florida before inauguration, 252, 253; "The man who," 253, 254, 255; his qualifica-

Jackson, Andrew, 128; onslaught on Supreme Court, 471
Jackson, Robert H., 487
Jacobs, Thornwell, 23
Japan, 110
Johnson, Senator Hiram W., 107, 296
Johnson, Hugh S., 370, 371
Johnson, Mayor Tom, 359
Johnston, Bill, 196
Jones, Jesse, 232, 378
Jones, Senator Wesley L., 298

Kalinin, Mikhail, 377, 378
Kaufman, Jay, 250
Keeler, O. B., 129
Keller, Representative Oscar E., tries to impeach Daugherty, 142
Kellogg, Frank B., 216, 218, 446
Kelly, Mayor Ed., 450
Kendrick, Senator, 142
Kenny, William F., 240
Kent, William, 92
Kentucky, WPA, political activity in, 534-9; see Hopkins and WPA
Kenyon, Senator William S., 171
Keys, William, 494
Key West, Fla., 1, 2
King, John T., 156
Kirby, Rollin, 342
Klein, Julius, 271, 272, 292
Knox, Fort, 378
Knox, Frank, 428, 460, 461
Knoxville News-Sentinel, 244
Kremer, Bruce, 321
Ku Klux Klan, 120-2, 181, 185, 186, 187, 191, 198, 240

labor, coal and railway strikes, 95-105; child labor, Coronado, minimum wage decisions, Supreme Court, 104; anthracite strike, 218; 30-hour-week bill, 369-70; Section 7-A of NRA, 370; gets opportunity under NRA, 371; Wagner Act, 371; Republican convention fight over constitutional amendment for state wage laws, 429; Supreme Court upholds minimum wage law, 472; Supreme Court upholds Wagner Act, 473

LaFollette, Philip, 364, 365, 457
LaFollette, Robert M., criticizes Supreme Court, 104, 107; introduces oil investigation resolution, 142; mentioned, 151, 163, 165, 167, 173; philosophy, 180; 1924 Progressive convention, 195-201; campaign for Presidency and results, 204, 205, 206; platform, 201; mentioned, 229, 274
LaFollette, Robert M., Jr., 197, 206; at 1928 Republican convention, 229, 230; bolts Hoover, 296
LaGuardia, Fiorello H., 163, 165, 166, 167, 179, 194, 274, 324, 326, 452
Lambert, John, 426
Lamont, Robert P., 279
Landon, Alfred M., 388; treated gently by Townsend convention, 418; leaders for, 422, 423; impressions of, 423, 424, 425; his philosophy, 424, 425; build up, 426, 427, 428; nominated, 428; a Teddy Roosevelt Bull Mooser, 429; fights for constitutional amendment permitting states to fix minimum wages, civil service plank, gold standard, 429, 430, 431, 432, 433; pulled and hauled by party's conflicting elements, 435; bad speaker, 435, 436; sentimental journey through Pennsylvania, 436, 437, 438, 439; on teachers' oath at Chautauqua, 439, 440; on taxes at Buffalo, 439, 440; Old Guard Republicans surround him, 440, 441; they lose interest after Des Moines farm speech, 441; big promises to farmers, 441, 442, 443, 444; inconsistency on national planning, 444; "cheese" boner at Minneapolis, 445; campaign hits downgrade, 446, 447; confident before election, 447
Lanier, Sidney, poet, 23
Lasker, Albert D., 101
Latonia, race track, Roosevelt speech at, 493, 494
League of Nations, Wilson and Harding discuss, 76; mentioned, 106, 107, 114, 115, 117, 124, 265
Leche, Governor Richard W., 406

555

Roberts, Roy, 428, 430, 431
Roberts, Warren R., 458
Robinson, Senator Joseph T., nominated Vice Presidential candidate, 231, 232; directs fight on Hawley-Smoot tariff, 265; leads fight for drought relief, 280, 281
Rockefeller, John D., Sr., 354
Rogers, Will, 439
Roosevelt, Alice, 148
Roosevelt, Archie, testifies in Teapot Dome investigation, 149, 150
Roosevelt, Eleanor, 237, 316; interview, 363; welcomed by women at Columbus, 453
Roosevelt, Franklin D., 200, 201; nominates Smith at 1928 convention, 233; attacked by Hoover for remarks on Supreme Court at Baltimore, 289-90; first inauguration, 309; conditions at time, 309, 310; man of the hour, 311; vague in campaign speeches, 312; 1932 convention, 313-25; criticized by Frank Hague as weak, 314; other candidates, 318, 319; fight over two-thirds rule, 320; critical moments, 321; nominated, 322, 323; addresses convention, 324, 325; conditions elevating to Presidency, 332, 333; power program, 337; experience with public utility holding company act, 337-9; on "money changers," 345; early days of New Deal, 361-3; could have been dictator, 362, 363; quote on emergency powers in inauguration address, 363, 364; best friend of capitalistic system, 364; banking policy, 365; his calmness and resourcefulness, 365, 366; press conferences, 367; dizzy period of reforms, 368-9; puts through economy bill, 373; on danger of loose fiscal policy, 373; on relief, 374-5; Russian recognition, 376-8; devaluation of dollar, 378-80; on Dust Bowl problem, 381, 382; visits North and South Dakota drought area, 386-91; visits Idaho reclamation area, 391, 392; visits

Grand Coulee Dam, 392, 393, 395; 1936 western campaign trip, 447-58; in Colorado, 447, 448; through Kansas, 448; campaign tour theme "four years ago and now," 449; trip through New Jersey, 450, 451; appears with Hague, 450; joie de vivre on Roosevelt campaign train, 453; his campaign manner and tactics, 453-6; his attempt to realign parties, 456, 457; Pittsburgh scene symbolizes whole political story of 1936, 458-61; explanation on budget balancing failure, 460; real meaning of second inauguration, 461, 462; Madison Square Garden speech, 1936, 462; social security distortion, 463; Supreme Court bill and fight, 463-84; Roosevelt's target, 464; surprise to country, 464; Congressional leaders, unadvised on Supreme Court bill, resentful, 465; reaction of Supreme Court, 467-71; great battle with Hughes, 471, 472; what defeated bill, 473; press conferences on Supreme Court after NRA declared unconstitutional, 477-80; "horse-and buggy-age," 477; Court nullifies AAA, 479; Roberts' decision, 480; Stone's lecture, 480, 481; reaction to AAA decision, 481-3; Republicans hope to use Court issue in 1936, 484, 485; effect on him of Court bill defeat, 485, 486; shoves Farley aside, 486; vindictive over Court bill defeat, inaugurates the "purge," 487; its course and results, 487-99; confusing, mismanaged and inconsistent, 489-92; aim to liberalize party, 489; his participation in Ohio, 493; in Kentucky, 493-4; in Oklahoma, 494; in California, 495, 496; in Georgia, 496-501; in South Carolina, 496-501; in Maryland, 501, 502; loss of prestige from, 501; split Democratic party wider, 503; surmise as to objective, 503-4; tries to break feudalism in South, 529, 530
Roosevelt, Franklin D., Jr., 387

Roosevelt, Theodore, visit to Atlanta, 13; mentioned, 71, 128, 274; F. D. Roosevelt voted for, 456; criticizes Supreme Court Justice, 471
Roosevelt, Theodore, Jr., appears in Teapot Dome investigation, 148-50; resignation demanded, 157
Rorabach, J. Henry, 421, 422
Ross, Governor Ben C., 412
Ruhr occupation, 112, 113
Rural Electrification Administration, 336
Rush, John C., 384
Russell, Lillian, 77
Russia, 6, 115, 116, 218; recognition of, 376-8
Ruthenberg, C. E., 197

Sabin, Charles H., 92
Sacasa, 218
St. Mihiel, transport, 113
Sandino, 251
San Pedro, 247, 248
Saperstein, David, 347
Sargent, John Garibaldi, 174
Saunders, Everett, 226
Savannah, 2
Sawyer, Dr. Charles E., 77, 134; in Veterans Bureau investigation, 145; see investigations, Veterans Bureau
Sawyer, Mrs., 77
Schenck, Hassil, 482, 483
Schwab, Charles, 99
Scott, W. C., 522
Sears, Dr. Paul, 382, 383
Senate Campaign Funds Investigating Committee, investigation of WPA political activity in Kentucky, 536
Sharon, Pa., Landon at, 437
Sheppard, Senator, 536
Sherman, General, 9, 70
Shipstead, Henrik M., 170
Shouse, Jouett, 320
Shushan, Abraham L., 407
Simmons, Furnifold, 237
Simmons, William J., Ku Klux Klan head, 121; see Ku Klux Klan
Simms, William Philip, 250, 251
Simpson, Kirke, 111

Sinclair, Harry F., investigation of oil leases, 142, 149; two jail sentences, 151, 152; acquitted on main charge, 152; see investigations, Teapot Dome
Sinclair, Upton, 409, 410
Slemp, C. Bascom, 422
Smith, Alfred E., Ku Klux Klan fights nomination of, 122; at 1924 Democratic convention, 184-7; 1928 Democratic convention, 231-4; his message to convention on prohibition, 233, 234; what he typified, 234, 235; his 1928 campaign, 237-43; attacks Mabel Walker Willebrandt, Senator Robert L. Owen, 240, 241; on McNary-Haugen Bill, 241, 242; visits Hoover, 253; contrasted with Hoover, 257, 258; Borah ridicules on farm issue, 264; Hague issues attack on Roosevelt on behalf of, 314; bitterness toward Roosevelt and reason for, 315; at 1932 convention, 315-17, 330; pleads with Roosevelt to run as governor of New York in 1928, 315, 316; announces at Chicago for himself alone, 317; urges repeal of Eighteenth Amendment and Volstead Act, 317; deserts 1932 convention when Roosevelt nominated, 323; Jimmy Walker stands by to end, 323, 324, 430; leader in American Liberty League, 457
Smith, Senator Ellison D., 168, 497, 500, 501
Smith, Representative Gerald L. K., 415, 417, 494
Smith, Gomer, 417, 494
Smith, Dr. James Monroe, 406
Smith, Jess, 76, 77, 89, 154, 155
Smith, Representative Martin M., 417, 418
Smoot, Senator Reed, 140, 310
Snap Bean Farm, home of Joel Chandler Harris, 13
Snell, Bertrand H., 431
soak-the-rich, tax bill, 419
South, international viewpoint, 105, 106; Roosevelt's "purge" there, 488; lack of democracy in, 488, 489, 529,

558

530; why "purge" failed in, 496-9; its political system, 505-7; migration of industry to, 508-30; low wages in, 516, 517; renascence in, 530, its caste system, 531-3
South America, 247-51
Stalin, Josef, 116
Standard Oil, compound, in shelling of Nanking, 215
Stanton, Frank L., poet, 55
Steiner, P. S., judge, 393
Stephens, Alexander Hamilton, Vice President of Confederacy, at college, 32
Steuer, Max, 156
Stimson, Henry L., 218
Stinson, Roxie, testifies in Daugherty investigation, 153, 154
stock market, Harding's interest in, 93; mania, 208, 209; crash, 263, 270-2; Senate investigation of, 345-60
Stone, Harlan Fiske, appointed attorney general by Coolidge, "kicked up stairs" to Supreme Court, 174; dissent in AAA case, 480, 481
Sumners, Representative Hatton W., 509
Sunday, Southern dinner, 18; observance, 21-3; school, mission, 25-7
Supreme Court, child labor, Coronado coal, minimum wage decisions, 104; LaFollette views on, 200, 201; Roosevelt's reform bill and fight, 463-84; Roosevelt discusses philosophy, 477-80; see Roosevelt, Franklin D.
Sutherland, Justice, 464, 470

Tabor, Silver Dollar, 125
Taft, William Howard, Chief Justice, labor decisions, 104; on prohibition, 117; gives oath to Hoover, 257
Talmadge, Governor Eugene, alliance with Huey Long, 404, 405; 1938 Senatorial campaign, 496, 499
Tammany, 451, 452
Tariff, Fordney Emergency, 82; Fordney-McCumber, 83, 170; Smoot-Hawley, 83; fight over, 264-7; investigation of lobbyists, 268-70; Hoo-

ver signs, 268; reciprocal tariff, Landon views on, 445, 446
Tarry, Gus, 69
tax, first Mellon bill, 95; on undistributed profits, advocated by LaFollette at 1924 convention, 200; soak-the-rich bill, 419
Tax Appeals, Board of, 176
Thaxton, G. A., 521
Thirty Dollars Every Thursday, 495, 496
Thomas, Senator Elmer, 378, 494
Thomas, Norman, 418, 419
Thompson, Carmi, 76
Thompson, John W., in Veterans Bureau Investigation, 146; see investigations, Veterans Bureau
Tidal Basin, 62
Toombs, Bob, commencement address, oak, 32
Townsend Old-Age Pension Plan, 408-20; convention in 1936, 412-20; pushes Roosevelt to left, 420
Tribune, Chicago, 449
Tucker, Ray, 215
Tugwell, Rexford G., rehabilitation work, 383-7
TVA, 337
twelve-hour day, conference on abolition of, 99, 100; Harding on, 125; abolition, 125
Tydings, Senator Millard F., Farley for his defeat, 492; Roosevelt campaign against, 501, 502

Uncle Reuben Comes to Washington, book, 89
Underwood, Senator Oscar W., 188
United Mine Workers of America, 371
U.S. Shipping Board, 101
U.S. Steel, 125
Unknown Soldier, 111
Utah, battleship, 248

Vandenberg, Senator Arthur, 294, 295, 428
Van Devanter, Justice, 464, 469, 470
Van Sweringen, 358, 359
Vare, William S., 225, 236

560